LIFTING
THE TABOO

by the same author

REFLECTING MEN at twice their natural size
(with Dale Spender)
JUST DESSERTS: Women and Food
WOMEN, CELIBACY AND PASSION

SALLY CLINE

LIFTING THE TABOO

Women, Death and Dying

LITTLE, BROWN AND COMPANY

A *Little, Brown* Book

First published in Great Britain
by Little, Brown and Company 1995

A CIP catalogue record for this book is
available from the British Library.

ISBN 0 316 91361 8

Typeset by M Rules
Printed and bound in Great Britain by
Clays Ltd, St Ives plc

Little, Brown and Company (UK)
Brettenham House
Lancaster Place
London WC2E 7EN

This book is dedicated to
EM MARION CALLEN

This book is also for BA SHEPPARD, with love

The book is in memory of my friend
CAROL KENDRICK
born 18 April 1950
died 13 July 1993

CONTENTS

ACKNOWLEDGEMENTS

A major acknowledgement goes to the many women in Great Britain and North America who talked to me at length, offered their attitudes towards death and their accounts of dying, bereavement and grief. Their names have been altered but their voices and views weave through these pages.

I wish to put on record my enormous appreciation to the judges of the Arts Council of England Writers' Awards for validating my faith in this work and giving me an award that bought me time to continue it.

I wish to express my deep gratitude to The Royal Literary Fund which awarded me a literary merit grant during a period of severe financial crisis and sickness so that I was able to finish this book.

For networking for interviewees, information, advice and research facilities, I wish to thank the following individuals and organisations: The AIDS Helpline (Cambridge), The Alder Centre (Valerie Mandelson), The Alzheimer's Disease Society (Clive Evers), Dr Eileen Baildam, Barbara Baker, Margaret Ball (Cambridge Library and Information Service), Carys Bannister (Booth Hall Children's Hospital), The Bereavement Trust, The Breast Care and Mastectomy Association of Great Britain, The Bristol Cancer Help Centre, The British Heart Foundation, The Buddhist Centre (Cambridge), June Burt, The Cambridge Centre, The Cambridge University Student's Union, The Cambridge Women's Resources Centre, The Cancer Aftercare and Rehabilitation Society, The Cancer and Leukaemia in Childhood Trust, Cancerlink, Carers National Association (Angela Herbert),

The Children's Hospice (Milton), Tony Chiva (Pre-retirement Association of Great Britain and Ireland), The Compassionate Friends (Jillian Tallon, Anne Pocock), Gwynneth Conder, Shirley Cooklin, Cruse, Alan Dowson (Chair of the Peterborough Perceptions of Living and Dying Group), Kay Dunbar (Director of the Ways With Words Literary Festival), Pauline Dauber, Dr Carol Ewing, Frontline Bookshop Manchester (Shamsa Butt, Alison Page), Foundation for the Study of Infant Death, Kay Goodridge, Christianne Heal, The Hen House Lincs, Hospice Arts, Hospice Information Service, Rosy Howden, Imperial Cancer Research, The Jewish Bereavement Counselling Service, Dr Eve Jones, Pat Kitto, The Lesbian and Gay Bereavement Project (Denni Jenno Lewis), The London Lighthouse, The Miscarriage Association, The Motor Neurone Disease Association, The Muslim Women's Helpline, The National AIDS Helpline, The National Association of Widows and Widows' Trust (Kate Johnson), The Natural Death Centre (Josefine Speyer, Nicholas Albery), Stephanie Oates, The Open University (Barbara Bilston and members of the Death and Dying Course Team), Pamela Oppenshaw, Helen Passant, Carole Plummer, Margaret Potter (Cruse Training Co-Ordinator), The Samaritans, St Christopher's Hospice Information Service (Avril Jackson), Dame Cicely Saunders, Carol Southern, The Stillbirth and Neonatal Death Society, Stretten Avenue Community Centre, The Sue Ryder Foundation, The Terence Higgins Trust, Beverley Walker Funeral Service, Waterstone's Bookshop (Cambridge), Weyman's Funeral Service (Mandy Walker), Harry Williams Funeral Service (Sally Smith).

For painstaking photocopying services, constant cuttings, articles and information I thank: Liz, Noel and Melanie at Prontaprint Cambridge, Pauline McCartney, Leslie Brett, Sophie Young, Hilary Bichovsky, Ngaire Jane Woodhouse, Janet Taylor. Lengthy audio-tapes were patiently and meticulously transcribed by Frances Ward (when bereaved herself), Beth Basham, Rosemary Smith, Leslie Dommett and most particularly Debby Taylor. An impeccable bibliography was achieved at high speed by Beth Callen. Her usual fine indexing (and inexhaustible personal support) came from Lowana Veal.

For space to write, many weeks' accommodation, and energising discussions, I thank Anne Gurnett (New York), Kathy Mullen, Robert Hess, Graham Metson and Cheryl Lean (Canada), Liz and Graham Dimmock (Cornwall), Jean Adams (yet again for the incomparable Sunset Heights), Linnie and Nick Price for letting me turn their Devon Barn into an interview centre, Alison West for her Todmorden cottage at a critical crisis, and Mary Twomey and Judith Emmanuel for their generosity in offering me house space at a point when we were all struggling with bereavement.

I thank Josie McConnell of the Cambridge AIDS Helpline, dear chum as well as colleague, who worked with me on the AIDS chapter until it passed her scrupulous scientific inspection. The Cambridge Women Writers (Joy Magezis, Chris Carling, Em Callen) read, criticised and imaginatively improved large sections of this manuscript. Laura Morris, my ex-publisher, kept bringing cheer and humour into the spirit of this book.

Hilary Foakes, my first editor, breathed life and enthusiasm into a highly challenging project. Richard Beswick, my new editor, is discreet and canny in his editorial rigour. Clare Chambers, herself a writer, my friend and former editor, copy-edited as always with imaginative understanding. My literary agent Barbara Levy's acute analysis of what was wrong with a chapter, and her affectionate display of what was right about me, is what any writer needs. My research assistant Louse Gilchrist's flair for research enhanced the study (most especially the cross-cultural issues) and her flexibility with my changing moods often quite literally kept me going.

Personal encouragement and intellectual clarity throughout this lengthy, often draining project came from Sue Benson, Kathy Bowles, Manda Callen, Anne Christie, Jane Jaffey, Joel Jaffey, Stella King, Wendy Mulford, Val Owen, Aliye Seif Al Said, Nicho Wooding, Miranda Williamson. Particular practical help and perpetual enthusiasm came on a daily basis from Angie and Chris North.

My family and extended family have again been a source of professional and personal strength. I thank my cousins Joan and Jonathan Harris for insights into Jewish bereavement, Elsie Sheppard for discussions on widowhood, my cousin Jane Shackman for reading and re-reading drafts with critical concern, Vic Smith for her magnetic ideas and irrepressible enthusiasm, my aunt Het (Harriet) Shackman for photocopying, finding articles, and giving unstintingly of her time and love. Ba Sheppard's generosity in sharing her knowledge of the health field, and her radical improvement of the Alzheimer's chapter, was this year's example of the sixteen years' emotional and literary sustenance she has given me. My daughter Marmoset Adler's professional help in providing references, contacts, cuttings, and networking for interviewees, has been backed by her constant commitment and bubbling ideas.

A book about death is a difficult journey. Mine was made easier by my good fortune in having as my travelling companion Em Marion Callen, who deserves more thanks than anyone. With writerly imagination she attentively proofread every chapter, and added creative touches to otherwise stringent editing. She debated each death issue, believed in the importance of this study, and at points when my own faith wavered, hers remained firm.

PERMISSIONS

The author offers grateful thanks to the following for permission to quote extracts from titles held under copyright: Chatto & Windus for *Nothing to Forgive* by Lyndall Hopkinson and *How We Die* by Sherwin B Nuland; Gerald Duckworth & Co for *The Collected Dorothy Parker* by Dorothy Parker; Firebrand Books for *A Burst of Light* by Audre Lorde; the *Guardian* for 'A First Person' by Clare Williams and the article on Funeral Directors (19 November 1994) by Sarah Boseley; Celia Haddon for her article in *The Times* (30 August 1994); Key Porter Books and Bella Pomer Agency Inc for *Charlotte and Claudia Keeping in Touch* by Joan Barfoot; Macmillan Canada and Georges Borchardt, Inc for *Memory Board* by Jane Rule; John Murray for *Perspectives on Living* by Bel Mooney; Tessa Sayle Agency for *Have the Men had Enough?* by Margaret Forster. Every effort has been made to trace copyright owners of material used in this book. Where acknowledgement has been omitted, the author is happy to make the appropriate acknowledgement in future editions.

BACKGROUND TO
THE BOOK

Why look at issues relating to death *now?*

Perhaps a book that breaks through our most sacred taboo, that splits open the silence, not merely surrounding mortality but shrouding women's relation to it, would always have been useful. Today, however, it is timely and urgent for several reasons.

The first reason is that it explores the unexplored. It takes out of the closet the specific relationship women have to the dying process, in order to comprehend their feelings and fears about their own deaths, their attitudes towards loss, their reactions and responses to their role of primary carers to the sick and dying.

A second reason is that it investigates our culture's uninformed attitude towards death. If we can lift the veto on death, we may be able to change the experiences of dying and bereavement from those of alienation and exclusion to those of shared understanding and communication.

A third reason is that the advent of AIDS is making us aware suddenly and sharply of our own mortality at a much younger age. Many women are of course AIDS sufferers. In addition, an increasing number of women, who are not necessarily HIV positive, are taking on new responsibilities caring for those with AIDS, either through private obligations or in public roles as AIDS workers or nurses.

The stigma attached to certain causes of death such as suicide, murder, and most emphatically AIDS, is a major means of both constructing and maintaining the taboo around death itself.

The word 'taboo' comes from Polynesia where it delineates areas of social life marked off simultaneously as sacred and forbidden.

The West, too, has ritual or religious restrictions around areas considered holy or unclean. What are regarded as forbidden subjects or behaviour in one society may be perfectly acceptable in another. For Jews and Muslims, pork is a taboo food. For most British people so is horsemeat. French Christians will eat both pork and horsemeat and regard this as normal.

All societies have rules defining certain foods, activities or topics of conversation as out of bounds, though often the rules that shape the way we think or act have been so successfully internalised that we are hardly conscious of them. The existence of taboos is universal but the content changes from time to time, from place to place. Breastfeeding, a routine public sight in one culture, must be done in private in another.

In everyday usage, taboos are enforced by custom rather than by law. If you are on a diet then jam doughnuts and cream are taboo. If you are taking tea with the vicar then masturbating at the tea table is *verboten*.

Sex and death have always been significant subjects but the openness with which they have been discussed has changed over the centuries. In the West, Victorians discussed death, but for them sex was taboo. The backdrop to the book's theme is that today we have reversed that situation, and women are uncomfortable with the reversal.

In this, as in previous books, I work within the standard sociological and literary tradition of interactionist interviews and case study methodology.

Although in *Lifting the Taboo: Women, Death and Dying* I offer for consideration several thanatological theories and begin to weave together the threads from my own discoveries into a theoretical exploration of women's special relationship to the dying process, throughout this book I also offer women the space to speak about death.

To tell their stories.

I do this in order to show firstly irrecoverable loss through the eyes of bereaved women; secondly to comprehend the process of terminal illness through the eyes of women facing death; thirdly to illustrate the challenges, the suffering and the joys of caring for or healing those who are dying, through the eyes of women whose public jobs or private duties are to act as medical experts or social caretakers; fourthly to investigate the role of the few women in the profession of dealing with the dead and arranging funerals.

My use of their stories not only legitimises their experiences but for the first time places the complex female understanding of death centre stage.

I am sometimes asked: Why do you tell stories? In cases where women face their own death or face the loss of those close to them, I believe that the stories survivors and patients offer are the starting point of our understanding. As Jung pointed out: 'Clinical diagnoses are important . . . but they do not help the patient . . . The crucial thing is the story. For it alone shows the human background and the human story.'[1]

If we are to perceive something of what it means in this society to be a woman who is dying of breast cancer, or is a suicide survivor, or is a mother whose only child has died, then stories may help.[2]

Before I began the research I had been somewhat concerned that the interviewees might find the experience distressing. In practice there was no need for any anxiety on *their* behalf. Even when they broke down or became upset, without exception, they all assured me that they had nevertheless found the discussions helpful. Many women said that it had been important to them that my own experience had included an attempted suicide and several significant bereavements. Ironically it was initially I who found painful the cumulative effects of several agonising stories in swift succession, the more so as they occurred during my own slow recovery from bereavement.

The rawness of feeling in some of this documentary material that arose straight out of immediate suffering called for fortitude from the listener/writer. Areas such as suicide and the death of children called for greater strength than on some days I felt I had.

Fortunately not every story was hard to bear or hard to hear.

The unsparing bravery and extraordinary optimism of my interviewees enlarged my own experience. It made of death a creative journey. It made the mutual collaboration between author and subjects less an academic exercise and more a feminist meeting place in which the jagged jigsaw of women's grief, women's loss, women's suffering and women's spiritual strength could be reassembled in an imaginative manner to create a new model of a world which includes but does not subsume women's perspectives on death and dying.

My own conclusions about the value of this work have been reinforced by the knowledge that other researchers in this field, such as Shepherd and Barraclough (1979), Solomon (1981) and Wertheimer (1991), also reported that survivors and bereaved people found it immensely productive to discuss death openly with someone non-judgemental and uninvolved in their personal crisis.[3]

Some of my interviews reflect Albert Cain's comment (on suicide research) that 'given the clamorous needs of many survivors for psychological assistance, survivor research will often acquire a strong action research flavour'.[4]

Part of the motive behind the eagerness of bereaved women and women facing death to be interviewed was related to their own needs. Their desire was to talk about death and dying. In a few cases, where the bereavement had happened six to ten years previously, they thought they had 'got over it', had not recognised their need for communication, and were shocked (although subsequently appreciative) when they broke down in tears during the session.

For many women recently bereaved, the interview situation provided a useful opportunity to talk about the person who had just died, an opportunity they said repeatedly that had been denied them in the society they moved in.

Sometimes after the interview the women would reflect further on the issues raised and send me additional notes, drawings, paintings, or taped material. Many interviewees wrote short stories or poems or began painting the death they had experienced. Several subsequently joined creative writing groups or painting classes to continue this work, later to expand their art into other areas.

Some women with terminal illnesses took the opportunity to discuss openly their fears and confusions about their imminent deaths, an honesty they felt was 'less permissible' with their families and closest friends whose suffering and intimacy often disallowed total honesty.

The most significant statement made consistently by the majority of the interviewees was that in addition to meeting their own needs, they felt that by taking part in this study they were helping to lift firstly the taboo around all forms of death, and secondly the silence around women's participation in the death process. Contributing to this book was a way of lessening women's isolation and validating women's experiences.

I interviewed 150 women then decided to draw extensively on eighty interviews. Some women were highly self-aware of their role as women in relation to the dying process. Others were less so. I also had several group discussions with women. All the individual interviews were taped. Each interview lasted between one and three hours. I saw some for a follow-up interview. A few women offered me hospitality. They were interviewed over a period of two to three days.

All interviews were confidential. In most cases the names of practitioners have been retained unless they asked for fictional names. In
all cases the other women interviewed have been allotted fictional
names.

As I was interested in looking at public roles and procedures as
well as private emotions and attitudes, I interviewed practitioners in
the field of death and dying, as well as women with experiences of
terminal illness, death, bereavement and loss, and writers and artists
who made images of death, or whose work had been profoundly
changed by bereavement or near-death experiences.

The interviewees included some Asian women, some African-
American women, some white Europeans, some Australians living in
Britain, and many North Americans, Canadians and British women.

The interviewees' religion, age, occupation, class and sexual orientation varied. They included Jewish, Christian, Catholic, Muslim,
Hindu, Buddhist, Agnostic and Atheist. Ways in which their cultural
and religious heritage affected and shaped their attitudes towards
death are explicated in Chapter Two.

I have drawn on the work of black women writers and interviewed many black and Asian women. I hope that there may be
issues other women of colour may wish to pursue, despite the fact
that this study predominantly reflects the experiences of white
working-class and white middle-class women in Great Britain,
Europe, and North America.

The respondents were aged between eighteen and eighty-four.
They came from the middle and working classes, they were lesbian,
celibate, bisexual and heterosexual, single, separated, widowed, partnered, married, divorced. As I was interested in investigating
mothers as a group, about two-thirds were mothers, one third child-
free.

Their occupations ranged from unemployed to self-employed,
the majority being employed. Practitioners included medical consultants, surgeons, general practitioners, paediatricians, nurses,
cancer nurses, acupuncturists, homeopaths, bereavement counsellors, AIDS workers, health therapists, Samaritans, Cruse workers,
Compassionate Friends workers, organisers of centres dealing with
the death of children, psychologists, bereavement art therapists,
child-care workers, hospice organisers and workers, and funeral
directors.

Non-practitioners included students, homemakers, factory workers, shop workers, bookstore workers, sales assistants, caterers,
secretaries, laundrette assistants, soda-fountain workers, Buddhist

nuns, Catholic nuns, doctors, nurses, shiatsuists, homeopaths, aro-
matherapists, therapists, dentists, health visitors, health workers,
rape crisis workers, rock climbers, university lecturers, teachers,
adult education staff, literacy workers, language teachers, medical
sociologists, sociologists, administrative assistants, publishers, edi-
tors, magazine journalists, painters, photographers, community
artists, writers, poets, scriptwriters, actresses, business and market-
ing co-ordinators, scientific technicians, scientific researchers.

In Great Britain and North America networking for interviewees
was made through a number of different channels listed in the
acknowledgements.

A small pilot sample of about fifteen Canadian women was interviewed during research in Canada for a previous book. Other
interviewees were identified through personal or professional contacts, or through women who had already come forward as
interviewees. It was usual after an interview for the respondent to
suggest several more potential respondents. Interviewees were a self-
selected group whose common thread was a strong wish to talk
about their attitudes towards death and dying or their experiences of
bereavement. That the great enthusiasm for this project was to be
expected was made clear to me by Dame Cicely Saunders, founder of
the Hospice Movement:

> Talking about dying is incredibly important. I've never had a
> reporter, or indeed anyone, come here yet, but in the course of
> their coming here to interview me, they bring up someone who's
> died in their family. People who have had a difficult bereavement
> are going to talk about it if they think there is a listening ear.

This book and this writer provided a listening ear.

I hope that this book will contribute to the body of women's experiences during this century, limited though it is by my class, colour
and religious upbringing. Perhaps the experiences and attitudes of
other women which I have recorded will reach out beyond the personal and political boundaries of my own experience as a white,
Western, Jewish, middle-class feminist, to offer new insights and
some reassurance to other women, and men too.

What then has been my own experience, both personal and professional, of death?

Professionally, I have been a member of the Working Party on
'Perceptions of Living and Dying' organised by Alan Dowson at the
Peterborough College of Adult Education, Peterborough, England.

In conjunction with the Pre-Retirement Association of Great Britain and Northern Ireland, in Guildford, UK, and PRISMA/Adult Education Institute, Noord-Brabant, Tilburg, Holland, the working party addressed the subject of preventative health education in connection with the trauma associated with death and dying.

It looked at aspects of learning for the end of life; end-of-life awareness; individual and group exploration of thoughts and feelings about death; considerations of the role of death work in people's lives and workplaces; and ways of developing this material in adult education in Cambridgeshire.

In addition to this formal work, I have also been informally associated with the Cambridge AIDS helpline, and have been a member of several workshops on Death and Dying during the period of this research.

In personal terms, death has been a significant presence in my life.

When I was nineteen, my father died. The death of a man, generous and kind in many ways, but from whom I had in my childhood, with good reason, shied away, came as an unadmitted relief. As many women in this study confessed: you are not supposed to feel relief when someone dies. I have struggled, as they have, during this research, to make sense of that guilt and those reasons.

A less complex but no less traumatic death occurred when my close friend Jenni, who was like a second mother to my young daughter, drowned having an epileptic fit over a bath while her newborn son cried in the adjoining room. In an earlier book I recounted the shock and the enduring consequence on my life, and the lives of those who knew and loved her.[5]

My literary entanglement with death started early.

When I was eleven years old I got my first poem printed in the school magazine. I also received a lot of flak as the poem was about death, and was considered 'unsuitable for a young lady'. I cared little. My career as a writer had been launched! Schoolmates were shocked. Teachers (no literary experts!) were impressed at its death-defying verve. People continued to quote it. This is how it ran:

> Razors pain you,
> Rivers are damp,
> Razors pain you,
> Acids stain you,
> And drugs cause cramp.
> Guns aren't lawful;
> Nooses give;

Gas smells awful;
You might as well live.[6]

Not only have people been quoting it ever since I wrote it, people were quoting it long before I wrote it.

The problem was I did not actually write it.

Dorothy Parker, dubbed America's wittiest woman of the 1920s, did, when she was twenty-seven. To her credit she wrote it after one of her several suicide attempts.

Call it plagiarism if you must. Though I'd rather you didn't. I prefer to call it a kind of dream memory, or wishful thinking. Had I read it earlier in my childhood? Had I learnt it by heart then sneakily forgotten its source? Did I then manage to raise it from the dead, so to speak, in time for the school magazine?

Whatever its roots, I did share two things with the immortal Parker (and with all the women I have interviewed): a fascination with death and a desire to speak out about it.

Dorothy Parker (given to saying she preferred living in hotels because all she needed was room to lay a hat and a few friends), was a born rebel who enjoyed thumbing her nose at the rules women were expected to obey. Death to her was a part of life.

Indeed it was an obsession. A tragedy. A source of humour. It is a crucial element in many of her wittiest stories. Her verses abound with shrouds, bones, graves, ghosts, worms and weeds. Her books have such funereal titles as: *Enough Rope*, *Sunset Gun*, *Death and Taxes*, *Here Lies*, *Laments for the Living*, *Not So Deep A Well*. When she was on the staff of *Vanity Fair* she subscribed to two trade magazines for undertakers. She named many of her characters from obituary columns.

Her active engagement with death was in direct contrast to other women of the past whose relationship to death, according to researcher/historian Gerda Lerner, was more passive.[7]

Parker spoke out and wrote out about death. For other women of her time, the theme of death, especially the death of children, although much in evidence, was less raucous, less belligerent. Notions of death appear in women's embroidery samplers, in needlepoint pictures, in journals and diaries, in correspondence between women friends, or between wives and husbands. In general however women, intimately involved in the process of dying, taught to prioritise the feelings of others rather than themselves, did not write out their emotions about death as vividly or as mockingly as did Parker.

A few hours after Parker's husband, Alan Campbell, died, a woman who was not overfond of Dorothy came to her house to offer condolences and assistance. How could she help? she asked.

'Get me a new husband' Dorothy replied without a flicker of expression.

The shocked woman said that the remark was the most vulgar and tasteless she had ever heard.

'I'm sorry' Dorothy told her. 'Then run down to the corner and get me a ham and cheese on rye. And tell them to hold the mayo.'[8]

Parker believed that death should be spoken about even in times of crisis. Indeed most especially in times of crisis. It should be whistled at weddings, made fun of at funerals, turned into lyrics, made into pop songs.

For Dorothy Parker death was not taboo.

How different an approach from that of the Canadian mother I met in Halifax, Nova Scotia. She told me that when her small boy asked her for the title of an Elton John song which he heard constantly on the radio, she lied and said she did not know, rather than tell him it was called 'Funeral for a Friend'.

'If I had told him the title,' she said, 'I would have had to explain what funeral meant, and I couldn't face it.'

Death in our society today is subjected to severe over-protection. As we see from the 'Funeral for a Friend' story, today, the questions children ask their mothers may go unanswered. A hundred years ago children would have received a very different response. Indeed they would not have needed to ask the question.

Unlike Parker, when I made a serious suicide attempt in my early twenties, I did not write poetry. For many months I did not write anything. I struggled for years with the awareness that I had seen myself to be perfectly 'sane' in making that deliberate choice, whilst those around me felt it appropriate to brand me as 'mentally disturbed'. In these pages, I look at some of the implications of making an anti-life decision within a particular cultural heritage, in my case Jewish – a religion that is perhaps the most life-affirming of them all.

My own suicide attempt came out of an abusive childhood spent sniffing violence in the wind and believing that death was on the doorstep.

During my childhood my mother, who sadly was not my friend until her final illness, talked constantly about her impending death. Although I now assume she was perfectly physically robust during my childhood, at the time I fell for her own delusion that she was extremely frail. This was largely induced by her decision to control me and my 'evil ways' by the constant use of the threat of her own death if I did not behave better.

It is a hard campaign to inflict on a child.

I feared that if I did not mend my ways my mother would die and leave me. She did not die but on two occasions she did leave which meant my notions of abandonment became inextricably entwined with ideas of death. This is an idea reflected upon by many of the interviewees.

Although seriously ill in her final two years, she lived until she was eighty-four, when ironically she too tried to kill herself. She was found in time, but died from the complications of attempted suicide some weeks later. Her death occurred during the initial planning and pilot study for this book.

As I continued to write this book, death continued to shadow its pages.

When I was writing the suicide chapter, I was appalled to learn that my former next-door neighbour had just committed suicide.

Then came what has been the most significant death in my life. During the writing and research of this book, my most particular friend, Carol Kendrick, a young and brilliant paediatrician, a life-enhancing woman, died suddenly and shockingly from a brain haemorrhage.

In our society, friendship bereavements are singularly less validated than those of family members. Yet for women, friends have a special and lasting importance. In the chapter on Unacknowledged Losses I show how bereavement is intensified for women when loss is not legitimated.

Professionally, Carol Kendrick's death has altered the shape of this book, because she was to have played a substantial part in it. As a paediatrician, Carol daily dealt with the 'untimely deaths' of babies and young children. She had agreed that part of my research would look at the daily routines, the situations encountered, the feelings and consequences upon her own life of such a job. Daily she was part of the grief and bereavement process as it affects parents, particularly mothers, to whom she broke the news of a baby's or child's impending death, discussed possible outcomes, and for whom she set up and was involved in counselling and aftercare.

We had made a start with some informal interviews but her own untimely death prevented us doing the major research work. I have however been aided in this project by several of her understanding colleagues, who deeply respected her work and who miss her professionally as I do personally. Their voices, their contribution to debates about discretion and disclosure, notions of care versus cure, and death as failure versus death as completion, will be heard in Chapter Three (Mortal Messages).

Carol's words will not have a place in these pages, but her spirit informs every line that I have written.

Chapter One

BREAKING THE SILENCE

There is no assurance that you will live to read the whole of this book.

I had no assurance that I would live to finish writing it.

These seem simple statements. Obvious statements. But nobody talks about their implications. Nobody talks about death.

I say this, having established that at least 150 women want to talk most seriously and most earnestly about death. They want to lift the taboo which they see pertaining to dying and bereavement and, more significantly, to women's participation in the dying process.

If this sounds contradictory, it is because the notion of a death taboo that needs lifting is both accurate but also contains within it certain contradictions which have been the subject of incessant debate for a decade.

On the one hand, we appear to have spent years learning cultural rules which tell us to repress, avoid, and deny death. A cultural confirmation of this viewpoint came in 1970 when commentator Malcolm Muggeridge stated: 'For most contemporary minds the notion of death is hidden away, unmentioned if not unmentionable.'[1]

Twenty years later, in 1990, a spate of articles such as this from the *Radio Times* reiterated 'Death – and talk about it – is the one great taboo of our age.'[2]

Last month, during 1994, a woman funeral director told me: 'People just don't talk about death, especially people with families, it's not the thing to be talked about. But because I am a funeral director, and I deal with death, they open up. Other people just don't want to open up.' (Sally Smith 1994.)[3]

Yet on the other hand, the quality press gives space to fashionable funerals, notable obituaries, and creative hospice work. People have showered me with news cuttings to illustrate that I am not alone in what they term my 'peculiar undertaking'.

Nor is this frequent discussion of a forbidden topic unique to the United Kingdom. Simpson's 1979 *English Language Bibliography* lists over 650 books on the subject, while his updated version (1987) adds a further 1700 books written between 1979 and 1986.[4]

Furthermore, despite general resistance to the topic, the Open University nevertheless as confidently assumed a large, enthusiastic studentship for their first death and dying course as I have assumed an enthusiastic readership for this book.[5]

The recognition of this taboo around death, however, meant that my decision to undertake the peculiar was not easy.

The first few publishers to whom I submitted the idea said hastily: 'Of course it is a wonderful project, a necessary project, but what it needs is a big bold publisher.'

They themselves were not big enough or bold enough.

I moved on. I found a big bold publisher.

'Of course,' they said, big and boldly: 'It is a wonderful project, a necessary project; wonderful, yes, necessary, yes, a project that *needs* to be done.'

(Being big and bold means they frequently repeat themselves.) They continued regretfully, 'But what it requires is a small, innovative, risk-taking publisher.'

I moved on. I found a small, innovative, risk-taking publisher. The risk-takers were too small to take the risk.

'Death isn't like sex,' they said nervously. 'Sex sells. Everyone wants to talk about sex. You can't talk about death.'

Ah ha! I remembered what people had said when I wanted to write about celibacy instead of sex. You can't talk about it![6]

I moved on. My book, and the women who want to talk about death, found a good home.

Despite this, there were still some obstacles. As Germaine Greer points out, if a woman admits that 'death is on her mind, it will be understood that something is wrong with her'.[7]

Choosing to write about death is choosing to be looked on as a freak. A worthy freak but still a freak. Choosing to talk about writing about death is choosing to swim against the stream. It is asking to be silenced.

Nothing is more of a conversation stopper than the mention of a corpse or two, a jolly graveyard where I often sit and write, a cemetery that I found suitable for picnics, a widows' group where we had a real laugh, a bereavement centre where parents who have lost children can rebuild their lives and where I began to understand mine more fully .

'Aren't you being a bit morbid?' friends asked hesitantly. 'Aren't you finding it depressing?' inquired my family with sympathy.

Thinking about death is itself considered to be a morbid symptom. Germaine Greer says that if the presence of thoughts about death in a woman are suspected, some brain-deadening treatment will be ordered. In my case, I and my book were effectively quarantined.[8]

'How is your *next* book?' people asked. 'You know, the one you are going to write after that . . . er . . . difficult one?'

What they are asking is if there is a life after death?

The truth is there is a great deal of life within death. The conversations I had with women about death and dying were often painful, usually moving, sometimes funny, always a challenge, filled with joyous good spirit.

It was hard to convince people that this was the case.

Death is under permanent veto. Those who are dying are kept under wraps. But grief too has a shelf-life and a talk-by date. Blinds are no longer drawn nor curtains pulled, nor mourning clothes worn when someone dies. In the past when we singled out the bereaved, we did not psychologically exclude or invisibilise them as we do today. We offered a respect for their mourning and gave them formal adjustment time.

Today we arrive late for funerals, leave hastily. To the bereaved we are perfunctorily polite, if we talk at all. Often we make a swift embarrassed exit. We expect the bereaved sharply to pull themselves together and get over it. We are a nation of brave citizens and self-admiring stoics. Low on emotion, high on judgement.

We are selfish in our terror. We underestimate the effect that even one ordinary raw death (a death we rage against) can have on our lives, an effect often as profound and positive as it is painful.

Our attitude has particularly harsh effects on women. In this society women are in a double-bind situation. They are socialised for most of their lives to be caring, nurturing, emotional, expected to act like vulnerable girls irrespective of their age. Then at the point when the caring is over, their emotions at their height, their vulnerability most intense, they are expected not to show it.

As women attempt to come to terms with individual or family

deaths, the world outside obfuscates, obliterates, sequestrates, screens and conceals the total death process. Pointedly people refuse to talk about the dead, as if they had never existed.

'My daughter was marvellous about taking me to the supermarket and getting the bank sorted out after her Dad died, but in the three years since his funeral she has never once mentioned him to me.' (Widow, seventy-nine.)

Many people I spoke to said they found grief embarrassing. It made them uneasy. The women I interviewed did *not* feel this way. They wanted to talk about grief, openly and at length.

He lived on the edge. He had an obsession with racing motor bikes. He crashed to his death in a very dangerous race. My son and my mother heard it on the radio and broke the news to me. I just simply screamed the house down. I wanted to get in the car, go somewhere and be with him. The coroner tried to stop me seeing him because of how he looked. But I had to. I didn't care how he looked. He was all dressed up in his coffin in a grey taffeta suit, he was an artist, he'd have approved of his shroud. I sat by the coffin for three days; it felt like a ritual. He'd gone so quickly that I needed to talk to him. I needed to cry with him. I needed to just be silent with him. I told him I loved him, I repeatedly told him I loved him, which I'd told him before. Later I became obsessed with talking about it. I wanted to talk all the time, to expose my grief, to expose myself more and more.
          (British homeopath whose partner died on racetrack.)

When my husband – he was a Greek American – died of cancer, I called up his mother. She entered the room and shrieked, threw herself on his body and just wailed. She shook him and she kissed him and she beat the hell out of him – and I just stood there. At first I thought she's gone round the . . . she's gone nuts . . . then I realised this must be what Greeks do. Greek women can wail. They're allowed to wail. We aren't allowed to wail. It must be a tremendous catharsis. That was exactly what I felt like doing, but no one would ever give me permission. I felt envious . . . then I wanted to talk, to talk all the time . . . but women here are imprisoned, we can't just keep on talking about our grief. Wailing, that's obviously a Greek custom. But women here, we should have customs of our own. Maybe one of them should be talking. *Talking could be our women's ritual.*
          (Ellen, New York editor, sixty, on death of her husband.)

The writer Alice Thomas Ellis, whose son Joshua died in an accident at nineteen, confirms Western women's attitudes towards the social limitations on grief. 'In this country certainly we don't grieve sufficiently when we should. I remember seeing, I think it was some Turkish women at a funeral wailing, swaying from side to side and all one's instincts tell one to do that, but you'd look so stupid wouldn't you, doing it all by yourself?' (Alice Thomas Ellis, 1992.)[9]

Resentment about a time schedule for grief, or feelings of rejection, do not necessarily imply women wish to get that grief *out* of their system: 'I don't want to talk my grief out. I want to talk my grief in.' (British landscape gardener, widowed at thirty.)

As I listened to women, I consistently picked up the notion that women's perceptions of death and grief were something internal, something inside them.

Equally significant to women was the making of images around death, or writing creatively about it. Many had taken photos of the person they loved at the point of death. Several women had taken videos of the open coffin. Many had made audio cassettes of the last conversations with a dying person. Even more had recorded the funeral or the memorial. Some women had made creative photo montages, some wrote stories, poems, or documentary prose pieces.

Some engaged with these art forms for therapeutic reasons, others used them as starting points for sustained work in art or writing. Professional artists and writers who had been bereaved spoke about how death changed their art, and how their art helped them come to terms with death.

At first, despite being an enthusiastic photographer myself, I felt a little uneasy about the idea of taking photos at a deathbed.

Then, during the writing of this book, when my particular friend, Carol Kendrick, tragically died aged only forty-three, I sat at her bedside, where in a coma she lay dying, for several hours. During her short life I had taken hundreds of photos of her working on the hospital ward (in the very hospital that was now the setting of her last hours), walking the Yorkshire hills, drinking champagne, relaxing quietly in her Manchester home, always laughing.

Suddenly I understood why the women I had interviewed felt the need to take photos. It was exactly what I wanted to do.

Yet still I felt constricted. With me, in those first hours at the bedside, were Mary, the friend who had taken her in to Intensive Care, and Carol's young and precious daughter Nicho. If I had been alone, I should have caringly taken a last image. I do not think Carol would have minded. She always told me she loved being photographed. But I did not want to do anything 'unseemly' or anything that might have further distressed Nicho. So we sat, the three of us, holding on to Carol, sad that Carol's partner J. was abroad, and I imprinted the image of my friend for all time in my mind.

My intense grief, throughout the research and writing of this study, did not impede the work, although of course it changed it. Many women interviewed said it helped to discuss bereavement with someone who was no stranger to it.

The evidence I have gathered suggests that women and men may have different grief patterns; that women, especially bereaved mothers, or women responding to suicide, do not feel their grief gets 'resolved' although they learn how to cope with its symptoms so that they may play a less embarrassing part in society.

These findings are interesting because they expand, even contradict, some major grief theories already available. This is less surprising when we remember that researchers in the area (Averill, 1968; Kubler-Ross, 1969; Parkes, 1972) were looking at the general population without any gender breakdown.[10]

Death revives passion, even or perhaps especially in elderly people. Others become uncomfortable. Grief is passionate. Women explain: 'Now he is dead I am in the grip of an obsession like a love affair. I want to talk about him all the time. I'm obsessive about everything he wore, or where we went, or what he said.' (American widow, sixty-five.)

'He was killed in an accident. They said don't come. I had to go to him. It was the only thing on my mind. I've been going to him in the cemetery ever since. He is my love and I am savaged by it.' (Canadian mother of a son, thirty-five.)

'She was my other half, she was my person. Her death was a mystery, she went missing for weeks, I searched, everyone searched, and I howled, then they found what was left of her beneath the rocks. This, what I feel now, must be the other side of what I thought love was about.' (British bereaved partner, thirty-five, whose woman lover died from a fall.)

The message women communicated was that grief and love are two sides of the same coin.

Are there some in society who wish that passion to abate? Is that one reason for discomfort? Certainly if the 'relic' (as one bereaved elderly woman termed herself) is old, then her fiercely impassioned grieving may be looked on as out of place.

In Chapter Three (Mortal Messages) I discuss implications of

evidence taken from women interviewed, which suggests firstly that
the loss of a loved person cannot ever effectively be resolved (already
hinted at by Littlewood, 1992); secondly, that a woman, rather than
fully recovering from that experience, simply becomes a 'new person'
with that death, that grief, inside her.[11]

> The sense of loss is a presence that is familiar to me. I shall never
> stop feeling their loss. Most of all I shall never stop feeling the loss
> of those two who loved me and who I loved. Theirs is a uniquely
> shaped loss inside my heart. What changes about grief is that at
> first I went right off the rails, then I got back on the rails, but they
> are different rails.
>
> > (Angelica, a poet who lost her partner, her mother, her
> > stepfather, her father, her close friend, all within five years.)

'Since Greg died I have had this burden, this rucksack of grief on my
back. I shall never be able to put it down.' (Annie, whose son Greg
committed suicide four years ago.)

Most women with private griefs made similar statements, but several bereavement counsellors to whom I talked felt the idea of 'not
getting over it' was 'bad for one's health'.

Several grieving women had been to grief therapists or counsellors.

> Those women who have a professional investment in grief are try-
> ing to enable people to get on in society so they teach women
> about managing grief. If you say that you never stop grieving
> they get angry. It is anti-social behaviour. They are out there in
> society helping women to get on in appropriate ways.
>
> > (Angelica)

Many women did not want to be controlled by what is seen as an
appropriate time limit for grief. Women have an ability to feel
intensely for a long time, and wish to be able to do so unhindered.

> When my Dad died I felt that loss was irreplaceable. It wasn't that
> he'd *done* much, he hadn't – only the garden, and his job at the
> water board – it was *who* he was that was irreplaceable. So I've got
> to live with that loss for ever. People don't like you to feel that, so
> though I'd like to feel I was free to say more about it, I'll just learn
> not to show the symptoms.
>
> > (Emily, bereaved daughter, fifty-two.)

Bel Mooney, the writer, whose second son was stillborn, wrote this:

> I would interrupt all the wise phrases of bereavement counselling,
> all the talk of 'loss', with this blunt truth: that when someone you
> love dies you might as well accept the fact that you will be
> haunted by that person for the rest of your life. . . . That is not
> morbid: it simply invested what happened with permanent dig-
> nity.[12]

As Karen Blixen, quoting William Faulkner said passionately:
'Between grief and nothing I choose grief.'[13]

Women in this study are choosing grief, but out of it they are
attempting to make something meaningful. They want the freedom
to mourn vividly if need be. To take photos, make audio tapes, show
videos, if those are their preferences. To mourn, for as long as it
takes, both in ways that are unique to each of them as one individual lamenting the loss of another special person, and also as women
who share a particular mode of grief.

Failure to mourn is to devalue loss. Grief and its ghost go on. A
proper haunting which may indeed be permanent does not necessarily need exorcism.

*Grief needs expression but it does not need the debasement of the
coinage.*

That, however, is what I see happening around me. I would argue
the case that, in some sense, death in the last decade has become a
fashionable topic. But by becoming trendy it has also become trivi-
alised.

A new breed of bereavement counsellors has sprung up with a
paid professional investment in other people's losses. In a capitalist
consumer society, bereavement counselling has become big business. Grief-teams run death workshops. Chain stores sell 'grief
management' manuals. Railway bookshops stock 'living gently with
cancer' books alongside Mills and Boon romances.

You hear phrases like: 'That was a healing experience.'

Or: 'Thank you for sharing your grief.'

Certain post-death phrases are used to minimise the mystery.

Somehow, the New Age packaging of grief has made us forget
that death, like love, is a monumental mysterious experience which
has captured the imagination of generations of poets, playwrights
and painters. Profound problems of the nature and purpose of existence have occupied the minds of philosophers and the imaginative
sensibilities of mystics since the beginning of history. Throughout

the ages, in every culture, the living have been as preoccupied with
death as they have with love.

Death like love, touches our emotions at our most vulnerable
moments.

Death, *unlike* love, is the only certainty our life holds.

It is an amazing and entirely natural process. Yet it is treated, in
this culture, as something unnatural, something to be feared. An
aberration to be clinically controlled.

The struggle to stay alive is as common to animals as it is to
humans, but only humans can contemplate and analyse their own
mortality. We reflect, we fantasise, we produce ceremonials and rituals around death which illustrate the value placed on life, as well as
our understanding of destiny or spiritual passion. We search for
meaning in the midst of unbearable suffering. We examine religion
for comfort. Or we do not, believing there to be none.

But often we stay silent.

Are we afraid to accept that death is an opportunity as well as an
end? Can we not trust in the suggestion that endings which are
most often viewed as a loss can be seen as a change? Is believing that
there are no other terms on which we can live except those of death
the stuff of visions and wonder? Is that belief too dramatic, is that
belief too highly coloured for this pizza-parlour culture, this mun-
dane existence?[14]

Does denial of death seem an easier route?

Loss is the fire this time. We cannot come through it unscathed.
When bereavement touches us, we look away, or we look inside. In
our everyday lives, we do not talk about death. We try not to think
about it. We invisibilise, sanitise, and neutralise a process we cannot
encompass and cannot come to terms with.

We rarely try to comprehend how it specifically affects women.
Yet it cannot be disputed that women's particular relationship to
dying, women's attitudes towards death, women's responses to loss,
have been shrouded in silence.

Women (like the working class, like black people of all classes),
have long known that silence is a symbol of oppression. Liberation
is speaking out, making contact, communicating how an experience feels for that particular group, which may conflict with the
understanding of the dominant culture, whose ideology in our society is masculist, white, and heterosexual, rooted in an emphasis on
coupledom and genital activity.

These ideological preoccupations adversely affect women who do
not adhere to them, as for instance in the case of widows, or

bereaved lesbian partners, or black women carers of the dying from
other cultures. These pages record how the taboo around death
together with the stigma that attaches to certain groups of bereaved
women, have implications for their participation in the death
process.

There has been a notable absence of serious discussion of the
gender issue. Despite three decades of feminist inquiry I have seen
very little debate on where and how women fit into the death
process, or the effect that a death taboo has on women's lives.

The impressive and highly researched Open University course on
death and dying consistently looks at religion and race, but only
occasionally analyses gender. This may be partly because they had a
very wide agenda, and partly because, like me, they were forced to
start from existing source material which is very low indeed on gender information.

In a rare analysis of gender differences that exist in the way people view death, Nicky James, a lecturer in nursing studies and
researcher in palliative care, observes: 'It is fascinating that despite
the pervasiveness of gender differences, even a scholastic and
detailed study of attitudes to death failed to address the issue.'[15]

It is less fascinating than predictable and disturbing.

What then are the reasons?

Talking about how it really is for women in many varied situations has been handcuffed by the lack of a language that feels
appropriate and by the lack of a space in which to communicate.

More significantly, women's response to death and dying has been
subsumed under men's relationship to death.

Every time I went to a literary gathering for work, or a social
gathering at home, and said I was interested in women's perspective
on death, I received the same response.

'Surely death is the same for everyone, men and women, isn't it?'

I expect the actual split second of encountering death itself is
either identical for every human or utterly different for each individual. We have no way of knowing. The travellers do not return.

But the lead up to death; the socialisation of attitudes towards
death; towards caring for dying people; towards loss and bereavement of children, of parents, of lovers, enemies, friends and family;
the response to one's own terminal illness and imminent demise, of
course these are not the same for women as for men.

The only people who could believe that must be the utterly
unaware, the totally misguided, the semi-conscious, the intellectually stunted, or those who through too long a sojourn under the

duvet have missed the sight and sound, the passion and fury of the Women's Movement, which has spent three decades systematically unearthing the differences in women's response to and perspective on all the major conditions of life.

The second wave of feminist theorists have spent thirty-four years breaking the silence around men's constructions and women's relationships to language, to food, to economics, to sex, to power, to education, to health, to religion, to violence, to pornography, to beauty, to housework, to peace, and to war.

The dying process is no more immune from patriarchal strictures, power imbalance or gender difference, than are any of these. The sexual politics around death has simply not yet been uncovered.

This book begins to remedy this omission.

The study is in the nature of a first exploration.

I hope other researchers may find something of interest that they can explore in greater detail.

Our sexual politics, as well as our cultural taboos and our consumer context, shape and structure women's roles and responsibilities around the sick and the dying. They affect women's attitudes and behaviour towards bereavement and death.

Death has always been a significant part of the historical experience of women since so much of the actual care of the sick and dying falls on women's shoulders.

Historically men and women have had a very different relationship to the dying process.

'Men experienced death by seeking it out or confronting it alone or in a predominantly male context: on sea voyages, in Indian fighting, in wars. Women encountered death in the home or went out to bring home their wounded and dying men during wartime.'[16]

There was, and is, one especially female mode of the death experience: death in pregnancy, death via abortions, death during and after childbirth. We can only surmise the complex effects, in the past, on women's psychology brought about by the inevitable connection between heterosexual activity and pregnancy at a time when it was substantially more likely for women to die in childbirth than it was for men to die violently in war. Lerner tells us: 'In the centuries before soldiers were drafted, a man meeting death on the battlefield or in Indian warfare usually had made a choice in the matter. Women's way of death, like women's lives, was cast in a passive mold.'[17]

However, in the present, women's voices throughout this study offer us an insight into the intricate connections between the processes of giving birth and responding to death, most especially the death of children. For women, the boundaries between life and death are blurred.

Women see death, like life, as 'inside' them. Men are more likely to see death as external or 'outside'.

Throughout life, males are statistically more likely to die than females. Up to age fourteen, the ratio of boys' deaths to girls' is roughly four to three, and up to this age deaths from external causes of injury and poisoning are in a ratio of two to one.[18]

Nicky James shows graphically how in childhood and early adolescence this is reinforced metaphorically in games children play, the boys revelling in miraculous escapes and revivals from deaths.[19]

The mortality figures suggest that boys take more risks than girls, a feature that is mirrored in their games. These physical risk-taking deaths appear to be consistently associated with 'outside' factors. Archer (1989) has suggested that boyhood emphasis on physical strength is an historical residue from preparation for the fighting role, another death threat from 'outside'.[20]

Although girls appear more immune from death than boys during adolescence, once they menstruate and encounter the possibility of pregnancy, they face a form of death outside boys' experience. Nicky James points out that as a female becomes pregnant and a life is growing inside her, the spectre of the death of the child is introduced.[21]

This may be the core of women's perceptions of death from 'inside'.

Of the nearly 690,000 babies born in England and Wales in 1989 very few will have come to term and been delivered without the mother contemplating the embryo's malformation or death. In 1989 there were nearly 170,000 recorded abortions for women between fifteen and forty-four years, and 803 were experienced by girls under 15.[22]

Raising questions about the integral nature of life and death as it does, abortion is a uniquely female experience, emphasising again death from 'inside'.

Parenting, which in our society socialises women into primary parent-carers, reinforces worries about children's accidents and their possible deaths.

Relatively recent social change means that more men are becoming involved in parenting which means they are somewhat more likely to experience the intimate knowledge of their child's development, which should make them more conscious of the child's life and vulnerability to death.[23]

Whether this will result in a slight shift in men's perceptions of death as an 'outside' event remains to be seen, though obviously for reproductive reasons they will not be able to experience the female insider's viewpoint.

From fourteen to forty-four males are nearly twice as likely to die as females, with the ratio of deaths from external causes rising to four to one, double that of childhood.[24]

During this period men are considerably more likely than women to suffer death from causes outside themselves, a proportion of which will be death by violence. The well established pattern of male violence, under patriarchy, has a direct influence on men's own handling of death, as in their suicide attempts, the majority of which are by very violent means. It also has severe repercussions on the women who are left to pick up the pieces. Sometimes literally. (Chapter Ten.)

Male violence moreover directly impacts on women's fears about deaths. Insufficient space and time for adequate research meant I have not considered in depth the issue of murder but I should like to point out how many deaths are directly attributable to male sexual violence against women. If today's increasing figures for incest, rape and battery are disturbing but well documented, what have been largely hidden, by virtue of their highly distressing nature, are the figures for female murder by men women know intimately. According to one study, wives constitute 41 per cent of all women killed as against husbands' 11 per cent.[25]

Jill Radford and Diana E.H. Russell who address the problem of femicide in the USA, England and India, explode one of the most pervasive myths of patriarchal culture: that the home provides a safe haven for women. They show clearly that the home is the place where women are at the greatest risk (a risk that not infrequently ends in death) when that home is shared by a man, be he husband, male lover, father or brother.[26]

What is striking about the limited history of women and their experiences with death at my disposal, is that it is overwhelmingly connected with their sexuality. As Beth Ann Bassein's research suggests, and this study confirms, women's involvements with death, both in fiction (Chapter Three) and in women's actual lives, invariably deal with some aspect of their sexuality, often the most brutal side of it.[27]

In Chapter Eight (Image, Sex and the Language of Cancer) I examine the links between women's bodies, sexual image and cancer. I explore the ways in which the taboo around death knits into the image taboo to make open awareness and assessment of breast cancer and other cancers more complex.

In Great Britain women die from breast cancer alone at the rate of five hundred a week. In the USA an estimated one in nine women will be diagnosed with breast cancer every year (1991 figures). It is the leading killer of women between the ages of thirty-five and forty-five in the USA.

I investigate how surgeons deal with women patients and analyse the differences between reported 'good operations' and 'bad butcherings'.

I also look at the doubly taboo areas of sex and dying and sex and death. While death is considered both serious and shaming, sex is counted as frankly frivolous. Many people believe (or pretend to themselves) that the dying partner/lover is 'above all that sex stuff'. Very often a dying woman is not! But if communication is poor, if women and men cannot speak out, the death process may well damage a love life also.

There is as much silence over the idea of a dying woman wanting sex as there is over a dying woman dying.

'My wife is dying and I hate to admit this but I just feel there's something unwholesome about the idea of sex with her now. She's got this deteriorating disease. Her whole body has changed. Quite honestly I just don't fancy it.' (Husband of wife dying at home.)

'I almost felt I would catch her death if I went too near her. Of course I never told her. I knew she wanted to make love. I couldn't even try. We never spoke about it. It was too heavy so you just stay silent .' (Husband of wife who died in hospital ward.)

There are other sensual and sexual problems:

> My lover comes daily. She knows how much I am hungering for her to touch my body. But because she is a woman, the staff don't take her presence in my life seriously. Sometimes when we draw the curtains around the bed, so that we can fondle or kiss privately, some nurses draw back the curtains as if they had every right. They would never intrude on our privacy if she was my boyfriend.
>
> (Female partner of woman dying in public ward.)

Fear of death, when related to sexuality, is another example of a woman's death experience being seen as 'inside' her, a very different situation from that encountered by men.

Such gender variations, reinforced by the gender division of paid and domestic work, and women's conditioning towards caring, support differences between the two sexes so that their life experiences, up to the point of dying (or caring for the dying) are significantly gender related.[28]

Substantial evidence illustrates that men see life as a series of achievements and revel unto death in 'things they have done'. Death of course stops the doing. My own research exemplifies that when someone dies, men focus their mourning on what the dead person *did*. This study of dying confirms my earlier research on sex, celibacy, food and power, and other research (Gilligan, Spender, Tannen) on language, power and sex to show that women's relational view of life extends to a relational view of death.[29]

Communication tools, and the ways in which women and men use them, bear this out. Deborah Tannen's (1991) research on women's and men's conversations shows clearly how men's conversations are activity-based whilst women's reinforce relationships.[30]

Women show how this works in practice: 'When his work partner died, my husband talked about his past achievements, what he'd done, what he'd achieved. When my best friend died last year, I only thought about what she'd meant to me, and to her other friends.' (Bereaved woman, thirty-six.)

Toby's brother was a sports star so I suppose it was natural to dwell on what he'd achieved. But somehow it seemed cold and egocentric when he did the same thing with Janet, our niece who died of leukaemia just after she'd got a place at Oxford. He kept talking about what she'd done to get there. I was thinking about how Janet had tried to keep her Mum and me from worrying even when she was very sick. I kept thinking how she might have affected all of our futures.

(Bereaved aunt , thirty-eight.)

Women's relational view of death sees dying as the death of hope, of optimism, of limitless possibilities. Women see the dead person as important for who they are, not only for what they did. It is the 'irreplaceableness' of that person, and her or his place in the lives of others, for which they grieve.

Whether we explain the forces shaping the roles of the two sexes biologically, socially or structurally, my evidence suggests that whereas the male experience of death is largely seen as an 'outside' event, for females, both life and death are intimately associated with females' psyches, expectations and their bodies, with the implication that both life and death can be comprehended and delineated as something 'inside' them.[31]

Over the last hundred years conflicting masculine and feminine experiences of death have taken place within a shifting context. Changes in population, health and community patterns, have had particular implications for the death process. I shall use Great Britain as an example.

At the start of the century women played a very active role in the formal death process. Chapter Two describes how in many towns local women laid out dead bodies, watched over them in the home, acted as 'bidders' or informants about funeral arrangements, became coffin bearers for dead women, and were responsible for preparing and serving the funeral teas.

At that time, the population of the United Kingdom was almost entirely white, Anglo-Saxon and Christian. Earth burial was the rule. Families were close socially, close geographically. When a death occurred, both the family and the local or religious community were involved. Dying, death, disposal and bereavement were an integral part of everyday life. Death was talked about as it was lived.

By today's standards, medicine and surgery were primitive. 90 per cent of deaths occurred at home. Children and young people were high risk groups. Less than 5 per cent were subject to coroners' inquests.

Today, Britain has become multi-ethnic with people from other cultures bringing their own customs and religious rituals. Cremation is the commonest form of disposal of corpses; the coroner investigates over one-third of all deaths. Dead bodies, no longer in the care of women, are the province of funeral directors, a profession still almost entirely male which I put under the searchlight in Chapter Five (Female Funeral Directors). What changes are made by women directing funerals? How does a funeral manager incorporate the death business into her home life? What kinds of rituals and spiritual memorials do women today see as applicable?[32]

Death has become a medical matter; current medical ideology sees death as the enemy, dying as failure. Death today is seen as so problematic that according to Philippe Aries scientists have 'conjured away' death.

Aries suggests that the medicalisation of death has involved firstly the use of 'clean' talk about illness in terms of cure, which is opposed to the disgust at the 'dirtiness' of death; secondly, the relocation of dying people into hospitals away from public view; thirdly the regulation and organisation of death by doctors who see it as failure.

He sees the history of dying as one in which both control of the dying process and place of death has changed. In the Middle Ages, control was either held by the dying person in the home, supported at the time of death by the community, or held by the dying person's family, in the home, supported by the family. By contrast, today control is held by the medical profession, in hospitals, where support at time of death is minimal, except for a small group of health professionals who, aware of the isolation of the dying, have tried since the sixties to defy the taboo and change the medical, psychological and social work practice.[33]

Certainly our tendency to label anything connected with death as morbid, irrelevant or in sheer bad taste, blows up into elaborate debates such questions as: Should a doctor tell a patient diagnosed as suffering from terminal illness that she (or he) is dying? The notion, surprisingly still prevalent, that keeping them in the dark is for the patients' own *good* is dependent on an ideology that says death is *bad*.

In Chapter Three (Mortal Messages) I examine this modern (irrational?) belief that death should be ultimately avoidable, a belief based on a strange notion of progress that provocatively suggests that advances in medical science might one day conquer death itself. Women surgeons, consultants, paediatricians and oncologists discuss the suggestion that this is a masculist scientific ethic and look at how such messages affect both dying people and doctors themselves.

Moving beyond the male medical model, and viewing death with a whole-person approach in order to regain its spiritual dimension, is the area covered in Chapter Twelve (Unacknowledged Losses).

In the years since the sixties counter-culture, several professional women have challenged the old norm that it was courageous for the dying and their carers *not to talk* about what was happening, by persuading people that it was courageous *to talk* about it.

In Great Britain Cicely Saunders founded the British Hospice Movement which is very much in tune with the expressive elements of the counter-culture. In America Elisabeth Kubler-Ross (1970) promoted in North American hospitals the right and necessity of the dying to talk openly about their feelings.

Associated with this productive personal expressiveness are three other cultural currents: the Green Movement and the Women's Movement, which though they did not set out to consider dying and bereavement have profoundly affected both; and the Death Awareness Movement, which flourished in the USA from the early sixties until the mid seventies. It facilitated humane programmes of care for the dying, it offered professionals and the community realistic courses in death education, and made a real challenge to the denial of death. Unfortunately the movement has lost momentum. Bureaucratisation seems to have taken place. New approaches are needed.

I look at the pioneering work of three women: Dame Cicely Saunders; Sister Helen Passant, a boundary-breaking complementary therapist, and Josefine Speyer, co-founder of the Natural Death Centre. I also analyse the impact of the Women's Movement on women's healing and rituals.[34]

Today we live substantially longer.

In the Middle Ages, life expectancy in England is estimated to have been about thirty-three years. By the nineteenth century this had risen to forty-one years. In the early eighties, 75 per cent of all deaths were people over sixty-five compared to 34 per cent in the 1920s. By 1986 most people who died in Britain were elderly. Figures for 1986 show that 79 per cent of all deaths were of people aged sixty-five and over and 55 per cent of all deaths were of people aged seventy-five and over.

Now that developing nations have made substantial progress in eliminating premature death, increasingly death is a phenomenon of old age. Western society in less than a hundred years has more than doubled a child's life expectancy at birth. The dramatic reduction in infant mortality means we have changed the face of death.

Until the advent of AIDS-related diseases, deaths outside the older age range were rare occurrences. When childhood deaths do occur, their impact is shocking. Both parents have special bereavement difficulties, but the grief of mothers is intensified both by their reproductive bond and their socialisation as primary parents. Problems faced are examined in Chapter Seven (Deaths That Haunt: Mothers Lose Children).

The gender imbalance in life expectancy between women and men is increasing. In 1906, average life expectation at birth for males was forty-eight, for females fifty-one. At seventy-five it was eighty for males against eighty-two for females. In 1985 the figures at birth for males were seventy-two, for females seventy-seven; at age seventy-five, figures were eighty-three for men, eighty-five for women.[35]

In general women live longer than men. This applies in each social class. 60 per cent of those over sixty-five are female and this gender imbalance increases with age. Amongst the population aged eighty-five plus, there are 250 females for every hundred males.

Women's greater longevity combined with the societal norm that women should marry men their own age or older means that women frequently find themselves living alone when old.

And dying alone.

In 1987 61 per cent of women over seventy-five lived alone, which carries implications for their access to informal care and support, and is a major reason for the increasing number of people dying in hospital.[36]

In 1989 in the UK, an analysis of deaths by cause showed that disease of the circulatory system caused about half of all deaths; cancer accounted for just under a quarter, and respiratory system failure accounted for between 10 and 15 per cent. All three diseases are characteristically (though not invariably) associated with old age. In the USA more than 150,000 Americans die of stroke each year, stroke (according to the World Health Organisation) being the third most common cause of death in the world's developed countries, only exceeded by cardiac disease and cancer.[37]

Over 85 per cent of our ageing population will succumb to the complications of one of only seven major conditions: Atherosclerosis, Alzheimer's (and other dementias), cancer, hypertension, adult-onset diabetes, obesity, and decreased resistance to infection.[38]

Of these I have chosen in Chapter Nine (Sons? Do I Have Sons?) to examine Alzheimer's because in certain significant ways it can be seen as a 'women's disease', a fact that has been very little documented.

Elderly people make up a larger section of the population (15 per cent today) than they did at the turn of the century (5 per cent) The proportion of 'very grey' people has grown, while the numbers of people who might take responsibility for providing informal care for the elderly infirm and terminally ill has proportionately diminished. This has resonances for women as major carers. It means they may become obligatory caretakers when they are old and frail themselves, possibly even in the early stages of a debilitating disease. Chapter Four (Dutiful Daughters: Private Caring) explores what caring involves for women who take on this task.

There is a bitter irony in the fact that women's greater longevity means elderly women are forced to live with death longer than any other identifiable group. Having faced the death of partner, peers and family, they then confront the seemingly endless prospect of their own death.

One group who face this situation in Britain are the 3 million widows and millions more bereaved partnerless women. Currently, widowhood is increasing for women under sixty. There are four times as many widows as widowers. Yet despite an estimated 15 per cent of women today being widows, neither the welfare state nor our death-taboo culture deals adequately with this fact or its consequences.

Many elderly widows still reported intense loneliness, 'difficulty in getting through Sundays', anxieties about their own deaths, and a desperate drop in income.

Younger widows, who did not daily observe their friends dying, were much more positive but still saw widowhood as a stigmatised state. Chapter Six (Widows and Other Leftover Lives) investigates their situation. Whether 'respectably' labelled 'widow' or whether as bereaved live-in lover or common-law wife, these women, in a culture that fears death while it affirms coupledom and genital activity, become a group trebly stigmatised. The special stigma and complex forbidden grief attached to lesbian 'widowhood' and bereavement is dealt with in Chapter Thirteen.

Coni, Davison and Webster, consultants in geriatric medicine at Addenbrookes Hospital, found evidence that (hardly surprisingly!) older people in general are more preoccupied with death than younger ones.[39]

'Death is a realistic concern of the old person, and he or she has a need to share his or her thoughts and feelings on this topic.'[40]

The problem remarked on by the elderly women I spoke to was the growing number of losses they experienced. As Lily Pincus in *Death and the Family* emphasises, it is difficult to *believe* in death, even one death.

'One of the major tasks of mourning, [is] accepting the reality of loss.'[41]

Older women, confronting loss upon loss, were even readier than younger women to talk in meticulous detail about death.

They regarded death with less dread than did middle-aged or young women; some because life had become less precious, some because they no longer felt an urgent need to complete their unfinished tasks, others because they felt they 'had done their bit' and could sit back and enjoy their few remaining years.

Many women over sixty had completed professional and family life cycles, though in many cases friendship and personal growth cycles were incomplete. In this, they differed substantially from older men, having often started their personal development cycle later. Unlike men most felt that they needed friendship cycles continuously.

If younger women feared death more, it could have been because when death arrived for those in their thirties or forties, it caught them mid life-cycle. Many felt cheated, some bitter. Often having started a career or a course of study later than men, or having found a new sexual expression, perhaps having changed their lifestyle from heterosexual to lesbian or celibate, they wished to explore these areas to their fullest possibilities. They yearned to conclude what was interesting and incomplete.

Death cut them short.

In most cases, young women in their twenties to forties did eventually reach an accommodation with death, but sometimes disbelief, shock or anger delayed or distorted the process. Often the question they asked was 'Why? Why me? Why now?'

The dominant question older women posed was no longer 'When shall I die?' (they felt it would be soon) but 'How shall I die?' or often 'Where shall I die?' Several older women worried they might die falling over, getting on or off a bus, or on the street, or even on holiday away from their house or apartment.

Parkes's research found that for many people, dying at home was their preferred option. He found only 24 per cent of those dying in hospital were said by their relatives to have wanted to be admitted.[42]

Ironically it is the difficulties of relatives that are more often a cause of hospital admissions than the difficulties of patients.[43]

Certainly 'home' was a vital concept to most elderly women. Almost all expressed a wish to die there. Sadly, the probability of that is not high. Although women in rural areas are more likely to die at home than city dwellers, in general we are all twice as likely to die in hospital as at home, a developing trend since the 1950s.

One hundred years ago only 50 per cent of deaths took place in hospital. In 1984 only one in four deaths occurred in people's own homes compared to almost half in 1954. In 1987 about 360,000 deaths in England and Wales (56 per cent of the total) took place in NHS hospitals as against 135,000 at home. In urban areas the proportion was as high as 70 per cent. Approximately 80 per cent of people who die in the USA do so in hospital. In Scandinavia 90 per cent of all deaths occur in hospitals.[44]

We die away from home. Often against our will. Often without witnesses who know us well.

Of the substantial number of the elderly who live alone, it is the increasing number of women living alone that is remarkable.

In 1987 38 per cent of women in the sixty-four to seventy-four age group lived alone, as did 61 per cent of women over seventy-five.[45]

Comparing two random national samples of deaths illustrates the amount of change that principally affects women.

In 1969 l9 per cent of women who died lived alone. In 1987 44 per cent of women who died lived alone.

Dying in hospital often means dying in a hectic acute ward where staff are not specifically trained in the care of the dying or in pain control, as they are for instance in hospices. Hospitals are primarily committed to curing people rather than meeting the needs of dying patients. There is too little time for the kind of emotional support and attention dying women need.

Many hospital nurses I interviewed felt their own training in terminal care was inadequate. 'I'd like to be able to spend more time with the ones that are dying, but there simply isn't enough time, and I don't feel confident about getting it right.' (Young nurse, twenty-five.)

Several older nurses confirmed Wilkes's suggestion that many acute medical wards were too busy to give dying patients appropriate attention.[46]

However, despite the acknowledged disadvantages of such a situation, as so many elderly women now live alone it may be that dying in a busy, albeit alienating ward may be more secure or less lonely than dying on their own at home. In certain hospitals where nurses are allowed more autonomy an air of greater informality occurs, and emotional involvement with dying patients becomes possible.

There is another change as startling as the modern medicalisation of death.

Melodramatic representations of death have become the fodder of the media. Death is exposed to us on television almost as much as sex, but what we see in the media is a constant portrayal of the horrific mechanics of death without experiencing its reality. Children, for instance, may be glued to the gore of video death, while few of them have ever seen a sister or brother die, or viewed a corpse.

An over-exposure to death imagery and our under-exposure to its palpable reality combined with the silencing around 'natural' deaths means that adults and children alike have a picture of death that is morbid, bizarre, extreme and fictitious.

This is another curious contradiction.

In 1971 an American study reported that by the time a child in the USA reaches fourteen, she (or he) can be expected to have seen, on average, 18,000 people killed on television, yet the same child will live, on average, for the next forty years without experiencing the death of an immediate family member.[47]

In 1991 David Widgery reported that by the time a Californian child is five she or he will have seen 2,000 deaths on TV but will know nothing of it first hand.[48]

Television floods us with violent and murderous images, yet the reality of natural death is removed, moderated, distanced and rarely discussed. Average women and men in the West today are less familiar with dying and dead bodies than in any other period of history. Death is outside many people's practical experience.

Despite the fact that today at any given moment, approximately one in four members of the adult population will have experienced the death of someone close to them within the previous five years, many will be experiencing their first encounter with death. For some it could be the start of a series of bereavements that could range from the unbearably distressing to the emotionally catastrophic.

Yet still silence surrounds what death has done, what death will do. Denial and avoidance characterises our attitudes towards death and dying despite the profound impact it has on our lives, on our very souls.

It is most strange.

We need to account for this curious situation.

Sociologist Tony Walter believes that many of us are reluctant to talk about death and dying primarily because we lack the necessary skills or the experience of death.

'Death is not very much present today. If the bereaved person finds others embarrassed, crossing to the other side of the street, I suspect it is not so much because they dare not, cannot, confront death, but because they have had little practice at it, do not know what to do, are scared of saying the wrong thing.'[49]

One study, interestingly enough of workers in the health field, confirmed this view. A study of student nurses showed that only one in ten had experienced a death in their family while over a third had never witnessed a death at all.[50]

Walter's 'lack of practice' explanation is one possible reason. But a number of writers have developed more complex theories to explain our wariness of death. Before we examine how women are affected by this wariness it is necessary to look closely at the arguments which attempt to explain its existence.

Geoffrey Gorer in his influential book *Death, Grief and Mourning* suggested in 1965 that death had replaced sex as contemporary society's major taboo topic.[51]

The idea that the mass media's avoidance of natural death is matched by their fascination with violent death is at the heart of Gorer's thesis. He focused on the 'pornography' of death and its presentation of dying in an unrealistic framework. Voyeurism has replaced realism. In Gorer's day the horror comic or the horror movie epitomised those trends. In our day, the way the mass media treats AIDS is an ugly example. In its early stages, AIDS, merely a *disease* was seen as 'the enemy'. Medicine waged war on it. The populace waged war on those who suffered from it. As Susan Sontag aptly points out, military metaphors contribute to the stigmatising of certain illnesses and by extension of those who are ill.[52]

Women in this study describe how having breast cancer labelled 'evil' in England and *male* in Italy, adds to their distress and makes them feel their illness is shameful.

For other women, and men too, throughout the Western world, the term 'plague' is the principle metaphor by which the AIDS epidemic is understood.

'Because of AIDS the popular misidentification of cancer as an epidemic, even a plague, seems to be receding.'[53] AIDS has made cancer appear banal.

AIDS is of course a very serious disease but it is *not* 'the plague'.

Today, although the elderly still form the majority of those who die, the dramatic increase in AIDS-related illnesses means that a new young group are dying. This presents severe problems not only for those youths who must come to terms with imminent death at a time when their peers are just embarking on bright full lives, but also for their friends, families, nursing and medical staff.

In late 1988 in the USA women composed 9 per cent of the 67,273 cases reported. Currently the major cause of death for women between the ages of twenty-five and thirty-four in New York City is AIDS. In Africa, where transmission patterns have differed from those of the northern hemisphere since the beginning of the pandemic, AIDS is as prevalent among women as among men, and some countries within Africa have reported more cases of women with AIDS than men.

I examine the special problems for female AIDS sufferers as well as the issues faced by the growing number of women, who may not be HIV positive, who are caring privately and publicly for those with AIDS.

The way in which AIDS is stigmatised today is an extreme version of the problem Gorer saw as attached to all deaths. Getting AIDS is not like getting flu. It is seen as bringing shame and disgrace upon oneself, upon one's family. With AIDS the scandal is linked to imputations of guilt. As Peter Tatchell (1986) points out about the newspaper presentation of the AIDS virus: 'To Fleet Street AIDS was a new cocktail which embodied all the ingredients on which sensationalist journalism thrives, homosexuality, venereal disease, disfigurement, disability and death.'[54]

Language is one element that helps to construct our modern taboo around death. It is not a neutral means of communication. It transmits attitudes, values, and models of behaviour. It sets the tone and decrees the ground rules. Language either conceals through suppression what is significant about deaths from natural causes, or through its highly coloured inflammatory metaphors, it stigmatises certain diseases and victims thus intensifying the spiritual disquiet which might be expected to come with human awareness of mortality. This manipulative device which ensures continuance of the death taboo is as prevalent in our day as it was in Gorer's.

Gorer's other argument is that society today has difficulty in discussing death because there is no general belief in immortality, unlike the Victorian era when constant reference to death was made within a religious framework.

Although there is some truth in this idea, it is both over-simplistic and overdependent upon white Western evidence. In Chapter Two I take into account the large numbers of ethnic and religious groups such as Jews, Muslims and Hindus who fully participate in this culture, bringing to it beliefs and practices that illustrate a strong sense of the religious significance of death.

In fact today, even amongst white Westerners, ritual, religion and a sense of immortality, which may not necessarily be linked to a specific faith, are by no means absent. Recent surveys in England, for instance, suggest that at least half the population has some belief in a form of afterlife, while a quarter has no belief and a quarter is unsure. Belief in immortality means different things to different people. In Davies' survey it meant at least the idea of a soul that continued, whilst 25 per cent of the believers surveyed had a concept of bodily resurrection and 10 per cent believed in reincarnation.[55]

In this study, most women who were practising Jews, Muslims or Christians subscribed to some version of a traditional theological belief in life after death.

The majority of women, who held no formal religious beliefs, expressed a sense of immortality sometimes ill-defined or vague, but with a strong awareness of continuity and connection. 'Although it's harder to think of a soul when you are dealing daily with a corpse that's fast going off, you could say everything is recyclable, plants, the earth etc., so why not us?' (Woman Funeral Director, 1994.)

Gorer's understanding of the connection between religion and people's ability to handle death may be too formal, simplistic and insufficiently geared towards female spiritual interpretations to be useful to contemporary women.

Later in the book I look at ways in which the existence of a connected framework (particularly in feminist circles), which may be that of shared belief but is more likely to be shared language and shared values, gives rise to relevant rituals which provide communities of women with the means to handle death.[56]

French historian, Philippe Aries, who has done extensive research (1974, 1983) on changing attitudes towards death in Western societies from the Middle Ages to the present day, is another writer who sees our modern situation as bleak.

He detects a marked contrast between twentieth century silence and an earlier era when death was familiar, public, and expected. He argues that the mid-nineteenth century saw the 'beginning of the lie': a process by which death was driven into secrecy and dying people no longer told their prognosis.

The isolation around death which as Aries emphasises, also affects the bereaved, was a point raised by most bereaved women in this study. As living reminders of the unspeakable truth of death they were often avoided rather than supported.

Aries (1983) identifies four models of dying today which correspond to the historical and social changes he detects. Women's place within these models is examined through these pages as are the different implications for women who are dying and women who are bereaved.

The first two models, from earlier times and other cultures, are set against models three and four which capture the way of death in contemporary Western societies. The models have the following features:

1) *The Tame Death* 'The oldest death there is.' Death here is sad, inevitable, but natural and a good end to life.

2) *The Romantic Death* Here death is the great 'heroic' event which confirms and deepens the meaning of the individual's life.

3) *The Modern Lonely Death* This involves the isolation of the dying and the mainly female carers. Here death is a meaningless

event which could happen to anyone anytime, where what is feared is not death but dying.

4) *The Modern 'Scientific' Death* This pivots on total alienation because death is simply ignored, subsumed in everyday routines. It is an event to be managed as cleanly, quickly, technically as possible.

My evidence suggests that as carers, within this death model, women are expected to be both 'loving and nurturing' but also to sublimate their strengths to men's 'superior' high-tech expertise.[57]

Critics of Aries have questioned his claim that there exists a silence about death in recent times. The British sociologist David Armstrong suggests that during this period there was not a silence but a new way of speaking about death, which Aries failed to hear. The new speech is largely a legal and medical language which focuses on dead bodies rather than on dying people.

It is certainly true that in hospitals, particularly in intensive care, around a dying patient's bedside, there are the constant whirr and ticks of life-saving machinery and other technical devices, matched immediately after death by the hubbub of voices as clinicians, pathologists, and coroners subject the corpse to detailed scrutiny.

I recall vividly when my friend Carol was dying, glancing constantly at the frightening amount of machinery to which she was attached, which recorded in minute detail the exact state of her damaged brain, her heart, and her bodily functions. At intervals the nurses (who otherwise could not have been more understanding or sympathetic), would come in, glance at the various dials rather than at Carol, then say quietly 'It won't be very long now.'

I found this new way of dealing with the end of life desperately distracting. In my journal that night I wrote: 'There were savage moments when I didn't want to wait for them to turn the ventilator off. I wanted to tear the whole damn contraption away and have you die naturally.'

The paradoxical thing is that if Carol could have seen how technically well she was cared for, being a doctor, she would, I am sure, have approved.

'They are doing the best they can, Sal. The best you can do is the best you can do.'

That was something she always said about her medical practice. I can almost hear her say it now.

I think that I, like Aries, believe there are dangers in listening only to technical sounds about death, of 'accepting death as a technical fact but reducing it to the state of an ordinary thing, as insignificant as it is necessary'.[58]

Aries, unlike Armstrong, fails to hear the new medical scientific way of speaking about death, because he is not interested in words that do not add to human dignity.

Words that do not express the significance of death do not constitute a humane response to death. By reducing death, such expressions reinforce the taboo.

There is lastly the argument that a denial of death is not a modern condition but a human condition. Ernest Becker (1973) suggests that the fear of the 'id' is not the fear of sex but the fear of death and the individual personality constructs a process of repressing this awareness.

Becker's view re-interprets Freud's argument that humans confronting the reality of death could not admit its finality, therefore constructed imaginary ways in which its reality could be admitted and its finality denied.[59]

Becker, like Freud and Kierkegaard, believes that all societies are premised on a denial of death, which would suggest that death is not problematic uniquely for contemporary society, but would account for the death-denying focus of the modern world.

Such a view could be the backdrop for La Rochefoucauld's famous line: 'Death and the sun are not to be looked at steadily . . . as with the sun, so with death: without staring at it, the wise person lives in its sight.'[60]

Many women I talked to held the more robust perspective of Prospero, Duke of Milan, who decided after his daughter was married to make every third thought a thought about death.

> Think about death daily. That way you really are aware that nothing is permanent. You appreciate that flowers are blossoming now, you see we are all part of a cycle, you have a good spiritual attitude. Discuss death over dinner, explore the losses in your life because they can teach you a lot, educate yourselves about the ethics of death here and in other cultures, reflecting on death will open you up to be more real with the people you are with, to have less regrets of what you've said or not said when they're gone.

This was advice from Josefine Speyer, Buddhist psychotherapist, co-founder of the Natural Death Centre. She saw it as excellent preparation for reducing anxiety about dying.

It is hard to take this advice when traditional medicine still largely sees death as the enemy, when popular culture is hardly a whit more friendly. Currently our cultural understandings of dying are still those of fear, evasion and superstition, when they are not (as on popular television) those of violence and pornographic mutilation.

The workings of the death taboo affect everyone. One of the worst consequences is that we shut off from others possible gifts of companionship and availability. In turn we may find we are shut off from ourselves.

One dying woman told me: 'I feel as if I'd died already, the way they exclude me.'

If we are to avoid that situation we have to learn to treat death as a usual part of life's events.

It is time for a change. Women in this study feel it is time to talk about death. To talk with passion and compassion about what it means to reach an ending.

Chapter Two

EARLIER TIMES, OTHER CULTURES AND RELIGIONS

Although death is universal, it necessarily occurs within particular social and historical frameworks, so that the ways in which it is handled and women's participation in the death process, vary enormously according to time and place. Grief, which I analyse later from a Western perspective, is classified differently in other cultures as are taboos around death. Religious rituals shape women's bereavement experience, their approach to their own death, and ways in which they care professionally for dying people.

In this chapter I make no attempt at large scale generalisations, but in order to illustrate some of the religious and cultural diversity which affects women's experience, I use a series of snapshots:

1.   Death customs in a British village at the start of the century.
2.   A brief depiction of some religious beliefs and observances which modify women's attitudes towards death and dying.
3.   A sketch of some cultures which offer different ways of grieving and different views on whether or not death is taboo.

Women's Role in the Death Process in Earlier Times

A formal history of death registration and its cause in the UK is relatively recent. It was women who were involved with the early form of death registration. Until 1836 there was no national system for keeping records, the only records being local 'Bills of Mortality'. Each parish appointed two 'searchers', almost always elderly women, whose duty was to inspect dead bodies for signs of infectious disease and record the number of deaths. It was a system of such inefficiency and inaccuracy that estimates reveal one third of the burials were unaccounted for, whilst the number of deaths due to epidemic disease were often wildly exaggerated. These jobs however gave women professionally the same working knowledge of how death decimated a community, which they had already accumulated personally in their role as carers for the dying.[1]

A case study by David Clark of how death was handled at the beginning of this century and in the mid 1970s in Staithes, a Yorkshire fishing village, is useful because it shows clearly the essential participation of women in the formal death process.[2]

In contrast to contemporary practice, which one woman summed up with the phrase: 'Now the Co-op has it all – tea, flowers, box – he'll put it in t'paper and everything'; at the start of the century it was the community, most particularly local women, who were actively involved.[3]

A group of women, recognised in the village as qualified, who took considerable pride in their task, were responsible for what Staithes called 'the lying-out'. They washed the body, tied up the jaw, wrapped the corpse in a white sheet, laid it on a board made by the village joiner (who doubled as the undertaker and made the coffin), put it in the centre of a double bed, covering the feet with white woollen stockings and the face with a large white linen handkerchief edged with Maltese lace. Finally they meticulously folded over the body a second sheet in a series of horizontal pleats and awaited the visits of kin and friends. As each visitor entered, the woman watching over the corpse would lift the face cloth so that the visitor could view the deceased before touching the body sympathetically 'to show they had always held out goodwill while the person was alive'.[4]

Women's activity within funeral preparations was significant. One woman known as 'the bidder', who knocked at every door to 'bid' or invite the household to attend, was employed to announce the day and time of the funeral, usually on a Sunday despite double burial fees. Women also acted as coffin bearers, generally relatives of the same sex as the deceased. Behind the bearers in the funeral procession came the women, often neighbours, locally known as 'waitresses', who would later serve the specially baked funerary food, who had already offered sweet biscuits and port to mourners gathered around 'the box'. Six or eight women, wearing black hats with white crocheted shawls and black silk sashes, walked in pairs, one wearing her sash diagonally from her left shoulder, the other wearing hers from the right, to form an inverted V pattern. Women bearers, wearing black skirts, white shawls and white hats, helped carry the coffin after the chapel service up a steep hill to the graveyard. Serving women rested at the foot of the hill before they served the meal in several different households, unless a very large house or chapel schoolroom was placed at their disposal. Smoked ham, fruit cake (known as 'funeral bread') and Madeira cake were the traditional foods.

This funeral tea was the first in a series of rites which brought the group together to acknowledge the death and prepare the bereaved for mourning then for their re-entry into community life. After the funeral, women would remove white napkins from mirrors and pictures and partially open curtains. Readmission to normal life was expected to be gradual. For women, mourning represented a protracted period of restrictions of movement and dress. Frequently women ceased to attend chapel for as much as a year. One woman said: 'Some never went for five or six years – they used to think it wasn't reverent.' Any appearance outdoors in the early months was considered improper and any woman doing so risked hostile comments. Permanent remembrances of death during the Victorian period were kept in the house for years, grim reminders to a community where death was a frequent and untimely visitor.[5]

By the late seventies such mourning customs had largely disappeared. Death as a communal and female event had been replaced by paid professionalism. The preparation of the corpse, even the teas, were done by funeral directors rather than by traditional female specialists. Bearers, no longer the same sex as the dead, were often male undertakers; the human voices of women bidders were replaced by impersonal announcements in newspaper obituary columns.

Only two features did not change, which differentiated Staithes from the new national pattern. Women are still called to lay out the body and while the rest of the country has largely turned to cremation, women-centred Staithes still prefers six of their ten deaths to be burials. The community of Staithes has never allowed considerations of time or cost to interfere with what they see as the right and proper way to bid farewell to the dead, but much of the suspicion of and resistance to cremation derives from these women. The trend towards a more clinical impersonal standardisation of death seems to be linked with the extent to which such mortal matters have been placed in the hands of male professionals. Although we must be cautious of generalising from one case study, it is worth considering the gender implications of recent professionalisation of death.

Religious Issues and Patterns

Death raises deep religious and cultural issues. As traditions associated with death vary widely between ethnic or religious groups (even within groups there is a range from highly orthodox to agnostic or atheist), this affects women's responses.

For those with strong faiths, the meaning of death and the meaning of life are inextricably bound together. Life may be a preparation for death or for afterlife. For Jews, their life-affirming faith means that preservation of life always takes precedence over any possible hastening of death. For Muslims, suffering and death are part of God's plan and will happen when God determines. Sikhs believe life is part of a seamless journey through life, death and life again, to a final merging with God. Hindus and Buddhists stress the interrelatedness of life and death so that death gives life its meaning.

Formal theology is, of course, only one part of a religious exploration of death, yet knowing someone's belief system makes us better able to comprehend the framework out of which speak the women whose stories texture these pages.

There are practical as well as theological issues. A non-believer's mode of death still has an impact on religious kith and kin. In my own family, when a non-practising Jew decided to be cremated with a humanist service instead of adopting the traditional Jewish burial, some family members found this distressing. For believers, non-observance of religious laws at the point of death when such things matter most, may cause anguish. This is more likely to happen in hospitals if health care staff are not sufficiently sensitive to religious or cultural issues.[6]

Christianity

One third of the world population is estimated to be Christian. Although this makes Christianity (comprising Anglican, Catholic and Non-Conformist churches with 1,700 million adherents) the largest world religion, not all non-conformist Christians from other cultures share our society's customs around death. This can present problems for white Christian nurses caring for patients from other cultures.[7]

Afro-Caribbean Methodists living in Britain, for example, may be more concerned with family structure than their white neighbours. If an Afro-Caribbean hospital patient is terminally ill, the close family (including grandparents who play a vital role in bringing up grandchildren), the extended family, church and community leaders will all expect to visit constantly.

> It took us by surprise to see how much space the relatives of this West Indian patient needed. Dozens of them gathered by the bed. When I told both grandfathers it was 'two visitors only by the bedside' they were horrified! While the patient was still able to be moved, Sister finally wheeled him into the day room so that everyone could be there. Later when he was dying it got very tricky.
>
> (British nurse caring for dying West Indian man.)

One West Indian woman described the family's feelings: 'It is a good hospital but we feel for us some restrictions. We shout or make noises from our emotions, it is too much for them. The doctors they don't always tell us what is going on.'

The patient's sister confirmed a characteristic language problem that further distresses non-English families: 'He have a consultant but we never get to speak to him. When he speak it is not easy to understand, then my brother he die. Then he tell us. We did ask and they give us a black sister to lay out my brother's body. She understood about the care for the hair, and the proper respect.'

There is no religious objection to staff of other persuasions handling the body of an Afro-Caribbean Christian but that remark of the patient's sister was typical of many community members' hope that the after-death rituals will be performed in a manner they can approve.

Christian nurses caring for non-Christian patients may have greater problems.

> We just don't get enough instruction. I knew something about the Muslim ways, but not that I wasn't supposed to touch a Muslim man when I was nursing him. He was in great pain, I wasn't very experienced, so I tried to make him feel I cared by patting his shoulder. He couldn't speak English but he got into a terrible state.
>
> (Mary, White Christian nurse, twenty-eight years.)

As rules surrounding physical contact between women and men are believed to have been given by God, their observance is integral to Muslim identity, so Mary's action was a complete violation of the man's religious attitudes. But Mary's experience is by no means unique. Ajemian and Mount (1981) emphasise that we must not assume that beneath differences of culture there are universal non-linguistic ways of approaching death. This is simply not so.[8]

Amongst Christian women, although family or ethnic traditions may vary, the major understanding is that death is in no way an enemy but a form of completion. The approach to mortality by the 'established' Anglican church is influenced by the Christian conviction that everyone shares in Christ's resurrection and eternal life. Catholics teach that this life is just a beginning; death is the important step to the next life. Christian meanings of death are dominated by the belief of Jesus's first friends that he had died on the cross, yet had been raised by God to a life after death. (It is worth remembering here that the Christian understanding of death began in a Jewish context with Jesus assuming the role of an independent and highly controversial teacher.)[9]

Several bereaved Christian women told me they were able to take Jesus's death into account when mourning their own loss. Anna Haycraft (novelist Alice Thomas Ellis), a Roman Catholic, when asked by an interviewer if she railed against God for taking her nineteen-year-old son Joshua who died in an accident, said: 'No, I never got cross with God . . . because He'd sent His own son to die that terrible death, it would have been a bit stupid of me to start complaining about mine.'[10]

What she did, as a Christian, was to redirect her anger.

> The anger was against death. I had a terrific sort of anthropomorphic vision of death . . . When we were in the country we kept seeing people with scythes, and I thought, 'There he is, there the brute is.' He was in our lives so much at that time because the year Joshua died two of my friends and I lost twelve people between us, close people. It was rather like living in a mausoleum, you could almost smell the charnel house.[11]

Despite this grim reaper figure neither Haycraft nor other Christian women to whom I talked saw death as threatening. 'After Janice drowned, I felt desperate but not angry with God, nor did I find death harsh. Death is just with me now. But believing means I have to think it will be all right.' (Mother whose ten-year-old daughter drowned.)

Children's deaths severely test the faith of Christian women but many are aided by the belief that they will see them again. 'I see

Mark quite clearly in Heaven. Strangely he isn't harmed, the way he was after the scooter smash. I know I shall find him when I die. If I didn't feel that then the loss would have no purpose.' (Bereaved mother whose sixteen-year-old son crashed to his death.)

This view of mortality pivots on Jesus's anticipation of his own death, his assertion that it is in and through death that the 'truth of God' will be unequivocally manifest.[12] It appears important to Christian women that by consistently calling himself 'the son of man', in the Judaic understanding of his time, Jesus implied both that he spoke and acted like any other human who was subject to the penalty of death, but also he spoke as one who believed that he would be vindicated by God beyond death. Terminally ill women saw this aspect as relevant.

Several bereaved Christians said they had 'faith' or 'trust' in a 'good ending one day'. They took comfort in the idea that God's consequences and wisdom are available to all sorts and conditions of women and men simply on the basis of faith.[13] The fact that Jesus did not evade his death seems to have important implications for Christian women.[14] Michele, thirty-eight, saw her thirty-year-old husband slip to his death on a ski slope.

> At first I howled with rage and anger. I kept saying his death could be avoided. Over and over again I wanted to yell: 'Why does it happen to me?' Then I realised I was getting nowhere, worse if anything. I went to Church a lot and thought about Jesus. He did not evade his death. He practically asked for it! I started saying why shouldn't it have been him? Why shouldn't it happen to me?'[15]

Trust in God not to abandon them, the way Jesus trusted, helped women who were confronting their own deaths. 'I *am* frightened of losing all control of my limbs. MND spreads fast. I worry my partner and the two girls won't be able to cope. Although I feel I'm abandoning them, I am not worried about being abandoned myself. I've always been a strong believer.' (Woman with motor neurone disease.)

As death approached, some practising Christian women asked for prayers or to be anointed with oil by a priest/minister. 'I have a lot of repentance to do. I'm going to need a bunch of forgiveness. They'd better get me Communion!' (British woman dying of cancer.)

Some non-practising Christians deplored these facilities. 'When you get to feeling this bad, the last thing you want is to see the

Vicar walking towards your bed. It makes the -last moment come a lot nearer!'

My evidence suggests Christian faith helps believers over death issues. The area of cultural conflict most often reported by Christian women was not in their role as patients but in their role as carers for dying people of other faiths.

Judaism

Central precepts in Judaism are belief in one God, a transcendent, omnipotent and omniscient creator, obedience to the Ten Commandments, the practice of charity and tolerance, and the importance of family life. The estimated 17 million Jews worldwide (of which between 350,000 and 410,000 live in Britain) whose spiritual centre is Jerusalem, whose faith is firmly rooted in revelation, will encompass a wide spectrum of religious observance, therefore a range of attitudes towards death and dying.[16]

Though there will be differences between Orthodox Jews who scrupulously follow the laws of the Torah (which contains rules for daily life, including dietary restrictions, which are seen as God's commands) and the more flexible Liberal and Reform Jews, all of them will adhere to the central notion that life is precious. Its preservation must take precedence over anything else. What if anything happens in an after-life is less important than the here and now.

'The ultimate aim of all human activity is to establish the Kingdom of God here on earth. "Pie in the sky, when you die" is definitely not a Jewish point of view.'[17]

A faith that states where there is life there is hope and opposes any measure to hasten death, offers a challenge to women doctors. 'Discretion versus disclosure about death to any dying patient is a big issue, but when someone Jewish is dying, you have to ask will telling them make them give up hope?' (Jewish woman doctor.)

Some of my Jewish patients are quite unconcerned about an after-life, it is this life that counts, so to tell someone they are dying may well put them in total despair.' (Christian woman doctor with Jewish patients.)

One consequence of a life-affirming faith is that suicide is not merely considered an act of violence but also an act of sacrilege. By many thinkers it is believed to be an even more heinous crime than murder itself.

'As it is God's prerogative to grant life, so it is His sole decision to take life: "Perforce were you born" say the rabbis of the Talmud, "and perforce must you die". One who takes his own life is a murderer, as is one who takes another's life.'[18]

The horror of suicide is not merely theological but also moral: the betrayal of family and friends. It is a default of all responsibility. This can put a heavy burden on Jewish women.

> My mother had terrible suffering from cancer. Often she asked us to help her die. My dead father had been very Orthodox so there was no way my brothers or I could see that as right. What could I do? I desperately wanted to help her out of her misery. I knew she'd begun collecting pills but I shut my eyes to it. I prayed a lot, and stopped talking to her. She'd gone inside herself, saying strange things, sounding mad. Did I know then she was getting ready to do it? It still came as a shock. My mother had killed herself! She'd gone against God, and she hadn't been responsible to us but yet I felt huge relief – at least she wasn't in pain now. But you are not allowed to feel relief so then I felt guilty. My brothers saw it as a sin. I think the pain drove her insane, so there is a small bit of comfort.
>
> (Anna, Orthodox Jewish woman.)

The reason behind Anna's 'small comfort' is that some contemporary Jewish commentators make a distinction between wilful or premeditated acts of suicide (always considered unacceptable), and those suicide acts carried out when the person is of unsound mind (where some leniency may be observed).[19]

If Rabbis label a suicide as 'intentional' then the victim will have to be buried at least six feet from surrounding graves, sometimes in a separate part of the cemetery. Despite any good qualities the dead person may have demonstrated when alive, no praise or eulogies are allowed at the funeral. Although the Mourners' Kaddish is recited regularly morning and night as for other deaths, Jews do not recite the Burial Kaddish at the graveside. Someone who commits suicide is seen as an outcast. Someone who attempts it is subject to stigma.

As a young deeply depressed woman in the sixties, I suffered this stigma when I attempted to kill myself. After weeks of planning, I escaped from the hospital where I was being treated for 'clinical depression', took twenty pills when I left the hospital grounds, went to the only place that still seemed like home, my first ex-husband's flat, in order to take the remaining forty. I let myself in with the key I still owned. It was 1.30. Neville, my ex-husband, was safely at work. I made in 'successful' suicide terms one mistake: in the bathroom was a bottle of sleeping pills. Neville, it seemed, was also having poor nights. Despite having swallowed more than enough pills, recklessly I took his too, then fell into the bed that had once been ours. The mistake was in not throwing away his empty bottle.

Neville later told me that at 1.30 in his office he was suddenly struck by a deep sense of foreboding. Something was wrong. He left work. Totally unexpectedly he arrived at his flat to find me in a barbiturate-induced coma. Believing I was asleep he decided not to wake me until later when he planned to drive me back to the hospital. Then he walked into the bathroom and noticed the empty jar. He summoned an ambulance.

Forty-eight hours later I awoke in Paddington General Hospital, to see at the bottom of my narrow bed, the small seething frame of my Jewish mother. I lay and looked at her, unable to take in the fact that I who had chosen death so carefully should seemingly still be alive. I who had chosen never to see my Jewish mother again should now find her looming at the end of a narrow iron bedstead. She screamed only one question: 'How could you do this to me?'

Neville led her gently away out of the ward. The next night, before he got there, she returned to reproach me with a second question: 'How could you do this to your father and his father?'

As my father had died when I was nineteen, as I had never known my dead grandfather, her second question seemed as much of a bizarre fantasy as the fact that I was strung up to tubes, desperately depressed at having failed to kill myself.

Today I realise that my mother's remarks meant that to my father's family, all practising Orthodox Jews, this act would have been untenable. I had brought upon them shame and humiliation. Neither then nor later did my mother and I ever discuss the tortured feelings I had undergone in order to come to such a bitter decision.

Ironically thirty years later my mother, eighty-four, sick, feeling that all quality of life had gone, asked me to come and discuss her own intention of committing suicide, which a month later she attempted. As I was not a practising Jew, I felt the decision should be hers alone, although I knew my relatives would see it as a betrayal of faith and family.

At the time of my attempted suicide and at the time of my mother's, I did not think of the way my Judaism affected my attitude towards death. But it is impossible to write this particular book without considering it now.

For years I have been lying low. For years Judaism has been lying in wait for me. You can be a non-practising Jew. I am certainly that.

A Jew out of practice. I am certainly that. A secular Jew. A cultural Jew. But I see no way *not* to be a Jew. In matters of death as in matters of life.

I do not think I would choose suicide today firstly because of the effects on my daughter, my partner, and the significant others in my life; and secondly because of my awareness of the life-affirming culture from which I come. Whether I practise or not, my people are Jewish. Six million of them died in the gas chambers. You cannot have that inheritance and deny your faith. As a contemporary feminist I quibble with Judaism's masculist particulars, and its sexist implications, but I can no more deny it than I can deny death. Being Jewish informs my attitude towards dying, just as much as my feminism does.

Many Jewish women today, like myself, have difficulties in reconciling a personal concerned Creator with the problem of evil in the world. 'Where was God when the Nazis burnt the Torah and compelled the Jews to dig their own graves? My father got my mother out of the concentration camp but my uncles and my cousins died there.' (Rachel, Jewish woman, fifty-three.)

Awareness of death itself often prompts the initial impulse towards religion. Awareness of the Holocaust and those unbearable deaths adds a complex element to the religious understanding of Jewish women involved in this study.

Islam

The word 'Islam' (the religion of the Muslims who form one fifth of the world's population) comes from the Arabic meaning surrender or submission to God. Muslims surrender themselves to God's will over death 'as if he or she were a feather on the breath of God'.[20] Through Shariah, the law, Islam's system of faith and behaviour emphasises twin concepts of peace and permission, drawing no distinction between religious and practical spheres of life or death.

The 2 million strong Muslims in the UK (like those scattered from the Adriatic to Malaysia), learn as a first religious duty from The Qur'an that there is only one God and that Muhammad (570-632) is his prophet. The other four religious duties are to pray five times daily (with rituals of purification), to give alms, to fast, and to make pilgrimages to Mecca.[21]

Rituals of purification, fasting and dietary restrictions (no alcohol, pork, lard, ham, carrion or blood, other meat only if slaughtered according to Halal blood-draining ritual) have implications for Muslim women dying in hospitals where their needs may not be sufficiently well understood. Many Muslim women have spent most of their time at home without the opportunity their menfolk have had to acquire skills in written or spoken English.

If sick, Muslims are not expected to fast during the month of Ramadan, but several women found eating during that period psychologically traumatic. Through an interpreter friend, a dying Muslim woman told me she knew food could not aid her recovery and she would feel nearer to God if hospital authorities allowed her to fast.

The Muslim attitude towards cleanliness is rooted in the importance of purity, which relates to dead bodies as well as to the living. Impurity arises out of the transgression of boundaries, especially body boundaries such as defecation and menstruation. Before a Muslim can address God such impurities must be removed by ritual washing. Women must wash hands, feet, mouth and face before praying; after menstruation they are required to wash the whole body. Fresh running water is critical so a shower is preferred to a bath. After urinating and defecating they must wash down body parts with water. Toilet paper is not considered sufficient. 'My mother was helped to a bath, there were no showers in that ward. There were no jugs of water in the toilets. The nurses did not understand her distress. I explained, but now she is very ill and on a bedpan, and they just can't remember to always bring a jug of water.' (Daughter of a Muslim patient dying in hospital.)

Several Muslim women confessed that their fears about not having private washing facilities in hospitals or hospices were greater than their fears about their illness.

Another critical issue for Muslim women dying in hospital is propriety. 'Should a Muslim be in hospital . . . first and most important is the modesty. Female patients should be seen by female doctors, and males by males.'[22] (Dr Abduljilil Sajid.)

In extreme cases of sickness, if a female doctor was unavailable, a Muslim woman might be permitted to be examined by a male doctor, but only in the presence of another woman and only with the patient's permission. 'All the Muslim women we have had on this ward have refused to see a male doctor. Their families supported this, so we just had to scurry round and find female medics. One woman refused to wear the gown for X-ray theatre because it wasn't modest enough!' (Christian nurse with several Muslim patients.)

These rituals, whose omissions or inaccuracies can worry Muslim women dying in hospitals in ways it is hard for non-Muslims to comprehend, come out of an Islamic understanding of death which teaches that suffering and death are part of God's plan; that life is a time of probation before the final judgement, at which point every action a Muslim has taken will be recorded and assessed. If a rule has been broken, it will be remembered. Death itself is not a punishment, but the termination of one stage in a much longer process culminating in the day of resurrection and final judgement.[23]

As death approaches, according to Dr Sajid, a Muslim leader in Britain, 'The important thing is that the patient's face should be facing Mecca which in the UK is 127 degrees southeast. The body should be covered with a white sheet so that respect is shown.'

Sometimes there are slip-ups. 'When I arrived at the bedside they had not moved my mother's bed towards Mecca, they thought she was asking for a bedpan.' (Daughter of dying Muslim woman.)

Soon after the death the ritual washing of the body is carried out. Only women may wash women, and men wash men.

For Muslims, as for orthodox Jews, post-mortems are forbidden. Islam teaches that the body belongs to God so no part of it should be cut, harmed or donated. If a coroner orders a post-mortem, the family often needs intricate explanations about why it is necessary, and reassurance that all organs will be returned to the body for burial. Funerals take place within twenty-four hours of death. Again, as in orthodox Judaism, cremation is forbidden (on the grounds that the soul is thought to remain in the body for up to forty days after death). In most Islamic cultures men take the body to the mosque for prayers and readings from the Qur'an; women take no part in the burial ceremony. Families stay indoors for three days while relatives bring food. Mourning lasts up to a month. The grave is visited each Friday for forty days while alms are given to the poor. Women's relationship to the death process is stringent. Widows who must shed their jewellery, wear simple clothes, are confined to the home, their movements restricted as they mourn for 130 days. At the end of nearly nineteen weeks widows are encouraged to rejoin society and subsequently encouraged to remarry.

Hinduism and Sikhism
Hinduism, rooted in a caste system with a central belief in reincarnation, is a set of complex beliefs, values and customs. Many paths to the same goal. The dominant religion of India, characterised by the worship of many gods, with Brahma as supreme being. Sikhs, members of a sixteenth century reformed Hindu sect, are monotheistic, with the Granth as their chief religious document.

Hindus believe we are reborn many times as part of a cosmic

cycle. During our lives good or bad thoughts and actions generate good or bad 'karma' which determines what happens after death. Holy souls reach God. Less perfect souls are reborn as humans (if they have been good) or as animals or insects (if less good). Unexplained suffering is understood as a person's previous 'karma'. Hindus prepare for death by meditation, prayer and by becoming less attached to family and possessions. Sikhs, who believe in both 'karma' and reincarnation, try to live life so that death does not take them unawares.[24]

As with Muslims there are often language problems within hospitals. Hindus and Sikhs are members of a family first and individuals second. It is essential that relatives are present so that death rituals can be minutely observed. Failure in this respect is believed to be damaging both to the dead person and their bereaved kin. Shirley Firth suggests that lack of sensitivity on the part of British doctors or nurses borders on racism which sometimes results in Asians misunderstanding the prognosis of the patient's illness, therefore failing to be there at the point of death.[25] 'Because my Uncle died peacefully in the night, the staff didn't phone and wake us. It is urgent to call all the family. As we believe in the after-life, it is important how we leave the world.' (Hindu bereaved niece.)

For Hindus, death is not a matter of anxiety, because in this long sequence of rebirth, death will occur frequently. Nor does death merit lengthy mourning. 'We try not to cry for a long time after the death. If we cry for too long we would distress the soul which has gone over.' (Bereaved Hindu woman.)

However because there are fewer taboos against both sexes weeping than in Anglo-Saxon society, at the actual moment of death great outpourings may occur from the relatives of a dead Sikh patient. Several British nurses reported they found this overt grief 'extreme'. Some said, 'It upsets other patients.' A Sikh woman who had a stillbirth in a maternity unit wailed loudly at the death of her baby as did her mother-in-law and two relatives. A Sikh nurse on the ward explained that such open distress was 'the "done thing" in a village setting at home but was regarded as abnormal here'. An English nurse disapproved of the whole family 'making a scene' and told them to 'keep your voices down'. The Sikh nurse felt strongly they needed to work the grief out of their system.[26]

Buddhism

Today there are over 311 million Buddhists worldwide (at least 20,000 in Britain) who pursue the goals of morality and generosity.

Their framework is an eightfold path encompassing:
1. Understanding of life
2. Right motives
3. Right speech
4. Perfect conduct
5. Right livelihood
6. Self discipline
7. Right mindedness
8. Perfect meditation.[27]

For dying patients the state of mind, which must be that of peace, is the most important consideration as it influences the character of rebirth. In Buddhist teaching all killing is forbidden. Many Buddhists who are vegetarian, and from a range of ethnic backgrounds, may encounter problems of diet, language and conflicting customs inside hospitals.

The Buddhist faith comes from a single source: the life of Gautama (sixth–fifth centuries BC, India) who, after his Enlightenment, became known as the Buddha, founder of a way of living. The Buddhist understanding of death begins with the familiar story of Gautama's rich and protected youth. Born in a palace, Gautama was saved from signs of poverty, harm or illness by his wealthy father. One day the young man ordered a carriage-driver to take him into the country. During the drive he saw his first disturbing sight: a sick person cowering beside the road. On his second drive he saw a second sight disruptive to his well-being: a very old person. On his third drive came a third threatening vision: a dead body being prepared for cremation.

The pleasures of the palace palled. He was haunted by the fear that such evils might occur to him. On a fourth drive, determined to find a way to resist disease and death, he met a shaven-headed ascetic in a saffron robe, one of a group that anticipated death by continually practising detachment from all worldly offerings. This, Guatama decided, was his path. He abandoned his wife and son, left the palace, and threw himself into a range of austere practices prevalent in India during the sixth century BC.[28]

'In a charnel-field I lay down to rest upon bones of corpses. And the cowherds came up to me, even spat upon me, and even made water upon me, spattered me with mud, even poked straws into my ears. Yet I cannot call to mind that a single evil thought against them arose in me. That far was I gone in forbearance.'[29]

Gautama went from one extreme practice to another in an effort to discover something inside him that would not be touched by death or decay. To no avail. Ultimately he realised even the sternest ascetic programmes could not grant immunity from death. There is nothing which is not subject to transience, change and dissolution. Nothing is permanent, not even a soul. Buddhist understanding of death is based on 'dukkha': this subjection of everything to change and impermanence.[30]

Buddhists do not believe that death is the final extinction; rather that some trace of the individual remains. There is a 'continuity of consequence' even though a soul is not reborn. Buddhists, who consider the consequences of all their actions and thoughts not to gain punishments or rewards (as in Islam's precise reckoning), but merely as a record of consequence, offer a middle way between the eternalists, who maintain that there is an undying unchanging soul, and the annihilationists who believe that nothing whatsoever continues from this present life. The law of 'karma' governs what is left, which is karmic consequence flowing from life to life.[31]

Throughout this study Buddhist women talk about how notions of impermanence and detachment help them to meet their own death and those of others. Here I focus on a major Buddhist meditation 'The Mindfulness of Death', which helped several Buddhist women give up attachments to life.

'You are asked to think about your own death in eight different ways. The first way is that death could appear like a murderer, sword in hand. You learn that from the moment of birth death has entered. I found this easy once my first child was born when I started to think about ageing and death.' (Sarah, Buddhist mother.)

This was significant because very similar points were made by women from other faiths: that as a new life grows within a woman, her own death and that of the child is envisaged.

'A second way we meditate on death is to see it as the ruin of success, health and youth. So you learn there's no point pinning your hopes on those!' (Elsbeth, Buddhist water-colourist with breast cancer.)

Several Buddhist women artists focused on a balance between the excitement of creative achievements with their inbuilt hope for permanence and the knowledge that at one level they are transient.

'We are asked to accept that death will never give a clear sign in advance of when it will come. As I am very into control, this part of the meditation is what I most need.' (Buddhist woman dying of cancer.)

A second meditation: 'The Mindfulness of the Body', an extraordinary thirty-two-stage review of the repulsiveness of the body, was mentioned by several women. Travelling from the soles of the feet to the top of the hair, it deliberately shows how ugly, unkempt, filthy, frail, and foul each part of the body is. The idea is to offer one sure way to avoid the temptation to cling to flesh or appearance.[32] One woman, terminally ill with motor neurone disease, spoke for many: 'My problem has always been vanity, which during my life I have struggled to overcome. This meditation is useful.'

This woman is not alone, for image is at the core of women's identity in a society where women are socialised to see their self-esteem rooted in 'beautiful bodies'.

Grief in Other Cultures

What is obvious from even a brief cross-cultural analysis is that neither modes of grief nor meanings and taboos around death are fixed. Some cultures count people as dead whom most Americans or British would consider to be alive or vice versa. For instance in Vanatinai (S.E. of Papua New Guinea) people who are unconscious are considered to be dead, whilst in other cultures the dead are considered capable of actively affecting the lives of the living.

Donald Irish's team, which surveyed ethnic variations in dying, death and grief, points out that no one grief theory applies to everyone. The anxiety and depression which we see as involved in grief are simply Western concepts based on Western beliefs. People from other cultures understand and classify grief experiences differently, placing them in the context of their own beliefs about 'the origin of events, the nature of the person, the proper way to behave, the meaning of losses'.[33]

The way of grieving seen as appropriate in one culture is viewed as 'abnormal' in another. Take Bali and Cairo. In Bali 'muted grief' is the form. Bereaved Balinese believe that God will not answer prayers unless the bereaved are calm, so they work hard to 'treat death lightly', supported by people who joke, tease, and distract in an attempt to redefine death as not bad, even desirable. By contrast in Cairo the acknowledged form is 'excessive grief'. The loss of a child is expected to cause 'years of constant suffering' to Egyptian mothers. People who offer social support are expected to encourage suffering and to dwell on pain and loss.[34]

By USA or UK standards both types of grief would be considered pathological. Muted grief would be seen as 'repressed' and excessive grief as 'morbid'. Along with theorists like Wortman and Silver

(1989) I feel critical of our Western 'pathological' approach to loss and grief. Evidence from other cultures offers us a range of grief expressions and mourning time schedules that indicate greater flexibility and less pressure could be productive for the bereaved in our society.[35] It is also the case, as Lillian Burke points out, that not all traditional cultural practices around death are beneficial to people in that society. A person from a 'stoic' culture actually may need to grieve at length.[36]

Death Rituals and Taboos in Other Cultures

From even a brief look at other cultures firstly we see that in some countries today women play the major part in funeral preparations (as they did in earlier times in England), lay out corpses, control death rituals, and have a key role in exhumations. Secondly we notice that there is a wide cultural variance from death as affirmation to death as taboo. To see how this works, insights can be drawn from rural Greece, China and Mexico.

Potamia, North Thessaly in Rural Greece
Loring Danforth, in a compelling study of the death rituals in the village of Potamia, shows how customs help villagers face the universal paradox of mourning. How can the living sustain relationships with the dead and at the same time bring them to an end, in order to live meaningfully as members of a community?[37]

In rural Greece, death rituals and mourning customs are both women-focused and women-controlled. After a death, female neighbours of the deceased or female relatives (who are not immediate family) tie the feet together, shut the lower jaw, close the eyes, then cover the body up to the waist in a white shroud. After they have washed the corpse they dress the body in new clothes. Close female relatives meanwhile devote themselves completely to grief by crying and singing lamentations, which are later repeated at the funeral. Throughout the area it is older women (who have learnt many lamentations through having experienced frequent deaths of relatives) who maintain this tradition of singing dirges. Some younger women see this as signs of rural backwardness or superstition and find it embarrassing. Women sing the same songs at funerals as at weddings as both are rites of passage marking a departure. A woman's wedding is seen as a sad occasion for her and her family as she leaves her own house to join her husband.

Following a death, women in the village watch over the corpse for twelve to twenty-four hours between the death and the funeral. Men pay quick condolences then go out into the yard while women sit around the corpse singing laments. The most conspicuous feature of death-related behaviour is undoubtedly women's mourning attire. Women must dress from head to foot in black, wearing black kerchiefs which cover hair, forehead and neck. The length of time a woman wears black is determined by her relationship with the deceased. Widows are compelled to wear black for the rest of their lives unless they remarry. Widowers can remarry quickly without criticism. Several men in Potamia remarried only forty days after their wives' deaths. Widows lead the most restricted lives: they must not go into the city to shop, they cannot attend village weddings or baptisms. Their major excursion is to other people's death rituals as this provides them with an opportunity to express their grief.

The mother of a young dead child must wear black for at least five years. Women mourning parents or siblings must wear black from one to five years, those mourning in-laws must wear black for a year, and for aunts or uncles six months. Close female relatives of the dead person are expected to care constantly for the graves, making daily visits for five years until exhumations are completed. They carry candles and oil lamps which they light at the graveside. Then they wash the marble headstones with sponges and detergents kept in plastic bags hidden in the grass by the graveyard wall. Some women realise the futility of this task and have been heard to mutter 'We are wasting our time', but the social pressure on women serves to enforce such practices, whereas restrictions on men are less severe and less strictly enforced.

Those in mourning are separated from the world of the living because of their contact with the world of the dead. Their seclusion reflects the isolation of the corpse buried in the ground.[38]

Women's mourning tasks do not end with the funeral. It is women who are expected to dig up the bodies of their loved ones some years after burial. Take the case of twenty-year-old Eleni, killed by a car in a hit and run accident. Five years earlier, her mother Irini buried her in the white bridal dress and wedding crown she had been unable to wear in life, then stayed inside their home for a year, leaving only to visit Eleni's grave night and morning. Irini wore black for the full five years, her sole occupation attending every funeral and memorial service in surrounding villages so that she could lament and cry. 'She knew full well, though, that the wound of a mother never heals, that her pain never ceases.'[39]

When her other daughter got married, Irini did not attend the wedding, and refused to allow singing or dancing in her house on the wedding day. After five years Irini is now to dig up Eleni so that she does not have to bear the weight of the earth on her chest for eternity, and so that her family may see what is left of her once more. Irini begins to dismantle the grave which will be destroyed, the marble monument being kept for the next villager who dies.

Relatives and close friends leave Irini's house in a procession to the graveyard. Eleni's father and two brothers are the only men present. Immediate family go first followed by distant female relatives carrying food, drink and a metal box for Eleni's remains. Over a hundred women surround the grave, the clothes of the women forming concentric rings of colour from black at the centre to blues and browns in the middle to a band of bright colours worn by those in the outer circle who are not so closely affected by the death.

Two women with shovels start to dig up Eleni's remains. Then as the women standing around shout and wail, an older widow with a hoe replaces the women with shovels. Some women shout instructions: 'More to the right. Find the skull first, then the ribs. Don't break anything.'[40]

Eleni's brothers have withdrawn to the outside of the circle of women where 'they stood quietly and awkwardly, men out of place in a women's world of death'.[41]

When the widow uncovers the skull, she places paper money on it before handing it to Irini. Irini herself kisses the skull, places more paper money on it and wraps it in a kerchief which had been embroidered by Eleni as part of her dowry. This is another parallel between an exhumation and a wedding, as newlyweds are kissed and money pinned to their clothes. While Irini cradles the skull, cries and sobs uncontrollably, more bones are uncovered and put in the metal box, the skull is passed around the crowd, and women throw coins into the box. The lamenting gradually ceases and women begin to exchange fatalistic comments about human mortality. 'That's all we are, a pile of bones. We were born, and we will die. Then we'll all come here.'[42] Finally Irini is persuaded to place the skull in the box with the bones. After the priest has arrived and recited the funeral service, the box of remains is placed in the ossuary, food is distributed, then the women return with Irini to her house and greet her and the family with the phrase: 'You have received her well', the same phrase used when relatives return home after a long absence. Irini has one more task: she must take her shovel and fill in the empty grave where her child had been buried. When she has done so she looks down at the empty grave: 'Eleni, my child, you have gone away too, but you will never come back.'[43]

China and Mexico: Taboos and Affirmations
China is a culture with a strong taboo around death. Traditionally Chinese people do not make wills, or plan for funerals, nor could they contemplate making decisions about a coffin in which they were likely to be buried.

'Not knowing the Chinese attitude to death, I talked about the prospect of their brother dying, and about funeral arrangements to the family. The worse thing was when I suggested he could be moved home to die. I got a terrible reception!' (Christian hospital social worker.)

In today's growing Chinese community in Britain, many come from Hong Kong, where traditions about death and dying are utterly opposed to those of British or American Christians.

> Other Western people may wish to die at home surrounded by their friends and relatives. Chinese people prefer the dying relative to die in hospital. This is partly because medical facilities are on hand in hospitals but more importantly because death at home brings bad luck to the house and family. In China and Hong Kong you can find people building bamboo towers around the window of the family house so that the dead body can be removed from the house without using the escalators and staircases because these are reserved for the living.
> (Thomas Chan, Advocacy Services Manager for a British Health Authority responsible for Chinese people.)[44]

He emphasised that Chinese people do not like to talk or think about death: 'We are concerned that the spirits of our ancestors do not pass from the living to the dead, especially young children, or an unborn child.'

Young women and pregnant women are very rarely allowed to pay their respects to the deceased.

'When I was waiting to have my first baby, first my father died here in hospital, then my mother-in-law she died in another hospital. My husband being British did not understand that it would be wrong for me to go and see them. He thought I was being disrespectful. (Chinese woman, twenty-six, married to Englishman.)

By contrast to China, Mexico is a vividly death-affirming culture.

Their extravaganza: The Day of the Dead, celebrated each year around All Saints' Day (November lst), an occasion for communication between the living and the dead, although dedicated to the remembrance of the dead, is quite the reverse of morbid.

It is a fiesta full of life, colour and cultural celebration. Women bring notions of nurturance and floral tributes by dressing graves of deceased family members with wreaths of orange cempasúchil marigolds (the flower of the dead) and placing food offerings and lighted candles before the souls of ancestors. Peasant families set places at table for their dead loved ones whom they believe will return to enjoy for a few brief hours the pleasures they once partook in. Small children play with tiny coffins and brightly coloured skulls made of sugar, plaster and papier mâché. Others dance about in death masks with toy skeletons and paper cut-outs of Death as a companion, a lover, a woman or a man. Death is confronted in every shop and on street corners in wild and whirling images, where cameras now outnumber candles, and tourists delight in seeing the dead disport themselves in demoniac dance. It is not fear children learn but familiarity: an acceptance of the inevitability of death and the permanence of the spirit which underlines Mexican celebrations.

Octavio Paz, in his study of the Mexicans' special relationship with death, suggests that the Mexicans' indifference to the gloom or morbidity of death may be due to the low value they set on life. Although he speculates that to the modern Mexican death has little meaning, has ceased to be the transition, the access to the other life which is more authentic than this one, he focuses on one highly relevant point:

> To the inhabitant of New York, Paris, or London death is a word that is never uttered because it burns the lips. The Mexican, on the other hand, frequents it, mocks it, caresses it, sleeps with it, entertains it; it is one of his favourite playthings and his most enduring love. It is true that in his attitude there is perhaps the same fear that others also have, but at least he does not hide this fear nor does he hide death; he contemplates her face to face with impatience, with contempt, with irony.[45]

Death in Mexico is usually personified as a woman. Maria Antonieta Sanchez de Escamilla, a nursery school teacher, who won first prize for her death installation at the 1989 fiesta, explains how death is depicted:

Often we portray her humorously, with scant respect. We show her as a sugar skull and we eat her clean away . . . We show her dancing, in accordance with our sense of fun and jollity. We like to see her as someone from everyday life . . . we clothe her . . . in modern jeans and old style frocks. This is our way of showing that we love her, that we are not afraid of her.[46]

Chapter Three

MORTAL MESSAGES

Institutionalised religions and varying spiritual practices offer messages about mortality that see death as *completion*, as change rather than as loss, or as part of the process that begins with birth. Death affirmation messages are common in cultures or religious groups which try to integrate the fact of mortality into their design for living. Buddhists for instance see the inevitability of death as a fruitful topic for reflection. Followers of Theravada Buddhism, which originated in Thailand, are encouraged to meditate first on deaths of those who led pleasant lives, then to concentrate on their own death.

'Constant reflection on death makes me see it as a friend, not as a hostile stranger. I try to dwell on the deaths of people I love before they die. When my brother drowned suddenly I was just that bit readier.' (Gillian, Buddhist.)

Women who were not aligned to a particular religion felt something similar: 'I see myself as spiritual rather than religious. Through my practice life has suddenly become this extraordinary gift because I know it will end soon.' (Elaine, dying of cancer.)

This message of acceptance is one point along the continuum of mortal messages, some of which actively help us acknowledge the reality of death, whilst others encourage denial.

The most combative, death-denying messages arise from our society's medical mindset about death. Central to this contemporary understanding of death is the message: *Death is Taboo* from which flow other mortal messages. In sociology and psychology we have the message: *Fear of Death as Universal*. In grief counselling there is the message: *Grief as Resolvable*. In medicine, where 'cure' is the prevailing ideology, where advances in technology have given rise to the notion that science might one day conquer death, the message: *Death as the Enemy* or *Death as Failure* is prevalent.

In what ways are women affected by such messages, and how have they begun to change them?

Fear of Death

Questions about the fear of death have preoccupied philosophers, theologians, psychologists for centuries. Religion helps some come to terms with fear but is not a necessary deterrent: 'Of course I'm afraid of dying! Of course this bloody disease has made me go off God! Look at these lesions: what a foul price to pay for a lifetime s beliefs.' (Woman with AIDS.)

'She hung herself from her hospital bed. How can you go on believing in Christ? I try. I do try. I need Christ to keep my own fear of death at bay. (Woman whose female lover with AIDS committed suicide.)

That many people *do* fear death is indisputable, but theories for its cause vary enormously. Ernest Becker believes that fear of death is universal, though for much of the time, for most of us, it is unconscious or hidden. He suggests that *all* fears are basically fears of death, that 'the idea of death, the fear of it, haunts the human animal like nothing else'.[1] Other researchers do not go this far but argue that death fear is a profound factor in our behaviour and appears disguised as neurosis, depression, schizophrenia.

In contrast, writer Erich Fromm proposes that fear of death far from being the ultimate reality is an expression of alienation from reality, a sign of an inauthentic lifestyle.

> The fear of dying is the fear of losing what I possess . . . my body, my ego, my possessions and my identity . . . To the extent that we live in the having mode, we must fear dying. . . . But it may be diminished, even at the hour of death, by our reassertion of our bond to life, by a response to the love of others that may kindle our own love. Losing our fear of dying should not begin as a preparation for death, but as the continuous effort to reduce the mode of having and to increase the mode of being.[2]

Certainly, as is evident from women's voices, some do fear losing what they possess, a fear perhaps intensified by powerlessness. Evidence however appears throughout this book of the way women see themselves as bonded to life in a continuous linked process from birth to death. Within this process, response to loving relationships is a marked feature. That this adds *regret* to dying is incontrovertible. That it may diminish fear is possible.

Several women writers see the focus on 'having' (like 'doing') as part of our patriarchal thinking, and suggest that when that focus moves from having or doing to being, fear of death recedes. Dorothee Soelle explains: 'Death can be accepted only by those who know what it means to live . . . The reluctance to talk about death with someone who is dying, the refusal to face up to death's reality are signs of life that has not been lived.'[3]

Some people are not afraid of death, they are afraid of the incompleteness of their lives. Many women told me that decisions to live fully made death seem natural: 'I don't want to shrink into death, I want to burst into it! So I'm doing as much as I can of what I want now.' (Woman with breast cancer.)

Certainly isolating the topic increases *fears* around death.

The available research on women's fears is curious. Vernon (1970) and Carroll (1991) suggest women are less fascinated with macabre imagery of death but tend to wish for death more often. (I have *not* found the latter.) They further suggest women fear decomposition of their bodies more than men: we should remember here that among the extremely restricted number of ways which society offers women gainful esteem, a major way has been to offer up bodies for male admiration. My findings confirm that women envision death in terms of loss and mourning, men in terms of violence and frustration; women's ongoing concern with pain and suffering is more extreme than that of their male counterparts. Although men dream about death more often than women, they are less likely to believe in life after death. One suggestion that women avoid thinking about death more than men do, but are considerably more willing to discuss it, was *not* supported by my findings. Women *were* willing to think as well as talk about death.[4]

Where death implies extinction, helplessness or alienation, fear of death generally can be divided into three major components:

1. Regret at leaving the world.
2. Anxiety that there might not be an afterlife, just mere nothingness.
3. Terror at the process of dying, a particular fear being attendant suffering or indignity.

I found that women over seventy have a strong fear of indignity. Some were scared about exactly how they would die: would they suffer loss of control or humiliation? Often this fear was less for themselves than for other women carers in their family, even for female strangers, whom they envisaged as paid carers. This confirmed other evidence about women's strong desire to nurture others even when dying.

If fear of losing control, or 'being a burden' was a major anxiety of older women, fear of leaving loved ones, particularly dependent children, was the anxiety most voiced by women of thirty or forty.

Women I interviewed identified five main categories of fear. These are:

1. *Religious fears*: of damnation, retribution, punishment in afterlife. Women with strong spiritual feelings avoided this.
2. *Fear of pain*: physical and psychological.
3. *Fear of separation*: being alone, being parted from loved ones, separation from familiar surroundings, or from their possessions. One woman who almost drowned recalls worrying about her gold bracelet and engagement ring. Several women worried about who would tend their rose bushes, who would care for their cat, who would cherish their books. An Italian survey which interviewed 964 people about their death anxieties, found that 54 per cent of women interviewed were most fearful about leaving loved ones.[5]
4. *Existential fear*: What will it be like not to exist? What happens after death?
5. *Domestic fears*: These include:
   - Shall I die before Christmas?
   - Shall I die before my son's/daughter's wedding/bar mitzvah?
   - Will my mind die before my body?
   - Shall I become so disgusting that he/she won't want to touch me/hold me/kiss me?
   - If I have a mastectomy before I die will my partner still find me attractive?
   - Will my body shrivel?
   - Can I bear all my hair falling out, or my skin shrinking?
   - If I become incontinent, who will have to change me?
   - What will happen to my children?
   - Will my partner/husband eat properly after my death?
   - Will my partner/husband find someone kind to replace me? Many women assumed their male partner would seek another

woman. Several discussed this with partners. Women with female partners rarely mentioned the idea of 'replacement'.

- Shall I be quickly forgotten?
- Have I time to change my will?
- What shall I be missing?
- Has my life been a failure? Women artists seldom voiced this.
- Will my writing/painting/pottery etc. live after me? Voiced by most creative women.
- Have my children loved me? Mentioned by women who had stormy relationships with offspring.
- Will there be enough to eat at my funeral?
- Will the funeral 'make sense' to my family or friends? Is it possible for it to 'make sense' to both so that there is no quarrelling?
- Will they invite the right people to my funeral?
- How will they mourn me?
- Will my children cope with the actual funeral?
- Shall I be buried alive?
- Why didn't I finish all those remaining chores?
- Will the people I love be here at the end?
- Will the person I quarrelled with, or want to make up with, get here in time?
- Do I actually want anyone here when I'm dying?
- How can I tell him/her that I don't want them here, without them feeling rejected?
- I need to talk about my fears. Who will want to listen?

The majority of these fears are related to appearance, housework, love, relationships, food, communication, nurturance, and concern for children, perceived of course as characteristic female preoccupations. Only one (anxiety about being buried alive) is fear of death itself. Only two (immortality through art and fear of being forgotten) relate to personal ego or self-esteem. One fear only: 'Do I actually want anyone here when I'm dying?' focuses on women's individual needs rather than on typical care for the needs of others. It appears that when dying, just as during life, many women's worries are for other people.

For some women, fear of death can be positive. Megan, a cancer nurse, is also a climber who confronts death in leisure hours as well as at work.

Climbing is the challenge of dealing with fear. I've learnt to say: 'this is a scary position to be in. Can I deal with it?' I'm concerned about safety but I'm prepared to take risks. There's a relationship between my climbing and nursing people with cancer. I've learnt not to be afraid, not to put things off, not to get to a stage where I think 'I wish I'd done that.' It's hard for women, so many of us put things off. Many dying women said to me that they know now housework isn't that important. If I don't learn from them, what use am I? If you want to live right you've got to think about dying!

I believe Megan is right. But because death is powerfully feared, because that fear is denied expression, it puts pressure on us *to do away with grief*.

What is grief, what theories account for it, and how do taboos around death affect the way women grieve?

I use the term 'grief' to refer to the experiences which arise after the death of a loved person. It is possible to be bereaved without feeling grief, but it is difficult to grieve without being bereaved of something, someone, or somewhere. Bereavement means we have been robbed of a close relationship; it is by definition a state of *loss*, and two components have been identified:

1) *Missing something*, whether it is a person, place or object to whom we were attached.

2) *Having to make changes.*

Grief can be seen either (1) as a biological response mechanism which compels grieving women towards anxiety or depression; or (2) as a socially constructed fear of separation from the group in general or from significant others in particular. As certain grief processes particularly attach to Western women who have been socialised to over-invest in partnerships, mothers, and children, I am interested in looking at theorists who work with the second model.

1) **John Bowlby offers a psychological perspective, focusing on attachment**. He believes that the tendency of humans to attach themselves to people and things, modelled on the primary attachment of the child for the mother, is as fundamental as mating. It represents our need for safety and security. Thus losing something/someone causes deep distress. Irretrievable loss (i.e. death) causes 'separation anxiety'.[6]

2) **Peter Marris offers a sociological perspective on the relationship of loss to change.** He suggests that in order to reduce uncertainty we all have a conservative resistance to change. We relate to our environment through familiar patterns called structures of meaning – we feel attached to objects or people from early childhood – and we carry those meanings from one situation to

another. So we might feel Chicago or Liverpool is our home because our parents still live there even though we do not. When they die or the house is demolished our structure of meaning changes. The way we adjust psychologically to that change which brings loss is what Marris understands by grieving.[7]

Both Bowlby and Marris, who suggest we need to *control* our environment in order to feel safe, see predictability as related to control. Loss or change such as death affects our ability to control and provokes the anxiety in which grief is rooted.

3) **Colin Murray Parkes, as a psychiatrist, combines both viewpoints.** He developed a theory of psycho-social transitions that uses three criteria to explain why some losses seem especially hard and lead to deep grieving.

    i)   If people have to undertake a major revision of their assumptions.

    ii) If changes take place over a short space of time so there is no chance to prepare.

    iii) If changes are lasting rather than transient.[8]

With death, our perception of our world, and our expectations have to be dramatically revised. With sudden death, or with self-chosen death, lack of preparation and the feeling we can no longer even take the past for granted, bring anger and guilt as well as shock.

It is useful to look briefly at a five-stage model of dying pioneered by Elisabeth Kubler-Ross (1969) about attitudes of dying people to death, because her stages have been applied to the grief process by Kalish (1985) and have implications for women in this study.[9]

Kubler-Ross presented a sequence of stages which she saw as common ways people responded to dying. Stage One is *denial*: statements like 'No! Not me! It can't be true!' are typical. Stage Two is *anger*: the characteristic feeling being: 'Why me?' Stage Three is *bargaining*: dying people try and make a deal with fate to put off death till Christmas, a Bar Mitzvah or the birth of a grandchild. Stage Four is *depression*: when physical or mental deterioration shows recovery is hopeless. Dying people may feel guilt or fear, or may withdraw from others. Stage Five is *acceptance*: depression may lift, or numbness set in, or peace may be achieved.

Her model has come in for criticism because people move at different speeds, may move backwards or forwards or in circles rather than in straight lines, or may not experience more than one 'stage' throughout a long process of dying. Kubler-Ross however, who succeeded in putting the emotional needs of dying people on the map, did not claim that everyone does or should move through every stage. Lack of structure and anxiety amongst health professionals working with the dying may have led them to apply her findings in too rigid a manner, giving themselves a falsely secure knowledge base, but allowing patients to see stages as the norm, and any deviation from them as pathological.[10]

However when this dying-model was applied to the grief process further problems occurred, as grief experiences are varied, contradictory, and difficult to organise in terms of a logical sequence. Several researchers, nevertheless, have theorised grief in terms of stages:

Table: Comparison of Theories Relating to Stages of Grief[11]

Researcher:	Averill 1968	Kubler-Ross 1969	Parkes 1972
Stages of Grief:	Shock	Denial	Numbness
	Despair	Anger	Pining
	Recovery	Bargaining	Depression
		Depression	Recovery
		Acceptance	

There are remarkable similarities in that Averill's despair stage encompasses Parkes's pining and depression, and Kubler-Ross's anger and depression can be seen as counterparts to despair and depression. All three conclude with resolution or recovery, which is the goal of bereavement counselling. A few women I talked to identified with the stages theory, but others found it a handicap. For them grief is not in stages, it is cyclical, a holistic process. They suggested grief works more as a series of conflicts and contradictions rather than as passing-through phases. Christmas, birthdays, holidays, familiar places, poems, old letters, all these can evoke wild grieving after many years.

Nor did *time* follow set patterns for women. Though Smith (1982) suggests intense grief should decline after the first six months and Glick, Weiss and Parkes (1974) suggest that if grief hasn't almost recovered after the first year it bodes ill for future adjustment, the women I talked to said they took literally years to recover if they recovered at all. *But they 'functioned' adequately and did not see themselves as maladjusted.*[12]

In a culture where death is taboo, it is not surprising that grief has a completion date. But culturally imposed grief messages take no account of women's feelings which emphasise that a time-limit should not be set for 'normal' grieving.

Jane Littlewood suggests that perhaps the loss of a loved person cannot effectively be resolved, therefore people never fully recover from that experience.[13] *Certainly most women in my study did not feel the label of 'resolution' or 'recovery' was applicable to the way they grieved.*

Doctors who treat children with cancer bear this out.

The pain of losing a child is enormous. It goes against all the rules of nature. Parents live with that emptiness for the rest of their lives. With help, sometimes it becomes manageable. The women become different people. They may accept the child won't come back, or there's still a reason to go on living, but often that's the most you can achieve.

(Dr Eve Jones, Oncologist. Treats children with cancer.)

Grieving however need not be seen as negative. Neurosurgeon Carys Bannister described a practice in the children's hospital where she works:

At one time, we had an extraordinary Sister on the ward who set up a bereaving group, with no time-limit. The anniversary of the child's death was extremely stressful, but seeing the parents after the second year we noticed a lot of laughter. People remembered happy things about the child. Parents never ceased to grieve that the child didn't go on to achieve the things they had wanted for them, but many said they would have been very sad not to have had the child. They've celebrated the life rather than grieved the death.

Female grief counsellors, and bereaved women, held contradictory ideas. Some counsellors felt women were better equipped than men to deal with grief: 'I feel more women than men are capable of resolving grief because given the right circumstances women will go into depths of emotion more than most men get a chance to.' (Jay, Bereavement counsellor.)

Others saw marked gender differences in clients' responses: 'Male clients expect to learn how to resolve and manage grief. Women want to talk about the death but they don't expect a resolution, and honestly I feel women's grief isn't resolvable in the terms we teach.' (Marsha, Bereavement counsellor.)

Caron, a counsellor whose parents both died within twenty-four hours from heart attacks, finds her own experience useful:

I don't think I shall ever get over seeing Mum and Dad go like
that. You just learn to accommodate grief. We talk about 'unresolved grief' as if it's a *failure* but there is no such thing as
'resolved' grief. You can't resolve something as momentous as the
loss of those you dearly love. You have a new dimension to your
life that accommodates that missing piece. All I can do is show
clients how to function with one limb less.

Many bereaved women reiterated this idea of missing limbs or special shapes to their loss.

Anna Haycraft (novelist Alice Thomas Ellis), whose son Joshua
died from falling through an asbestos roof, said whenever she picked
up a book and saw his name scribbled inside she was suffused with
an 'awful burning sensation . . . I did feel for a long time as though
I was living in the middle of a furnace of pain . . . I suppose if you
lose a limb you come to terms with it but it's never going to come
back.'[14]

'I did not resolve my grief over Mary, my partner's death because
I couldn't "work through" it the way the books say you should. It's
four years ago but her death still lurches inside me. I miss exactly
who she was. Nothing, no one fills up that space. I seem to function
okay with that grief inside me.' (Marge, fifty-three, bereaved of
woman partner.)

Other women likened grief to backpacks, heavy loads, or con-
tainers. Alice Thomas Ellis said she felt as though she was 'simply
like a container for grief; that was all that I was; that seemed to be
my only point and purpose, just to carry this load around'. She said
her grief 'went on for years and I've never felt whole since. I've never
felt a complete person. I still feel like a sort of empty thing.'[15]

This sense of incompleteness is a characteristic feature of mothers'
griefs. Those who described grief as burdens felt they could grow
from it but to do so they had to keep carrying the load whilst
expressing their feelings.

Several elderly married women, irrespective of whether their grief
contained bitterness or affection towards their deceased husband,
reported visual or auditory hallucinations which lasted up to two
years. Some saw their dead husband's body, others heard his voice.
Most hauntings concerned the division of labour within the home.
Male ghosts were heard advising widows on where to sell the car,
how to mend the lawnmower, or in what order to pay the bills.
None of the elderly women found these hallucinations in the least
disturbing.

As I indicated in Chapter One, many women compared bereavement to grief over a broken relationship. Although some were
adamant that the two were not comparable as death was final,
substantially more women reported that grief from divorce,
desertion, or relationship break-up was *worse*. 'When my first husband betrayed me with this young Chinese girl, I was desperate.
Eventually I found happiness with a man who suddenly died from
a heart attack. What a terrible loss. But I haven't felt that rejected
feeling, that perpetual gulf in my stomach. (Bereaved partner, forty-
two.)

Many women find relationship break-ups harder because death
(except suicide) is not chosen. If there's been acrimony, women can't
grieve while that other person is still there.' (Relate and Bereavement
Agency Counsellor.)

> Last year my best woman friend died but I also left a long rela-
> tionship with Peter. Both were traumatic. Losing Peter was worse.
> It's the same process, somebody dying, losing somebody, it's loss
> you're talking about. Death is one aspect of loss. Relationship
> loss is underestimated. You can rationalise death, you can develop
> a picture of that person that stays. You can resolve your initial
> anger with the dead person, but with someone who's alive what
> do you do with that? You have guilt and failure, and it doesn't feel
> legitimate.
>
> (Marny, thirty-five.)

The problem with certain forms of death counselling, whether in
person or books, is that they use a kind of therapy-speak in which
grief is perceived as a disease that needs careful treatment, even as an
aberration in need of control. Courses are offered in how to accept
the unacceptable that is death. These are timid answers, an attempt
to domesticate passion (for grief *is* passionate), to tame the violence
of grief. Women to whom I talked were finding new ways to navi-
gate. They were prepared to meet grief head-on without drugs or
'management'. We *cannot* manage the unmanageable. We must find
our own comfort within its stone walls. For some it can be productive: 'When death touches you closely, suddenly in a stark moment
you know who you are. Your identity is somehow on the line.'
(Woman whose partner died in car smash.)

With a contemporary phrase like this, we see the Greek view of
mortality: that death is the supreme moment for bringing person-
hood into focus, that feelings about death are monumental, not the

instant commodities they are visualised as today. As Adrienne Rich pointed out:

> At the San Francisco airport, early March 1991, you could buy *A Gulf War Feelings Workbook for Children* in a bright spiral plastic binder. An out-of-date commodity, soon, no doubt, supplanted by yellow ribbons, which like flags, are safe and static emblems; they leave no question open, they keep at bay doubt, confusion, bitterness, fear and mourning.[16]

Grief changes but it may not disappear. We change with our grief and are changed by it. We cannot escape grief. It is our ghost. Within its imminent haunting will be our fears and mourning. Women are not afraid of grief, do not feel the need to shut it away. Many have grown, have become the strong new women mourning has made them.

The Medicalisation of Death

Messages: Death as the Enemy/Death as Failure

Death, once in women's hands, is now in the hands of professionals, namely funeral directors and doctors. It is interesting to speculate whether this professionalisation is also in part its masculinisation. Certainly the traditional connection between birth and death was severed when the 1902 Midwives Act forced knowledge of midwifery, once passed down from mothers to daughters, into male hands: those of undertakers and medical professionals.

Though most of the practical care for the dying is done by relatives, death itself is seen as needing professional aid. It is the doctor who is first summoned, and death thereafter is defined as a medical event. The medical profession has the power to say that death has occurred and what caused it. But in a wider sense the medical profession controls how death is managed and spoken of. That the medical model has a substantial hold on people's perceptions of death is a pivotal reason for analysing the medical message.

At other times, or in other cultures, death was and is *not* classified in terms of physical causes but often as an act of God, or the result of social or moral causes. (We do see this here with lung cancer or AIDS where the dying are said to have 'brought it on themselves'.) This apart, however, the dominant framework remains medical. Aries saw the medicalisation of death, with its progressive concealment through regulation and organisation by doctors for whom death was a failure, as 'the beginning of the lie', part of the process of secrecy and denial.[17] The most pervasive expression of the medicalisation of death is the notion of *death as disease* rather than as the natural and expected limitation to life. As long as death is seen as disease the atmosphere will be one of combat rather than acceptance. Where hospitals are committed to curing people, there will be practical implications such as ward routines which (unlike hospices) are hardly geared to the priorities of dying patients.

Because it is well established that many professionals in medicine, who seek to keep control in their own hands rather than in those of dying people, have masculist clinical attitudes, I asked women doctors about whether their medical training had reinforced gender stereotyping as well as inculcating the death-as-failure message.

I approached neurosurgeons, consultants and doctors who worked with dying children within paediatrics, as paediatricians are often described as 'a different breed of doctors'. More than half of the doctors working in the British paediatric service are women. Figures for women consultants in British medicine are disgraceful (about 8–10 per cent) but in paediatrics more women become consultants than in other areas.

> For a long time I was the only woman neurosurgeon practising here. One lady did it during the war, then she died in 1955, then there was a gap, then me, only me. But in the last five years two or three other women have been appointed consultants. I'm enormously grateful because I would have thought I'd put everybody off! There is a difference in our practice because you must incorporate the parents otherwise it doesn't work. Looking after infants is like veterinary surgery. You are looking at your patients partially through the eyes of the parents.
>
> (Carys Bannister, Neurosurgeon.)

Other paediatricians echo Bannister's comments: 'Paediatricians are trained to look at the predicament the child is in, whether that is the illness, the social setting, or their past experiences. It is more holistic than say a surgeon who focuses on one part of the body, treats that, but the rest doesn't really matter.' (Dr Eve Jones, Oncologist. Works with children with cancer.)

These women doctors see communication and caring as central. 'With technical skill you also need that special ability to communicate not only with the child but also parents, colleagues, doctors and social workers.' (Dr Mary White, Paediatrician.)

'Gender stereotypes still exist in specialities like surgery. It's less in paediatrics because we've all had more of a parental role, tending to be caring, and male paediatrics are fatherly. It's accepted that women have as much of a role here as men.' (Eileen Baildam, Consultant.)

For some female doctors, even consultants, gender is still an issue:

I could talk to you for a week about gender stereotyping! I've always been aware of it so I've always fought against it, but quietly because qualifying in 1978 I knew it would be an uphill struggle to get to be a consultant if I was openly assertive. When I was a medical student we had an orthopaedic surgeon who wouldn't talk to female medical students at all. He just talked to the men. We weren't worthy to be taught!

This doctor feels the old message lingers on:

Recently I was expecting my third child, was under huge pressure to carry on day to day work which I was doing as well as everybody else. But one of my male superiors didn't like to see pregnant women in the role of doctors. He felt you should be at home. He tried to force his view on me that if you want to be a careerist you should give up any idea of having kids. You should have a one-track mind. I didn't deal with that as well as I might have done because I felt vulnerable, tired most of the time, and because he was in a superior position. I ensured that all the work was done then I shied away from actual confrontation with him.

(Carol Ewing, Consultant paediatrician.)

The prevailing stereotype that cure was the province of doctors while care, compassion and communication was left to nurses (a stereotype that fortunately is changing) had its roots in early medical training. In the past, as Carys Bannister explains, 'we were taught nothing about the coping, telling, dealing with parents and patients'. The quest for diagnosis is often seen as more important than care for the whole patient, though it is less common where dying children are concerned. 'In hospital medicine the idea of cure as success and death as failure is incredibly strong. For example with very premature babies who in the long term have a poor quality of life, there are times when we strive to keep them alive when really it would be better to let them die.' (Carol Ewing, Consultant.)

Others reinforced her view but see positive changes:

Our training as doctors makes us see death as a form of failure. It's difficult for anyone working with children to see them die and *not* feel you've failed. Living with that sense of failure is often the hardest bit. Your whole aim is directed to cure but with children with malignant diseases, some you are not going to cure. So you live with the threat of death even when the cure rate for oncology is wonderful. Because of that the attitude of death as the enemy is changing.

(Dr Eve Jones.)

When I trained the idea of death as the enemy was not something anyone ever said, but it's an unwritten assumption. You train to be this great person who is going to heal everything. Paediatrics is different: it's more realistic. Because we deal with fatal congenital abnormalities, you have to accept that it is not always possible to cure.

(Eileen Baildam, Consultant.)

Today many women medics break through this rigid message, hold on to the notion of care, see the patient as critical as the treatment. 'Caring is the most important skill. You want to help children and parents and that manifests itself by being able to listen and empathise. Try and be in that situation with them. Some of us are better at listening to the parents than we are at listening to the child.' (Eileen Baildam. Consultant.)

Though the simplistic distinction between medicine as 'curing' and nursing as 'caring' has been surprisingly widely incorporated into the nursing ethic (though the caring-curing contrast does not work in palliative medicine which does not aim to cure), the tough medical message does not leave all nurses immune. Indeed some feel they have benefited from it. Twenty years ago Jeannie was taught to be hard about death:

On that first day, I'd had a two-year-old child with leukaemia. No way to save him. I had to lay him out. A babe, a babe. I thought I might faint. I went to cry in the staffroom. The Sister came after me, hauled me to my feet angrily: 'This is your life, Nurse! Stop crying! If you can't stand death, if you're going to show tears or be weak this is not the job for you. You'd better give in your notice now. Make up your mind. You have to lay out this death or go!'

Jeannie decided to face death and life without tears.

In those days laying out the dead was horrible. You had to pack wadding up their back passage, in their front, down their ears and nose. A right smelly job! It's all changed now because of post-mortems, they don't want to waste their valuable time unpacking them. I got hard enough so I never fainted, never cried again. Being peripatetic, I got the order of the most deaths on any ward in a week, never less than eleven, sometimes twenty, no flinching! But learning to be hard has helped me live my life. When my Joey died I was a young mother with a large family. I wanted to die then I thought of that Sister. 'If you can't stand this death, Jeannie, this isn't the job for you!' Either I gave in my notice, tried to die, deserted my kids, or got on with it.

She got on with it. Highly successfully. Other nurses today, however, find the masculist ethic hard. Megan, a cancer nurse, explains:

We had 200 women a year with cancer. Some doctors I worked with were fine. But other doctors were not prepared to talk with patients about how long they had to live. I felt dishonest within the medical profession, trying to put women's interests first. Some doctors wouldn't use the word 'cancer'. With one consultant it was tricky because you'd forget he didn't use the word. Sometimes I forgot and called it that. One patient said: 'How dare you say I've got cancer? I haven't got cancer. If I had the doctor would have told me!' Obviously if it's important for a patient to deny, then you go along with that, but many women want to talk. I tried to get patients to maintain hope, fight for the present, but try to be realistic about the possibility of death.

Several studies suggest that the death-as-the-enemy message has been internalised by doctors so that as a group they have a high personal anxiety about death. 'I think doctors are anxious. Doctors look at their family trees. You can tell from them what the likelihood is. I know I'm likely to die from a coronary in my sixties. It's learning to live with that. I do fear death and dying. I want it to happen quickly. I don't want to linger.' (Carol Ewing.)

'Doctors make rude jokes about death, call it "turning up the toes" because they find it scary. I've seen limbs thrown around and medics laugh. It's fear they won't talk about.' (Dr Mary White.)

Gary L. Grammens, haematologist and oncologist, writing in a book on ethnic variations in dying, death and grief, suggested that the science of medicine is 'an exponential fight to stay on the cutting

edge of technical progress'. Grammens believes that for most fresh-
men medical students, 'their first hands-on contact with any
human is a dead one – a startling beginning.' Grammens says that
as a student 'there was an unwritten taboo against dwelling on
death. Patient rights regarding cardiac resuscitations, intubation,
and other such heroic and often futile efforts in the terminally ill
patient were not even considered. Patients almost had to earn
their way out of this life by enduring a barrage of mechanical and
chemical insults.'

Grammens felt that nowhere in any medical school course, postgraduate residency, fellowship training, continuing medical
education class or even self-directed readings 'is there to be found
the secret success of looking into another human's eyes and with
compassion and sensitivity explaining what the end of their life will
be like and offering physical and emotional support until the very
end'.[18]

> Anxiety? I think you've put your finger on it. However we try and
> skirt round it, we try to treat patients, keep them alive. Death is a
> failure, we may have to accept it. We may have to accept that our
> role is to treat the patient well to death but it *is* a failure. There are
> some doctors who once it becomes obvious to them, they pull out
> of the care.
>
> (Carys Bannister, Neurosurgeon.)

Ms Bannister however is one of several doctors who does not see this
as a mistake: 'It may not be wrong. It may be better done by other
groups. Certainly the nursing staff because of their much closer contact with patients and relatives have a role that is much more
intimate than doctors.'

One doctor talked for many when she analysed the silence around
death.

> Sometimes that silence inside medicine is a good feeling.
> Sometimes there's this sheer revulsion and horror, it's traumatic,
> people don't want to feel that more than they have to. You've got
> a war inside. You've been there, seen how horrible it is. So on one
> side it's this terrible death that should never have happened, on
> the other side it's natural. We try to bring those two contradictions
> together. If the death happened to a child with a terrible neuro-
> logical condition you might say 'thank God that's finished' but if
> it's a road traffic accident, all you want is to fight the death. So

there's the fighting and the accepting, and the silence while you
sort it out.

(Eileen Baildam.)

Many women doctors told me they found their emotional health in
jeopardy when they were required to mask their pain. Yet doctors,
even in conversation with colleagues, seldom speak of death.

There is very little open conversation. Unless you are with a group
you know and trust, death is not talked about in depth. When I
was in psychiatry we had a psychiatric registrar who committed
suicide. People didn't know how to handle it, couldn't talk about
it. Fortunately we are more open in oncology.

(Dr Eve Jones.)

This conspiracy of silence means that some doctors use language
that obfuscates death issues. 'Some male doctors have problems
putting issues about dying into accessible language. Men do it to
protect themselves. I've had no difficulty, I'm not aware of other
female members of the team who have. You have got to sit down
with a family, if their child is dying, and make sure they understand.' (Dr. Pat Johnson.)

Consultant Eileen Baildam offers a balanced view. She suggests it
is a case of pitching the language correctly. Assessing what knowledge the patients or parents have. 'If it's renal failure or a
neurological problem they'll be expert in that condition and using
non-medical terminology is counter-productive. You don't want to
insult them.'

If death-as-the-enemy is the theory, then distance and avoidance
become the practice. How do women doctors deal with this? Carys
Bannister sees the first interview about a child who is dying as the
most important and often the most stressful.

I have never avoided stressful situations even when patients or
relatives may not want to know. Many details of brain surgery
and operative procedures are quite frightening. You feel you've
done it well if you have been sympathetic, understanding and
compassionate, but we don't always feel up to it because we too
are human. You could be anxious or concerned about other
patients too. But you can't ever backtrack on that first difficult
interview. I don't avoid it but if I really feel I can't do it then I
postpone it.

Younger women doctors go further than Ms Bannister in their analysis of distance versus closeness. 'Feelings do have a place but you must recognise where it is. I am always emotionally involved with patients but I see myself as their protector too.' (Dr Pat Johnson.)

'I don't have any mechanism to keep at a distance and I don't want to. Of course you must have some way of coping with the involvement, but distance is counter-productive. The one thing you can do to help children is actually not to have a distance.' (Eileen Baildam.)

Consultant Eileen Baildam focused on the breaking of bad news to parents. Once in a job interview for a consultant's post she was asked to pretend that the interviewer was a mother with a baby who had Down's Syndrome. 'I was about to break the bad news to her. "What are your first words going to be?" asked this interviewer. I said: "I'm sorry. I'm not going to do it, not here, not now. Because it isn't a matter of the first words or any words. It is the way you come in, it's through touch, it's your face, your expression."'

Other doctors saw practical measures as an important start to the interview: 'I always say "Can I get you a cup of tea?" to the parents before I begin. Often parents will say as you walk in "They're not dead are they?"' (Dr Evelyn Peters, Paediatrician.)

One woman doctor I know well, who had not been able to save a little girl's life, broke down in tears and hugged the mother when she told her. The mother later told me how appreciative she had been. How do other women doctors perceive this behaviour?

> That's unusual behaviour but it isn't inappropriate. I've actually cried buckets with parents. I think that's fine. I'm sure my male colleagues would find that difficult because it isn't a male thing to express your emotions. They are supposed to be seen as coping in every aspect so it's a sign of failure.
>
> (Carol Ewing)

'I often have tears with parents. I don't mind being physical. I won't cry sort of uncontrollably but I always need a tissue. As a medical student I was told "Don't get involved with your patients." I just think that's rubbish!' (Eileen Baildam.)

There are, however, barriers that should not be crossed for the patient's sake. One doctor issued a warning:

> Women often get more emotionally involved which can be both good and bad. If you're too emotionally involved you can't help the families. If you're too isolated from the feelings that are

around, the parents will be aware. I feel most parents open up more to women, though having said that I know several men who were very good at it. It's no good you falling apart if everyone round you is falling apart. The time for you to fall apart is when you're away from the situation with people around to support you.

(Eve Jones.)

The time when doctors need the greatest support, during their own bereavements or losses, may often coincide with difficult cases, when generally they are not expected to express grief or are not offered time for private grief or recovery. In an article in the *Guardian* (5 April 1989) Jane Martin, a junior hospital doctor, described her conflict when her father suddenly died of cancer.

When I returned to work, I was informed that part of my 'compassionate leave' would be deducted from my annual holiday entitlement. It was difficult to comprehend the mentality that could conceive of the nightmare through which I had just lived as being interchangeable with a *holiday*. With this dawned the realisation that nobody at work was going to acknowledge my desperate need for time to reflect, to grieve for my father . . . In re-donning the white coat, it seemed, I had covered up my claim to be a human being with the capacity to be hurt and the right to crawl away and lick my wounds.[19]

Some doctors confirmed Jane Martin's bitter experience: 'If you have a private loss you're still expected to hide it, deal with it and get on. The other day a doctor friend was bereaved. I heard someone say in a tone of shock: "You know she's been off work a week!" (Eileen Baildam.)

'Part of the problem is we don't get adequate counselling about death. Individuals may go to a few workshops, but it's not part of the curriculum.' (Dr Pat Johnson.)

'When it comes to loss, doctors are reluctant to go for counselling. There's that feeling that somewhere you've *failed*.' (Dr Eve Jones.)

In some children's hospitals a more optimistic note was struck about doctors' personal bereavements. Several said they saw themselves as a community which shared experiences of loss. One paediatrician said: 'Someone is going through a loss now. It's okay to express those feelings. We don't have to put on a mask.' Where there *is* a feeling of failure, if a doctor expresses grief, it is linked to the notion of the doctor as expert.

'Being looked upon as an expert makes me want to learn more. I want to be absolutely sure I am doing everything I can for the patients. It has widened my knowledge.'

'Having got to the level of consultant I realise that you're not an expert at all.'

'I accept I have more knowledge than the people I'm advising on this one bit of life, there are millions out there who've got a lot more knowledge about the other bits of life.'

'I hope I don't make parents or patients think I'm such an expert that I'm not approachable.'

Is Jane Martin correct in assuming that donning the white coat (the traditional costume of distance and avoidance) dehumanises doctors and further reinforces the message of detachment about dying?

Although I did see a few paediatricians in white coats, it does not have to be worn within paediatrics. 'I don't wear a white coat so the human with feelings is there and yes there are times when there are tears in my eyes and times when I've cried with families.' (Eve Jones.)

'In other branches of medicine I wore the white coat and felt like I was some expert but not myself. It is easier without.' (Dr Pam Victor.)

'I was geared towards paediatrics because I knew I shouldn't have to wear a white coat. I felt it was a barrier between me and the patient though I do see a lot of patients wanting me to have a white coat because then they have more respect.' (Carol Ewing.)

'We don't wear white coats because we don't want that barrier for the child. When I went back to an adult rheumatology ward and wore one it felt strange. It's security, you're in a role. When I don't wear it I have to find out if they want me in that role.' (Eileen Baildam.)

In a lighter vein, the last word must come from neurosurgeon Carys Bannister, who keeps herself sane by running a smallholding with sheep, donkeys and a dog, which frequently accompanies her to work. 'The patients love my animals and the stories about them! I absolutely do *not* wear a white coat. *I wear my anorak!* It has been seen in many places, high and low. I've been mistaken for the cleaner. I'm often asked who the hell are you? Very rarely do they think I'm a neurosurgeon, that's for sure.'

She might be right! There is certainly a wonderful anecdote told about Ms Bannister at the hospital. Apparently soon after she moved into her house in the country, the postman tried to deliver a parcel. He tried repeatedly but never located her. She was obviously off with her animals. When he finally caught her at home, he asked her where she went.

'I go the hospital,' she said. 'I'm a neurosurgeon.'

The next day the postman visited her neighbour. 'You want to watch that one,' he said. 'You know the one with the animals. She's been saying she's a neurosurgeon!'

Although I cannot vouch for the veracity of the anecdote, I can vouch for the affection with which it is told and retold, and the enormous esteem with which Ms Bannister's unique blend of scientific brilliance and compassionate accessibility is a model for women doctors everywhere.

Chapter Four

DUTIFUL DAUGHTERS: PRIVATE CARING

Neither publicly nor privately have we re-adjusted the balance in caring between men and women. Women are so socialised into nurturing roles that it comes as no surprise to discover that they are the chief carers (often at high emotional cost), both public and private, of the sick and the dying.

Here I focus on private caring. I am curious about the ways in which a daughter's care for a sick mother is different from her care for a sick father; in the way her reasons for nurturing are rooted firstly in the expectations our society has of women; secondly in the complex relationship between mothers and daughters.

Every woman is another woman's daughter. Of all the roles women are required to take on, daughterhood is universal. Even if she becomes a mother, she still remains somebody's daughter. Every woman, even in the nineties, is expected to become a mother or at least to act in a maternal manner. The mother role is the one for which women are most often blamed and least often relinquish. As Adrienne Rich pointed out, to have borne and reared a child is to have done what patriarchy and physiology together render as the definition of femaleness.

Motherhood in the sense of an intense reciprocal relationship with particular children is only one part of the female process, but the institution of motherhood has rendered it an identity for all time.[1] Given that the institution of motherhood is not identical with the bearing and caring for children, motherhood as it is set up and experienced is a strange and contradictory process.

We know how mothers are *expected* to act. Most of us remain burdened with the knowledge that much of the time we have 'done it wrong', 'not mothered our children enough', 'mothered them too much', failed to 'let them go' at the appropriate time. Yet beneath these prescriptive edicts, to our surprise, we are often swept by sharp surges of love or anger, fiercer than passions we feel for other adults. 'If anyone touched my kid, I'd kill him!' was a phrase used by many mothers in this study. A phrase not used lightly.

Mothers feel this for sons as well as for daughters, but the relationship with daughters has deeper conflicts. Deeper roots. It colours daughters' motives for nursing dying mothers. It adds a special dimension to the way a daughter feels when her mother dies.

Many women told me their desire, or obligation, to nurse sick mothers, had strongly *physical* roots.

Women can feel wildly unmothered yet still retain the need to physically 'mother' a female parent. 'In later years she didn't hug me or touch me very much. I didn't feel mothered enough. I made do with the memories of her touching me a lot while she braided my hair before school. Now she is in a wheelchair, I plait up her long hair, and wash it very carefully.' (Wendy, daughter, forty-six.)

One woman's mother (now dying of cancer) had frequently left her during childhood. Clinically depressed as well as over-burdened with the impossible demands of an impoverished working-class woman's routine, she divided her small daughter and her four sons between relatives when she voluntarily entered a mental hospital six times.

> I am left with the legacy of feeling abandoned. But I have an essential need to make it up to her. I resent the demands she makes on me, but sometimes I think I still smell her skin, as I smelt it when she held me on her return from the hospital. I have a kind of body feeling that I should care for her. So I decided to take her out of the nursing home and care for her.
>
> (Allie, daughter, fifty-one.)

This mutual need for physicality is hardly surprising. The first awareness any woman has of nourishment, comfort, sensuality, mutual closeness, comes from her mother. Growing inside a mother's body, created from her blood and cells, a child is touched and touches with an intimacy never replicated. Even women who have no desire to mother, if they become pregnant will find their bodies nourish a developing child even against their inclination. Many women later feel that the original enfolding of one female body around another should be shaken off, denied, seen as over-possesiveness or as a claustrophobic prison from which they must escape. But they do not find it easy to disremember that once it was their whole world.

Most women (apart from the few brought up by fathers, servants, relatives, caretakers) will have been physically handled by mothers during their earliest years. The process of touching seems to imprint bonds between mother and daughter. (Interestingly many daughters I interviewed complained they had not had sufficient physical caressing; many gave and received it sometimes for the first time in many years when their mothers were dying.)

Certainly boy children also receive initial physical caring from a mother's body. But institutionalised heterosexuality and institution-alised motherhood demand that a daughter transfer those first feelings of dependency and eroticism from her mother to a man in order to become what has been defined as a 'normal' woman; whereas sons are allowed to carry those feelings over into other 'normal' relationships with women.[2]

In a society that degrades women, daughters and mothers are kept apart. Daughters find it hard to respect either themselves or their mothers. Mothers still socialise daughters into the narrow roles of wife and mother. The profession of motherhood has low status, is unwaged, rarely validated.

At present there is a difference between the mother-daughter relationship which grows golden from a natural mother-bond, and the grey, cold relationship fostered by an oppressive culture in which mothers teach daughters to be less than they could be.

For these reasons feminists have for some years been trying to redefine this relationship. But they have discovered that the stormy push-and-pull of this mother-daughter relationship can explode and undermine their efforts.

In order to understand daughters' devotion to dying mothers, or their denial of those obligations, we need to explore the complex issues of duty, martyrdom, guilt and care.

Writer Phyllis Chesler, in her introduction to Judith Arcana's brilliant study of mothers and daughters, confesses that when she read an early draft of Arcana's book she wanted her mother to read it first. She felt the book might break the silence between her mother and herself. Might give her the courage to rethink their typically unfinished business in a new way; with less fury, less despair, without the 'Blame-Mommy-it's-her-fault' explanation so popular but useless today.

Chesler says in her Introduction:

I took this book home to my mother. 'Please, mother, read this book. It will make everything – everything – clear. Then, you'll say you love me. Only me. For my strength. For all the ways I'm *different* from you. Then we'll embrace. Prodigal Daughter. Prodigal Mother. We'll speak only words of love to each other. Nothing superficial will ever pass our lips again.' 'You're so melo-dramatic,' she says. Putting on her glasses. (This conversation didn't take place. But we're closer to it every day, my mother and me.)[3]

Chesler, as a daughter, wanted her mother to read that book first. I, as a mother, want my daughter to read this book first. (Well, for goodness sake, at the very least this chapter!) However my daughter, Marmoset, like many writers' daughters, rarely reads my books. She says: 'I don't want to find out intimate things I don't know from a book offered to the public! I want *you* to tell me those things. I am your daughter!'

Writing is not only what I do. It is an intense part of who I am. Just as mothering is. For me they are entwined. I feel challenged by her decision to go her own way, make her own choices. Is it that I want her to be 'dutiful'?

Simone de Beauvoir has no doubt about the answer.

'My mother's whole education and upbringing had convinced her that for a woman the greatest thing was to become the mother of a family; she couldn't play this part unless I played the dutiful daughter.'[4]

Simone de Beauvoir wrote that in 1958. Thirty-six years later these roles are still being played out in sickness and in health. If duty is the traditional daughter's role, then martyrdom is traditionally the mother's. Frequently I have fought down a Jewish-motherly martyr impulse. When my daughter as a child would not eat cab-bage, I would think: 'So, you don't like my cooking?' I would mean: 'So you don't love me properly!' Now that she is grown-up (and I am not) I am still stuck with: 'So, you don't like my writing eh?' I mean of course: 'You don't love me properly.'

Fleetingly, I wondered, would she care for me if I were sick? Recognised immediately the absurdity of connecting two such dis-parate ideas, but had to acknowledge that, however irrationally, it had crossed my mind.

Both of us struggle to get beyond this prison of properness: I as bossy parent, she as dutiful daughter. To treat each other as people.

We try, with great difficulty, to see ourselves as women in the same situation within an oppressive society that has created a particular breach between mothers and daughters.

In a society that has made of women second-class citizens and nurturers of men, daughters cannot respect mothers, even if they empathise with their frustration. Some daughters will reject their mothers for acceptance or connivance. Some daughters will feel guilt that they cannot be 'proper mothers' in life, or more significantly when death looms, any more than their mothers could.

As Adrienne Rich imaginatively pointed out: 'Mother-love is supposed to be continuous, unconditional. Love and anger cannot coexist.'[5]

The impossible institution of motherhood, which has degraded and ghettoised female potentialities (which must be separated from *the experience of mothering*, that potentially joyous relationship of any woman to her powers of reproduction and to children), has institutionalised ideas that tell mothers they love daughters by definition, and tell daughters that they can expect approval, affection, acceptance unendingly no matter what they do or how they behave.

When a mother is dying, many of these strains and conflicts show up.

My case studies illustrate a curious unanimity in women's understanding of the role of dutiful daughter and point up the difficulties mothers have in rejecting matryrdom but not rejecting their children. Many daughters *wish* to care for dying mothers; few daughters, however, who don't, can escape the statutory feeling of obligation.

Daughters learn through adolescence that to be 'acceptable', they should offer parents, especially mothers, unconditional affection (displayed through appearances on family occasions, Christmas, weddings, eightieth birthdays); they should marry (if at all possible), bear children (visit with them); become efficient cooks and housekeepers and, at least in some social classes, do well academically. As parents age and become sick, daughters' duties may include physically looking after them.

Obviously the extent to which daughters actively involve themselves in caring tasks depends not merely on the way they perceive the mother-daughter relationship as 'satisfactory' or 'lacking', but also on their own family ties and financial circumstances. What I discovered is that regardless of the nature of the relationship, most daughters feel an *obligation* to care for a dying mother, whether or not they carry it out.

Mum was ill for fifteen years. Ended up with Alzheimers. We'd always been close particularly during the war. From the age of six I was aware of being progressively drawn into responsibility for her. As a child I remember her vomiting and going down the doctor's to get medicines. So at forty when she was dying of cancer, it was no different.

(Bessie, daughter, forty-five)

I don't ever remember having a good relationship with my mother. Dad beat her up, kind of imprisoned her. With hindsight I see she was envious of my youth and figure. My freedom. My father started using me as hostess for his dos at the House of Commons when he was an MP. I thought she hated me. She couldn't tolerate me around her. She'd say, 'Oh get out of the kitchen you stupid girl.' I felt I wasn't as important to her as my brothers. When I was married, she still excluded me. But then she got ill and phoned me. I felt: 'It's always me that does the caring.' Before I got there she'd had a stroke. All the way to the hospital I was saying: 'Please die Mum. Please die. I don't want to look after you. Oh God I can't look after you, we get on so badly together, it would be intolerable', but I felt it would be my role even though she liked my brothers better.

(Sandra, Jewish, daughter, forty-seven.)

Although different cultures exert varying imperatives on women, there are interesting similarities.

I come from a large extended family, the pattern in the Indian subcontinent. I wasn't trained for anything. You just had to look after someone, first my mother who was dying, then the other children. She'd been ill since my brother was born in 1967. She wanted to die. She had severe diabetes. Was virtually blind. She kept asking us to kill her, us little children. It was against our religion as Muslims. The idea from our culture is to accept everything God brings. She couldn't accept all the pain. I couldn't accept her dying. But what could we do? I left school at fifteen with no qualifications because they said to me at the hospital: 'Your mother is dying. Either you look after your mother or you value your education.' So I left school to care for her. I don't resent it. I was her daughter.

(Lehora, Muslim, thirty-two.)

Race, rebellion, spiritual practice affect how daughters see obligations but daughterly duty seems central.

> At seventy-six Mother had cancer though they didn't tell her she only had a few months to live. They just told me. Then they got it wrong, she lasted two years. She wanted to be cared for by me at home. I wanted what she wanted. There had been areas of me that had wanted her dead but I didn't want her to be away in a hospice while she was dying. If she'd been dead I wouldn't have had to constantly take her into consideration. I hadn't done what she wanted. I wasn't rich or respectable. I'd led her a merry dance. I'd had my children with a black bloke. Then I was an anarchist, got into black and women's politics. But she'd given me tremendous support. The GP said she was so ill she must go into a hospice. She would be a weight. I said she wasn't.
>
> (Nessie, daughter, sixty-two.)

> I'd been a Buddhist nun in this community for eleven years before my mother got ovarian cancer. It was a closed community in the sense you couldn't come and go as you please. But as I became more senior I took on teaching engagements, went on pilgrimages. The relationship between my mother and me which had been difficult got better. When we irritated each other, I meditated on it and realised this was the karma of our relationship. I had to get beyond pressing the mother and daughter buttons. When she was told she would have only a few months to live I decided to leave the monastery. It made all the difference. She didn't want to feel she was standing in my way but I was happy just to look after her. Being a Buddhist, I accepted what was happening on a deep level. As a nun I'd learnt how to be supportive. I could help her better than anyone, with her horrible symptoms, she was sick and I'd have to clear up the mess, but I didn't mind, it was such a relief to her.
>
> (Sophie, Buddhist, daughter.)

A major myth is that mother love is supposed to be continuous and unconditional. The mother is expected to be constantly available to nurture regardless of the number of offspring she might have, her financial situation or her own needs. She is moreover expected to have understanding and sympathy that never fails. At the push of a shift button, motherly words should show up on the screen that would do justice to the amazing Marmee in *Little Women*.[6]

The daughter myth is that the daughter will always come first with the mother, who will require on her part sacrificial obedience, long after such a term is in any way appropriate. As Judith Arcana points out, there is no form for the mother/daughter relationship other than that which serves when the daughter is a child, 'so mothers continue to desire dutiful obedience from their grown daughters as they continue to martyr themselves.'[7]

In her novel *Have The Men Had Enough?* novelist Margaret Forster suggests that sons do not feel the same need to martyr themselves for sick mothers. In the book Grandma is inexorably dying of Alzheimer's. Grandma's single daughter Bridget insists devotedly, against opposition, that Grandma be cared for at home. She herself shares a flat with her and does much of the physical caring. Grandma's married son Charlie feels (weakly) that Grandma should now be in a Home, but (weakly) supports Bridget by paying the bills, maintaining Grandma's flat, financing a team of helpers, and getting his wife Jenny to share physical care with Bridget. Jenny agrees with Bridget, is harassed by Charlie's importuning, remains guilt-ridden.

> What do I do, after all?: I bring Grandma along here for two hours three times a week; I shop for her; I do her laundry; I look after her on Sundays; I supervise the helpers. What does Charlie do: he pays the bills and looks after the flat. But Bridget, Bridget sleeps with her two nights a week and lives beside her, always on the alert. Her life is dominated by Grandma. And most of all Bridget suffers, whereas we do not. We suffer tedium and irritation and boredom. Bridget suffers real pain. She cannot bear to watch Grandma disintegrate, to see her helpless and lost, wanting only the love of her family. 'Men', Bridget says with Grandma about Stuart and Charlie . . .

Stuart, the other married son, thinks his sister Bridget is a foolish martyr. He is implacable that Grandma should be put in a Home. Now. He resolutely refuses to help the family keep her at home. He pays nothing and does nothing. On one occasion Charlie, going away for a Silver Wedding, leaves Stuart's phone number with the Grandma-sitter, who in an emergency rings it. Stuart is furious. Charlie phones Stuart to apologise:

> 'Stuart . . . we went to this Silver—'
> 'I know where you went . . . what I'm referring to is telling that

woman to ring me . . . if you'd *thought* you'd have remembered I'm not in on this . . . I'm not having any more of my life messed up by Mother and I've told you straight.'

'Well, normally the system works quite well but with Bridget being—'

'Don't mention Bridget to me, don't try that blackmail . . . if Bridget wants to be a martyr then that's her affair but count me out . . .'

'She's our Mother, Stuart and—'

'Good God, I *know* she's our Mother . . . I know she's old and sick, I know she can't help it but it's the other bit I'm not having, the bit where Bridget says it's our duty to look after her. I don't see it Charlie . . . I admit she was a good mother, very good, but that doesn't mean I have to go on paying for it all my life. She should be in a Home and that's that.'[8]

Eventually the male view predominates and Grandma is placed in a Home where she dies. Some of the family suffer guilt. Bridget suffers pain. Bridget, and to a lesser extent Jenny, illustrate the traditional role of *any* woman, which includes strong elements of self-denial and other-nurturance. Stereotypical mother-daughter roles merely heighten and extend the ways in which *most* women are expected to live. In order to receive the approval and love mothers and daughters need from each other, they continue to struggle to satisfy each other's demands, often unable to acknowledge that some of these expectations may be contrary to their dispositions. In the face of death, both groups of women revert to roles in the hope that it will provide security.

Approval is the core. Every daughter I interviewed, even if estranged from mothers, wanted their approval.

No more obvious proof of devotion can be given than when a mother is dying. After eight years of tense silence between my mother and myself, when she wrote that she was ill and needed to see me, I responded at once, despite having long given up on gaining her approval. For months I commuted between Cambridge and London to spend time with her, care for her, and finally try painfully, and not altogether successfully, to communicate with her. When friends asked in amazement why was I doing this, I used the same phrase I later heard from many of my interviewees: 'I am doing it for me as much as for her. It seems like the right thing to do.'

This concept of 'the right thing to do' arises from two different roots. Firstly our society's socialisation system, which restricts

women to nurturing roles, has established a public practice of professional carers and counsellors and a private practice of daughters
(sisters, wives) feeling a duty to care.

Secondly, although male culture has separated women from each
other, mothers and daughters still retain emotional bonds that are
stronger than role impositions. These bonds are based on an unspoken recognition of women's sameness: the closeness of similar
bodies, spirits, experiences, often co-existing with an antagonism of
tastes and ideas. This means that on a subliminal level they never
stop wanting to share even as they rage against each other.

An acceptance of dutiful structures into which women have been
fitted will turn daughters into carers of both parents (sometimes
more easily into carers of fathers), but it is an awareness of these
more complex bonds with mothers which engages daughters with
the emotional feeling that 'it is right'.

It is worth noting the facts which surround caring to see where
daughters and other women fit into the picture.

The 1990 UK General Household Survey of (informal) Carers
(which identifies both carers of living-in dependants and also carers
of dependants living elsewhere) analysed the 15 per cent of adult
carers over sixteen to show clearly firstly that although both sexes
care for those inside their own home, women carers are in the majority; secondly that 'women are more likely than men to look after
someone outside the household; thirdly that 'it is true that the number of women caring [3.9 million] is considerably greater than men'.

The report confirmed that societal expectations mean that
'women are more likely than men to take the *main* responsibility for
looking after someone and to devote 20 hours a week or more to caring . . . one in ten carers was devoting at least 50 hours a week to
caring.' The report acknowledges that women 'are more likely than
men to devote *long hours* to caring'. As I show in my examination of
Alzheimer's Disease, many women carers spend up to eighty hours
per week in this exhausting activity. Chief among these are dutiful
daughters, and daughters-in-law caring for somebody's parent.[9]

Although both sexes care for relatives other than parents, the survey discovered, what most women already know, that 'women were
more likely than men to be caring for parents and non-relatives'.
Researchers suggested that the likelihood of someone taking up an
unpaid, often unappreciated, caring role, depends not only on the
extent to which the sick or dying person is in need of help but also 'on
whether he or she is willing and able to undertake the caring role'.[10]

My study lucidly illustrates that daughters, sisters and other women, whether or not they are 'able' (often they themselves are poor, sick or both), do feel an obligation which puts them in the 'willing' category.

The peak ages for caring are forty-five to sixty-four. In 1990 27 per cent of women in that age group were caring for an elderly, often dying person. My case studies showed this burden falls more often on single women (usually daughters) who are seen to be 'free to do it'. The General Household Survey confirmed that single women in the peak age-group were more likely to be carers than married women.

Friendship networks are essential to single women of all ages, so it is no surprise to discover that a considerably higher proportion of single women cared for friends and relatives other than their parents.[11]

The type of all-day care women are expected to give to sick dependants includes washing, bathing, dressing, using the toilet, aiding the bed-to-chair struggle. Women supplement these tasks by shopping, cooking, housework, gardening, and in many cases administering medicines or bearing a substantial brunt of nursing care. When a mother is dying, such tasks are intensified.

> I did the whole process of looking after her. We became closer as she was less able to do things for herself. It was like we became almost one being. I felt I was doing the things she couldn't do for herself. I was like her arms and legs. I think we both felt that. I lifted her on to the bed pan, helped her brush her teeth. On the last night, when she couldn't drink, I kept putting little bits of ice in her mouth. I swabbed with this lemon and glycerine stuff.
>
> (Sophie, Buddhist, daughter.)

Some women learn as children to be their mothers under crisis situations.

> When my Gran died I was sixteen. She wanted to be nursed at home by Mum and me. I did all the cooking and most of the cleaning. Spooning food into her. When she died I helped our neighbour lay her out. Bowls of hot water, on and off with the nightdress, clean sheets, on with the cotton gown she was buried in. Washed out the nightdress. I was numb with shock. My Gran was buried two days after my seventeenth birthday which was quite overlooked.
>
> (Lakey, West African, grandaughter.)

First death I can remember was the lady next door. When I went round with my Mum the thing that shocked me was this great chamber pot full of urine. I thought that's never going to happen to my parents. I'm a nurse so when Mum was dying, I did everything, mopping up vomit, mopping her, but I was most terrified she would die alone. So when I needed to go to the toilet I would wait till the very last minute, rush outside pulling my undies down, terrified in case she needed something while I was away a few minutes. Tearing back, pulling them up, doing it in reverse. I did not want to lose one intimate moment.

(Moira, daughter, fifty-two.)

Sometimes this clearing-up continues after death, even when a male relative has been there and might have attended to it.

When I returned from hospital after she'd died from the stroke, she'd been incontinent all over the floor. No one had touched it. I suppose it was too awful for father, who had found her. I'd always dealt with the grot. The mess was stinking. Two days it had been left. I cleared it up, then I found all the vomit on the sheets. I changed them in case my brother wanted to sleep in her room. He didn't, so that night I slept in her bed.

(Marge, daughter, fifty-seven.)

The invisible nature of women's caregiving is at least established for the white population. Black women's personal caregiving appears intensified but more scantily recorded. McCalman (1990), unusual in undertaking a survey of informal carers from black and ethnic minorities, contacted Asian, Afro-Caribbean and Chinese carers in Southwark, to discover that twenty-one of the thirty-four were female. These women not only spent eleven hours *per day* caring for elderly sick and dying relatives, but all reported that they had 'spent a considerable amount of their lives caring'.[12]

There is a particular problem for black women. The notion that care in the community for black households (especially Asian households) usually resides in care by the family means that black women's acknowledged commitment to caring for disabled or dying relatives is assumed to be greater than that of white people, to the extent that service provision thinks it need not concern itself with black people's needs. As 'family' care most often means 'women's care' for black as well as for white households, the lack of adequate service provision specifically affects black women.

The prevalent idea that black people dying of cancer or other life-threatening diseases can comfortably be looked after by their 'large extended family' rests on a huge misconception. Although the traditional pattern in many Asian communities is to share responsibility among family members, research into the circumstances of black families suggests that the supportive extended family network is largely a myth. Changes in household structure, and geographical dispersal of close and extended kin, means there are still a significant proportion of Asian people who live alone, with few relatives in this country. Research (Cameron, Atkin, Fenton) shows 'extended families were common, but by no means universal'. Cancerlink argued that the commonly held view that Asian people look after their own, have self-supporting networks, was simply not true. They concluded that the most revealing finding of their research was the shattering of these assumptions.[13]

McCalman (1990) observed in her study of Asian and Afro-Caribbean families that when someone was sick or dying the main responsibility fell on one family member. Year after year, research project after research project shows that (as in white families) responsibility fell on the one 'family member' who was a woman. Where a child is desperately sick or dying, as Walker (1987) showed in a study of fifteen Asian families caring for ill children, the mother always assumed responsibility for all aspects of care.[14]

My research shows that in the absence of a mother, the obligation falls upon daughters.

First it was the mother, she took a turn, they said it was cancer, nothing to do but for us to help. Three of us daughters, two married so it was mainly me doing all that washing, shit everywhere, toilets I hate them. Then her brother, he was living with us, had one of those strokes. Couldn't hardly move. Upstairs and down, though I was rocking with pain. Then our father had a stroke too, they'd always competed. No one to give me a hand. I had to be like an oak tree. But I wanted to collapse, wanted someone to look after me.
                    (Anja, Afro-Caribbean, daughter, thirty-three.)

As a Muslim with an arranged marriage at fourteen, my mother felt marriage was from God. When my Dad divorced her, two weeks later she died of heart failure. I was just fifteen, completely broken-down. But my job was to feed and wash and clothe the other children.
                              (Shushi, Asian, Muslim, daughter.)

Black women as the main carers of the dying in their communities have even less help from outside sources than do their white sisters. Research on white carers of the dying, borne out by my study, shows increased levels of emotional strain. Although there is a lack of systematic exploration in relation to black women, evidence available suggests the disadvantages of loneliness and isolation (increased by communication difficulties) associated with ethnicity intensifies emotional costs. Racism compounds the situation. Cameron's research showed that black women carers felt restricted to their houses through fear of an 'alien' outside world where their own norms, values and social skills, were often regarded as inappropriate.[15]

For mixed race families there are additional strains.

You can't walk out arm in arm with a black man and not be abused. You can't live in a racist society without having problems bringing up kids who are black. My three girls' father is African. They've had rough times. But they've done well. My middle one is the second woman and the first black woman to qualify as a sound engineer. But they've had problems with their white Grandmother. Even when she was dying. She likes the rebellious aspect of having black grandchildren but she can't rid herself of the idea that it's the white man's burden to educate the black. It made it difficult looking after her when she was vomiting from cancer. Just us looking after her. She had a gross mastectomy, half her armpit taken away. She needed a lot of nursing at home, and my three girls had to develop great honesty and understanding. All four of us women were changed by that long suffering.

(Nessie, daughter.)

Black women carers, already handicapped by women's low wages in general, suffer further deprivation from even lower wages. McCalman found that none of the eight Asian women she interviewed was in employment yet all eight had sole financial responsibility, because of the severity of their husbands' disabilities or terminal diseases.[16]

These pages show how daughters from many cultures cope with good heart with the tough tasks of caring for dying parents. But public acknowledgement of black and white women's private caring has been sparse. For too long women's care has been subsumed under the neutral non-controversial term 'family care'. Women carers need to break this silence, before the work breaks them. This study gives them a space.

We need – and do not have – a vastly improved service provision for carers of the dying, which is both racially sensitive and has gender acknowledgement.

Given that these unacknowledged physical tasks of care for the dying are often back-breaking and sometimes spirit-splintering, do daughters regard such tasks as burdens?

'The doctor said I could put her away. I didn't need to have this burden. I said to him, "Maybe I don't look on it as a burden!"' (Nessie, daughter, sixty-two.)

> It was hard work, but she tried to be undemanding, make it easy for me. In order not to keep asking me for things, she'd try and ask for lots of things in one go. She didn't want to feel she was taking up my life. I didn't feel her to be a burden. So that was something we had to work through. She would say 'Why don't you go out?' So once I went to a friend's. When I got back she wasn't complaining but she had been too exhausted to give herself a liquid nutrition drink. So I felt awful. It was more of a burden not being there.
>
> (Sophie, daughter.)

Nessie and Sophie's views were echoed by many daughters. Sophie's persistence in discussing difficult issues was a way of honouring their relationship. She felt that her training as a Buddhist nun had helped her.

> I had a strong sense of purpose beyond the material mundane level of survival which helped me become more patient with the annoying trivialities. Buddhism showed me how to develop compassion and kindness. My mother and I worked with that. Part of the training of a nun is integrational unity. In the monastery I learnt the integration of caring for the physical side along with the emotional and spiritual. So when she snapped at me and said 'Why did you do that?' I realised it wasn't personal, she wasn't being impatient with me. She was just this person with a tendency towards impatience and a terrible illness.
>
> (Sophie, Buddhist, daughter.)

At the moments before death do daughters choose to talk to their mother about the fact that she is dying?

'We never discussed the fact she was dying. I regret it now. There was too much taboo. It's a subject that filled me with horror at every level.' (Babs, daughter.)

'I talked to Mum about the fact her cancer was terminal. While she was having radiotherapy she relaxed into awareness she was not going to recover. She was frightened then angry. It was better to talk.' (Nessie, daughter.)

'Talking about her actual dying helped us both. She admitted she was frightened. Then we put our arms round each other.' (Fern, daughter.)

'I was afraid to mention death but she had no such fear. She said she was frightfully curious. Had always liked adventures. I was amazed. It made me laugh.' (Tamsin, daughter, forty-six.)

'Being Christians helped talking about dying. My sister and I sat by her bed. We said prayers together then strangely we looked at some old children's books and tried to discover what death meant to us all.' (Phillippa, daughter, fifty-one.)

Unresolved feelings and guilt play their part in discussions. Sophie explains:

> In those last few weeks we did talk about death. She didn't have much unresolved. She and I knew her death was near. My father denied it more. We talked about guilt, her guilty feelings about my father's first wife. We said how her dying affected our relationship. It was me more than her that needed to say things. I was able to voice that she had been a wonderful mother. She said she couldn't have asked for a better daughter. I'd been so difficult as a teenager, and she'd often been annoyed. She said death didn't frighten her, not like painful fighting for breath. She said it was strange living with the uncertainty of not knowing how long you had. That was good from a Buddhist view. Because it was so uncertain, she just lived day to day.

Though life outside a monastery weaves webs of silence around death, inside the monastery walls death is spoken of constantly.

> Our daily reflection was: 'I am of the nature to die. I have not gone beyond dying. And all that is mine, beloved and pleasing, will become otherwise, will become separate from me.'
>
> Saying that every day gave me a preparation for my mother's death. The Buddhist sense of unconditional love became linked to hers.
>
> (Sophie)

Just as a Buddhist training gave one daughter tools with which to cope, so a feminist consciousness can throw another daughter's relationship with her dying mother into a startling new perspective. 'I got involved in the Women's Movement two years before my mother got breast cancer. I had to stop seeing her as some bossy rival, as someone who drained me emotionally. I realised we had both been oppressed – it wasn't her oppressing and upsetting me.' (Annette, daughter, thirty.)

> Once I'd become a feminist I wanted to drag my mother into the light. Get her to see her situation from a feminist point of view. She was very slowly dying of cancer, she tried, but she was too ill to think about much except the slow poisoning of her body. But we made it as friends for about six months then she was gutted with poison, lost all control, I practically had to mother her.
>
> (Phoebe, daughter, forty.)

Though some daughters want very little to do with their mothers, many others like Phoebe want to take care of their mothers, a process that may begin as early as the menopause.

Phoebe's words link two key issues: that of friendship and that of daughters mothering mothers. Some women saw mother-daughter relations and friendship as mutually exclusive – they criticised mothers who tried, even on their deathbed to be friends to their offspring. Many daughters, however (a greater number amongst feminists), had been trying to transcend stereotypical roles. Where they had already attempted to relate to their healthy mothers as women in a shared situation, they found dealing with their death less problematic though no less painful.

The second issue of the daughter-mother role reversal was a common phenomenon.

> They told her it was gallstones. They told me she had six months to live. One night she was dancing, the next night she was hallucinating. Those last six days she couldn't do anything for herself. She messed the bed, couldn't feed herself. It was heartbreaking just to see her use a feeder cup. She used to drink about fifty cups of tea a day. Not to be able to do that, she was desperate. She'd move the feeder cup to her mouth, it would take half an hour, then she didn't want to have the top on, it was a terrible thing for her pride. So she'd say 'NO! I can do it!' So I'd take the top off but

it would all spill down her, so I'd have to feed her, just like a mother with her child. She would cry, she was so upset.

(Babs, daughter, forty-one.)

It was like being a mother instead of a daughter, trying to find small bits of food my mother could swallow. She had to have a commode quite early. But she was brave with a lot of grace. The pain was too severe for her to be touched. So the last time she had a bath we were both in tears. After that I washed her feet every day in warm water. I dry shampooed her hair. She was a woman who was vain. When she became incontinent and had to wear pads, she would only accept it because I was washing her night-dresses every day. Just like a child. I said: 'It's much easier if you do pads than if you leave me with a load of laundry. I can't wash laundry in the sink. So you've got to co-operate. I can manage these baby knickers and your nightie but not sheets!' She'd say: 'Of course. I'm a baby now. I'm a Belsen beauty and a baby. Look at me!' It was true. She was thin as Belsen.

(Nessie, daughter, sixty-two.)

Doing motherly things for her was like doing them for myself. She didn't have to put on a brave face. If she was sick she knew I didn't mind clearing it up. Whereas with my brother and father she was embarrassed. She felt she had to make an effort for them. One time she stopped my brother from coming because she didn't feel up to it. She was relieved if I was there doing motherly things. Anything she needed she could ask me. Having that sort of ease and love between us was wonderful, it felt like a real fulfilment of being a daughter.

(Sophie, daughter.)

The concern of Sophie's mother to protect the men in her life was uniform. Many dying mothers reassured daughters that with them they 'could be themselves', that they 'did not have to put on a front', they felt 'no need to put up a good show'. One daughter whose mother died in hospital said: 'She kept up all her social obligations until Dad and my brother left. Then she relaxed enough to die peace-fully. She didn't have to go on protecting them.' (Lana, daughter, thirty.)

If many mothers felt free to be themselves while daughters min-istered, the reverse was also true. Babs spoke for many: 'My mother was the one person I could be myself with. I didn't have to justify myself to her. Though she was incredibly demanding, she thought the sun shone out of me.'

When a mother dies leaving a very young daughter, the daughter may never face a role-reversal, but she will be subject to fear of appearing different. 'At school I felt everyone was going to look at me because I was different. They'd say: "Look at her. She's lost her Mum." I felt odd, not like the others at school. They didn't talk about it. No one at school mentioned it. They thought: "She might cry! She'll be upset." So nobody talked to me.' (Caroline, British daughter, bereaved at eleven.)

> Mum died of a brain tumour when I was a young girl. I wanted to continue as though nothing had happened. But Dad and the family said: 'You can't go back to school. People don't go back to school after their mother's died.' So I knew I was different. The Minister and his wife took me for a drive, tried to get me to talk about my feelings. I was desperately trying to be a regular person, trying to think of something social to say, about my homework or sport.
>
> (Carmel, American, daughter, bereaved at sixteen.)

Self-blame is a common characteristic of youthful bereavements. 'What I missed was that the house was empty when I came home from school. She'd always been there. I found it hard and creepy. Had I done something wrong that I had to be without a Mom?' (Eve, American, daughter, bereaved at twelve.)

'I blamed myself when my Mum died. It didn't seem natural being so young and not having a Mum, so I reckoned it was my fault.' (Esme, British, daughter, bereaved at thirteen.)

Fathers and brothers tend to rely on very young daughters once the wife/mother is dead, just as they do on adult daughters: 'I grew up very quickly. One day I was a little girl of eleven. The next day I was the woman of the house.' (Candy, British, daughter, bereaved at eleven.)

'I'd been running the home since Mom's death when I was fourteen. I started going out with guys. Dad panicked. He said he was worried I'd leave him, go away, get hitched, then what would he do?' (Jennie, American, daughter, bereaved at fourteen.)

A few fathers decided to get paid help. Sometimes this added extra feelings of guilt or exclusion to a young daughter's desolation. 'There were these housekeepers coming in. I was excluded. Then I was sent off to college. I became very promiscuous. I don't know if it was guilt. It was related to my mother. I wouldn't have dared to behave in that way had she been alive.' (Carmel, American, daughter, bereaved at sixteen.)

Several women told stories of sudden promiscuity, which started after their mother's death (often from a feeling of abandonment) which they repeated after a partner's death (often from a feeling of anger or betrayal).

In the face of death, mothers as well as daughters often act in surprising ways. A few become untypically self-assertive.

Mum had had this stroke. When she had a slight remission the hospital let her go home for the last weeks. In the hospital she'd put lots of two and twos together, sussed out who Dad had been having an affair with for twenty-three years. On her first day out of hospital she staggered with her zimmer frame and her leg in a caliper to this woman's flat, staggered up nine flights of stairs, there was no lift. Then she hammered on the door and said to this woman's husband: 'Your wife has been having an affair with my John.' All hell was let loose! It meant she finally took control over her life when she was in her sixties and dying.

(Leanne, daughter, forty-eight.)

What fears or desires do mothers have as they wait to die? **The most common fear I encountered was the fear of losing control of their physical functions; the most common desire was permission to die.**

She wasn't frightened of death, she was frightened of losing her self-control. She was scared of losing her bowel movements. The first occasion it happened she was absolutely devastated. She didn't speak the rest of that day or night. The next day she'd regained control of her bowels. It was another 8 months before she lost it again. That was will power, spirit over flesh. She said: 'I'm not having that again until it's absolutely beyond me.'

(Nessie, daughter.)

Writer Celia Haddon reports the same fear when her mother was dying: 'I could also see her distress each time she had to pee in the bed. I would lean over her and say 'It's all right to do it here, Mum', but her face would look anxious and she would move her thin-stick arms about as if she was desperately trying to get out of bed. The potty training held its force even at the gates of extinction.'[17]

When my own mother was dying in a nursing home, that was her fear too. A nurse attempted to reassure me:

'Don't worry about your mother weeing in her knickers. She's got paddy pads on and we don't mind changing her and keeping her clean.'

I tried not to raise my voice. 'It is not me that minds. It is my mother. She says she is not incontinent. She still has all her mental faculties and if she says it, I believe her. She says because she can no longer see properly, she can't always find the bell when she wants to go to the toilet. Because she is losing her voice, she cannot shout for help. So sometimes she is forced to let go. She is finding the situation intolerable. Can't you see how degrading it is for her?'

'Is that what she says dear?' the nurse asked kindly. 'You know a lot of them don't like to admit they've lost control! It's our job to clean up after them.' Then, with forced jollity she said: 'Quite a lot of the time we manage to get the commode to her so that she can open up her bowels!'

That night I asked myself how long would it be before Mother could not wait to shit into the pan? How long would it be before the nurses gave up trying to reach her in time? Would Mother die while she could still control her own shit? Suddenly this question seemed of immense importance.[18]

Mothers often need families' permission to die.

'What sticks in my mind is Mother looking at all the family round the bed and saying: "It must be time for you to go home." One of them said: "We're going to stay with you till you get better." Mother said: "Oh, can I go to sleep now then?" She never regained consciousness but she'd kept her social obligations going until someone gave her permission to go.' (Leanne, daughter.)

Permission also conditioned several daughters' regrets. 'I regret not asking the family to leave so that I could be on my own with her. I felt I needed their unspoken permission and I didn't get it.' (Owen, daughter, forty-one.)

'I wished I'd had permission to get into the hospital bed with her and cuddle her.' (Anita, daughter, thirty-eight.)

'I took a tape recorder with me, to record some of her last words, all those stories, then I felt I needed someone's permission to use it. I deeply regret being such a wimp.' (Deanna, daughter, forty.)

Sometimes the pain their mother was going through was so

intense that daughters would do anything to relieve it. Anything except help her die.

Lyndall Hopkinson, the agnostic daughter of Catholic novelist Antonia White, sat by her mother's deathbed, watching her ward off the invisible blows and horrendous screams of threatening dreams, and prayed to Antonia's God to release her.

> I who until so recently had not believed in anything . . . flung all the frustrated spiritual fervour of years of agnosticism into pleading with God: 'Please don't let her suffer any more. Please let her die now, in her sleep, on her birthday with the sun shining, her hand in mine. Surely she's made amends enough. Please PLEASE . . . But her irregular laboured breaths continued to mock my prayers. God was as stubborn as Antonia that day and in no mood for simple endings.[19]

Writer Celia Haddon believes that nothing had prepared her for the full horror of her mother's last seven days in which she died inch by inch, moment by moment, organ by organ.

'I feel as if the experience has darkened my life. For our society denies death. Men die nightly on the television screen, but for the most part they die with unrealistic brevity. The pain and squalor is never shown and most of us have never seen a dying person in the decaying flesh.'

As her mother literally decayed away, as squamous cell carcinoma of the tongue spread its cancerous way to the pancreas, as she finally stopped drinking and began dying of dehydration as well as cancer, Celia Haddon felt that neither she nor her mother could take any more.

> I tried to moisten her lips with a mixture of cider and lemon juice . . . she began to choke. By now I wanted my mother to die. I could perhaps have helped her along by making her choke. Yet I could not bring myself to kill her in this way . . . Raging ideas began to plague me – why not smother her with the pillow, or go round the corner to the do-it-yourself shop, get an axe and just axe her to death, or strangle her with her dressing-gown cord. Anything to stop the pain I felt at her pain.[20]

Where there had been a stormy relationship before a painful death, daughters were left with anger or unanswered questions.

'There were things I wanted to say. I felt angry with her. Stuff in

my adolescence. My father was an alcoholic, no one spoke of it. My
mother was paranoid, she thought people were trying to poison her.
I was left wondering what was normal what wasn't. No wonder I was
angry.' (Babs, daughter.)

> She was never there for me. She was absent when I was beaten by
> my father. He'd send me to the shed to choose a cane. So you'd sit
> and look at the green ones, that were thin and sharp, and you'd sit
> and look at the brown ones, with knobbles on. You'd have to go
> and bring it back. He pulled your trousers down and did it on
> your naked bottom. I suppose that my mother was probably off
> crying somewhere in helplessness, but at the time she never
> stopped him. She never came afterwards to comfort me. I was
> excluded from everything in her life. When she was in her last
> coma, my older brother and his wife were there. At one point
> Mother seemed to smile at them. I was so angry that she wasn't
> smiling at me. I felt left out and cross that I was dealing with such
> childish emotions. I had so many questions to ask but I'd been
> excluded. I sat outside intensive care for two hours. No one
> allowed me in until after she had died. However the year after she
> died I talked to her a lot as if she was there.
>
>   (Sandra, daughter.)

Whatever the nature of the relationship, many daughters felt it was
a time for reconciliation. Celia Haddon who had watched with relief
the chaplain finally administer extreme unction, was suddenly
shocked out of her distress by a small miracle.

> One of my mother's hands lay outside the coverings. It was bluish
> in colour. I took hold of her hand and as I did so, it grasped back.
> She was holding my hand. I felt a great joy. We stayed like this for
> 6 hours. I talked to her, I told her of my love. I believed she could
> hear me. Her hand turned from blue to pink and she did not
> die . . . Her breath no longer rattled . . . It occurred to me that per-
> haps I had called her back and I stopped holding her hand. Besides
> by now her breath was so foul, that I could not sit close to her
> without wanting to throw up . . . One of her ears now had red
> blotches from the pressure of the pillow. One of the blotches was
> turning black. She was rotting . . . Seven days later . . . something
> changed . . . I walked over to her, and picked up her hand . . . Dead
> cold. Quite different from the cold of the living hand which had
> held me as a baby. I sang her a hymn. I told her how much I loved

her. I sang to her the lullaby she used to sing to me. 'Golden Slumbers Kiss Your Eyes'. One long intake of breath and she stopped breathing for ever.[21]

Lyndall Hopkinson for years had suffered an uneasy relationship with her novelist mother Antonia White, always believing, because her mother told her, that it was Susan Chitty, her half-sister, who was the favourite daughter. However when her mother was dying in a Catholic nursing home racked with osteoporosis, cancer, a broken hip and bouts of obsessive depression, it was Lyndall rather than Sue who was with her, but Antonia, assailed by ghosts from her past, did not recognise Lyndall.

> Sometimes she thought I was Sue, her favourite daughter, a Catholic and a writer like herself . . . Whoever she thought I was, my voice and touch seemed to comfort her. Once when I was stroking her she insisted I was 'touching filth' as if she were pleading forgiveness. But although I *had* forgiven her, I was afraid to say so, for she might still have leapt back fiercely and demanded: 'Forgiven me for what?' And I would have been too cowardly to answer, 'For the way you never bothered to find out who I really was, because you ignored me in babyhood, terrorised me in childhood and slighted me in adolescence' . . . I cried for what had been, for what had not been and for what might have been: for the mental suffering her almighty ego had inflicted on herself and others, particularly on her two children. I see now there was as much self-pity as commiseration in my tears.

When her mother no longer had the strength to swallow, Lyndall dampened her tongue with wet cotton wool, read and talked to her. Recited poems learnt in the fifth form, hardly suitable for a literary lioness struggling with death.

> So I stopped quoting and told her I loved her. Was I being hypocritical? . . . How could I be sure this new emotion was not compassion in disguise? Certainly I had never been able to love all those unhappily conflicting personalities who had once combined to make up my impatient, hot-tempered mother. But that mother was as unrecognisable in this helpless wreck on the bed as she was in the pretty eager girl on the poster advertising the Virago edition of the works of Antonia White which someone had pinned to the wall over her bed.

In the middle of Lyndall's musings, Antonia suddenly murmured the last words her daughter would ever hear her say: 'Which one?'

> For a second I hesitated: should I pretend to be Sue, who might not get back before our mother died?
>
> Why end on a lie? I had told her so many in the past to protect her feelings or mine.
>
> 'It's Lyndall,' I said.
>
> I'm glad I told the truth. She squeezed my hand lightly then very very slowly dragged her other on towards it across the humps and hollows in the duvet. When it finally reached mine, she started to lift my hand, but if it had been made of lead it could not have cost her more effort . . . She halted at her mouth – 'Perhaps she's trying to show me she's thirsty' I thought – then she pressed my hand to her lips and held it there a long time before kissing it . . . It took all my efforts not to let her hear my sobs. With one gesture, which seemed to convey affection and remorse, gratitude and apology, she had placated the past by acknowledging me finally as her own.[22]

At the moment of death, some daughters used tape recorders to retain memories of their mothers' last words; others were not brave enough to defy the taboo: 'We sang "Bye Bye Blackbird" which she had taught us to Charleston to. How I wish I had that on tape.' (Leanne, daughter.)

Some daughters took photographs of their mothers' last moments, or even after death. The family of Sophie, the Buddhist nun, allowed some of those photographs of her mother Sasha, Lady Young of Dartington, herself a writer and broadcaster, to be printed in the *Guardian*. One photo, of Sasha the day after she died, being ministered to by her writer husband Michael Young, her daughter Sophie and her son Toby, caught the public notice and shocked many readers by its intimacy. Sophie and her family hoped it would bring dying into the light, that the open image of love and devotion would make some people rethink their taboo ideas.

Lord Young publicly supported Sophie's decision by explaining that Sasha too had been a Buddhist, that in the Buddhist tradition, where there is no taboo about death, it was customary to have the body on view so that friends and relatives could pay their respects. Part of that respect was this photographic memento.

Once the mother is dead, what do daughters feel? If both parents die simultaneously, daughters feel as if their history has been wiped out.

'Mum died of Alzheimer's, Dad died very soon afterwards. Suddenly I seemed to have lost my whole history. I felt like a holocaust survivor.'

My parents died within half an hour of each other! My mother had a stroke, I nursed her right through it. Then my Dad, who'd had carcinoma bowel, but had partially recovered – I'd cared for him as well – he came in and saw her expiring. He just stood there and said: 'Poor Mum, poor Mum', then half an hour later, he said: 'I must get in my armchair. Help me across the room.' He stumbled, fell in my arms, and was dead. Just like that. He had just loved her so much. He couldn't go on. So he had this massive coronary.

   With both parents dying, your life has been wiped out from underneath you. Where is your history? I had this frantic need to write down family stories, family trees.

(Moira, Nurse, daughter.)

Some women felt equally historically bereft when it was their mother alone who died: 'Once she had gone, my history had gone. It was the death of a generation. I moved up. You go from being a child to being an adult. It's the end of a cycle, you have to make your own history now.'

Some who felt strangulated by their relationship with their mother were able to breathe more freely when she died. 'My nails had always been short, bitten, childish. When my mother died my nails grew long.'

'She had always been so much more than I was. Now I can grow in my own way.'

Other notions that came up frequently were feelings of abandonment (one woman in extreme bitterness over her mother's suicide said: 'How can I exist if she is dead?'); feelings of guilt ('Remembering Mom wasn't perfect helped lessen the guilt I had about not being perfect towards her!'); extinction of any rivalry, and the disappearance of pretences that may have been maintained for years. 'When my mother died I no longer had to pretend or play down all the things I'd done or did, which she hadn't had the opportunity to do. She was nursing her own mother at twelve and had to leave school to do it.'

Sociologist Jane Littlewood emphasised that many women in her study of adult bereavement associated persistent sadness following a mother's death with their perceptions of their mothers as having experienced 'a hard life'. They compared their own relatively privileged position directly with their mother's. Many felt they had tried to 'make it up' to their mothers and anguished over her deprivation once she had died. Littlewood emphasises that 'relatively few sons made similar observations in connection with their mothers' deaths.'[23]

A virtually unanimous feeling amongst bereaved daughters was that of being orphaned.

'When your Mum dies you get this feeling you are an orphan. I only got it when Mum died, not when Dad died.'

'Losing your Mum, you're on your own now, even if your Dad is still alive. You're an orphan really.'

'You are suddenly adolescent even if you are grown up when she died. Yet at the same time, you have to be grown up. I felt that orphaned feeling even though my Dad was still alive.'

'After your mother's death you have to grow up. Before you'd always been a daughter. But now you're a mother without one, like an orphan.'

Many women said it changed their own relationship with their own children.

'I became more possessive of my children. I was on red alert.'

'I became more responsible, more watchful of the kids. I was the one looking out for them now.'

'My mother had always told me how to run the house and children. I'd resented that. But funnily once she was gone, I did a lot of things with the children like she said.'

My friend Nicho whose mother Carol died when Nicho's baby son was just a few months old said: 'One of the saddest things is that when he grows up, he won't know or have any memories of Carol who was part of my life, was my life, who I am.'

Having privately cared for one or both dying parents for years, several women found a new strength in becoming professional carers.

'Her death pushed me into bereavement counselling.'

'I was already a nurse, but after caring for her all those years, I decided I would train in geriatrics. I felt I now had something to offer.'

'Without looking after her I would never have become a cancer nurse.'

Desolation over a mother's death was only one side of the coin. Feeling death as a gift was the other. American writer Joy Magezis explained that her mother's gift to her was the feeling that once dead her mother was contained within her.

When Mom died peacefully I was sleeping next to her on the cot. When I cried in the nurse's station, I felt Mom petting my long hair down to my shoulder. That was when I began to feel she was with me, somehow inside me . . . A month after Mom died I went to the sea, went swimming. I suddenly discovered that I could float effortlessly. It was something I'd admired Mom for being able to do. I always had to keep moving my arms and legs or I'd sink right down . . . Now that she was inside of me I was able to float peacefully.

Other women reiterated Joy's impressions of death as a gift.

The gift she gave me in dying, in talking about dying in those last days, was to take away fear. Death is feared because it is denied. It isn't talked about. We talked. So now I see it as part of a cycle, not a failure, part of the deal of being born.

The one treasure I got from her death is that the worst has happened. Now I am more fully in my life. I live each day as if it may be the last. I try to stop worrying about the washing machine breaking down or the cat being sick on the duvet.

In the last year I've forgiven both parents for their terrible lack of parenting skills. I think my mother's death was one of the biggest opening doors in my life. I feel her dying was a gift to me. It somehow released something so I could start to look at myself and heal myself. I felt more cared for when she died than when she was alive.

If a door opens when a mother dies so that a daughter may achieve her own identity, a breeze also blows. Broadcaster-writer Mavis Nicholson described the feeling she had when her mother died: 'I was on the edge of a cliff, my feet were secure enough, it was very windy. When my father died I was extremely sad. When my mother died I did feel the wind blowing around me because you are next.'[24]

For some daughters, a new identity, within a structure without a mother, seems life without hope. For others it appears as a new life on the edge of challenge.

There seems no point now that she is dead. It is highlighted for me by the fact that I don't have children and don't want them.

Even though I am happily married and couldn't ask for a more understanding husband, nothing seems the same. There is this huge *gap*. She used to be in that gap, she would protect me from whatever, now she has gone.

'I am not the same person. I shall never be the same person. Is it that there's this *gap*? Or have I fallen in it?'

'As a Muslim, I know that Mother's death came from God and there is still point to life, but without my Mother I feel life is pointless. There is a gap in my life and I am in that *gap*.'

These last statements forcefully echo the words of that remarkable writer Maya Angelou who talked on television about the death of her mother. Asked by the interviewer if the death had been worse than she expected, she said:

Much. You can never prepare for that . . . We know that the mother stands in the *gap* between earth and it. Whatever it is, there is a mother who stands in the gap and you have to somehow get through the mother to get to the descendant, to the child, the woman, the man . . . When the mother is gone the gap is cavernous. Cavernous. Suddenly I am in the gap. There is nothing between me and it any more . . . And if you have the blessing, the responsibility, the privilege, and the burden of being a mother, then suddenly, you who thought you had been so responsible, so long, raising the kids right . . . suddenly you are in the gap; and it is crushing, it is exulting, but one wonders am I capable, am I strong enough to stand here?[25]

Maya Angelou's powerful and resonant writing leaves no doubt of her strength as a writer, mothered or motherless. It stands as a symbol for the many creative and caring daughters I spoke to.

Chapter Five

FEMALE FUNERAL DIRECTORS

At the start of the century women played an active role in the death process. Dealing with the dead and caring for the bereaved were both women's tasks. Often, quite literally, it was a hands-on job.

Today there is a sharp divide.

Whereas paid professionals in the bereavement business are almost all women, those who care for the corpse are almost all men.

Bereavement counselling, resplendent with respectability, is seen as 'useful caring work' (i.e. work that is underpaid and fit for females); undertaking, seen as 'difficult heavy work', is dovetailed for males.

'Male undertakers constantly tell us we are too delicate to lift bodies, and too feminine to conduct and arrange funeral services. Congregations wouldn't like it. They want to see a proper man heading the dead. They don't see us as suitable!' (Woman funeral director, 1994.)

Funeral Meanings and Female Funeral Direction

If death is seen primarily as a disruptive limitation on life and relationships, funeral rites are attempts to find ways through the limitations of death both for the dead person and for those bereaved. Death rituals are frequently about boundaries and connections. In many parts of the world funerals are an expression of solidarity amongst those affected by the death. A celebration of the journey on which the dead person has embarked. Death rites for Muslims and Jews are instances of community events rather than lonely and isolating happenings. Of course if we look at anthropology we can see that no one explanation fits all cases of mortality. The Hopi Indians of North America, for instance, have very elaborate ceremonies for most of their life-cycle events but allow only meagre and quick rituals for funeral occasions, restricting them to immediate households and a speedy despatch of the corpse.

Religious beliefs alter both methods of disposal and funeral rites. Buddhists bury or cremate according to local custom. Within three to seven days of the death a service may take place in the house prior to the funeral ceremony at the cemetery or crematorium. Monks may be invited to remind mourners of the impermanence of life.

Both burial and cremation are seen as appropriate for Christian funerals. Roman Catholics and some Anglicans may hold a church service with a Mass or Communion. At more Orthodox funerals the casket may remain open during the service though at most Protestant services the body will not usually be visible.

Muslim practice ensures the body will be washed and cared for by relatives and appropriate prayers said. Islam forbids cremation. Ideally compulsory burial will take place within twenty-four hours of death. Male family members carry the coffin either to the mosque or directly to the cemetery for funeral prayers. Women do not attend the burial. The body is buried in a deep grave facing Mecca. Sometimes the body is embalmed and taken back to the country of origin for burial.

Hinduism requires cremation as soon as possible, with the exception of children under three who are buried. Part of the service takes place at home. The pandit (priest) chants from scriptures and the chief mourner (usually the eldest son) performs the rituals. Herbs, sandalwood, clarified butter (which purifies the body and helps it burn) and flowers are placed on the body. Ganges water and 'tulsi' (basil) are put in the mouth, together with a coin, symbolising payment of the ferryman crossing the river of death. Mourners walk round the open coffin, which is then closed and taken to the crematorium for further prayers. Among the Gujaratis, women are not allowed to follow the coffin.

Sikhism, like Hinduism, requires speedy cremation. The body is brought back to the house for a last viewing and prayers. The dead person must be dressed in the traditional five Ks, symbols of faith worn at all times by initiated Sikhs. They are 1) uncut hair, *kesh* (spirituality); 2) the comb, *kanga* (discipline, neatness, cleanliness);

3) the sword, *kirpan* (readiness to defend the faith, the poor, the oppressed); 4) the steel circle, *kara* worn on the right wrist as a reminder to use the hands only for good (symbol of divine unity and infinity); 5) shorts, *kachh* (restraint, modesty, purity).[1] Family, female friends and female neighbours circumambulate the coffin which is then taken to the 'gurdwara' (temple) where prayers are said and family, male friends and male neighbours pass round the coffin.

Orthodox Judaism decrees burial as soon as possible in a simple wood coffin. Returning the body to the earth while the soul rises to God is a pivot of Judaism. Some liberal Jewish communities now permit cremation but it is not encouraged. Flowers are regarded as inappropriate. Charitable donations are suggested instead. The service takes place in a Jewish burial ground, prayers are said first in the small chapel then at the graveside. Although women now attend burials, male mourners recite the prayers and place the coffin in the grave. Primary pallbearers should be male children or brothers of the deceased. No non-Jew is allowed to handle the casket. Curiously, personal enemies of the dead person are allowed to help carry the coffin as their efforts are seen not as hypocrisy but as a form of regret. The service is starkly simple, aimed at honouring the deceased rather than comforting the mourners. Community leaders, close relatives and friends (including women if they are chief mourners) help shovel the earth into the grave after the casket has been lowered. The shovel is not passed from hand to hand, but each person shovels in earth then replaces the spade into the ground. Jews believe that each individual thud of earth is psychologically beneficial in proclaiming finality and helping overcome any illusion that the person still lives. As someone who has held the shovel for both her mother and father I can vouch for the feeling of finality but not for any psychological benefit.

Funeral rites are rich with meaning. They focus on the relationship between the individual and the community. They pivot on questions about the very nature of life and death.

A funeral can stop you in your tracks. Just like death.

Bowker believes that the actions performed at funerals and the particular way a body is disposed of can help people to see death in terms of change and continuity.[2] Burial in the ground for example could carry associations of burial of seed and growth of new plants. The burning of a body through cremation could be seen as destroying decay, liberating the spirit or releasing new energy into the air.

When my mother was dying I'd watch this beautiful maypole tree waving in our garden. The family decided to have it cut. Its roots were undermining the foundations. I saw the top branches coming off and I screamed for them to stop. When my mother died of Alzheimer's followed immediately by my brother's suicide and my father's death, that tree became a symbol of my family tree. Our roots, our beginnings, how our spirit moves out from the top of the tree. It's changed me from wanting cremation to deciding on burial. Burial helps nature's cycle.

(Patty, bereaved several times.)

In this sense funerals can be vehicles of life, as they move the dead and the mourners on to a different form of existence. A 'good' funeral is more than just the disposal of a corpse. It can reassert the continuing life of the group who remain. As Dutch anthropologist Arnold Van Gennep suggested, it can strengthen the bonds between all those who have been touched by one person's death.[3]

If this highly integrating social function works – and it certainly does *not* always work in this way – a funeral can help people recover from their loss. Of course many funerals will not meet this need. Some funerals are grim. Some farcical. Skimpy and hurried. Few attenders. In no way relevant to the dead person's life or character.

My mother's funeral was like that. A brief and perfunctory affair. She was not a one for friends and it showed. As the chief mourner I was part of the tradition of 'keriah', the rending of the garment which has echoes of the biblical story of Jacob rending his garments in despair when he saw Joseph's coat of many colours drenched with what he thought was his beloved son's blood. Today such rending is a controlled opportunity for psychological relief, anguish or even anger by means of a controlled religiously sanctioned act of destruction.

At my mother's funeral, I stood erect in the correct posture for accepting grief, as my borrowed jacket was torn vertically on the left side over the heart (the correct tear for a parent's death), to the dismay of the non-Jewish friend who had lent it to me! I felt simultaneous relief that my mother's painful life was over and bleakness at the pain she had caused me. And doubtless I her. There was one optimistic note: even that funeral bonded some of us younger ones more closely (and I am sure more lastingly) after my mother's death than had been possible during her life.

After the funeral, on the first day of Shiva (the statutory seven days mourning), I sat as custom required on a low stool, shoes removed, eating the condolence meal of bread (which symbolises the staff of life) with hard-boiled eggs in salt (to symbolise the cyclical or continuous nature of life). I thought, yes, Van Gennep and the Torah are right. Funerals can help one recover, move on, even hope.

The strict formality of that funeral lent the right distance to a situation of a mother and daughter who never achieved closeness. By contrast the subsequent funeral for Carol, my close friend, was memorable for its intensely personal nature. Everything she and I had shared in her life was there at her death: shared values, feminist politics, women friends, several hundred photos of her at work and home, most of them showing her laughing, drawings by children who had been patients in the hospital where she worked as a doctor, wonderful luxurious food, and more flowers brought from allotments, gardens, florists, and fields, than I have ever seen at a celebration. Indeed the funeral and the three memorials were a celebration of her life.

The funerals remembered by other women with affection were similarly relevant to the dead person's life.

My friend was a Buddhist poet and weaver. At her funeral her weavings and tapestries were hung on the walls. People read her poems. A pianist friend set her favourite poem to music. Nuns and monks chanted. Two of her children spoke about their mother. There were built-in silences so that we could reflect on what she had meant to us.

(Woman weaver who had worked with the dead poet.)

Some women, not so lucky, recalled funerals as bitter. Or as black comedies. 'Mother was a big woman. Big and wide. So was the coffin, bigger than most and very wide. My brother and I watched the pallbearers straining with her weight and we started to giggle. Nerves I think.' (Sandra, on the death of her mother.)

My daughters and I were all on benefit. So it had to be paid by the social services. They wouldn't come and take the corpse until they had their money. The £500 grant got you the coffin, hearse, one car following, the laying out and keeping Mum in the mortuary. But they had to keep her twenty-one days waiting for the social security. In the end I had to borrow it so she could be buried on the appointed day. I had to shout and shout. I'm tough and I don't mind making a fuss but it seems unacceptable to have to make that fuss for your mother's funeral.

Finally we got a piece of paper saying we were entitled. When they sent their men round for her body, they kept calling my two girls 'Sonny'. One has short hair, one dreadlocks. They've both got strong faces! The men kept calling: 'Excuse me sonny, wait in there!' and 'Move out the way sonny, stand with your brother!' The day after the funeral the money arrived.

(Nessie, on her Mother's death.)

Fear of funerals may be rooted in the modern distancing of the living from the dead. Although in certain parts of Ireland today the practice of children kissing a corpse continues, this is rare elsewhere compared to the Victorian era when most children would have been encouraged to touch a corpse with either reverence or affection.

Grandmother's was my first death. She didn't like me because I was a girl. When she choked to death with a muscular disease, I wanted to kiss her corpse. I was fascinated by the stillness of a person left in the shell. I have a great curiosity so I didn't feel daunted by death, I wanted to see and wanted to know. By wanting to kiss her corpse I wanted to get closer to what was going on. To say farewell. But the women in the group tried to prevent me from doing that. They thought it was not nice.

(Sandy, Shiatsu practitioner.)

Some years later, Sandy, in her early thirties, was able to kiss the corpse of her Great Aunt Bessie. Sandy had taken on the role of frequent visitor, so was the first to be informed of her heart attack and demise.

She'd been a remarkable woman, on the fringes of Bloomsbury, clever and interesting but always held in contempt by my father, who, like my grandmother, was particularly scornful of women, more if they were plain like Great Aunt Bess. I loved her and felt a great sense of loss. When I arrived her body was still in the bedroom. I had an hour with her on my own. As with my grandmother I felt this intense curiosity about what was left of her. She had gone somewhere else. It wasn't the end. I believe that everything that animates and gives life is somehow separate from the body. She'd told me she had money in the flat and to make sure I found it. I talked to her and kissed her. I found £450 in five pound and ten pound notes in about thirty different handbags and purses! I counted the money and told her I loved her, that I would miss her, that I'd enjoyed her company. It was a proper conversation, a proper farewell. I tripped over her foot at the bottom of the bed and apologised to her corpse. After that I felt okay at her funeral.

The element of curiosity that Sandy recalls from her childhood is a central feature in children's more open responses to death. Edward Robinson, who collected memories of childhood experiences of death from a series of adults for a book called *The Original Vision*, documents curiosity as one of the chief ways in which children contemplate death.

For some women, a funeral remains the most poignant occasion of their lives. Moira, whose parents died within half an hour of each other, was one:

> Because my Mum died in her bed and my Dad had a massive coronary from grief as soon as he saw her, and fell dead in the hall, the doctors and everyone kept me away from them. They robbed me of time with my parents. When they'd lifted Dad onto the bed with her they let me in. My parents always slept the same side of the bed, and the doctors had put my dead parents on the wrong side of each other. I kept saying: 'They're on the wrong side. You must put them on the right side.' I was terrified that would happen at the funeral. They were laying on the biers in the funeral. Distraught though I was the first thing I checked was were they on the right side? Finally they got it right. Everything went quiet in this little country church. Then from nowhere two birds appeared, flew up the church, over the two coffins, then down the church. Two birds like a release of their spirits. At the graveside they lowered my mother's coffin, then put this sort of sheet of paper, then lowered my father's on top of her. I thought: 'He's heavy. He'll hurt her.'

At the centre of the modern Western funeral is the funeral firm. Undertaking, more than most jobs, is seen to be tainted by death. A stigmatised profession. A masculist profession. Once a simple sideline of the carpentry business, where the undertaker merely contacted different suppliers for goods ranging from mourning hats to basic caskets, cakes and ale; today professionalisation and commerce have transformed it into big business.

The concept of a 'respectable funeral' has been changed into a materialistic extravaganza. Undertakers will organise the removal and care of the corpse, completion and arrangement of medical and legal documents, purchase and preparation of graves, provision of coffins of assorted colours, styles and fabrics and monumental masonry for memorials in marble or granite, hire of hearse, several limousines, insertion of press announcements, ordering, receipt and care of floral tributes, production of printed service sheets, receipt and distribution of charitable donations, internment of cremated remains, and organisation of catering which can range from simple sandwiches to a cordon bleu banquet.

As one firm of funeral directors, whose slogan is, 'We're here to help you', proudly tells its customers: 'The formal ceremony is of little value or comfort if you are left with the feeling that something, no matter what, has been left out.'[5]

They leave nothing out. Except sometimes in the initial discussion with grieving clients, the cost, which can rise from £700 to more than £2000.

Sometimes, within these escalating figures, it is hard to locate the spirit of the event.

I was curious about whether female funeral directors felt there were any ethical issues about discussing coffin costs with grieving clients.

Sometimes selling the practicalities, the coffins, seems difficult, not immoral though. Funeral directing is a business. You've got to make money. We actually get commission on the coffins. The better quality the better commission. But I'd never rip anyone off. If someone came in and said 'My Mum has died', I'd never say 'You must have our best because I shall get £15 commission!' I say: 'Here's the coffin brochure. I'll go right the way through it with you, then the decision is yours.'

(Sally Smith, Assistant Funeral Director.)

Sally Smith sales-talked her way enthusiastically through her coffin brochure with me. 'The Warwick is plain simple veneered oak. Most people have the Warwick. You get a hearse and one car for £837. The grandest is the Kenilworth solid oak casket at £1500. That's just the casket, hearse and some fees. The rest of the costs bring it to £2300.'

Sometimes I feel embarrassed. People are crying and you have to start mentioning coffins. Normally I say: 'Do you have a preference as to which wood you'd like?' If they go for cremation I always suggest veneered. What's the point of burning solid wood? If they're having burial, solid wood is better because it lasts longer in the ground. You have to broach it gently before you go into prices.

> (Mandy Walker, Assistant Manager and Funeral Director.)

Mandy Walker's prices and patter were as polished as her colleague's:

> For £837 we do a traditional white coffin, veneered oak, which includes our administration costs, hearse, limousine, body collection, funeral direction, the lot. The Knightsbridge mahogany veneer, more ornate, goes up to £937. We do several solid woods, pricier obviously, a Tudor wood which is environmentally friendly. Nowadays people ask you for that! Then you rise to caskets up to £1595.

Do not however be beguiled into believing that this sum will buy you a complete casket funeral. 'No it won't! Your complete funeral always costs more because you have two doctors completing cremation papers, minister's fees, paying for press notices, all your flowers. Hygienic treatment is extra of course.' (Mandy Walker.)

As Beverly Day Walker, who runs her own funeral business in Ely, said: 'Obviously a funeral business is in one sense like any other business. I see it as a service we offer that is a necessity. We all enjoy it and get satisfaction from helping people so, no, asking for the money isn't a problem.'

Women undertakers who are members of the National Association of Funeral Directors will provide if required a basic funeral service.[6] Many items however are not covered. 'Our basic at £532 only gets you collection from hospital, coffin, hearse, bearers, but you can't get your whole funeral for basic because on top you've got church or crematorium fees, doctor's fees, a following car, any embalming, any flowers – yes, it will probably cost you around £800.' (Sally Smith.)

In their business-like attitudes, female funeral directors resemble their male counterparts, but across the board they do not receive equal pay for their professionalism. By contrast with funeral costs, wages for undertaking are generally low. Through a series of manipulative devices, such as relabelling jobs, shifting the focus of tasks done by men and women, these wages are often considerably lower for women.

'It annoys me. The money is rubbish. I'm a trained funeral director, passed every exam, but because I don't conduct they don't give me the title of funeral director, my wage is only £750 a month which with stoppages is a take-home pay of £600 a month.' (Sally Smith.)

It's a badly paid job. In our firm a coffin bearer gets £8600, a funeral receptionist about £9000, as assistant manager I get nearly £12,000. In most badly paid jobs you rely on tips. We don't get tips. I'm trained to conduct and I have done so. The first was my friend's father's funeral. But even I had to ask permission to conduct it. Women are almost never allowed to conduct, so they earn less than men. They won't willingly let me go on removals either. They say women aren't built the same as men! If you hurt yourself it would be the firm's fault so they try to stop you. On my police removal I started to lift the body off the bed onto a stretcher – there's nothing to it – when a policeman rushed over and said: 'I'll do that! You go and talk to the family.'

(Mandy Walker, Assistant Manager.)

In one firm another woman trained as a funeral director is not allowed to call herself that because if she did she would expect a director's wages. Currently they employ her as a receptionist, but she calls herself a funeral assistant. Despite the menial label, her work covers all areas of funeral directions. But no conducting.

Middle-aged men is the done thing for conducting. I do it but it's rare for women. This is my own firm. We each pay ourselves. But I don't earn as much as I would if I were a manager. The average for that job would be about £12,000 to £15,000. Women will earn less because it's custom that they don't conduct (which I do) and are usually not on call (which I am).

(Beverly Day Walker.)

Not all female funeral directors however wish to conduct.

You can only take tradition so far. It's hard for a woman. You need to be solemn and straight, very respectful in dress, not wear leggings or make-up. Perhaps a woman of fifty-plus who was tall, straight and sturdy could do it, but she shouldn't have a shapely figure and high-heeled shoes. My Mum wanted me to conduct my Dad's funeral but I couldn't. I was too involved emotionally. I still think it's nice to have a big strong man conducting. I wouldn't have had the same sense of security if a woman had conducted. At a moment like that men make you feel like a little girl. It feels like: the man down the road has chased me but Big Ron is here to protect me. Probably sounds a bit stupid!

(Sally Smith.)

The central issue for women wishing to become funeral directors is the difficulty of getting a job in the first place. It is virtually taboo for women to enter undertaking in a management capacity.

At the National Association of Funeral Directors, publicity officer Mary Stewart assured me:

> This is a totally non-sexist profession. Of course women are encouraged to enter. In the UK including Scotland there are 3,600 funeral directors. How many women? I have no idea. We don't have a gender breakdown. But we do have a great many family-run firms with husband and wife teams. They will obviously sort out their duties. If women become directors then they have to conduct.

These are heartening words. But the practical experience of the women I talked to appears to belie them. The few strong-minded women who have broken through this taboo to use a woman-centred approach in a traditionally male profession have all encountered rigid resistance from male undertakers and clients. 'I've had several bereaved ring up and say: "Can you send Mr X, the funeral director, out." I say: "I am the funeral director. I will be the one who comes over." They usually say: "Oh dear, I didn't think it would be a woman."' (Mandy Walker.)

Some men will not deal with me at all. "I don't want to deal with a bit of a girl." I say, "I'm a fully qualified funeral director. My papers are on the wall!" The man will say: "I don't care. I don't want to deal with you!" That man would have nothing whatsoever to do with me. Plenty more like him.' (Sally Smith.)

In several other funeral firms, women directors reported the phrase: 'I'm not going to deal with a slip of a girl like you.' In a profession still resolutely resistant to women in leadership capacities, Beverly Day Walker encountered so much opposition to her ambition that finally aged twenty-four she set up and today successfully runs a one-woman funeral business.

> I know of only fifty female funeral directors in the country. It's an impossible occupation to enter. They always give a *physical* reason. They say women can't lift much! I tried for years to get a job with a funeral firm. At sixteen, there were small family firms who said they wouldn't take anyone outside the family. At twenty I tried again. The new large companies. They wouldn't take women because they said they couldn't lift. It was a vicious circle. They

aren't officially allowed to discriminate so they just said 'No vacancies'. Finally I advertised in a national magazine. Offered myself for work experience free of charge. Nobody would have me. I got no answers at all. So I set up this business which I run single-handed with help from my parents. I employ six part-time bearers. Dad drives the hearse. I sit up front. There's no part of the job done only by men. We have a body hoist so that even I can lift a twenty-five-stone man on my own. When I sat my British Institute of Funeral Director's Certificate, there were only a couple of other women.

Even fewer women take the F.D. Diploma which covers aspects such as Scottish law, cremation and burial laws, coroner's cases, exhumations, burials abroad, bringing bodies back from abroad, even pre-paid funerals by the deceased. Funeral Directors also learn the intricacies of ethnic funerals, mass disasters, and procedures for cases resulting from HIV or AIDS. Beverly was still studying for her Diploma when she opened the doors of her funeral firm to the public. 'We took a risk opening with me conducting – people came up to me and said: "A woman! Oh how unusual!" But it's paid off!'

Two female funeral directors fell into the business accidentally.

Five years ago, Sally Smith, thirty-six, married to a car trader, with two daughters, started part-time work as a secretary with a funeral firm. Today she has trained and qualified, deals regularly with ethnic funerals, has found her work and her ideas daily changed by the AIDS cases she deals with, and is on the local disaster team. Mandy Walker, thirty-seven, married with two children, was a freelance hair stylist eight years ago when she saw an advertisement for part-time typing in a large funeral firm. Within weeks she was made full-time, then moved up to administrator; today she is a qualified funeral director and assistant manager of the firm.

If death was taboo in their childhood, this conditions both their families' attitude to their jobs and their own responses to their first corpse.

At first my family said, 'Oh God! You don't want to do that job.' Jumped back a pace. That's because they never talked about death. When my grandmother died in my bedroom I was fifteen but I was told 'Stay away from her'. So your heart jumps, the first corpse you see. I went down the mortuary, there was this body on the slab with a white sheet. My heart fluttered. I'd heard several true stories about ladies who'd been taken to mortuaries in

America. In each case the lady sat up and said: 'Can I have a cup of tea!' In each case the mortician had to be taken home in shock. So I thought what am I going to do if that moves? I'll scream and be gone! But after that first time it was fine.

(Mandy Walker.)

'Death was hush-hush in our family, so when I came for my interview and was taken straight to the chapel of rest it was my first dead body. Oh my God this man's dead! It felt creepy. I was horrified but didn't show it. The interviewer rang the next day to say I'd got the job!' (Sally Smith.)

'I'll never forget my first corpse. It was a man I'd met the week before at the stroke club. "You won't be having me for a long time! So see you next week!" he said. I did see him next week. Put him in his coffin.' (Beverly Day Walker.)

Beverly took the plunge and conducted that first funeral. 'No one spoke up that first day. Later a lot of men came and said how unusual it is to see a woman conduct. But everyone now knows they'll get a woman-designed service so if they don't want it they go elsewhere.'

At work, all three dress with 'respect'; cautious conservatism. 'At home I wear jeans and leggings. Never at work. Trying to get hold of clothes for female funeral directors is nearly impossible. I conduct in either a black jacket and trousers, or grey striped, with a white blouse, a tie of some description, and court shoes. (Beverly Day Walker.)

They regard people's attitude to their work with amusement. 'I get a kick out of telling people. I like to see them step backwards as if I'm contaminated! First off they assume you're a secretary when we are more qualified than the men.' (Mandy Walker.)

'Endless curiosity about what really happens behind those closed doors. Bombard me with questions. Today I tend not to tell people what I do when I first meet them.' (Beverly Day Walker.)

People are intensely curious. If I'm on holiday and I tell people I'm a funeral director they go, 'Ugh how could you do that?' Or 'That's odd for a woman!' 'What's a body look like after a car crash?' 'What happens to coffins?' I don't want that. I want to get drunk. Let my hair down. So nowadays I say I work in an office.

(Sally Smith.)

Male and female clients differ in their attitudes:

Little old ladies are very pleased I'm a woman. They say: 'That's lovely. A woman. I didn't want a man to come especially with all those rapes and murders.' Sometimes *little* men are comforted by a woman funeral director because she is more sympathetic. I'll sit and hold a little man's hand, chat about the children and the garden. My male colleagues perhaps haven't got that compassion, or they don't make the time. Both sexes tell you their secrets. A bereaved will say, 'You know Gladys and Arthur weren't married but their two children don't know.' Or 'She had an affair for nine years, that's not his baby!' You have to listen. They tell us because we are funeral directors, knowing we won't say anything. It's like a confessional. Maybe they tell us women more.

(Sally Smith.)

Certain skills they see as particular to women: 'Women will listen, not butt in. We are compassionate, go with their moods. Some are pleased Auntie Doris has gone because she was in pain. But when someone's lost a child that's absolutely devastating. A woman can go with that.' (Mandy Walker.)

Several directors use skills from previous jobs. 'I use my old skills as a hairdresser. People bring in photographs. "Mum had her parting on this side. She's got short curly hair." So I take in my heated rollers and make it look like her.' (Mandy Walker.)

'In my other work I've run community centres and bars, always dealt with people. This is a big help.' (Sally Smith.)

Beverly ran a guest house before she opened the funeral firm and sees certain similarities. 'You are dealing with people. You get some funny customers. You need the same friendliness, tact and compassion only more.'

Communication and compassion were the phrases I heard repeatedly. 'Compassion is the main attribute women directors have. They are more understanding especially with children. If they are mothers it gives them that bit extra that male colleagues don't have.' (Sally Smith.)

'Women are good at communicating. People want you to listen right through from the first moment when the body was taken ill to the actual moment of death. Patience is essential. A few men can do it but many others can't.' (Beverly Day Walker.)

Accepting that 'the dear departed' is soon a pile of bones makes them rigidly realistic yet they still exude warmth. Beverly attempts to add a physical comfort, a feminine influence, to her firm's surroundings. 'I've tried to make it more homely. Get away from the

black and purple. Our Chapel of Rest has matching carpet and curtains. Pink and flowered.'

Female funeral directors confirm my evidence that men and
women grieve in different ways: 'Men won't cry. They're hard. A
man will go for a walk round the block rather than cry in front of
me. If a man does break down then I excuse myself. We are not there
to embarrass them. If it's a woman on her own who cries I'd walk
round the desk, put my arm around her or hold her hand.' (Mandy
Walker.)

'Men are more reserved emotionally. Women more observant.
They will notice if you've combed the deceased's hair wrongly. If
there are any worries women will speak out, men won't.' (Beverly
Day Walker.)

'Women cry more readily. Men are too embarrassed to cry. Many
male clients are angry. It has to be someone else's fault!' (Sally
Smith.)

They all prefer to plan funerals with the bereaved rather than
with the dying. Protection of men becomes part of the plan.

I find women protect their men even when they are dying. I
arranged a funeral with a woman who'd been given a fortnight to
live but lasted six weeks. It was distressing because she was so
young and because I spent those six weeks with her. She chose
her own flowers, the coffin, hymns, everything. Her husband left
it entirely to us. When she died he phoned and said come and get
her. I picked her up and told him to leave it to me. She protected
him while she was dying. I protected him after she died.

(Beverly Day Walker.)

A significant feature of spending time with women in the death
trade is how soon talk of corpses ceases to disturb. Yet those on the
outside, intrigued and interested, besiege directors with questions.

'People ask do they sew your bits up? How long does it take to
cremate? The favourite question is whether the coffin is burnt with
the body?' (Sally Smith.)

'How do the dead look they ask. Obviously if a body's been left a
long time it will form maggots. The mouth will be full of maggots. In
the ears will be maggots. The tummy area is the first to go. It goes
green so you know there are maggots in there.' (Mandy Walker.)

'Are the coffins waterproof? People worry especially if there are
natural springs in the area. They are waterproofed, lined and sealed.
Nine out of ten people ask about the newspaper. They want it in the

paper. They won't talk about the death but they do want it noticed.' (Beverly Day Walker.)

People make extraordinary requests, desire the strangest mementoes to be placed in coffins. Anything at all can be buried with the dead, but if the coffin is to be cremated, then aerosols or pressurised objects are not allowed. Treasures must be monitored.

'Some coffins get filled up. A builder had his electric sander put in. Several cans of beer, his cigarettes, his lighter and some loose change. He was known for his loose change when he was alive. (Beverly Day Walker.)

'For one Dad's funeral the children put in teddy bears and photographs of themselves. The youngest said Dad would miss out on Christmas so made him a card with Father Christmas in heaven! A gardener died so his family put roses out of his garden into the coffin.' (Sally Smith.)

'Can we have her dog's ashes scattered in the coffin?' Or 'We've had the cat stuffed. Can that go in with Mum?' You can't act shocked. You just say: 'Well I can't see any reason why not.' You have to get permission from the crematorium but if there's no law against it, then you can't stop it. One young girl who refused to believe her boyfriend was dead, but wanted to put photographs, cigarettes, lighter, even his front door key amongst the ashes. She said: 'Because he's going to come back and he'll want to get in. When he comes back I want him to be able to just walk into the house. I'll be sitting there and he'll walk through that door.'

(Mandy Walker.)

Decisions about what clothes clients wish their deceased to be buried in are discussed with directors.

Many men like their women to be buried in sexy nighties. Often red. A man who'd only been married a few months asked for his wife to be buried in her wedding dress. Kiddies are often buried in their favourite wellies. Hells Angels are buried wearing their leather gear and crash hat.'

(Sally Smith.)

'People say, "Bury Mum or Dad in their own clothes". Then they give you a suit and tie or shirt and shoes. But they never think about underwear or socks.' (Beverly Day Walker.)

The most bizarre request was from a little chap whose sister died wearing a 22-carat gold wedding ring. He said: 'Take it off! If you can't get it off, cut her finger off!' I said: 'We certainly will not cut her finger off. We will try and cut the ring off.' We had a request from a dying woman who was worried we would bury her when she wasn't really dead so could we cut her throat to make sure she was dead! We told her executors we wouldn't do that but we would embalm her. She'll certainly be dead once she's embalmed!
                                                            (Sally Smith.)

Embalming is integral to the undertaking business. Melanie Hunnaball, once a doctor's receptionist, now a funeral director, married to Trevor Hunnaball, this year's President of the National Association of Funeral Directors, explains how her husband engaged her interest in embalming.

'He said, "Let me show you a transformation." He showed me a little old man – nothing nasty – just old and worn. Then I went away and he did the embalming and then took me in again. He looked wonderful. After that I started peeping round the door while he was doing it. And now I'm hooked.'[7]

Trevor himself, who runs a family funeral firm, in which his twenty-one-year-old daughter Polly has just done her first funeral, describes the embalmer's almost god-like ability to bring back the appearance of life. 'This guy had a facial cancer. We had a female embalmer called Ruth. She rebuilt this guy's face with wax and cosmetology. There was a hole in his head you could have put a child's fist in. He had to be transported back to Greece and the coffin was going to be opened the other end.'[8]

Mandy Walker currently assists in embalming though she has not yet concluded her five-year course for a full embalming certificate.

People are curious about how embalming is done. You lay the deceased on the slab unclothed. For ordinary embalming, cut into the neck, under the arm where the veins come through, then pump the preserving liquids into the veins. That's just hygienic treatment which cleans up the system and preserves. Full embalming to preserve indefinitely is done in depth with injections at various points. You take out everything in the tummy, put into formulae, you've got a bare carcass so you put the fluid through the veins of the carcass. You embalm the insides separately. Then you pop it all back. The head is a bit horrendous the first time you see it, because they cut the back of the head, peel the skin off and put it down over the face, so they can get to the back of the head. When I first walked in after working there three years, all I saw was a person but no face! I couldn't believe it! It was frightening, like a Steven Spielberg film. A space creation, perfectly smooth, the inside of the head wrapped back totally smooth.

Embalming is carried out if the funeral is delayed for several weeks or even months. 'Sometimes we embalm if it is hot weather for more than 10 days between the death and the funeral. Of course we ask first. Obviously if you get a piece of meat out of the fridge and leave it sitting it's going to smell. Bodies go off just like that!' (Mandy Walker.)

Contrary to popular prediction, the stress of the job lies not in such ghoulish touches but in the anti-social hours and the frenetic nature of the work. 'I'm never off duty. I'm there in the morning before the phones start ringing and often till late at night.' (Sally Smith.)

It never stops. Before you, I had to put a shroud on a lady. After you is the family viewing. Then I have to pick up a body, see two vicars, hassle with a hospital. Later I have to bury a vicar's ashes in his old churchyard. Then I have a couple coming from Buckingham Palace to arrange a funeral. I used to live in the flat above the office. People were utterly inconsiderate. They phoned or called Christmas Day, middle of the night. I was a drop-in-centre! Now we live a few hundred yards away. I'm always on call so they can speak but they can't get in!

(Beverly Day Walker.)

Female funeral directors, though sympathetic, preserve a necessary detachment. Unless the deceased is known to them, the client's grief is not their own. When the funeral is for an intimate it is harder to stay detached.

When my friend died at forty-eight, playing badminton, I felt deeply shocked. The same when my schoolfriend's dad died suddenly of shingles. It showed me I've still got feelings. You can get too blasé about death. You need a little shock from time to time to put death back into perspective.

(Beverly Day Walker.)

Women directors, more so if they are mothers, admit they do become emotionally involved with children's deaths.

> Children's funerals are emotionally charged. Impossible to forget. If I've done a baby's funeral, when I next see my sixteen-month-old grandson I give him a bigger hug, a better kiss. One child died because an electric window went up in the car and strangled her. Now I say to my eldest girl: 'Don't let him in a car with electric windows.'
>
> (Sally Smith.)

> The hardest part of my job is a child's funeral. It affects your home life. I've just done one for a little boy who was run over. The mother and child were walking on the pavement, a car went out of control, hit them, killed the one-year-old. The mother was still alive in hospital so I went to talk to the father. He didn't know what they wanted, he didn't know anything. I had to put their minds at rest that I'd do everything, take it all over.

The coroner told Mandy Walker that if the child was his he wouldn't want to see him. He suggested she advise the family not to view the baby.

> That worried me more than anything. I wanted the parents to see him. As a mother it's what I would have wanted. They'd laid the baby in the fridge so I went to see him when no one else was around. He had a lot of discolouration, so I asked the parents for a set of his clothes and a pair of mittens. They couldn't find any, so I asked their permission to use my little daughter's mittens. I got the embalmer to try bleaching the skin but it didn't work. Every time I was with the baby on my own, someone in the firm turned up to stop me. They thought I was going to break down. I'd already thrown an angry wobbly at the men in the firm because they'd got the coffin wrong. They felt I'd got too involved because it was a baby so they wouldn't leave me on my own with the child.

A death in their own family can also cause a female funeral director's mask to slip.

> After five years on this job I thought if someone in my family

died I'd handle it well. But when my Dad suddenly collapsed with an aortic aneurism and died a few hours later, it was hard. Because of my connections the hospital moved fast, gave me all the facts. My Mum had hysterics so I had to be calm to look after her. But then I spotted one of our own morticians who now works at the hospital mortuary. As soon as I saw him the tears started to flow. It was as if 'one of my colleagues is here so now I can let go'.

(Sally Smith.)

Sally Smith's funeral firm dealt with her father's death. Her mother and brothers wished to see the body so she went there first to see if he needed touching up.

Hair brushed the right way. Checked on glasses and teeth. Touching up corpses is what you can do to comfort the relatives. Make sure their face isn't screwed up. Right colour lipstick and eyeshadow. But I let the others do a lot of the work for Dad. I know what happens to bodies. The day after the family saw him Dad started to deteriorate. In summer bodies deteriorate more quickly. In a thunderstorm they'll turn overnight. The eyes are the first place to go. They turn a greeny colour. Once the nose and mouth start the whole face will go. It goes green then black. It's like if you leave a piece of pork out in the kitchen, it smells. It's not nice at all. You can inject it with formalin, but once I'd detected that first sign, I just couldn't bear watching my Dad rot.

Despite their intimacy with what they still merrily call the Grim Reaper, I discovered that female funeral directors are a bantering witty crowd. They find the work heartening and often amusing. They recalled farcical moments.

It was mid winter. Thick ice. Snow. Freezing fog. They'd got the grave dug. I'd done the funeral. Then the Minister stepped forward to say the words of committal. He slipped on the ice and fell in the grave. My colleague Malcolm went to dig him out and fell down the grave with him! They put the coffin down on the side. One of the bearers went to help then he fell in! By the end the other bearer had slipped in! There were four in the grave! Half the mourners collapsed with laughter.

(Sally Smith.)

It was only my sixth funeral. For an American airforce man. The airforce people draped the US flag over the coffin and put his hat and gloves on the top. They insisted on bearing and shouldering the coffin whereas we use wheels, on the grounds that once it's on wheels it won't go astray. It was a tight-aisled Methodist Chapel. The Americans decided they couldn't fit in six men, so they used one at the head, one at the feet. They went to put the coffin on the trestles at the far end of the altar and missed! They dropped the coffin onto the wooden floor. The echo went right through the building. I shook like a leaf. Our reputation's gone! Nobody will come to us again! Then I started to laugh. Realised it was the airforce at fault. I shouldn't have let them take over. I wouldn't do that now.

(Beverly Walker.)

Female funeral directors genuinely love their work. They talk of little else. That these women receive deep satisfaction from their job was beyond doubt. But in what exactly does it lie? 'I can't see myself ever doing anything else. I feel I help people at their lowest ebb. You can't get any lower than the way you feel when your loved one dies. To help someone through that, to find at the end of the day they phone you up and say, "I couldn't have coped without you," that says it all.' (Sally Smith.)

'There is no other job I would rather do. My reward is satisfaction because families are so relieved when it is all over. I feel I have helped them when they haven't a clue what to do.' (Beverly Day Walker.)

Like women bereavement counsellors, whose immersion in grief is something they too often take home, female funeral directors say the support of their partners is critical. Husbands and lovers to whom I talked appeared to be casually familiar with their partner's profession and – to a greater or lesser extent – at ease with its funereal intricacies.

Three years ago, Mandy Walker married a man she'd known for a decade, who expressed himself 'perfectly happy' with her job. Beverly Day Walker who married her electrician husband also three years ago said: 'Fortunately I'd started the job so he knew what he was letting himself in for! He isn't interested in the funerals but he's not hostile. He doesn't come down to the office and never to the preparation room. He wants to picture me in my home.'

My husband Dave is brilliant. He's been down the Chapel of Rest and is fine about that. He's my friend, he's my companion, my lover, everything. He's always there. I can go home and scream at him if everything's gone wrong. I can cry. He's always there to say 'Tell me about it.' I can talk to him about anything: *Financial Times* index, period pains, corpses. With that sort of relationship at home I can cope with the stress at work.

(Sally Smith.)

Their children's attitudes towards death and dying is of paramount importance to the women:

Death is an open subject in our house. Deena, my seven-year-old daughter, hears me talk to her stepdad about death, she knows what I do at my job. She hasn't yet seen a dead body but she will. Ross my fifteen-year-old son has. He comes to chapel appointments with me. He's going to do his school work experience with our funeral firm. We had a beautiful little girl die, too good for this earth. I took Ross down to see her. He wasn't unduly upset. He said how pretty and nice she looked. He sat and thought about it. 'I'm here and she's not,' he said. It's given my kids a different and very positive outlook.

(Mandy Walker.)

My kids aren't remotely afraid of death. The youngest has been coming here since she was four years old. She'll come to the Chapel of Rest, lift up the cloths and say: 'Look at this little old lady. Isn't she sweet?' My eldest won't come near the funeral home. She hates the place and thinks it's an odd job for her mum to do, but she's not scared of death.

(Sally Smith.)

Inevitably all the female funeral directors whom I met have made careful death plans. Some of them contrary to my expectations. Although several funeral firms assured me that decomposition made speedier by expert air-flow through the coffin, is today more environmentally friendly than cremation, burial was not some women directors' choice.

Being in the trade I've told everyone what I want. I'm not going in the ground. I'm going to be cremated. Not by my firm either! Certainly not if I'm young. I don't want them looking at my bits! If I was old and past it I wouldn't care so much. Colin and I have talked about our deaths. He's sure he'll go first. If he does, I'm going to bring him home, put his ashes in pride of place! When I go, I'll be cremated, tipped into the same ashes casket as Colin. Someone's got to stir it so he can't ever get away from me. Then we're going to be buried together at Trumpington church yard. We'll have a headstone which says 'Weep not for us because we have loved and been loved.'

(Mandy Walker.)

'When I die I want my firm to handle my death. I know I shall be in good hands. I'm not afraid of death, but I don't want to leave my family and friends.' (Sally Smith.)

'I don't want to go in a cold hole so I'll be cremated. My husband wants cremation and wants my ashes buried with his, whereas I don't care where mine are scattered. If he died first I'm not sure I could conduct his funeral. That would be quite a test!' (Beverly Day Walker.)

Female funeral directors have learnt a great deal about themselves through dealing so intimately with death. 'It's changed my philosophy. I never wait till later. I want to make the most of what I've got while I'm here. I always say what I mean. I hate it if Colin goes off to work and we've had words. I now always say what I mean before we part. I don't like being stroppy when I go to bed.' (Mandy Walker.)

'I am much more aware of my parents' mortality. I now take each day as it comes. I never plan for anything too far in advance. I no longer look forward to next summer holiday. If we want a break we take it this very weekend. I measure in weeks because if somebody dies today it will be their funeral next week.' (Beverly Day Walker.)

The only advance plan Beverly holds on to is the advent of her first baby due in a few months.

I have only ever thought of myself as a child. A daughter. Now I must think of myself as a mother. Temporarily it will change things in the firm. I shall swap some roles with my Dad. Initially I shall come back to work part-time. During this stage I shan't conduct and arrange because I see conducting and arranging as part of a unified process. I know this funeral firm has my stamp on it, but it also has my family's stamp, and it will be in their hands until I return. When the baby is a bit older I shall return full-time. I intend to be absolutely open with my child about death. I want to encourage children to come to funerals.

Perhaps when more women, already open about death and dying, arrange and conduct funerals in a woman-centred way, they will again become places of meaning, without fear for children or avoidance for adults.

Chapter Six

WIDOWS AND OTHER LEFTOVER LIVES

Some years ago there was a salty series on British television about three women whose bank robber husbands all died in one raid leaving the feisty female trio to carry on the family business!

The series was called 'Widows'.

The drama offered women strong independent roles. It focused attention on bereaved women who had guts, gallantry, and a great support system. It was on prime-time television. It had large audiences.

Widows, you could be excused for thinking, must be in the nature of a top pop group.

The truth is they are not. Although widows in a television drama may appear racy and amusing; off-screen widows are seen as a stigmatised section of our female population. It is a stigma we need to lift.

The truth is that over three million widows in Britain alone are not getting their needs met, their special problems solved, or their lines of communication to others opened and maintained. They are treated like women in the shadows.

In the shadows the group grows.

Every year in Britain alone two hundred thousand women are widowed. Women over fifty make up one of Britain's biggest groups, being 17 per cent of the population. Half of that female population over fifty is without a male. Three quarters of a million of these women have never married, half as many are divorcees, the rest of this group over fifty – more than four times as many – are widows. Over one quarter of women over the age of sixty-five are widowed. In the USA too widows are a predominant group treated in a similarly cavalier fashion. The fact that many widows are elderly means they may be subject to ageism as well as to the death taboo.

They have become a rising population of outcasts. Women who disturb the social order. An order which constructs three prescriptive ideologies, around death, around coupledom, around sexual activity, all three of which constrain women, all three of which widows contravene.

Whereas death on television is a matter of fascination and fear, discussion and debate, death in the domestic arena is prescribed as unmentionable. The taint of death that attaches to widows marks them out as a socially abhorrent group, as surely as stigmata upon their foreheads. In most societies those who had a close relationship with the person who has died see themselves and are seen by others (for different time lengths depending on the culture) as 'touched by death'. To some extent the way in which a society characterises the dead also shapes how it treats the bereaved. Widows I interviewed wanted to talk about it.

Nobody wants to listen.

After Kostas, my second husband, died, I felt I was in the grip of an obsession, like after the divorce from my first husband. I became obsessive. I thought about Kostas all the time. All I wanted to do was to talk about his cancer. Talk about his treatments. Why they had failed. What I had felt. When Kostas died I tried in vain to find books about what women want to know about death. There weren't any. Being an editor I know about books, because I'm a widow I know about death. I feel the key to your book is that women want to talk about grief. I wish I'd been Greek like my mother-in-law who shrieked and threw herself upon Kostas's body. That's what I felt like doing but no one ever gave me permission. She had people to talk to, I didn't. Talking and wailing is their custom. Maybe talking should be our women's ritual.

(Ellen, New York widow, sixty-two. Widowed at fifty-four.)

Five months after Kostas's death, Ellen gave a dinner in memory of her husband who had been a wonderful cook. To remember him with good food. To remember him in good conversation. It did not work out that way.

I cooked his favourite dishes for our friends. The dinner Kostas would have prepared if he'd been alive. I wanted them to reminisce about his cooking, about his life. I wanted them to say: 'Ellen, this is nearly as good as a Kostas spread!' Or to say: 'I wonder what Kostas might have cooked today?' I wanted them to say *something* about him! They said nothing! Not one person mentioned his name. Course after course. A terrible silence around his name. They talked about everything else but not about my husband, their friend, in whose honour and memory I'd made this meal.

Finally a brave guest mentioned the word death though he did not mention Kostas. 'I thought: "Thank God. At last." I had planned to give a toast to Kostas but by then I was too upset to raise my glass. I said it to myself. But I let the glass stay on the table. I sat through the meal, paralysed, horrified and hurt.

Across the water, in Britain, talking about death is taboo too:

Immediately after John's death I wanted to tell people how his angina had got worse. About the shortness of breath, the increasing pain, how brave he was. I wanted to tell them about what it was like him suddenly rushed into hospital, then suddenly home again. Never knowing which visit would be the last. The last day when I arrived I heard the alarm bells ringing. Before I could see him, his heart failed. A nurse came to say she was sorry. Would I like a cup of tea? She didn't stay to talk.

(Enid, seventy-nine, British widow.)

That was eight years ago but Enid still tries to talk about John. People around her resist. 'My son shies away if I talk about Dad. My daughter has never mentioned his name in the eight years. Perhaps it has gone too deep for words. But it is there, that silence, between us.'

Some partnerless women have discovered a strategy to make it easier for other people.

If you can cross their barrier of fear, then they may talk. I tried to make it easier for my people to cope with me. In the greengrocer's when the assistant said: 'How are you my dear? I expect you feel very sad?' I would answer: 'Thank you for saying so. Yes it is sad. I hear your daughter has another baby coming.' I'd say something to divert the conversation away from death.

(Roberta, British widow, forty-eight.)

The taboos around death which construct such sad silences, affect *all* bereaved women. In our society widows, as living reminders of the 'unspeakable truth of death', are ignored or excluded from activities. But for the partnerless, the warning sign set on those touched by death is compounded by two further constraints. A couple-oriented society sets a stigma on those women not in couples, and an ideology which sets a high status on genital activity blacklists those women no longer seen as sexually active.[1]

In a couple-focused culture widows face the low social worth accorded to the leftover female half of a once approvable partnership. At social events where people are still largely asked in pairs, a once-partnered woman on her own appears pitiable or threatening. Their narrative concludes when their relationship with their man is finished.

> People say they are kind but if you are invited where there are couples, they shun you or they feel threatened. They didn't stop asking me out, oh no. But I stopped going. For two years I become a recluse. If I go out and their boyfriend he talk to you, then you sense they are frightened.
>
> (Mania, Jamaican widow, forty-nine.)

> After David died from a brain tumour I hated going out on my own. But I went to a Christmas party. I knew them all. I'd catered their parties. It was hell. All those couples. In a funny way they seemed afraid of me. I'd only been there an hour and a half when I said: 'I really must go home. I'm expecting a call.' My hostess said: 'You can't run away, it's not going to change things.' But I couldn't stay. They could have changed things if they'd been less couply.
>
> (Georgina, caterer, British widow, sixty.)

A year later, Georgina, feeling stronger, rallied her resources.

> The family thought I should go on holiday with a widowed friend to a hotel in Greece. It was torture! Everybody was there in couples. Dancing! Every night there was dancing. You hear the music and remember you used to be with your husband. I dug my nails into the palm of my hand to stop myself going crazy.

As Georgina makes clear, professional independence does not necessarily mitigate personal loneliness.

Professionally Kostas and I were independent, with successful
separate careers, I as an editor, he as a film critic. But our social
life was couples. Suddenly I was the odd woman out. Only fifty-
four. They all had each other, I was the reminder that one of them
might die. If they didn't see me, they were not reminded of their
own vulnerability. Finally the loneliness became unbearable so I
started cultivating single people I met through work. I felt less
lonely. But still I was the different one, there was them and then
there was me. I had suffered death.

(Ellen, New York widow, sixty-two.)

This focus on coupledom is matched by an onerous insistence on
sexual congress. As I showed in a previous book on female celibacy
our culture's assumption is that we should all be eager consumers of
genital activity which is regarded as valuable and health-giving and,
more significantly, normative. Celibacy is assumed to be in the
nature of disease. Women who are celibate are seen as failures,
whether they choose this situation or whether they have it thrust
upon them. Many widows are of course celibate. Some, accidentally, through deprivation of their sexual companion, feel distressed.
Others, intentionally, through a passionate autonomous choice, feel
more fulfilled than they felt as part of a genitally active couple.
However, whatever their reasons, they will be accorded the same
negative status.[2] 'My couple friends are always trying to get me off
with some guy. They're sure it's bed I miss. After all I'm only thirty-
six! But it's not sex. I kinda like my celibacy. What I miss a whole lot
is the guy's company. He was great to talk to.' (Lou, New York
bereaved partner, thirty-six.)

When Sam died there was a hole. We'd been Sam and Sammi for
years. We ran our consultancy together. Sammi and Sam. Bright
blue letters over the door. There was no way I wanted another
guy. They wrote me off as celibate, as not being one of their
crowd. It became one more topic of conversation they shied away
from. I guess it made me more lonesome.

(Sammi, Montreal widow, thirty-nine.)

In our culture, being partnerless and being celibate are seen as second best. Being touched by death is seen as something to be avoided.
That is, if you are a woman.

Widows are a taboo group. Widowers are not. This is a sex difference and deserves attention.

Widowers in our society are not similarly tainted. On the death of a wife, a widower is seen as an object of concern. A man in need of nurturing. Usually by other women. On the death of a wife, a widower immediately becomes available, interesting and sexy. Women encourage him to talk. Draw him out.

On the death of a husband, a widow is seen as an object of pity, perhaps a little distasteful. To be avoided. She is suddenly unavailable, uninteresting, either seen as sexually uninviting or as predator. She is rarely encouraged to talk. Sometimes silence ensues because the bereaved widow reminds others of their own or their partner's death.

Organisations which befriend and advise widows consistently confront this pattern of silence. I talked to some of the women who work with widows.

> Some widows are sad, others bitter at having no one to talk to. Some resent women still with partners. One widow seeing lovers on a park bench muttered: 'Oh leave each other alone, you buggers!' Half of our widows have been carried all their lives and want it to go on, the other half have never been carried but would like it to start now. They rarely lose the feeling their deceased husband is there. Some sleep with his jacket on the bed so they can still smell him. If they meet a new man they say there will still be three in a bed.
>
> (Kate Johnson, National Association of Widows.)

They point out that for many widows the deceased had been their best friend as well as their sexual partner.

'They did everything together. Out shopping they still say: "Will Fred want that? I'll get Fred this." It's like losing your arm or your leg. They are totally diminished and they want to talk about it.' (Kate Johnson.)

> We were playing scrabble when he had a stroke. We played twice a week through the winter. He'd roast the chestnuts, and I'd pour a little port. We had the best friendship of anyone we knew. He died while he was winning. I tucked him up with the tartan rug, then I sat and held his hand. I wasn't frightened. I could have sat there for weeks.
>
> (Winnie, British widow, seventy-six.)

Some neighbours, helpful initially, later retreat. Several widows described the feeling of being 'seen as a drain'. 'I was suddenly that

manless woman who needed favours, like help with mowing the
lawn or taking to the supermarket. Well if that was what their withdrawal was about I'd soon sort that out! I learnt to drive and I
bought a new light mower.'

The most outrageous example of the silencing of widows
occurred to an eighty-year-old woman friend. She and her partner
had planned a summer holiday in the sun. They left London with
their luggage and high hopes. Set off on the Gatwick Express for the
airport. Suddenly he had a stroke. Within seconds he was dead. She
called the guard who said there was nothing he could do until they
reached Gatwick where an ambulance would await them. My friend
sat in shock and disbelief for forty minutes, next to the body of her
dead partner in a crowded railway carriage. Not one person talked to
her. Not one person went to her aid.

Sudden death is a most seriously debilitating bereavement. Sudden
death in a context of avoidance is a trauma never to be forgotten.

Research shows that isolation is the most prevalent theme in widows' bereavements.

'Widows, especially the older ones, ring us with all sorts of surface
problems, sorting out pensions, help with benefits, but underneath all
they need is a chance to talk. No one talks to them so isolation is their
biggest problem.' (Lynne Davis, National Association of Widows.)

Writer Margaret Powell said that when she was a door-to-door
canvasser she met many widows pathetically grateful for someone to
talk to. 'One middle-aged, quite well-to-do widow assured me she
always filled in every form sent to her by the council or government
because she said "for a brief while it gives me the feeling that I'm
alive and my existence is noted somewhere."'[3]

Bereaved partnered women (both lesbian and heterosexual) who
have not been legally married, face similar social censure as widows,
but are dealt more iniquitous legal treatment. Later I look at some of
the emotional problems of lesbian bereavement; here I recognise
that the legal and financial problems are, in this society, simply left
untreated. Neither bereaved lesbian nor bereaved heterosexual partnered women in Britain are entitled to widows' statutory benefits.
Excellent organisations seem powerless to help them.

'We can talk to partnerless widows. But unless they have been
married they cannot become members of the organisation. Often gay
and non-married women in bereavement who have lived for years in
couples are desperate for help and we have to send them elsewhere.'
(Kate Johnson, Welfare Officer, The National Association of
Widows.)

Many women refuse to join widows' organisations because they do not wish to be identified stigmatically as 'widows'. Writer Jeanette Kupfermann says that during her own journey through widowhood she was unable to use the word. 'Widows were other people, they were not me.' She saw them as sallow faced mediterraneans in black with 'ferociously blazing eyes' or women with blue rinses, living in hotels in Eastbourne. 'I was always running into them on trains, travelling to see their daughters in Plymouth or Aberdeen. Most widows I've ever met seemed to be permanently on the move – shuffled around from relative to relative – a sort of forgotten regiment of women in transit.'[4]

Indisputably the word has ugly connotations. Widowhood's rich semantic history provides shocking clues to the way patriarchy views widows.

The Old English 'widewe' originated in the Indo-European root 'widh' meaning to be empty or separated. The Sanskrit 'vidh' means destitute or lacking. Joseph T. Shipley in the *Dictionary of Word Origins* points out that 'since marriage has made two of one, a widow is a woman that has been emptied of herself'. Other writers confirm this notion: 'She was a widow, that strange feminine entity who had once been endowed with a dual personality and was now only half of what she had been.' These meanings are not similarly affixed to widowers.[5]

Cross-culturally silence and celibacy are intertwined with ideas of widowhood. The Hebrew word for widow is 'Almanah' from the root 'alem' (unable to speak) so the widow becomes 'the silent one'. Bonnie Bowman Thurston, who analysed the position of widows in the early church, points out that Jesus's positive attitude towards them was unprecedented, as generally they had no legal power of speech.

The Hebrew interpretation of widowhood was 'the fate most feared and bewailed by women'. A husband's death before old age was considered a retribution for his sins, this retribution was apparently incurred also by the wife. To be left a widow was a disgrace.[6] In Ancient Greece, the widow had few legal rights. She could look after her husband's property only until an heir was established or her children's guardian had taken charge. The Greek word is 'chera' from the Indo-European root 'ghe' meaning 'forsaken' or 'left empty'. The word 'chera' also designates a celibate woman.[7] Certainly an early ideal was that a widow remained in chaste mourning faithful to the memory of her late husband until her own demise. The key problem was the widow's status, for she has always occupied an anomalous position in society. If the 'virgin maid' was the property of her father and the 'wife' the property of her husband, to whom did the widow belong? To whom was she expected to offer obedience? Margaret Wade Labarge, researching women in medieval life, suggests that, if poor, the widow remained the dead husband's property, but as common-law meant that the medieval widow was entitled to one third of her husband's holding, if she had resources she was suddenly in a more powerful position than most women of her time. Although she could not dispose of it and was often subject to intimidation or violence from those anxious to overthrow her legal rights, nevertheless many a widow 'regained her legal personality, and for the first time in her life, could make independent decisions'.[8]

By the sixteenth century the word 'vidual' (from the Latin 'viduus' meaning destitute) entered English to denote that widows were again seen in a state of destitution. On the one hand they were expected to conform to a code of chaste passive behaviour, on the other hand it was a commonly held assumption then (as indeed it is now) that once a woman has experienced heterosexual sex she would wish to keep it up, death or no death. Thus did the term 'lusty widow' enter the language with its curious mixture of fear and envy. Once again money was the key. The more wealthy was a widow, the less convenient – for men – was it to insist on her chastity or fidelity to a dead spouse.

Writing about women in the seventeenth century Antonia Fraser suggests that to 'those with something to gain from a woman's remarriage, notably her prospective second husband, no spectacle was more stirring than that of a wealthy widow. A Tally-Ho would go up when one of these creatures was sighted, followed by a pursuit which can only be compared to the contemporary chase after an heiress; except that the fox in this case was older and therefore wilier.'[9]

In this picture the widow begins to re-emerge as a woman of strength. It is the word not the woman which has negative undertones. The politics of naming means that women adjust their lives to meet the requirements of the labels. Fortunately some women rebel. Lynne Caine is one.

Widow is a harsh and hurtful word. It comes from the Sanskrit and it means 'empty'. I have been empty too long. I do not want to be pigeon-holed as a widow. I am a woman whose husband has died, yes. But not a second class citizen, not a lonely goose. I am a mother and a working woman and a friend and a sexual woman and a laughing woman and a concerned woman and a vital woman.[10]

Lynne Caine is strong, has the rage of will, bashes on regardless. I'm with her all the way.

Unfortunately lonely goosedom and second-class citizenry are two particular features of partnerless bereavements which this study attempts to show up.

In Lopata's 1979 study of widows in Chicago bereaved for an average of eleven years, half of them said that loneliness was their biggest problem.[11] Loss, deprivation and loneliness are inseparably bound up. All the widows interviewed cited at least an initial loneliness, all of them saw as the root cause other people's unwillingness to let them talk about death. *Avoidance* maintains that silence.

> People cross the road when they see me coming. I still live in the village where we knew everyone. Friends and neighbours would buy my plants, stop for a chat. But no one wants to talk to me since my William died. My old Mum said: 'Talk to the plants, it will make them grow!' Now I talk to the plants about William. I decide where he would have placed them, what fertiliser he would have used. I am so lonely I am thinking of moving.
>
> (Janet, British widow. Runs gardening shop. fifty-four.)

The age of the widow appears to make significantly little difference to their treatment. Mania, the Jamaican nurse, who became a recluse in her twenties after her young husband's death, explains:

> I'm twenty-five when my husband he pass away shockingly from the heart. My daughters were still in Jamaica. My husband had come here for a job as a builder. I followed him here and bore our son, just two when my husband he took a bad turn. When I get to the hospital, there he was gone. Now I nurse the old people dying, no one to talk to. All leaving me to myself.

In the area of avoidance age appears to make little difference; research suggests however that age does affect the type and length of suffering widows feel. Studies by Sanders, Parkes and Weiss suggest that younger widows suffer more psychologically in the short term but older widows have more long-term problems which often manifest physically.[12]

One elderly widow described difficulties she encountered in visiting her husband's grave. 'It is a long way out so I take a cab. When I say the name of the cemetery the taxi drivers are absolutely silent or whistle away to themselves in embarrassment. I feel I have to cheer them up.'

In studying bereavement in terms of risk factors, age is certainly one factor, but no risk factor can be taken in isolation. It is their interaction with other factors (such as social support, economics, religion) which influences the way women survive grief. A major problem at any age is low social support. Fortunately many older widows today have a good pool of other widows, who have been through similar circumstances. I discovered the most positive and friendly lives were led by a group of widows over sixty-five who lived in a small city estate of independent maisonettes and houses.

If isolation and silence is not hard enough, the economic position of most widows is reprehensible. Nor are these distinguishing marks of social disgrace and scandalous poverty confined to particular countries.

Worldwide widows are shunned. Worldwide widows are poor. Many counsellors hold that anger over money is one of the greatest contributory causes to pathological grieving. Many widows had left finance to their partners and found it frightening to be left to cope with insurance, banking, debts.

Widows are penalised by the sexual division of labour. If they have worked full-time in the labour market they will be typically at the lower end of the wage scales. Many elderly widows will have been more likely to have worked part-time (if at all) which would not give them benefits. Most frequently, older widows did not work and therefore lost not only their partners but their major source of financial support. Widows are amongst the poorest groups in our society.

Let us take a hard look at economic considerations.

In Great Britain, three million widows are amongst the most impoverished sections of society. Despite an equal pay policy, most employed women remain in less remunerative female-intensive labour sectors. If a young woman's husband dies she is immediately expected to go out, retrain, then find a job in this low paid area. Since 1988, a woman widowed under forty-five will *not* receive a Widow's Pension unless she has children still at school. She will receive only a small Widow's Payment, a one-off payment of (at the time of writing) £1000.

If a widow is under forty-five but has dependent children for

whom she is still receiving Child Benefit, she will be entitled to a
Widowed Mother's Allowance, but only until the children leave
school. Then, according to the Widows' Advisory Trust, she *may* be
eligible for a pension but only if she is forty-five or over. If a woman
was widowed between forty-five and fifty-five she is entitled to a
poverty level Widow's Pension of which the full amount is £56.10
per week (plus £9.75 for her first dependent child, £10.85 for every
other child). However the Widow's Pension is not paid in full unless
the woman was widowed at fifty-five or over. This means that middle-aged women between forty-five and fifty-five who lose their
husbands also lose out financially. Their age-related pension is
reduced by 7 per cent for each year they are under fifty-five at the
time of widowhood.

Widows in differing circumstances may face similar financial
debts. They will not however be compensated by the state in the
same way. The rate of the pension is dependent upon the age of the
woman when she is either widowed or when her Widowed Mother's
Allowance finishes. Significantly if a woman was not entitled to a
pension when she became a widow (or when her Widowed Mother's
Allowance finished) then she will *never* receive a Widow's Pension.

Currently, the British National Association of Widows is trying to
start a campaign for a child allowance so that if a widow remarries,
money for her children will still continue. However, as the organisation which has widows' interests at heart is as underfunded as
widows themselves, the campaign is only in its infancy.[13]

Britain is not alone in offering a poor economic deal to its widows.
In Canada almost 60 per cent of all widows live below the official
poverty line. In the USA Leslie A. Morgan looked at the National
Longitudinal Surveys Cohort of Mature Women and concluded: 'The
experiences of the NLS women as they exited marriages suggested
that systems of postmarital income support for women remain inadequate for a substantial minority of the widowed, separated and
divorced.' One year after being widowed 23.5 per cent of widows
were labelled 'poor'. Eight years later 34.5 per cent were poor.[14]

In New Zealand, as Maori writer Ngahuia Te Awekotuku and
New Zealand politician Marilyn J. Waring point out, men are
regarded as complete persons with potentials and rights, whereas
women, particularly Maori women, are defined by the functions
they serve in relation to men. Widows are defined even more specifically by their association with death and their association with dead
men.

The Matrimonial Property Act (once praised as enshrining a value for childbearing and home maintenance), actually perpetuates a status dependent on the principle income earner, still overwhelmingly the husband. In 1984 Waring and Te Awekotuku wrote: 'After fifteen years of marriage and three children, the work of a pauper's wife is worth nothing; after fifteen years of marriage and three children, the work of a millionaire's wife is worth half a million dollars. The work of a widow is still worthless.'[15] A decade on the sums are different but the work of a widow is still seen as economically insignificant.

In Pakistan, in the absence of adequate social services, isolated widows, like deserted wives, may be financially bereft. Miriam Habib, a leading member of the All Pakistan Women's Association, a former member of the Pakistan Women's Rights Committee, tells how she met a young widow whose active young husband had suddenly died leaving her distressed, ill-educated, without property, with three small children. Bravely she attempted to sustain them by skills with her needle. Day and night she embroidered velvet uppers for evening shoes at the rate of three rupees a pair. There was no way she could make a living. This young widow's plight is characteristic of many. Between chores, at home, widows perform piecework.

And miracles. They embroider shawls, crochet tablecloths, run up gold and silver threadwork to delight tourists. For local buyers they produce the famous Baluchi mirror work The middlemen reap the profits while the majority of Pakistan's widows live on the edge of poverty in a vain attempt to support an average of seven children per family.[16]

Similarly, in Sudan villages widows act as petty traders selling their own and other women's products, unable to make more than a basic living. In a study done in the Omdurman women's handicraft market it was found to be mainly middle-aged widows who sat in huts or under tree shades, displaying fresh agricultural produce or beautiful but unprofitable homemade crafts.[17]

In societies where men marry younger women, a youthful bereavement means young widows will have to bear many years of financial hardship. In Iran, for instance, 23 per cent of women aged between forty-five and fifty-four are already widowed. Among women aged fifty-five to sixty-four the proportion rises to 48 per cent.[18]

Poverty, as we see, is a predominant characteristic of widows worldwide. What is invigorating is to discover that it has not broken women's spirits. Older women with lined and lived-in faces. Younger ones with vulnerable eyes and stories to match. Life has betrayed their expectations but not their hopes. Few have retreated.

'I never knew anything about money when Bill was alive. He did the tax forms, paid bills. Now I have very little but I've learnt the hard way how to keep it, even save it, and know where it all goes.' (British widow, sixty.)

'When he died I didn't know what an invoice was. Three years later I joined his brother on the board of the family dress business. I market the Paris-copy fashion lines.' (British widow, fifty-two.)

'I was real scared. I'd been like a doll! Had to bring up my kids. I knew I had to start over. I went back to school. Took an accounting course at College. Got my confidence back.' (American widow, thirty-seven.)

Lack of money is debilitating but it may not be the most devastating feature of a widow's life. Jeanette Kupfermann, herself a widow, talks about a widow's 'spoiled identity'.[19] That widows are looked on as 'unclean' or untouchable, that they, like their grief, are hidden away, could have more serious consequences. Rarely are they seen as independent beings, merely as the sexual property of a dead husband.

In Japan the effects of impoverishment on many widows are compounded by the psychological effects which result from a combination of the death taboo and a sexual oppression founded on women's central role as homemakers. Japan's restrictive marital ideology means that a woman's perspective on her own life is short, her financial outlook, should her husband die, appalling. In her youth she can rarely plan beyond her early twenties. After that, she must follow her husband then her children.

Most Japanese wives are totally economically dependent upon their husbands, emotionally dependent upon their children. Should her husband die, the Japanese middle-class woman may probably have to go on relief because she has had no income of her own.

The difference between the status of wives and that of widows is considerable. Once her husband is dead the widow is regarded as useless. She is culturally prohibited from taking an interest in anything but her family. That pivot removed, she may fall into depression or senility. A survey by a Japanese gerontological research institute shows firstly that more older women (the majority being widows) than men become senile, secondly that this widespread senility of widows reflects the history of Japanese females who have been restricted from cultivating their minds or talents.

Japanese journalist Keiko Higuchi reveals older women still believe that 'women live in order to care for men' in a culture where the suicide rate of old women is higher than in any other country.[20]

The treatment of widows in Japan is mirrored in other places, despite differing customs. Across the centuries, across the globe, we see a history of widows as second-class citizens, caught up in a complex network of sexism, ageism, and a denial of individuality.

As early as 1936, writer A. L. Cochrane in a paper entitled 'A Little Widow is a Dangerous Thing' discovered that widows in mourning among the Shuswap of British Columbia were secluded and forbidden to touch their own bodies. Cups and cooking vessels which they used were not allowed to be handled by other people. To ensure their enforced isolation from the rest of their group, they were compelled to build a sweat house by a creek, where all night they sweated and bathed regularly, after which they had to rub their bodies with branches of spruce. Their shameful penance was further increased by the use of thorn bushes for bed and pillow, whilst around their beds more thorn bushes were laid. So unlucky was their presence deemed, that hunters were forbidden to come near them.[21]

The Shuswap are not the only group for whom widows spell danger. The Agutaino widows of Polawan may only go out at an hour when they are unlikely to meet other people because anyone who sees them is thought to die a sudden death. To prevent even an accidental tragedy of this nature, the widow has to knock in warning with a wooden peg on the trees as she goes along.[22]

Richard Huntington and Peter Metcalf who looked at the Berawan of central northern Borneo in 1979, describe widows who on the death of their husband are cooped up for eleven days in a tiny cell, next to the corpse. They may not bathe, must defecate through a hole in the floor and can only eat poor food. Hertz, an anthropologist, suggests the widow is contained partly because she is polluted but also because she must be made to suffer because the deceased has a 'vengeful soul'. By her suffering she deflects the dead's malice so she is sharing his condition metaphorically in order to avoid it literally. Widowers are restricted too but they are not physically confined.[23]

What is the situation today in contemporary cultures?

In Ghana, African writer, former Secretary for Education, Ama Ata Aidoo, tells us that the exclusive marks of womanhood are regarded as dirty. So during menstruation, the first forty days after childbirth, and more significantly the period immediately following widowhood, a woman is regarded as untouchable. Whereas a widower is left alone for at most forty days (often much less) after the death of his wife, a widow is put into seclusion for a whole year.[24] In Kuwait widows under Islamic jurisprudence must obey the ritual of Idda: a compulsory period of seclusion of four months ten days.[25]

Zara, a young Muslim woman, explained.

'We see it as protecting the widow's virtue. If she is carrying her dead husband's child, then Idda for four months ten days will ensure that no one can think the child belongs to another man. Men see it as a mark of respect to their dead male relative. Of course if the wife dies, widowers do not have to be secluded.'

An interesting legal case about the social role of an African widow who wanted control of her dead husband's remains and a say in where he should be buried recently came to light. David William Cohen and E.S. Atieno Odhiambo (1992) tell the story of what happened after the death of distinguished Kenya lawyer Silvanus Melea Otieno known as SM. For six months there was a heated struggle between Virginia Wambui Waiyaki Otieno, his widow, and the Umir Kager, her husband's clan, about whether she could bury him at the farm where they had lived near Nairobi or whether the clan would retrieve his remains and bury him in his birthplace in Western Kenya.

Debates raged about the legal, historical and social grounds governing disposal and about what rights widows should be allowed. Virginia Wambui firmly announced she was burying him at their farm, it being her husband's wish and her own. When this failed her counsel claimed that SM lived outside Luo customary law, that the couple had a 'modern marriage' which gave Virginia Wambui absolute rights to her husband's remains. The court of appeal however ruled in favour of the clan and Wambui declared that women, especially widows 'are discriminated against in Kenya . . . I have been denied the right to bury my husband.'

Wambui was respected as one of the leaders among Kenyan women, a political member of the National Council of the Women of Kenya, a radical fighter in the fifties for Kenyan independence. However none of this was made clear during the court case. Her counsel chose to ignore her political standing and used the 'good wife, good husband, good marriage, modern family' line of argument. She lost.

The authors argue that the widow Wambui was 'silenced' by judicial discourse. 'As her husband's dead body was invested with life, so Wambui in pressing her claim for his remains became socially dead.' In court her husband's clan argued the case that one could not entrust a widow with the authority to arrange the funeral of her spouse. Because women marry and form households in many different locations geographical chaos would be introduced into the burial and remembrance of the dead.

Her husband was buried in his birthplace. His widow stayed away from the funeral. Although she lost all legal rights and the emotional cost was terrible, in one sense her abstention from the funeral was seen as a triumph for women in Kenya. Because she refused to attend, SM 'could not be ritually reconstituted into the domain of death through the rituals of being mourned and buried by the widow'. A Luo woman social worker commenting on the iniquity of the case said: 'Perhaps as a man, the president was concerned that precedent not be set of women lording it over patriarchal custom.'

In some parts of Western Kenya widows have a great deal of sexual freedom. Nandi widows, unlike wives, do not have to be reserved in their public demeanour, they can go to beer halls and debate with men. They may decide to take a lover. They have freedom from domestic duties and can own property in their own right through the Nandi house property system.[27]

By contrast some East African widows are still considered as the 'wife of the grave'. When a husband dies the wife is expected to marry a relative of her dead husband.[28] There are different systems for matrilineal or matrilocal societies. The Bantu-speaking matrilineal Kwaya allow widows the choice of remarrying, remaining single or living under a leviratic union (the practice of a widow marrying her dead husband's brother). But patrilineal societies such as the Nilotic-speaking Luo and the Bantu-speaking Kwia do not allow widows to remarry because wives belong to their dead husband's lineage so must be cared for by their brothers-in-law. Those who attempt to remarry outside the prescribed kin group are treated like prostitutes and labelled 'bad mothers'.[29]

This idea, common globally, that a widow must become a 'wife of the grave', that she is defined as the sexual property of a dead male partner, can do strange things to a woman's self valuation.

We saw in Chapter Two how Greek widows in Potamia are required to wear black clothing for the rest of their lives. Throughout Greece widows tend to adhere to this custom. Margaret Papandreou, co-founder and former President of the Women's Union of Greece, who was also wife of the Prime Minister, suggested that 'the status of widow is revered, but the clothing is a warning that other men should stay away, that she is re-wedded to the man who died and must remain faithful to him. That would seem to me the ultimate in patriarchal demands . . . fidelity after death.'[30]

This fidelity-after-death feature is strong too in Palestine, a society like other Arab Islamic countries that considers sexual relationships acceptable only between a married couple, though in practice the standard is relaxed for men.

Israel is interesting in terms of the symbolic meanings it attaches to widows. Under traditional Levirate law, a widow without children was automatically remarried (whether she desired it or not) to her husband's brother. Although today this custom is rarely practised, in principle no widow is free to remarry unless the husband's brother releases her through the ancient tradition of 'halitza'. The widow and her brother-in-law exchange phrases and spit on the floor, then the widow kneels to take a shoe off her brother-in-law's foot. If he consents this then frees her from her duty to marry him.

Shulamit Aloni, author, political columnist, former Knesset member, believes that in many ways Israeli widows are still considered as their dead husband's property. Even today brothers-in-law can refuse to give consent: 'The least that the refusal of "halitza" entails is that the woman is not free to remarry. Blackmail is implicit in this state too, because the dead husband's brother is his heir, and can refuse "halitza" unless he receives a share of the widow's property, including pension and any other compensation she may receive.'[31]

In the nineties this patriarchal practice is predominantly symbolic, but the coercive sexism inherent in such a symbol, harms the self-image and self-respect of all widows. It should be found least in a modern democratic society like Israel's which prides itself on equal rights for women and men.

Historically many societies have taken the symbols of exclusion, isolation, and eternal fidelity to a dead spouse to the horrifying extreme of suttee or sati, the practice that condemns widows to be ceremoniously burned alive on the funeral pyres of their husbands.

In India this ritual was largely confined to upper caste widows, though it did spread downwards. The social context for this sacrifice of a woman's life was a religion that forbade remarriage while simultaneously teaching that the husband's death was the widow's fault because of her sins in a previous incarnation if not in this one. Often the sacrificial widow was little more than a child who had been married at ten or eleven to a sixty- or seventy-year-old man. Katherine Mayo in her controversial book *Mother India* tells us:

That so hideous a fate as widowhood should befall a woman can be but for one cause – the enormity of her sins in a former incarnation. From the moment of her husband's decease till the last hour of her own life, she must expiate those sins in shame and

suffering and self-immolation, chained in every thought to the
service of his soul. Be she a child of three, who knows nothing of
the marriage that bound her, or be she a wife in fact, having lived
with her husband, her case is the same.[32]

In countries which support sati, in many cases the widow is driven
to suicide by intense pressure from her in-laws. If she resists the idea
of killing herself, she may be pushed into the fire with long stakes,
ostensibly for religious reasons but often with the motive of repos-
sessing her inheritance portion or possibly gaining control of her
children.

Despite this well-established fact, many Western male scholars
display by their language a verbal complicity in these gyno-crimes by
terming this abuse 'ritual suicide' or saying a widow 'adopted the
practice', making the female victims through a grammatical sleight of
hand appear as agents of their own destruction. Mary Daly has accurately renamed this practice as female slaughter.[33]

Although suttee was legally banned in 1829, although there has
been repeated legislation against this practice, it persists with terrible ferocity, most routinely in many parts of India and other
countries on the Asian sub-continent. Far from being an outmoded
foreign custom – that mistaken notion with which we in the West
sometimes comfort ourselves – ritualistic widow-burning has for
years been widespread, appearing in Asia, Africa, America and
Australia, and according to Cochrane, Parkes and other researchers,
in Europe also.

Small cause for comfort or congratulation here.

Feminists, however, are struggling with the problem. Gail
Omvedt, writing in 1990, reports that 'the last few years have seen
dramatic revivals of the ancient custom of sati' and confirms that 'the
issue of violence against women has been the most pervasive theme
of the new women's liberation movement in India'.[34] Nepal, primarily a rural society, has a vigorous feminist movement which fights the
age-old Asian patriarchy. But ancient traditions are difficult to combat. Surveys carried out by an Indian Committee on the status of
women revealed that a large percentage of the population still
approves of such oppression of widows.

Widow-burning is still believed in fundamentalist Hindu religious observance to further the progress of the dead husband's soul.
That such a bizarre belief can still exist despite contrary evidence
which illustrates that nowhere is such a practice even mentioned in
major Hindu holy texts (the 'Sastras' and the 'Laws of Manu') serves

to show us the intensity with which the idea of woman-as-dead-man's-property has taken hold. In a study of women in India and Nepal, writers Michael Allen and S.N. Mukherjee found that the widow's position in Hindu caste society is still ambiguous. Though alive, her close identification with her deceased husband meant that she was socially dead, subsumed in her relation with him and highly polluted.[35]

Despite the banning of suttee, despite new legal reforms, the situation of Indian widows even when no longer burned alive is hard. Although the Hindu Re-Marriage Act gives some legal provision for remarriage of widows, a large percentage of the public still believe they should not. Shashi Jaln who studied the perceptions of 400 Hindu, middle-class, married women in 1988, found that though 82.5 per cent of her sample favoured remarriage for 'unconsummated widows' (those who had no children and were probably celibate), only a quarter were in favour if the widow had offspring. Of widows in the respondents' own families only 3.5 per cent had actually remarried, and this low remarriage figure seems typical.[36] Too often widows are stripped of their possessions, forced into permanent seclusion, and at the mercy of unsympathetic in-laws. As Germaine Greer points out, whereas in some cases a middle-aged woman with a husband might be a powerful and auspicious woman, a middle-aged widow, should she survive her death penalty, is an outcast.[37]

Faced with these facts, what is wondrous, what is worth recording, is how well, how valiantly, most widows cope.

For some widows, strength comes from the gaining of a new identity. The characteristic sense of incompleteness, the sudden shakiness, the confusion about one's social status, the insecurity relating to one's self-worth . . . all these have to be processed into a new woman. But widows reveal that emerging from grief can bring a fresh feeling of confidence. There could be new opportunities. New friends.

> I have lost perhaps 30 per cent of my friends and acquaintances who had only valued me as Jacques' wife. Mourning completes all relationships – not only your own with the person you have lost but other people's with you . . . The friends you make after bereavement are very special. They are part of your new identity. They have never known you as part of a couple.[38]

For other widows, strength comes from old friends, usually women,

whose loyalty lasts through decades, divorces and deaths. Genuine
friendship is their linchpin. Many widows found a new kind of passion, a source of constant sustenance.

In Joan Barfoot's new novel *Charlotte and Claudia Keeping in
Touch*, Charlotte, who has never married but has had a string of
affairs, and Claudia, who has remained faithful for forty-seven years
to Bradley, her husband who systematically and viciously betrayed
her, are two such friends, now in their seventies, whose good times
and intense secrets roll back to their childhood. After Bradley's truly
horrible death, Claudia is released from a bitter marriage into what
could have become a tragic widowhood. She writes to Charlotte,
whom she has not seen for the last five years, to tell her of Bradley's
death:

> Have you ever spent time with a dying person? . . . The skin
> changes. It loses moisture or mobility, something, anyway, so it's
> not quite alive any more . . . But oh, Charlotte, what I didn't
> know about, what was worst, was the smell! His breath, his body,
> all changing and terrible. As if he was dead before he was dead . . .
> Whatever you've thought over the years, he was always in my life,
> one way and another. I don't think I knew until recently how
> huge that was, his part of me . . . I do feel as if there's been some
> kind of amputation: some large limb or organ has gone missing,
> and if it wasn't exactly essential, I am somewhat crippled without
> it . . .

Claudia reminds Charlotte about how their friendship started when
they were six.

> Did I ever tell you how utterly blissfully thrilled I was when you
> asked me to be your partner when we lined up to go outside for
> recess or for skipping, or for walking home from school? Truly
> you know, I don't think I was so excited when I first fell in love . . .
> I think, you know, that past a certain point it's too hard to make
> real friends. There's too much missing that they can't know (and
> that you can't know about them). It gets impossible to fill enough
> details and blanks for them to catch up.

Claudia concludes by admitting "'I'm lonely, Charlotte, I feel all
alone. Not just because Bradley's gone, but because I'm scared.'"
Charlotte's response is immediate. She invites her to stay. They meet
excitedly at the railway station.

Claudia sets down her cases. Charlotte, at last! . . . Oh look at that smile. She didn't realize until they smiled and headed for each other that she was frightened something essential might have changed. 'Oh Char, I'm so *happy* to see you.' She feels herself almost dancing. They stand at arms' length. Claudia sees tears in Charlotte's eyes, and feels them also in her own. They hug. People skirt them, and some smile.

Claudia need not have worried. Nothing has changed in their friendship. But everything suddenly changes in their seventy-year-old lives. I shall not spoil Joan Barfoot's elegant surprises but I shall say that widowhood within the warmth of good women friends can be a celebration as well as a time for grieving.[39]

Chapter Seven

DEATHS THAT HAUNT: MOTHERS LOSE CHILDREN

It is not useful to measure one bereavement against another.

This I know.

What is productive is to examine the impact of a particular death on the special group it affects. To try and understand their needs.

This I know.

And yet.

I have talked to mothers, many mothers, whose child has died. I think of the death of a child.

I am the mother of a bright twenty-seven-year-old daughter. She is healthy and thankfully very much alive.

And yet.

I cannot but think of her death.

For a decade I have cared for and helped bring up three other girls. One now back at college, one in the army, one, with a child of her own, working with animals. All of them healthy. Vivid. Alive.

I cannot but think of their deaths.

I have been involved in step-parenting two stepdaughters and a stepson. All of them now grown-up, two live abroad, healthy, brimming with life and excitement.

Impossible to think of them dead. Impossible now not to think of their deaths.

I imagine what is unimaginable. I think what is unthinkable. It is foolish to fantasise. It is not useful to measure any one bereavement against another. Each death is unique. Each grief special to the woman concerned. But I find I am panicking. Reach for the telephone. I ring up my daughter. She is busy at work in her publishing office. I tell her: take care of yourself.

'Mum! I always take care! What's the matter? Did you think because I was stressed-out last weekend, that I'd go jump off a bridge?'

I gasp.

She reassures. 'Hey, it's a joke! It's only a joke. I'm fine.'

Realisation dawns on her. 'Oh don't tell me, it's *that book!* Death really is getting to you. Now calm down. Talk to you later.'

Yes, it's this book. Well, it is this particular chapter. It is not insignificant that one possible death is getting to me. The death of a child is every parent's unspoken terror. It leaves those who face it completely unprepared. This is true whether the death is sudden (a train crash, a fire, a boat capsized, an instantaneous heart attack, a fall from a cliff), or whether the death is from a long drawn-out illness. This is true whether a baby is stillborn, or a child is at primary school, a teenager in turbulence, a young adult comfortably into a job or – as so many today – angrily waiting in a dole queue.

A mother's grief takes no account of age or stage.

Existing research shows that the trauma of a child's death on both parents appears more complex, the bereavement longer lasting, than any other deaths. Jane Littlewood suggests that:

> Whilst grieving is universally acknowledged as painful . . . the loss of a child is a uniquely devastating experience for the child's parents. In contemporary Western societies such deaths are almost always viewed as untimely because they conflict with people's taken-for-granted assumptions and life-cycle expectations. It is now reasonable to suppose that children will outlive their parents . . . Consequently few parents actively anticipate the deaths of their children.[1]

Because the natural order is to precede our child in death, it is the feeling that it is an 'unnatural act' which is the most disturbing element.

The Compassionate Friends, an international organisation of bereaved parents, suggests that these women and men 'face a future which leaves their dreams and aspirations unfulfilled'. As every worker and counsellor within the organisation has to be a bereaved parent, their experience creates the belief that there is 'no death so sad', a slogan which is their mast-head.[2]

C.M. Sanders in an empirical study which compared the loss of spouses, parents, and children, concluded that those bereaved of a child experienced the highest intensity of grief as well as the widest range of reactions. One reason for diverse reactions could be the differing circumstances which surround children's deaths.[3]

My research shows that the shock of a child's death on the *mother* has particular implications that make her bereavement and expression of grief different from that of the father.

The biological experience of childbirth combined with the social role of motherhood, which in this society establishes mothers as the primary parent, is what makes the difference. Having other children, or deciding to have another baby, does not diminish a mother's grief over her child's loss. Researchers have found that mothers who lose one baby in a set of twins grieve just as intensely as mothers who lose a single baby. When a mother loses her only child she also loses her role as a mother. When one of several children die, the bereaved mother loses her family as it was because death has irrevocably changed that family structure. **Bereaved mothers do not 'get over' their loss, they rebuild their lives around that loss.**

For both parents, the psychological and social consequences and changes that follow a child's death will vary with the child's *age*, the *cause* and *context* of death, and the parents' *character* and *life experience*. Research suggests that the first two factors are more important than the third. But there is a fourth significant element; that of *gender*. It is mothers for whom the death of a child is part of the special female mode of experiencing death from inside. There are intricate connections between not merely the process, but even the possibility, of giving birth and women's response to death.

Journalist Anne Chisholm had long loved and often looked after her sister Clare's four-year-old son, Jess. When twenty-nine-year-old Clare was dying of cancer, Anne, who had suffered several miscarriages, decided that in the event of Clare's death (which occurred a few months later) she would become formally responsible for bringing up Jess. 'So there was a strange sort of subtext to her dying which was the life of this child and the two things are very interconnected for me. Her life ebbing and my taking on the responsibility for his life.'[4]

When a woman's child dies, she may look back and see these connections heightened. 'I didn't fear much till I had the two girls. Then of course you fear for them. You're their mother. It's your job to care, and when you care you fear. But with Lizzie having her special condition I tried not to be too fearful, even let her go on big rides at the fair.' (Juno, thirty-five. Nursery nurse. Daughter Lizzie died aged nine from long term immune deficiency.)

In a terrible way you know as a mother yourself that we are all born to suffer. We suffer from the moment our children are born. We worry about them when we put them in the cot. Are they going to be alive in the morning? I'm an optimistic person, but when Ben was born I started worrying. He pulled the iron down, fell off a step, had concussion from a bike fall, I worried and just tried not to look! The strange thing is I worried right up until he was eighteen when he went on his last voyage. Suddenly I stopped worrying. How bitterly ironic. He never came back.

(Shirley Cooklin, Writer. Son Ben died aged eighteen at sea.)

Before it happened four years ago, I was a reasonably calm mother. As an ordinary mother with five kids, sure, I did fear my children would have accidents or be run over . . . a lurking horror that came in with my first pregnancy, with Greg. Before that I'd done things like ride on the back of people's motorbikes. The minute I became pregnant with Greg I became cautious, especially about travelling. I think it is one of the last unspoken things about having children. That with the children comes this great fear.

(Annie, Mother. Son Greg committed suicide.)

Dorothy Jones, bereavement counsellor, bears out these women's words.

When my first child was born I became fearful as a parent. Once I was pregnant I felt I was introduced to a form of death that men do not experience; it was the fear that my child would die. Almost the minute she was born there was a cosmic responsibility. It was as if my mother's persona had descended. So death became something inside. The fear for my children was to do with my psyche rather than external forces. I've heard the same story from many women patients.

A major achievement of Western society has been to reduce the level of infant mortality. Although approximately 10,000 children die each year in the UK (more than half from accidents on the road or in the home, the remainder from life-threatening illnesses), death in childhood is not the common experience it was earlier this century.

That deaths from AIDS and its related diseases now bring death to the young, has not acclimatised us to this enormity. In the West we still view youngsters' deaths as untimely. We find the deaths of children shocking. It affects the way we relate to parents of dead children. It affects the way we treat children in relation to death and bereavement.

The fact that childhood deaths have substantially decreased will not of course console grieving parents, for whom there will now be fewer other parents who can share their experience, and who will be surrounded by those with living children whose greatest fear is the death of their offspring. That fear means we talk even less easily to dying children than to dying adults. Many parents did not use the word 'death' but said that 'Grandfather had had a long sleep' or that the children's favourite Auntie 'had gone on a long journey and wasn't coming back'. Not surprisingly some of these children developed travel phobia or became afraid of bed.

If children are reared in a house where death is a mystery, and if a child who is dying, or a sibling whose sister or brother is dying, wishes to express fears or last wishes, they may be prevented from doing so. Occasionally mothers would arrive at the hospital bed where one child lay dying 'protected' by her other children or relatives so that open conversation between mother and child became impossible. 'I regret this now. I wish we had talked about her dying. But she was only seven, and I'm not sure who was saving who!' (Mother. Child died of leukaemia.)

This same fear means we talk less easily to those whose children have died than to other bereaved people. A.T. Rando, who researched into parental loss, describes other people's reactions as 'uniquely strange and callous'. Parents often complain that they feel like 'social lepers'.[5]

It is more frequently mothers rather than fathers who wish to talk constantly about the death of their child.

> I know my sister needs to talk all the time about Tony's death. He was fourteen, the same age as my son; they were more like twins than cousins. Tony was killed in a car smash, my son survived with bruises. I feel guilty so that makes it hard for me to listen to her. I've stopped going to her house as regularly as I used to.
>
> (Mother, thirty-six.)

How does the age of the child at death affect both the silence around the subject and the response of the mother?

Mothers whose living children die between the ages of one year and adulthood at least have such deaths legitimated and their parental grief acknowledged.

Foetus and infant deaths however are largely unvalidated; consequently mothers' griefs may go unattended.

These deaths include:

Miscarriages

Induced abortions

Stillbirths

Perinatal deaths (these occur within seven days of birth)

Neonatal deaths (these occur within twenty-eight days of birth)

Sudden Infant Death Syndrome (Each year about 2000 babies in the UK die suddenly and unexpectedly, of which 1500 babies are diagnosed as SIDS.)

How to deal with the effects when professionals and friends alike lack understanding? How to cope with a loss when there is no social acknowledgement that each loss is a 'real' death? Women report it is hard.

Miscarriages and Induced Abortions

These early losses are often (though *not necessarily*) traumatic, because most women, from the beginning, think of pregnancy in terms of a live baby. If the pregnancy miscarries, then it represents the loss of everything a baby meant to them. This is true whether the loss occurs early or late in pregnancy. As Nancy Kohner points out, it is the personal significance of the loss, not the gestational age of the baby, which determines the extent of grieving.[6]

A child may die at twenty-eight days, twenty-eight weeks, or twenty-eight years. A mother's distress however takes no account of time.

Acknowledge that.

Then it is obvious that support and care offered to the mother must be determined by a precise understanding of the meaning of that death, not by the stage of pregnancy at which that death occurs.

Even after a very early miscarriage, mothers may be helped by seeing the body. If there is a body. In the absence of a body, mothers can be aided by being given as much medical information as possible. Unfortunately with many miscarriages, with many abortions, there is no body. 'That's what stressed me, my miscarriage was my child dead. But I saw no body. It was treated almost as a non-event. It was my *child* that had died, not a non-person!' (Woman with early miscarriage.)

It is vital to treat with caution distinctions between one kind of

loss and another, such as the meanings attached to early or late miscarriages. The timescale does not always imply a similar response in
different women. If the early miscarriage was the third or fourth to
a woman desperate for a child, this could have more significance
than a very late miscarriage to a woman who was from the start of
the pregnancy ambivalent about the birth.

What is consistent is that where there are feelings of loss they are
often prolonged, sometimes delayed until months, even years afterwards, each loss emphasising, again, women's perceptions of death
from inside.

If the death was from an induced abortion (of which in the UK
alone in 1989 nearly 170,000 were recorded for women between fifteen and forty-four, and many more went unrecorded) there are
often additional problems arising from either social pressure or personal guilt.

I look back at my journal of thirty years ago. Find the entry for
the week I had an abortion. What is uncanny is that I recall the experience today almost exactly as I wrote it then.

> I drove to Harley Street. I saw the gynaecologist in his silky
> green-curtained waiting room. I stepped gingerly on his green
> velvet grass. He talked about his fee. I talked about pain. My fear
> of it. Needing a general anaesthetic. 'Please agree to do it our way,
> dear lady,' the smiling specialist said. 'It is the time factor you see.
> We simply cannot give general anaesthetics to all our ladies and
> still get them out for their next appointment on time. Our dear
> ladies, like ourselves, like yourself, lead such terribly busy lives.
> What we use is a wonderful dreamy pill. You won't notice a
> thing!'
>
> He did not notice my tears messing up the green velvet grass.
> I trod in my tears so they would not show. The butcher was still
> talking about fees or sharpening his blades, one or the other.
> 'Dear lady, believe me, there is nothing to worry about. It is only
> a minor repair job after all.'

The following week I returned to his green-carpeted blood palace.
This time accompanied by the man who had been my lover. He and
the specialist counted out the money. Then the man who had been
my lover left, promising to see me later that night. I was alone in a
room with eight or nine other women. They were on their own too.
Obviously this was not a place for men. Some women came in with
men. They all left without them. The journal continues:

The secretary-nurse woman was staring at me. How odd, I thought. I am not here, so she cannot possibly see me. The woman said curtly: 'Follow me downstairs.' I followed down two flights, through a room with three little beds, into a large white surgery.

There was a big stainless-steel bin just inside the room. Protruding from it was a black plastic rubbish bag. As I stumbled past it, I glanced in. The secretary-nurse said sharply: 'Don't look in there. The last girl was stupid. Far too far gone. There's no point in looking!'

She was too late to stop me. Inside the black rubbish bag was a mess of flesh. Like assorted amputated knees. The top lump was very large. Different from the rest. Recognisably shaped. It was *not* like a baby. I had seen babies. They were fat and round and stupid. They were red and wizened, gurgly and alive.

This was more like a grotesque miniature old man. This was also stupid. This was also red. Very red. Very wizened. This was not alive. This was not a baby.

I wanted to run but could not move. I was sick over the specialist's expensive green pile carpet. The vomit was green pile too. I wondered idly about mix and match. The icy nurse-woman was furious. She shovelled up the vomit and put it in the same black plastic bag. Then she said sharply to the doctor: 'She's brought up her dream pill Doctor. Is there time to give her another?' His voice was smooth and luxuriant like his salon. 'Of course not,' he purred. 'We are running ten minutes late already. We must not keep our ladies waiting any more than they must keep us waiting.' Sharply his purr cut off. 'Get her in the chair nurse.'

I recall the chair was of padded leather with a frame of steel the colour of the nurse's eyes. There seemed at the time to be a great number of people all with magnified arms and legs holding down my legs, strapping down my arms. Pulling my feet up into a harness. The journal recalls:

The nurse picked up two shiny instruments and handed one to the doctor. She did this with great care. They were all careful people. No wonder the man who had been my lover had brought me here. He was a careful person. Suddenly I heard someone scream. Someone near me. The screams were loud and terrible. The nurse carefully handed over the second shiny instrument. It looked like a knife. The woman was screaming again. I was sure it was a woman. Only a woman would be so careless as to break the peace of this tranquil salon with such loud and terrible screams. I was sure they would punish the woman. Suddenly someone slapped me across the face. 'Stop that screaming. Sit still! How can the doctor work properly?' The nurse was being reasonable. I, it seems, was not being reasonable. If that other woman's screams were mine, then that other woman's pain must be mine. It must be me they are punishing. I tell the other woman, who may be me, there is no way of knowing, to be quiet. Ten minutes or a life later I was outside the room. The minor repair job was over.'

What I never fully got over, like many other women, was the feeling that a child of mine was dead. In the last three decades there have been changes for the better in the methods and treatment of abortion but whether it was 'badly butchered' in the sixties or 'skilfully performed' in the nineties, many women's memories stay locked into that death. Today, in general, the pain (if it is felt, and for every woman the experience will be different) is not of surgery but of loss of part of herself.

Stillbirths, Perinatal Deaths, Neonatal Deaths

The doctors told me my baby was dead but I couldn't take it in. I decided to call her Karen and I went right on buying her baby clothes. Even during the labour I kept hoping they were wrong. 'Don't let her die, don't let her die!' I kept screaming. When she was born dead it was the worst shock in the world.

(Mother, twenty-eight.)

This mother's statement was typical. The advance medical forewarning had been met by denial. Many mothers, also forewarned, went on to give their unborn children names. Had nurseries decorated for the baby. Would later talk about 'Stephen's room' or 'Shirley's nursery'. I discovered (as did Jane Littlewood in her study of children's deaths) a general predilection amongst mothers to experience their child's stillbirth as a *birth* followed by a *death* rather than as a foetus which has been born already dead.[7]
Sometimes the forewarning is so early that it turns what might have been a joyous pregnancy into a horror movie. One mother was told at five months that she was carrying a dead baby. She was

advised that it was 'safer' to go through with the pregnancy and labour. Her remit was to deliver a dead child. It may have been physically safer but by the time of the 'birth' (or death) she was in peril. No safe state hers. She delivered the dead baby. Left the maternity hospital. Three weeks later voluntarily entered the psychiatric unit of a general hospital.

Another problem attached to stillbirths is that 'pre-viable foe-tuses' are without legal status and therefore more subject to silence and invisibility. In the UK currently at least one baby in every hundred is either stillborn (i.e. born dead after the twenty-fourth week of pregnancy, according to the Stillbirth (Definition) Act 1992) or dies shortly after birth. 1990 UK figures (when the legal definition of stillbirth was a baby born dead after twenty-eight weeks' gestation) show that 3,721 babies were stillborn and 3,616 died within the first four weeks of life. After a legally defined stillbirth, the law requires certification and registration, and the baby's body must be buried or cremated. Such basic requirements provide both a framework for managing the death, which may help mothers, and imply certain moral obligations which are the consequence of recognising the status of the foetus. However when a baby is born dead before the legal age of viability there are no such requirements. No official statistics. No generally accepted practices.

> When we see a babe born dead say at twenty-one weeks, we feel it could have lived. We feel helpless, as if we've failed. Mums see it that way too. It's her baby that died. But in the eyes of the law it's just a non-viable foetus. We don't have to do anything! In our hospital there is good practice. We let the Mums hold the baby, say goodbye, we even give a medical certificate, which we aren't legally required to.
>
> (Nurse, British hospital.)

Jenni Thomas, a bereavement counsellor attached to a maternity and special baby-care unit, emphasises the importance played by photographs in the grieving process. Even if parents don't ask for a photograph, Jenni Thomas suggests hospitals take one anyway as it is only later that parents realise they have no record of their child. Mothers also need maximum information about exactly what was done to save their child. Choice of words is critical. Mothers need to hear their baby is 'dead', not 'lost' which implies carelessness.[8]

Today several hospitals have amended their practice. Some routinely photograph stillbirths, give parents photographs, the baby's name tag, or a lock of hair. Jenni Thomas has helped set up the new Child Bereavement Trust which offers emotional support and resources to bereaved parents as well as counselling skills advice to professionals involved in children's deaths including miscarriages, stillbirths, neonatal deaths and termination for abnormality.

Yes, there are improvements.

But more, much more, needs to be done.

Again – as in every death studied in this book – I saw breakdown over communication.

Researchers Stringham, Wolff and Bourne all record this post-stillbirth conspiracy of silence among hospital staff. This silence confirms the mothers' feelings that such a death was 'unspeakable'.

This low level of verbal acknowledgement can extend into the community. Many general practitioners are reluctant to discuss still-birth reactions with their patients. They, and sometimes family or friends, act as if the deaths had never happened.

Although perinatal and neonatal deaths share with stillbirths the lack of social acknowledgement, also produce feelings of guilt or helplessness, the fact that the child lived, albeit for only a few days, often means more involvement from the medical staff.

Sudden Infant Death Syndrome (SIDS)

Self-blame was again the most common characteristic I noted in women's accounts. Researchers Donnelly, Raphael and Littlewood all found that guilt was especially intense following a death from SIDS – the most common cause of death during a child's first year – which peaks amongst the two to four-months age group.[9] The cause of SIDS is still unknown. Nor is it possible to predict which babies will be at risk. Often infants appear supremely healthy prior to the death, the suddenness of which is a major contribution to mothers' grief.

Unfortunately other hostile factors complicate women's reactions. Police are called. In the absence of an obvious cause of death, they may suspect child abuse. Both officials and relatives may relent-lessly question the parents about events immediately preceding the death. Even if the mother gradually becomes reassured that neither she nor (if there is a second parent involved) her partner are in any way responsible, the sheer inexplicable nature of the death may leave her helpless.

Fortunately two voluntary organisations, The Foundation for the Study of Infant Death (FSID) and the Stillbirth and Neonatal Death

Society (SANDS), have developed in response to these mothers' special needs. More than mere support agencies, they campaign, engage
in research, provide advice and information, determined to raise
public awareness.

Deaths of Children, Adolescents, Young Adults

The age of the child and the manner of death has specific repercussions upon the mother. What is significant however are the patterns
which are the same for each bereaved mother irrespective of age or
cause.

To take some differences first.

Accidental deaths, sudden and unexpected (the most common
cause of death for fifteen to thirty-four-year-olds) leave survivors
totally unprepared, shocked and vulnerable. Anger is added to grief,
often an eruption of a high degree of anger because these deaths
involve some degree of responsibility. Raphael shows how normative
this is for both parents:

> Extreme anger about the accident – a hatred of the driver of the
> car, for example, a desire to hit out and get revenge – may domi-
> nate the parent's response. This may be directed towards other
> agencies or towards the husband or wife. A traumatic neurosis
> effect is common if the parent was present at the death or in any
> way involved.[10]

Several *fathers* I interviewed whose children had died in accidents
felt this outrage. Desired revenge. 'That bastard on his motor bike
took Tommy's life away. Seven! The kid was seven! He shouldn't be
allowed to live! He shouldn't have arms to drive a bloody bike.'
(Father. Seven-year-old child died in road accident.)

Deaths which occur in adolescence may be particularly stressful
for mothers if there have been struggles over autonomy and independence. Road accidents (very common in teenage years) also led
to attempts by parents to allocate blame. Jane Littlewood found that
it was fathers particularly who directed anger against wives, unable
to see children's deaths as accidents.

> One man reported that he blamed his wife for neglect, following
> his three-year-old daughter's drowning accident. However, upon
> attending meetings of Compassionate Friends he found that many

fathers whose children had died tended to do this, and made a conscious effort to see the death as an unfortunate, unforeseeable accident. Nevertheless he was further annoyed at what he saw as his wife's irrational behaviour. She had been present when her daughter's body had been found in a neighbour's pond and was phobic about the sight of anything floating in water.[11]

I talked to a mother whose eight-year-old girl pulled away from her hand, rushed into the road after their dog which had slipped its leash, and was knocked down by a bus. Died in hospital. The mother's self-blame was terrible. She has been unable to travel by bus ever since. Her self-blame was common to many women whose children died in accidents.

The behaviour of those mothers may be described as 'phobic', seen as 'irrational', but it is a common and understandable response to the fear and chaos engendered.

Deaths from varying cancers, particularly following long periods of uncertainty often result in severe psycho-social stress. Several studies show at least 50 per cent of parents required psychiatric help after the death. In one study 8 per cent of mothers attempted suicide.[12]

Recent medical advances in the treatment of childhood cancers now means that there are much better chances of survival. Childhood cancers are more often seen as chronic life-threatening diseases rather than terminal illnesses. In these cases mothers have to adjust to sustained periods of uncertainty. Where children do finally die, research indicates that more positive ways of coping with cancer deaths can be related to three key factors present during the child's illness:

1. Open and honest information and support given to the child throughout the illness.
2. At least one ongoing supportive person for the primary parent during the illness.
3. A consistent philosophy of life as meaningful held by parents during the illness.[13]

I discovered that where mothers helped care for their dying children, their subsequent feelings of helplessness were substantially reduced. This most often occurred when mothers looked after dying children at home. Several women reported that the more they participated in the caring tasks, especially if they were allowed to help wash or even help nurses administer medicines, the less guilt they felt.

For mothers who had day-to-day home care of a terminally sick child, there was no denial of death. What they felt was a desperate need to talk about the precise stages of the cancer.

Writer Janet Taylor who looked after her sixteen-year-old daughter Brigie at home in the last stages of her cancer, did exactly that. After her daughter's death she wrote a meticulous detailed account of every moment of the illness because she had 'a compelling need to share this experience with a much wider group, with all who fear death, especially for the young'. She regards the experience as profound, as one which strengthened and bonded her entire family. Her honesty is moving. She makes no attempts to gloss over stress or difficulties between a caring (careworn) mother and her dying daughter.

In the last stages of the disease, Brigie became confused. The doctor thought she had cerebral secondaries and put her on diamorphine. Often Janet could not understand her daughter's needs. Brigie gave up trying to explain, would sink back with a 'resigned look or with silent fury'. The frustration on both sides reached its climax after they had finally settled to sleep, Janet desperately tired after several continuous broken nights.

> Brigie could not get comfortable and I couldn't understand what she was saying . . . We changed positions several times and we tried the commode. She started giving me hostile looks and saying 'Mum' in tones of freezing fury . . . She leaned down and got hold of my sleeping bag, indicating she wanted to sleep on the mattress . . . There was nothing I could do but prop her up with all the pillows but I knew it would be bad for her breathing. It could not be for long, but I lay down on her settee, longing for sleep. Five minutes later we were up again. By now, my patience was running out, and when she got back to the settee I let fly. Anger might be effective where long-suffering was not.
>
> 'Now look here, Brigie, I know you're ill, and I'm very sorry. But I've got to have some sleep tonight so that I can look after you tomorrow. So let's stop all this messing about and settle down!' It seemed to clear the air and we slept.[14]

The conflict between a mother's needs and those of her dying child, the clash between a natural urge towards impatience and a feeling that it must not be expressed, were dilemmas encountered by many mothers.

It is time to look at these and similar patterns.

Main issues which repeated themselves in every mother's accounts were:

While the child is dying
  1. Mothers' relationship with doctors; medical language
  2. Home care versus hospital care
  3. Issue of uncertainty
  4. Support systems.
  5. Siblings' behaviour; father's behaviour
  6. Mutual protection of mother and child; anger, guilt; discussing death with dying child
  7. How bad news is broken
  8. Need to have maximum information about last words, last moments
  9. Need to touch and hold dying/dead child

After death
  1. The need to talk, make videos, take photos, have appropriate funerals, memorials
  2. Grief experiences: different from fathers'; marital difficulties
  3. Feelings of amputation, loss of competence, loss of self
  4. Support systems/attitudes of friends/professionals
  5. Spirituality
  6. Acceptance of death
  7. Consequences of death on mothers; changes in character

In order to look at certain key features, I shall use four women's accounts which stand as models for many more.
1. *Shirley* Writer. White, middle-class, divorced, single parent. Son Ben, eighteen, drowned at sea.
2. *Mania* Nurse. Black, Jamaican, working-class, widowed. Son Peter, twenty-three, died of heart attack.
3. *Juno* Nursery nurse. White, working-class, married. Daughter Lizzie, nine, died of immune deficiency disease.
4. *Netty* Lawyer. White, middle-class, single parent. Daughter Frieda, alive today, at age four diagnosed with aneurism in the head, almost died. Left with life-threatening illness.

Issues While a Child is Dying

When a child is dying, mothers need *support*. Personal as well as professional. Juno was lucky. 'My work mates were brilliant. The Mums at Lizzie's school they did a rota. They'd bring in packed lunches, flasks of tea; if I felt chilly, cardigans would appear from nowhere.'

Mothers also need to *talk*. But whether or not to talk about death to a dying daughter or son is a decision each mother must make according to her own strength and her relationship with her offspring.

> We always talked positively to Lizzie but we never got around to talking about dying. Even when she was on a ventilator for the ten days before she died, they said she might be able to hear us, so we always said positive things. Before that, when she'd stopped fighting, I thought about mentioning it. Then she came back from theatre twice and said 'You won't let me die?' So of course I said 'No! No, you'll be all right.'

Siblings and fathers of a dying child can be another cause of concern. Throughout Lizzie's illness, Juno and Tommy had always rigorously shared the child care.

> When she was in hospital we did two nights in hospital, two nights at home, splitting it. But towards the end Tommy couldn't stand to stay in hospital. He was running away from it. So he came and visited every evening but I stayed all night. He couldn't handle that. Mums do it because it is expected of you. I didn't ever think it was hard work. It was my job. I was her mother. I carried on going to work while her Dad sat with her. I did a few hours' work a day. Then he'd phone work and say: 'She's in too much pain. I can't look after her. You'll have to come in.' For some reason he thought I was strong. *You end up being strong*. Any parent can't stand a child in pain. But she did need reassurance. She didn't need a blubbering mother.

A second child in the family brings additional problems.

> Nancy felt pushed out. She was only eleven and for eighteen months she hardly did any work at school. We didn't know really because we weren't really with her. I felt I'd let her down but

we've got there in the end. Now that she has all of our attention since Lizzie's death, she's doing really well.

If a child is in hospital a mother's relationship with doctors is critical. As is her understanding (or not) of medical language.

Juno's problematic relationship with the medical profession started early. Her daughter Lizzie was immune deficient from birth but wasn't diagnosed until she was five.

For years she had chronic chest conditions, ear infections, chicken pox three times. Her immune system simply didn't work. But it was years before the doctor told me what she had. She was researched but never labelled with an illness. We were both unemployed with a constantly sick child but we couldn't claim the benefits because Lizzie's illness didn't have a name.

In 1990 Lizzie fell off her BMX bike and landed on one leg. She contracted a severe bout of shingles. Then a second bout. Then a chest infection. Finally a mark on her lung, originally treated as an abscess was found to be a tumour.

The doctors didn't tell me for ages how serious it was. The tumour growing. The consultant never lied to me. But I didn't have a clue about the language. I never understood him. I never felt confident enough to say: 'Can you tell me what you're saying again?' The thoracic surgeon was better. He talked to me so I knew. He said we'd have to open her, but opening someone with a lung tumour would make it spread. But without opening it they wouldn't know what it was. Either way they couldn't save her! Not that he quite said those words but they said if we don't open it and it's a tumour she'll be very ill anyway. If we do, and it spreads it will be even quicker. I understood. My husband Tommy just walked away. He didn't want to understand those words. Nor did Nancy, Lizzie's sister. She walked away. She said to me: 'If I run away, it won't happen, cos Lizzie wouldn't die until I came back!' I think her Dad was doing the same thing.

Juno was fortunate in having one paediatrician who was open, honest, and prepared to show her own emotions.

Carol was wonderful to talk to. She was the one doctor I called by her name. She was my good friend. She was a very physical person. She'd always touch you, even if she just hung on to your arm, or got eye contact, you felt you had her total attention. She never rushed away. You don't need someone rushing in and out. She always talked to Lizzie about her illness. Lizzie responded well to her as she liked her very much which for anyone who knew Lizzie was an achievement. She was an extremely fiery independent pest. She was strong and stubborn. Gave us hell. She was a fighter. That's why it was terrible when she gave up fighting. Carol understood Lizzie's fears. Treatment was never forced on her. But Carol and the nursing staff could always talk her round.

Juno, initially shy and confused, struggled with unasked questions.

As Lizzie got weaker, I got stronger, asked more. Lizzie can't fight for herself so I've got to. Carol was one doctor who listened to me, hugged me, wherever possible went by my wishes. She shared her fears over Lizzie's health. I believed in what she said because I got direct answers. She never avoided issues. She wasn't just a doctor caring for a sick child, she was someone like me, who had emotions. She was one doctor who always came forward with the information.

How bad news is broken is something mothers always recall. Lizzie was in intensive care. As Juno waited for 'the worst to happen' it was Carol who came in with the consultant.

The consultant was talking, talking, talking about I don't know what. 'Lungs and got bigger and done everything we can, and it's up to Lizzie now.' To me it didn't mean an awful lot. Did he mean Lizzie could fight and live or did he mean yes she's going to die? He didn't say. But Carol cried. The consultant left. He left Carol and me crying. Then I thought, yes she's dying. I didn't have to ask her. There weren't any words needed. I was so grateful she showed me how she felt.

That was at twelve noon. Lizzie died at seven that night held by Juno. *Holding a child, touching a child, is vital.*

Grandparents, uncles, aunties, loads of people and the priest came to say goodbye. But Nancy ran off. Tommy was awful. He collapsed in intensive care. 'Don't you let our Lizzie see you like this,' I said. Really stroppy. 'Come on! If she's going to go, let her go!' But he was in a bad state. He wouldn't hold up. The nurses suggested Nancy came in to see the ventilator so she wouldn't be scared of some horrible machine. Nancy lasted six minutes which wasn't bad. Then ran out saying: 'Don't like it! Don't like it!' Lizzie died in a nice way. She wasn't starved in another country or killed. She was on my knee. 'Are you cold? Do you need a blanket?' I asked them to turn the beep of the heart machine off. It was driving me mad. You're waiting for someone to die and it's going beep beep. So I said 'Leave the machine on but turn off the noise. Turn it away so I can't see it.'

I know exactly what Juno meant. Two years later, in the intensive care unit, in the hospital where Carol had helped Juno over Lizzie's death, Carol herself, Juno's doctor, my friend, lay dying. We, her friends, her daughter, sat by the bed, waiting for her to die, listening to the beep beep. None of us had Juno's strength and self-assertion to ask them to turn the noise off. It is a noise you do not forget.

Netty, the lawyer, whose daughter Frieda almost died, and whose prognosis is problematic, confronted several of the same issues as did Juno. Netty, now thirty-nine, became pregnant by artificial insemination, at thirty-one. Since Frieda's birth she has lived on her own with her child but has the regular once-a-fortnight child care support from a woman friend who lives in the same market town.

Obviously at first my parents had problems about the birth, but once the child is there it is different. Frieda is the apple of their eye now. But I wouldn't look to them for support. Before Frieda was ill I felt isolated. But as soon as she became very sick everybody crawled out of the woodwork. During Frieda's first illness, women ran rotas, made meals, talked, helped me while I stayed with Frieda in hospital. It made me realise I am part of a community.

Frieda's first illness was at eighteen months. A blood disorder following a virus. The body carried on producing antibodies which destroyed the red blood cells.

Her blood vessels burst. A red dotty rash everywhere. Then blood in her shit. Her blood count went sufficiently low for them to take her into hospital. I felt guilty. Was it something I'd done? What I focused it on was HIV stuff which was ridiculous because I hadn't done anything. Finally I had a blood test to prove to myself my fears were groundless. I'd given her really good care. I couldn't understand why this happy baby suddenly had a body that was ceasing to function properly. It was like she wanted to give up living. I decided that spiritually it was stuff she'd brought with her. Some issue she had to deal with.

Netty had to deal with it too. Frieda recovered. Temporarily. For two years, although perhaps frailer than other children, she played and ate, was good and bad. Then at four years she fell off a slide in the park. She banged her head badly. Then she caught flu, never recovered, became limp and listless. Something was very wrong. She was admitted back into hospital.

She had a rare condition. An aneurism in her head. It blocked the channel the spinal fluid went down. It's like a bulge in the blood vessels. Like a pool of blood. Two consultants, a neurologist and a surgeon with a scan identified it. First they inserted an external drain in her head to relieve the pressure on the brain that was making her so listless. Then they operated a second time and inserted a shunt which drains the fluid internally from her skull down to her tummy. They say she's had it since she was born. She'd got permanent brain damage, but up to now her brain has been compensating and using different parts of itself for that part that is damaged. But the doctors have said the prognosis isn't very good.

For some of the small number of children with aneurisms, there are operations. But because of where Frieda's aneurism is situated, they cannot operate. The risks are too great.

Fancy surgery might not work. She could die. So they are going for quality of life instead, even if that life turns out to be short. If she becomes very ill again the future is indefinite. She could have a minor disability, physical or mental or both. She could die. It could be anything between those two extremes. It is difficult not to overprotect her. It makes it hard when she's difficult. It's hard to demand my own life because I'm conscious that something awful can happen tomorrow. I just have to think she will grow up even if I'm not sure she'll be here for long.

That diagnosis was the start of Netty's ongoing relationship with the medical profession. In one respect she was luckier than Juno. Her profession, her education, her self-assertiveness aided her.

I think I was given appropriate information. Initially I struggled to understand, to learn as much as I could. But it's complicated. These doctors have spent years in science, while I haven't even got 'O' level biology. I do trust their judgement. The fact that they said 'We don't know' makes me feel they won't do things just for the sake of technology. I would have chosen a good quality of life, even if shorter, against not so good a life because she was brain damaged. And that's the line they've taken. Of course being coher-ent, being middle-class, means that we share a language, that I'm sufficiently like them for them to be able to accept that in their terms I give her good care. The first time she was in hospital my job was in my notes in big letters. They tend to treat me a bit cau-tiously. The first time she had to have a test on her spine, they were taking marrow and she needed an anaesthetic. The anaes-thetist was completely freaked by the fact that I asked questions. So to freak him more, somebody told him I was a solicitor. Then while we were chatting I said casually 'Oh yes, I do medical neg-ligence work as well!' It was him who wrote that in my notes. But that was the only time I felt I was getting different treatment because I might sue them.

One noticeable difference is the understanding acceptance by hos-pital staff of Frieda's unusual birth.

I've had to explain that I don't know who Frieda's father is because she's a self-insemination baby. I've got brownie points because I can actually find out any medical facts that are necessary, so they accept me as a responsible parent. They've accepted the fact that Frieda has a wide, supportive, unconventional family, mainly women. They're impressed by that which is a great credit to them. Some people would be put off. They also accept that I am always accompanied by my friend Celia who is Frieda's guardian. They've always included her in all discussions.

Netty, like Juno, had to decide whether to talk to her daughter about dying. Like Juno, Netty has decided to make each day important, to offer constant reassurance, not to discuss death. But she feels there is an unconscious level at which Frieda is aware of her frailty, her nearness to death.

It's not at a conscious level, but after she'd been ill she lived with the kind of ease and strangeness as if she knew she was only supposed to live until four. It is like she could give so much because her life was supposed to be short. After she was ill it felt like she was in limbo as if she was thinking 'Right, I've done my life, I've done what I was sent for, what am I supposed to do now?' She got over that after eighteen months, but each year at the anniversary of her illness, she wobbles. She's had a couple of fits. When they put the shunt in, the blossom was coming off the trees. Now it's been two years. As the blossom came off each time, she suddenly went downhill. I think her spirit knows but she doesn't actually ask me the questions that require me to say 'Yes, you almost died' or 'No, I don't know what may happen.' Interestingly unlike other children she won't talk about the future. I took her to a hands-on museum where children draw a picture of what they want to do when they grow up. She just wouldn't have anything to do with it. I don't put fear in her head. I don't lie. But I don't talk about the future. I avoid the issue completely.

One practical measure Netty has taken to safeguard the present, if not the future, is to take Frieda to a healer. 'I felt the flame inside her, which had begun to flicker, become stronger and steadier again.'

Netty feels her own support is talking to other women but this too presents problems.

Non-mothers don't understand. They could intellectually understand but they couldn't empathise. Until you've had a child and feel emotionally she is the centre of the universe it isn't the same. Mothers with children who are healthy understand but become nervous because of the threat. Mothers with children who are badly disabled also find it hard. Their children have brain damage, are still in nappies at twelve, need wheelchairs. It's a real insult to them to ask for help with my worries over Frieda's future. The same with mothers whose children have died. I am emotionally exhausted dealing with the fact that my child might die. But she is still alive. Their losses are what could happen to me.

For Mania, the Jamaican nurse, and Shirley, the British writer, whose sons both died suddenly, from heart attack and drowning, there was no expectation of death, no chance to build up reserves of strength.

Mania's husband had a heart attack at thirty-five. She was widowed at twenty-five. Her baby Peter, with her in Britain, was just

two. her two older daughters were still in Jamaica. First she protected Peter, then the balance shifted.

> He was my husband's spitting image; I put him in his place. There
> was so much love between us it gives me pleasure to talk of him.
> His first steps, his first teeth come through. You don't have that
> with anyone else. He grew to be the head of the family even
> though the youngest. He was my very best friend. The girls and I
> relied on him. He'd sort out my cars. He'd even sort out my men.
> 'Look Mum, let me vet him first before you go any further. You tell
> him if he mistreat you I'm coming for him!'

One man Peter was too young to vet was his stepfather.

> I leave my fourteen-year-old Sandra in the house studying for
> school exam. That night I get home. Back door open. Daughter
> gone. I panicked. Maybe someone kidnap her. I phone police.
> Then it's seven but my husband not come home. That night
> Sandra phone from New York. They'd run off. They'd been hav-
> ing an affair, here in my house and I didn't know. Months later
> she comes back, knocks on my door with a suitcase. I took her
> in. I'm her mother. But Peter my son wouldn't speak to her. He
> so upset for me. My second husband he said all the sorry in the
> world. He said it was my daughter's fault, that she come on to
> him! But it broke up my second marriage. That was another
> death. So I depended more on Peter. I always expect I die before
> him. A mother she expects that. We used to joke that he could
> put me in a home when I got old. He'd get cross. 'Mum don't
> ever say that! I can't have two Mums. What you've done for me
> nobody can do. I would never put you in a home. That's my
> solemn promise.'

When women's expectations of outliving their children are over-
turned so is their world. The day before Peter's death, mother and
son met twice. Her last memories are of laughter.

> I called to my regular pub on the way to work. A few minutes
> later Peter appear. 'What are you doing here Stinky?' I say, always
> calling each other names, so close we were. 'I've come to see how
> you are', he say. I told him take care. That night I stopped at my
> elder daughter's after work for coffee. Then Peter and Dorry, his
> girl, they call in. 'Why you keep following me all over the place?'

I say. 'Shut up Stumpy! You too small to argue. I'm checking up on you!' he say.

Peter walked Mania to the car. At the gate he kissed her. 'Mum, I love you very much,' he said. Mania answered 'I love you too Babe!' They arranged to meet at the weekend. The next morning at work Mania received a call from the hospital Chaplain.

'I'm sorry to tell you, Peter is dead.'

Later Dorry, his girlfriend, told Mania that she and Peter had gone straight to bed that night. At midnight she awoke to hear 'funny sounds' from his voice on the floor. Sleepily she said 'Get up!' Then she fell asleep. Peter may have tried but acute chest pains sent him into a coma. He was found by Dorry when she awoke. The ambulancemen failed to resuscitate him. By the time they reached the hospital it was too late. Mania tried hard not to blame Dorry but anger erupted.

If he'd got some quick response when he was lying on the floor, if she'd called an ambulance then, they might have done something. I don't want to blame her. She's suffering. She's got that guilt. All I ask is when you hear my son on the floor you just get up to see what's wrong. Then I would say at least you did try.

Mania's religious faith eventually translated anger into acceptance. 'Really there was nothing she could have done. If that's the way he was born to go, God knows that was the way he was born to go. But one minute full of life. Just like my young husband, his father. The next minute, the heart and gone. Just like my husband.'

In any sudden violent death, bereaved mothers will experience complex grief reactions. However, if the death occurs in a major disaster (such as a fire, an accident at a sports ground, an aircraft crash, a sunken boat), grief is intensified. As all parents view the deaths of their children as untimely events that have occurred outside the 'natural' order, bereavement by disaster is a double blow because disaster too is an event outside everyday expectations or control. Some parents may actually witness the disaster on television, or see it replayed after the event. Others may hear the news on the radio.

Shirley Cooklin has been there. Knows the terrain. Heard the voice of the radio bringing death into her front room.

Shirley had been for a walk. The rhododendrons were in bloom. It is the rhododendrons she remembers. She came back for lunch. Switched on the radio. 'A news flash. Twelve words: "A British square-rigged cutter sank today off the coast of Bermuda." There were only nine survivors. I waited frozen for the announcer to give out the name of the boat. He said *The Marques*. Ben's boat. I knew he would not be one of the nine.'

Sailing had been her young son Ben's life. He was just eighteen, had taken his 'A' levels, was realising a dream: to sail the high seas for the Caribbean. Competing in the Tall Ships Race. A month earlier he had crossed the Atlantic in a small boat without automatic pilot. Shirley had been frantic with worry. '"How long are you going for?" I'd asked. He got cross. Said "I don't know! Three years or forever!" A real don't-interfere-with-my-life attitude.'

This time, with Ben on a bigger boat, with radio contact, certificated as safe by the Department of Transport, Shirley's anxiety lessened. He'd phoned her to say they had won the race. Once they reached Canada he would fly home.

He called collect. Just for once I didn't say 'This call is costing me an arm and a leg!' I said: 'Do you still love me Ben?' He said: 'Yes. Tell the Old Boy I love him too!' That was unusual. It was a very final conversation. That night I didn't sleep a wink. I was literally storm tossed. I think I was in that storm with him. But having heard his voice, on the surface I'd stopped worrying.

For days after the radio announcement, Shirley lived in an ocean of uncertainty. When they finally received the names of survivors Ben's was not amongst them. 'One of the painful things about losing someone at sea is there isn't an actual moment when you know you can mourn. When you know your child is dead. My daughter went on believing for months that Ben was on a desert island and would come back.'

Mothers who cannot recover the bodies of their children, need desperately to know everything about their last moments. Shirley went to meet the survivors at London airport.

All the fathers had hip-flasks, we all needed it. I went up to this blond eighteen-year-old boy. Just like at a cocktail party I said: 'How do you do? I'm Ben's Mum.' He looked at me and said 'I was his brother!' Then we both burst into tears. It was terrible for them, they'd watched their friends go down before their eyes. The last thing I'd sent Ben was a pair of khaki trousers and tee-shirt from a surplus store. Now I know I sent my son his winding sheet. I had to find out what he'd worn. Whether he ever washed.

How he'd coped with eating fish. He hated the bones. I needed to know accurate details. They said he'd been trapped on board. It was a lie. He was swept overboard.

Shirley (like Annie whose son killed himself) had to deal with more lies. Major inaccuracies. On the death certificate the details were wrong. The age was wrong. The next of kin was wrong. More significantly the fact that the boat had been inspected and passed as safe was also wrong. Shirley was determined to turn grief into action. To establish exactly how her son died and who was to blame.

Shirley successfully fought to get two inquiries (one public, one internal Department of Transport) to establish the unseaworthiness of the vessel, and the danger of letting the race begin in stormy weather. She also sued the Department of Transport and the owner.

I had to do it on legal aid. I had no money. In this country the death of a child is not counted to be any loss to you unless that child was supporting you. Officials say you haven't lost anything. I would not accept it was an Act of God. I didn't grieve. I'm a doing person. I couldn't say the word 'death' for months, until I'd written articles about it, brought cases, made it public. I could see Ben standing there with his cross little face saying 'You can make a fuss for other people; if you can't for me, it's a poor show.' I made that fuss.

Issues After Death of a Child

Immediately after Death: Care of Child

The priest took everyone out of the ward into the chapel. He kept it jolly. But I didn't want to see all these people. I wanted to know where would Lizzie be that night? Down to the Chapel of Rest then to the mortuary because her rare condition meant a post-mortem. They asked my permission. But in that stage of grief you've no emotion at all. It doesn't matter what they ask. You say yes. You're not in your own life. It's like walking alone in somebody else's life.

(Juno.)

'When Peter was alive sometimes I see him twice a day. When he die, I see him twice a day. I used to go down to the Chapel of Rest morning and evening. Just on the sofa and look at him. If I didn't do that maybe I would go to pieces.' (Mania.)

Funerals: Often a Mother's Responsibility

I wanted to pick the coffin. Five friends came to the undertakers to support me. They were a wreck, crying non-stop. I was fine. It's a cold business. They give you a catalogue. If the child's under twelve the coffin is paid for by the government. You get your hearse paid for. I said: 'I don't want what the government gives me! I want a white coffin!' I asked the hospital priest to do a funeral mass, then we organised a celebration of Lizzie's life. The kids came from school and sang her favourite hymns. 'We are the fisherman and you are the fish'. Every parent was asked and said their kid could go. They all sat sobbing in three rows. To this day those kids will talk to me in the street about Lizzie because they took part in her service. They talked about her in the celebration. They got her off to a tee! Said she was stubborn and self-willed. I didn't mind because she *was* awful! Everybody told their memories. Like how she told the priest when she was seven that she was pregnant.

(Juno.)

The day of the funeral I have the coffin open all through the service. I was standing over it. Looking at my son. Dead. Sometimes a coffin is open but people they sit. I just want to stand there with him, that was my comfort. I just stood and looked and I had it videoed as well. If I didn't have it videoed I would feel something's not fulfilled. Often I play it back. In my old age, if I still got my wits about me, I can sit and look at it. It's strange but it's comfort for me.

(Mania.)

To Mania having a headstone for Peter was even more important than the funeral. 'I worked double shifts from 7 a.m. till 9 p.m. to save the money. Finally I'd saved £850. I planned to go and pay for the headstone, then take the flowers I'd bought to put on his grave.'

The sun streamed in through her car windows. The flowers on the back seat wilted. Mania decided to reverse plans and take the flowers to the cemetery first. She left her handbag in the car. Locked the doors. Walked to the graveside. Only five minutes was she away. But in those few minutes thieves broke in through the car window, took her handbag, removed the £850. 'It is one pain after another. That was all my savings. I could have had a holiday. I needed that break. But I like to give Peter his headstone first.'

Talk and Support

> Right at the beginning is when you need to talk most. You want to keep on talking so you don't lose anything. Your memory goes on lapse. You keep thinking 'I'm going to forget what she looked like, sounded like.' Of course you don't. But we've got photos of Lizzie everywhere. Other people don't want to talk about her unless you bring it up. It's a fear of their own. I've found the best is talking to other women.
>
> (Juno.)

The taboo around death means listeners are scarce. 'When I was ready to talk the rest of the world wasn't. I tried going to Compassionate Friends, but it was a big group that intimidated me. Some had been grieving so long I didn't feel I was in their league. I'd sit there thinking: 'How do they cope? Aren't they good?' (Juno.)

> We always talked about Ben. We laughed about him a lot because he was such a card. It's nine years ago and we still do. Most people have reached out and put their arms round me and shared. I even had wonderful letters from people I'd never met. I've supported myself by writing about it. I wrote several articles and a play for the BBC.
>
> (Shirley.)

> There was so much love between us it gives me pleasure to talk about Peter. But some people, call themselves friends, especially neighbours, they turn their head the other side. I want them to talk to me. At work they all pleased to see me back . . . I say it's ok to mention his name, but one lady never said a word. Not 'how is things?' not 'how you feeling?' not 'sorry'. Why is she acting like this? Is she blaming me for my son's death?
>
> (Mania.)

Siblings' Reactions and their Importance

> Nancy collected everything she could find of Lizzie's, all her pictures toys and books and every time she looked at them she

cried. She kept asking them at school: 'What's it like to be an only child?' In the end one said 'You'll never know Nancy, you've always had a sister, even if she's not here so it will be different for you.' She accepted that. But we had a health visitor who wouldn't believe it. She kept telling me how siblings suffer. How they feel pushed out. I worry more about her now. Just as she does about me. I don't know what I'd do if she wasn't here. If I hadn't had her I would have killed myself. I wanted to die to see where she was. To see someone was looking after her. I wanted to go for five minutes but I wanted to come back. Nancy is my link to keep me on earth.

(Juno.)

The effect on the sibling isn't sufficiently understood. It was very tough on my daughter Rebecca. As a parent you have to accept your child has been loaned to you. But he was her whole family and her future. I worry more about her now. I fear for her going on tubes. I fear for her because there is violence towards women. She'd mucked around till Ben's death. Suddenly she decided to do something socially useful. She has that extra understanding of having suffered.

(Shirley.)

Anniversaries and Other Triggers
'At first toys and photos used to set me off. Now it is seasons. She died Jan 29th so Christmas Day is my worst day. It's lonely. People say it's jolly and festive but people stay to themselves, they don't visit anybody else. I'd rather go out, be in a crowd.' (Juno.)
'I used to be unable to go up to the Heath and see people flying kites. He was a great kite man. Then I kept recalling him as a small boy. I'd become tearful in the market when I saw small boys.' (Shirley.)

Spirituality
'We're Catholic so I know Lizzie is in the after-life. But my religion has gone out of the window. If there's someone up there, why do they have to let all these people suffer? Her spirit is here. When there's a crowd of children playing outside, I hear her shouting in the middle of them.' (Juno.)
'I'm not of any practising religion but I believe in something more than the here and now. I believe that ultimately there is goodness in human beings. That goodness must live on in some way. I believe in

some sense I shall see Ben one day or be with him again. His spirit is alive.' (Shirley.)

Grief

Grief over a dead child is complicated because a mother does not merely cope with the loss of a unique individual but is also seriously affected by what that child represented to her. Children may represent some or all of these:

Part of the self, part of the body

A basic source of love

The mother's connection to the future

Missed expectations

Some of the mother's own talents or characteristics

A loss of the mother's power, competency

Feelings of Amputation, Loss of Self, Loss of Competence

'Even though Lizzie was definitely a separate person from me, I've got a piece missing. There's a whole piece of me gone missing.' (Juno.)

'When your child is gone you sit and think, now was I a good mother? You try not to blame yourself.' (Mania.)

Only a woman who has lost a child can understand. *We all feel we have the mark of Cain.* I feel there is a part of me that is completely dead. In many ways it makes you hard and tough. My friend's sister was dying of cancer. She was quite old. I was brutal. 'Well she's not eighteen is she?' I said. When I heard ambulances it used to cheer me up. Because it was somebody's pain. But I used to think it's not Ben. It can't ever be Ben. Nobody can hurt him again. I've lost part of myself in losing him. I feel more competence not less. Nobody can ever take anything away from me again. What can you do to someone who's lost their only son?

(Shirley.)

Mothers and Fathers Grieve in Different Ways

I discovered that in general mothers tend to express their grief more than fathers, regardless of the age of the child. Bereaved fathers appear to express less emotion, but it is unclear whether they actually experience less emotion or whether their grief is not given expression. 'Ben's father grieved openly. I was envious of him. I remember hearing him howl with grief. A mother's grief is probably different from a father's because you always feel responsible for your child's life, that feeling of obligation.' (Shirley.)

I saw many fathers withdraw from the trauma of seeing their children die from a long-drawn-out illness. Many more were adamant they did not want to talk about death or grief. Juno's husband was typical.

Tommy showed emotion in intensive care. He's never shown any since. He loved her, they were close, he must miss her, but he never says. He just gets up, goes to work, comes home, gets up. That's his whole life. Doesn't show his grief. That's men the world over. In one way he hasn't changed at all. He's still placid, still on one level. Tommy talks about Lizzie in the past tense. Concentrates on what she *did*. He never says the word 'dead'. He never talks to me about how he feels. He's happy so he should be left. Whether it will come back to him in years to come I don't know. He's open with Nancy. He'll always answer her questions to the point but he won't have a long conversation.

Other fathers' comments echo Tommy's:

Of course I felt the loss of our youngest. Any father would. She was a smasher. Seven with the head of seventeen! Red curls. There she is on the picture. But talking about it didn't help me. I'd never been a one to talk. I said to my girlfriend: 'Talking isn't going to bring her back. The bastard who ran her down on his motorbike, he's the one to bloody talk to!' Crying isn't me, and it wouldn't bring her back.

(British father, partnered, forty.)

Julie crashed off the slide in the big guys' pool. Shouldn't have been on it. God her head and face were mashed up. It was the first time I cried since I was a kid. Not then. Not at the time. Too much to do. I had the other kids to see to. But later on this camping trip. I took the two little guys. Julie should have been with us. Would have been her first Wilderness Camp. She'd have loved it, little toughie! Doing the barbecue, all of us singing, nobody mentioning Julie, that's when I realised I was kinda sobbing.

(American father, single parent, thirty-five.)

Anne and I couldn't grieve together over Tim's death because we went about it in such different ways. She was a great Mom so it cut her up. It wasn't that I didn't feel a great deal, but I never felt like showing it. She cried all the time. I tried to get her to *do* more, I felt that was a way to get over it.

(Canadian father, married, thirty.)

Sometimes grieving in different ways means couples cannot support each other. Sometimes that lack of understanding can break up the relationship between parents. Researchers Feeley and Gottlieb point to this particular risk of marital breakdown. They identified four factors in this lack of verbal understanding:

1. A decrease in the overall communication
2. An inability to discuss the death with one another
3. Difficulty in sharing feelings about the child's death with one another
4. Inability of the marital partners to actively listen to and empathise with one another.[15]

Grief: Getting Over It, or Not?

According to psychoanalytic theory, 'normal' grief follows a set process. First comes shock and numbness and a sense of denial. Next comes realisation which brings intense pain. Finally, suggest theorists, there should be resolution and the reorganisation of life.

I've read all that stages of grief stuff. I've read everything on death and dying. I can relate to what they say but none of it is me. Mothers don't get over their grief. They don't do it in stages. You just cross over and go back. It's like a circle, when you go round it once, you go back round it again. You do your own thing. I felt guilty over the pain, that it wouldn't go away. Now I accept it won't.

(Juno.)

Many psychoanalysts and bereavement counsellors believe the process of grieving should be 'worked through' in what they call a 'reasonable time'. They regard failure to do this as pathological. Too much grief or too little is seen as a failure to adapt. People, however, grieve in ways that do not accord to patterns. Some suppress or inhibit grief for months or years. Others continue pining or yearning for the lost person long after those around them may feel is 'appropriate'. The truth is that for mothers I talked to these patterns overlap. There is no sequence. Often there is no end to grief.

I am critical of this pathological model of grief and loss (as are researchers Wortman and Silver). I see a paradox in the theory. The assumption that the bereaved person should experience certain feelings at a certain time, that failure to do so represents denial and repression which in turn is judged abnormal puts heavy expectations on women about what is and what is not 'normal' functioning. It also conditions expectations people have of one another in times of crisis.

Although the literature suggests that those who immediately express signs of deep distress will adapt more successfully to life, while those who are unable to let go will have severe problems later on because that suppressed grief will resurface in a problematic way; new evidence suggests the opposite. I saw several women who showed great grief early on but were also depressed later. Mothers whose children died in infancy, who failed to exhibit early distress, did *not* necessarily have greater subsequent difficulties.[16] Their lack of immediate grief was often one way of coping not only with their own loss, but with the loss of those around them for whom they still continued to care. Shirley's case is an excellent example:

> After I'd been fighting the court case for two years someone said you'll have to face up to grieving because you've never done it. But I couldn't let somebody kill my son and sit back and say it doesn't matter. If you've lost a child, you've got to know the truth, it's a need. That's the lump of me that's gone, missing, dead. But there are others to think of too. My responsibility. As a mother I haven't got over my grief. I don't think I would ever want to. Because that would mean I had forgotten the person. They would no longer be part of your life.

Similarly the idea that prolonged immersion in loss is an instance of 'chronic grieving' and may similarly be labelled maladaptive again takes little account of individual character or of gender differences in response to grief.

Changes in a Bereaved Mother's Character

> I used to be very quiet, introverted until we lost Lizzie. Nothing can ever happen to hurt me as much as that. Now nothing else can ever really matter. There's no point being scared of anything. The worst thing in your life has happened. So now I'm self-assertive. A strong person. I always speak my mind.
>
> (Juno.)

I'm much harder. I have an antipathy to moaners who moan about trivia. I feel I have to get on with life. Death was the most real thing. Someone I loved was taken from me for no reason. Life is a gift and we have to appreciate every day we are alive and use it to the best of our ability. I feel I am now living for two. I have a duty to make the best use of my life because Ben can't enjoy it. In a sense I'm more positive, more invulnerable. I want to see more children having adventures, not less. That's why I started the Ben Bryant Trust to give disadvanataged youngsters the chance to learn to sail in safety. To give them an alternative to trouble with the law! To show them how to live!'

(Shirley.)

I'm a strong woman now. People at the funeral said they didn't know where I got the strength to stand calmly and look into his coffin. Where do I get the strength to carry on? My strength comes from Peter. I have got it from him to carry on a good life.

(Mania.)

Do Bereaved Mothers Fear Dying?
'No, not any more. If Lizzie can go the way she did, bear her illness, then I can do it. But I don't want to go suddenly. I want time to say goodbye. I have such good memories of Lizzie's funeral that I want to plan my own.' (Juno.)

'I don't fear death in the way I did before. Which is not to say I want to die. But I feel I might be with Ben again. That he has gone before. So I try to live every day for today. Live each day more fully. To have peace in my life.' (Shirley.)

Lichman, Wortman and Williams (1987) who studied the long term effects of the loss of a child (or a spouse) in a motor accident, found that a great many of those bereaved were still profoundly distressed seven years later. They argued that it is extremely difficult to fix a time for grieving to be resolved and suggested that a good many people are *never* resolved to their loss.[17]

An ending to grief is a lie to which we all conspire. Mothers live the lie with strength and spirit. They laugh or they rage. Their life goes on but bereavement never stops.

Chapter Eight

IMAGE, SEX AND THE LANGUAGE OF CANCER

There are two languages attached to cancer.

The language of the medical profession. Coldly clinical. Mainly male. Rich in rhetoric. Low in understanding. The language of the body. Symbolising shape. Signed in sexual expression. Attuned to appearance. Every illness intensely internalised. Not women's fault that when cancer writes itself upon the body, it is the body that speaks. Speaks a woman's language.

Listen first to a male surgeon's words. A rodomontade about the body. Bodies with cancer. Desire diseased.

'Bin that breast. That's what we must do. Disease, it is full of disease. There has been a malignant infiltration into your body. Breasts like that need binning or burning. Don't worry, you won't be stuck with that one much longer!'

Breasts need binning. Malignant infiltrations. Breasts need burning. Suitable for incinerators. Cold and clinical. Male medical tongue. (For clinical read brutal.)

Listen to the patient.

I couldn't believe he was speaking to me like that about my body. He just kept staring hard at my tits. He never once looked at my face. It suddenly reminded me of the awful time fifteen years ago when I had my abortion. The surgeon at the time said to me that 'they'd incinerate what wasn't wanted'! Then when he saw my face, I was gulping and crying, he said, 'There, there, it was just a joke.' But he had been talking about my body and what could have been my baby. Now that I've got cancer this one talked about my breast as if that wasn't wanted either!

(Penny, woman with cancer, forty-four.)

Penny is not the only woman with cancer in receipt of this kind of anti-body language. Listen some more.

'The consultant didn't say what I had, he said what he'd do. He handled my left breast really roughly between his finger and thumb. Then he said: "That tit is tainted. We'll have that one off. We've got places to put it. Better there than on your body."' (Ali, British. Breast cancer. Forty-two.)

Tits that are tainted into the incinerator. Best places to put them. Better than on the body.

Male medical language asks us to think of the parts of our body as expendable, exploitable, unconnected to the self. 'I worked a lifetime learning to accept my breasts, to believe they were beautiful, and now I am told I should just accept having them cut off.' (Woman with breast cancer, 1991.)[1]

Two weeks before her fiftieth birthday, writer Audre Lorde was told by her doctor she now had liver cancer, metastasised from the breast cancer for which she had had a mastectomy six years previously. In her cancer journal which she kept for three years, she wrote:

Twenty-two hours of most days I don't believe I have liver cancer. Most days. Those other two hours of the day are pure hell, and there's so much work I have to do in my head in those two hours, too, through all the terror and uncertainties. I wish I knew a doctor I could really trust to talk it all over with. Am I making the right decision? I know I have to listen to my body. If there's one thing I've learned from all the work I've done since my mastectomy, it's that I must listen keenly to the messages my body sends. But sometimes they are contradictory.[2]

Contradictions are evident in cancer, and in the language depicting it. No plain brown wrapping round women's bodies. No plain brown messages. Contradictory communiqués.

To take the cancer facts first. The facts are straightforward. They bring dis-ease.

At the turn of the century, cancer of all kinds accounted for only one twentieth of the total deaths in the USA. In 1900 cancer accounted for only 4 per cent of deaths in America. Now it accounts for 23 per cent. It is the second biggest killer amongst all diseases; it threatens to overtake heart disease and become the biggest killer; one out of three Americans will have to face some form of cancer at some time in their lives. Of these two out of three will die from the disease.[3]

In the UK cancer affects one in three of the population and approximately 75 per cent of those cancers are estimated by epidemiologists to be dietically or environmentally induced. The food we eat and the pollution that we inflict upon ourselves (or that which is inflicted upon us) are the most common contributory factors. Breast cancer is one of the cancers where an inherited predisposition (having a close female relative who developed the disease before the menopause) puts women at a considerably increased risk.[4]

It is breast cancer therefore which has become a rapidly rising women's issue. Hardly surprising. In the USA an estimated one in nine women will be diagnosed with breast cancer every year, where it is the leading dealer of death for women between the ages of thirty-five and forty-five (1991 figures). In Canada, breast cancer remains one of the three big cancer killers. For women it has long been number one, ahead of lung and colon cancer. Lung cancer deaths, which are rising dramatically, now compete for first place.[5]

The mortality rate for breast cancer in North America has remained stable at between 33 and 50 per cent (depending on how statistics are calculated) while the incidence appears to be increasing.[6] The average age of the onset of breast cancer is dropping with more and more women under thirty being diagnosed.[7]

Breast cancer, if detected early enough, is considered one of the more 'survivable' cancers in both the USA and UK. In the UK women with early cancers who are treated promptly have a 30 per cent chance of cure and a good long-term survival rate: 84 per cent will still be alive after five years. In Canada survival rates from breast cancer are 74 per cent. It is, however, the sheer number of deaths annually that is staggering.

So many women.

Set against North America's one in nine women, here in the UK each year 25,000 women are told they have breast cancer, a rate of 500 a week. In the UK breast cancer is the major form of cancer among women, among the highest incidence rate in the world. One in twelve women will develop it at some time in their life. The UK also has the highest death rate in the world: 28 per 100,000 women;

and breast cancer is the major cause of premature death in women aged between thirty-five and fifty-four.

In the UK breast cancer in 1992 accounted for:

26,000 new cases per year

16,000 deaths per year

5,000 deaths of women under sixty-five

One in five of all cancers among women.[8]

Frightening statistics.

Behind each statistic there is an individual woman whose life and happiness is threatened when she hears a cancer diagnosis.

Yes, throwing tits into the incinerator is big business. Yet it is a secretive business. An issue for women, that women have difficulty in discussing. Firstly because few people talk about it at all, secondly because of the rhetoric of medical discussion. Medical language, which has helped construct the taboo around all deaths, is at its most outrageous in its labelling of cancer. As several doctors showed (in Chapter Three), medicine's semantic stigmatisation of what is after all merely a disease as 'evil', 'malignant', or 'the scourge' is *not* helpful to women who suffer from it.

Rarely is cancer given its name.

Researching in Italy, I discovered women talk about *male* meaning 'evil'. Many Italian doctors frequently inform a patient's family that she has cancer but infrequently inform the patient. In British hospitals, male doctors systematically tell women they have a 'malignancy'; women who received this information reported that they had no idea whether or not they had cancer.

A contemporary consultant, American, male, a surgical expert on death by cancer, recalls his predecessors referring to cancer as 'the stinking death'. He explains: 'Until mastectomy became a common operation less than a hundred years ago, the most dreaded complication of breast malignancy was not death but the fetid running sores it produced as a hapless woman's chest wall was digested away. This is precisely why the ancients referred to "karkinoma" as the "stinking death".'[9]

Ah, the ancients. Not frightfully enlightened.

Our contemporary consultant, American, male, our surgical expert on death by cancer, is surely wiser. Perspicacious. Vigilant to women's feelings. Honest. Open. Would call a disease by its name. Would allow hapless women to know what is what. Let's read his words again.

Ah! I see: not 'cancer' but 'breast malignancy'.

Perhaps history helped him. Let us move forward, away from the

ancients. In the late eighteenth century, Giovanni Morgagni, author of
a landmark text of pathological anatomy, described the cancers of his
patients as a 'very filthy disease'. Two centuries later Sherwin B.
Nuland assures us that '*malignant tumours* continued to be viewed as
repugnant sources of self-loathing and decay, a humiliating abomina-
tion to be concealed behind euphemisms and lies.'[10] (My emphasis.)

There is no cancer. There are only euphemisms and lies.

What do the lies lead to? What effects does misnaming have on
the women?

The surgeon is knowledgeable.

'Women with breast cancer withdrew from friends, secluded
themselves at home, and lived their final months as recluses, sometimes even from their own families.'[11]

Ah! But that was the Past. Terrible things happened to women in
the Past. Women with cancer. Women approaching a 'stinking
death'. Surely not now.

The surgeon is hesitant. Puts on his ritual gloves. Straightens his
mask. Ponders on the Present.

'As recently as the period of my training . . . I saw a few such
women who had finally been prevailed upon to come to the clinic
because their situations had become intolerable.'[12]

I am sure in his upright clinically concerned way this consultant
(American, male, an expert on cancer) faced the truth and helped his
patients face it.

'We still hesitate to utter the word "cancer"' in the presence of a
patient or family assaulted by it, the residual heritage of its odious
connections is the one most difficult for our generation to
expunge.'[13]

'Assaulted'? Did he say 'assaulted'? In this violent prophetic disclosure of disease, women who contract it are indeed assaulted.
Demoralised not merely by the disease itself, but by the knowledge
that their particular disease is treated as sinister. Their bodies bale-
ful. Their habits heinous. Patients deemed putrid are labelled 'the
cancer victim'. The central structure of the cancer cell is known as
'the evil-eye nucleus'. As surgeon Nuland acknowledged: 'Of all the
diseases they treat, cancer is the one that surgeons have given the
specific designation of "The Enemy".'[14]

Under such tirades how can women believe they have merely
contracted an *illness*? They can't. They don't. Listen to this woman's
account.

I was forty-three years old on the morning when I discovered my cancer. My husband of nearly twenty years had recently left me, and I was still staggering from the shame of the rejection and the new, draining struggle of surviving as a woman alone, with two teenage children . . . Cancer: it's a terrible word. The very thought of cancer gives rise in nearly all of us to fear and loathing. It is a sinister thing that grows and consumes, mutilates and kills . . . It has become the core of a deep anger in me. Cancer – still our modern metaphor for evil.[15]

(Judith Brady, American, forty-three, 1991.)

It is the language and the images of evil that often lead to avoidance. In discussing what he calls the 'malevolence of cancer', Nuland, our surgeon (only one of many similar) cannot get out from under this language. Cancer, he roars, is 'this dreadful courier of death'. The twin characteristics of 'autonomy' and 'anaplasia' define the modern medical understanding of cancer. When Nuland, as a modern medical scientist, uses the word 'autonomy', he visualises its cells behaving 'like the members of a barbarian horde run amok – leaderless and undirected, but with a single-minded purpose: to plunder everything within reach'.[16] By anaplasia is meant 'without form' so the anaplastic cell gives birth to anaplastic offspring. It has an unlimited capacity to grow and generate new tumours, so Nuland and his colleagues see it as 'immortalised'.[17]

Cancer is amoral because it knows no rules, and immoral because it knows no purpose other than to destroy life. Cancer has been immortalised as the assailant.

Women become impaired and impotent. Women are scared, sapped and silenced. As much by this fire and brimstone battering as by a disease more sanely viewed as one of altered maturation, the result of a multistage process of growth and development having gone awry.

But surgical language is *not* sane. Nuland's terminology, characteristic of male medical depictions of cancer, is savage and metaphoric. Serves only to encumber and distort the responses of women who must deal with the illness. Listen to his apocalyptic scenario of cancer as plague, cancer as enemy, cancer as evil invader of women's bodies.

Cancer, far from being a clandestine foe, is in fact berserk with the malicious exuberance of killing. The disease pursues a continuous, uninhibited, circumferential, barn-burning expedition of destructiveness, in which it heeds no rules, follows no commands,

and explodes all resistance in a homicidal riot of devastation . . .
The cells of a cancer are wicked in ways far beyond what is
implied by the scientific connotation of the word 'malignant'.
Malevolent, in fact, says it better, because it bears the implication
of an element of ill will.[18]

The vindictive vituperation of much modern medical terminology
which views cancer as 'murderous cells' with a 'murderous infiltration', has its roots in the descriptions of early Greek male physicians.
They based the name of the hard swellings and ulcerations which
they commonly saw in the breast or protruding from the rectum or
vagina on the evidence of their eyes and fingers. To distinguish them
from ordinary swellings called 'oncos', they used the term 'karkinos'
or crab derived from the Indo-European root meaning 'hard'.
'Karkinoma' designated a malignant tumorous growth. At the time
karkinoma patients were said to be 'melancholy'!

With I suspect good reason.

Nuland recalls the second century AD description of cancer by
Galen, the foremost interpreter and codifier of Greek medicine. One
of his heroes. (Not one of mine.)

The appearance of this creeping, infiltrating stony mass, ulcerated
at its centre, which he so often saw in the breasts of women, is
'just like a crab's legs extending outward from every part of its
body'. And it is not only the legs that are digging farther and
deeper into the flesh of its victim – the center, too, is eroding its
way directly through her.[19]

In recent years military metaphors, as writer Susan Sontag pointed
out, have infused all aspects of the medical situation today, focusing
on AIDS as well as cancer. Disease is seen as an invasion of alien
organisms, to which the body responds with its own military operations, such as the mobilising of immunological 'defences'.

The language of chemotherapy has become the language of
aggression.

Abuse of the military metaphor implements the way dreaded diseases are envisaged as alien 'others'. The move from demonisation of
illness to the attribution of fault to the patient becomes inevitable.
Susan Sontag, who suffered from cancer, shows how myth and
superstition have long prevented patients thinking clearly about
their disease.[20]

In past years, tuberculosis was often regarded sentimentally as an

enhancement of identity. It was seen as a disease that struck the talented, the hypersensitive, the over-passionate. Today these are
thoroughly discredited beliefs. But similar 'fictions of responsibility'
and of a patient's characterological disposition to cancer have taken
their place.

'Cancer victims' are credited (or blamed) for their repressed anger,
their unexpressed sexual feelings, or their psychological and spiritual defeat. Even though the word 'victim' may be used conjointly
with the word 'responsibility', even though 'victim' implies innocence, by the inexorable logic which governs all relational terms,
innocence soon suggests guilt. Women are made to feel guilty for the
illness they suffer from.[21]

This is not to be countenanced.

Male military metaphors massively contribute to the stigmatisation of certain illnesses and by extension of those who suffer from
them. When Susan Sontag was a cancer patient, what particularly
enraged her 'was seeing how much the very reputation of this illness
added to the suffering of those who have it'. Many fellow patients
during her initial hospitalisation, and those she met while a
chemotherapy outpatient in several American and French hospitals,
displayed disgust and shame at their disease.[22]

The metaphoric trappings that deformed the experience of having
cancer had very real consequences for the women she met during
her period as a patient and for the women I have met during my
period of research.

They make it harder for women to lift the taboo around death.

They inhibit women from seeking treatment early enough.

They restrict women from making greater or more persistent
efforts to get competent aid.

They encourage irrational fright about useful measures such as
chemotherapy.

They lead to unproductive self-blame.

They encourage the idea that cancer equals death.

What metaphoric harassment always does lead to is what Erving
Goffman called a 'spoiled identity'.

Those with cancer see themselves as blemished. Disgraced. To be
avoided. Those without cancer see cancer victims as blemished.
Disgraced. To be avoided.[23]

Women patients need to regard cancer as a disease. A serious disease. But only a disease. Not the serpent's tooth. It is not a curse. It
is not a punishment. It should not be a matter for embarrassment or
a signal for shame.

It should not lead to these accounts.

My family saw my breast cancer as a stigma. I went to see my mother a few days before the mastectomy. While I was there I got on the phone and told everyone that I had cancer. I needed to mobilise support. My mother said she hadn't told anybody. She said she didn't realise you *could* talk about breast cancer. Once I told people in her village, like the Vicar, and a cousin in the choir, my name was put down on the prayer list. People knew then what I had but they wouldn't say the word.

(Merle, Health Visitor. Breast cancer. Forty-seven.)

After the first breast was cut off, my sister and mother unwillingly talked about it because I told them they had to. We're not talkers in our family. Nasties go under the bed. I needed to scream aloud and have someone listen. Then I was told the second breast would have to go. I needed to discuss it sensibly. I knew there was almost no time. The surgeon panicked me. He intimidated me but he didn't discuss any choices. 'I can't take the lump. It isn't wise. You must have that one off! And fast!' He pulled my shirt up and down without looking at my face. I wasn't a human to him. He did not treat my body like he would want his body treated!

My sister was abroad. My Mum said it made her cry to talk about that kind of thing. 'It's such a nasty word. Try not to use the word when your Dad is about.' I was psychologically shattered. I'd have drowned if I hadn't had the children. I felt it would be wrong to talk to them, they were fourteen and seven. No adults came near me. I felt I had the plague. He took the second breast off and I returned to work where people hoped I was better but shied away at breaktime. There are only two women in our office. The architects are all men. One of the two women shunned me as if she was frightened she'd catch it! You're the first person who's wanted me to talk about cancer.

(Anne, thirty-eight, Architect's assistant. Breast cancer.)

It should not lead to these accounts. Or to thousands like them. But it does. It does because male medical consultants maintain and feed upon that 'residual heritage of odious connections'. Dr Karl Menninger assures us that 'the very word "cancer" is said to kill some patients who would not have succumbed (so quickly) to the malignancy from which they suffer.' Dr Menninger exhorts fellow doctors to avoid plastering patients 'with a damning index tab'. (For

Damning Index Tab, popular abbreviation DIT, please read cancer).

If the tag, or tab, caught on, eminent surgeons would not have to label women as patients with cancer but merely label breasts as DIT TITS.

Dr Menninger, medical paternalist, strong on secrecy, avows unctuously: 'Our function is to help these people, not to further afflict them.'[24]

But women are afflicted. Afflicted further than they need be, by secrecy and medical 'protection'. 'I lived with my mother. She was over seventy and had Parkinson's. I did most of the caring. We used to talk about everything. Then I developed breast cancer. I knew I had to keep it a secret from her. Everyone in her generation thinks of it as the Plague.' (Woman, forty-four. Breast cancer. 1994.)

I know I've got cancer though the doctors never used the word. I felt too overwhelmed in the hospital to ask. Doctors don't seem to have much time for us patients. I don't know what they've told my sons, but no one is using the word in the family. I suppose it is to protect me, or maybe themselves. I know what I've got, and I'd like to sort out things openly before I die. But I can't seem to break through this constant: 'Don't talk like that Mum! You've years yet! You'll see us all out!'

(Woman. Cancer. Sixty-eight. 1994.)

Writer Audre Lorde, whose experience as a black woman suffering and fighting cancer for years led her to spearhead the construction of a feminist political discourse on cancer, acknowledges that: 'cancer survivors are expected to be silent out of misguided concerns for others' feelings of guilt or despair, or out of a belief in the myth that there can be self-protection through secrecy.'[25]

There is no real protection through myth or mystery. Self-healing cannot come through misguided secrecy.

As long as there is no cancer, only euphemisms and lies, death and its diseases will remain taboo. Euphemisms for cancer, lies to cancer patients, lies by cancer patients to families and friends, all these are a gauge of how formidable is the task of coming to terms with death.

'Outside the radiation lab or the doctor's office, we [women] are invisible to each other, and we begin to be invisible to ourselves. We begin to doubt whatever power we once knew we had, and once we doubt our power, we stop using it. We rob our comrades, our lovers, our friends, and ourselves of ourselves.'[26]

Silence seems to offer a safer course, but the silent are powerless. AIDS activists have recognised this social reality in a way that women with cancer have not yet managed. Ironic in the face of massive numbers of women's deaths from cancer as compared to women's deaths from AIDS.

Women with cancer need visibility. Women with cancer need to regard it as a disease. A serious disease, but only a disease. It is not a curse. It is not divine justice, or execution for a crime. Cancer is a punishing illness but it is not a punishment. It should not be a matter for embarrassment or a signal for shame. It should not lead to these accounts. It should not lead to such distress.

But it does.

It does because women doctors too are recipients of that residual heritage of odious connections. Shy away from cancer. Hide behind malignancy. Cuddle up inside a euphemism.

There is no cancer. There are only euphemisms and lies.

Cancer is a conjuring word. Perhaps that is why my doctor did not use the word cancer when explaining my condition. Instead she told me, 'Your results indicate a gross malignancy on the lower portion of your colon.' I couldn't believe what she was saying.

Is she telling me that I have cancer?

'Your tests indicate that the tumour is several centimeters and is located in the lower segment of the bowel,' she continued, drawing a pencil sketch of the colon which to me looked like a curvy snake poised to strike.

Is she telling me I have cancer?[27]

(Janice Coombs Epps.)

What do women doctors have to say?

Doctors don't always use the word 'cancer'. Perhaps we are being protective by saying growth or tumour. We all do that until we are quite sure about a diagnosis. I don't know whether it is just to protect us or to make it easier. The word 'cancer' still has um, er, well it has connotations that are more serious, more depressing, we step aside from those things. Rather go for something more hopeful. So we may actually use something like 'your leukaemia' rather than 'your cancer' because you feel that could be fought with, it is more positive.

(Eileen Baildam, Consultant.)

I used to tell patients they had gross malignancies or I'd say words like 'dangerous' or even 'possibly terminal'. It was partly my training and partly my own fears and worrying about the patients' fears. Trying to explain it to them a bit at a time. Then I got breast cancer myself. I knew just how important an open honest diagnosis is so that I could get the right support.

(Dr Helen Hoffman.)

Malignancy is a general term for disease which is not benign. A growth is a tumour and you can have a malignant tumour or a benign tumour. It's true that lots of doctors say to patients that they've got a tumour, or even a growth, and in my view that's protecting themselves. It's not protecting themselves in case they've made an error, but protecting themselves emotionally. It's telling the patient half the truth. It is sometimes very difficult to tell the patients the whole truth. Some are not ready for it in one session so it's a question of going back and going back. So they get it in little pieces. When one tells parents their child has got leukaemia, one should always say that it is cancer of the blood. So that they know it's cancer from the word go. I actually tape interviews so that the family can take it away with them and play it back. Otherwise sometimes they go away without hearing the word cancer. But some doctors do want to protect themselves and they may not always put it in words the patient understands.

(Dr Eve Jones.)

Habits like this, language that misleads, that implies a particular disease is shameful, makes realistic conversation about cancer and possible death even harder for women.

Fortunately some women doctors and psychologists like Stephanie Oates, a psychologist at a cancer centre, run group discussions where cancer is talked of in a gentler manner.

I felt we had achieved something when we made people giggle about the way others talk about it. One woman said somebody phoned her up and said: 'I hear you've got cancer! I do hope you have a happy end!' Another woman reported that a friend came up to her and said: 'You're so courageous because if I had what you've got I'd shoot myself!' No one mentions the name. Finally we managed to giggle about it. We are not the problematists. It's them out there. It's their lack of understanding. They've got the problem!

Pat Kitto, counsellor and healer at a cancer centre, tries to deal with that problem:

> Cancer is the most hated word in the dictionary. It always has been. When my mother had colon cancer, the doctor wouldn't use the word. He said: 'We'll just take your Mum in.' With my patients I try and open it up. We do imaging and visualisations, and visualise the cancer in the body but not necessarily as something vicious eating the body up. We don't think of women with cancer as 'dying people' but as living women.

Pat Kitto is one of many healers who believes that sometimes the impossible becomes possible.

> One day a woman came into the natural health centre with a lump on her breast. She had always been frightened of cancer. She was due to be taken into hospital to have a biopsy and probably removal of the breast. Sometimes even when they are not absolutely sure, they say it's better to take it off. Men are very good at taking things off women. We visualised the lump and actually saw it disappearing. She worked very hard on this. She went into hospital. Some time later I received this extraordinary letter: 'Well, I'm out of hospital. The doctor said "Let's see where this lump is." They couldn't find it!' This is not as unusual as you might suppose.

Kitto suggested that women respond more quickly than do men to ideas of visualisation.

> When you tell a woman to visualise making an omelette, they see the pan and the eggs before they do it. Whereas men often tell me they don't know what visualisation means. On the whole women are more connected to their bodies. For women having parts of their body cut off is not mechanical; with breast cancer their image is 'This is where I cuddled my child', or 'This is where I fed my child'.

The language of cancer is written on the body. Women's bodies. Breast cancer particularly has profound implications for the sex that is locked into an image taboo as well as a death taboo.

Listen to the women. Facing the stereotypes.

> I'm slightly vain, worrying about when it will be time to stop dyeing the grey hair. But appearance has come up much more

since the mastectomy. Obviously being a health professional my main worry was about whether it had spread. How long would I have? Hard, hard worry for Dan, my partner. I worried about his reaction to my possible dying.

Then I got sadder than I suspected about losing the breast. What would I look like? How would Dan feel? Those feelings started to come up after the operation. To start with I felt euphoric. For six weeks I went around showing everyone who wanted to have a look. Then when I got the prosthesis it hit me! A terribly insensitive woman did it. I went right down. I felt much worse about my shape than I ever thought I would. I hated walking past a mirror. So much of what I've read is about how you were not how you are now. People want you to feel you can look exactly the same as you once were if you wear a prosthesis. But you aren't the same. The best article I read was in *MS* magazine which had a full page photograph of a one-breasted woman who had tattooed a rose over her scar and on the other side was a long poem: How to make love to a one-breasted woman. They were beautiful. It was good to see photos that were women as we are not nice ladies with two breasts in typical poses. I have to come to terms with what I am. I have to be told the truth. To know that I am not the same. But women are not helped to come to those terms. Women in hospital who have had mastectomies are advised to wear falsies under their nighties. To take them home and lie in bed with their partners with this bit of foam. To make other people comfortable!

(Merle, Health visitor. Breast cancer.)

Other people's comfort. That's the crux. Prosthesis or no prosthesis? That's one decision. Society that sets a priority on a model of female beauty that is small-waisted, slim-figured, and above all two-breasted, distorts this decision. The fact that our culture surrounds cancer with shock and silence means that women, taught to nurture other people's feelings, may do just that. May disregard – or not even be aware of – their own.

'The reason I'll get one is to avoid questions from strangers. I'd like to say "Yes I've had a mastectomy", but I'm afraid I'll put the other person in a difficult position. Guys are the worst. They just can't take it.' (Emma, Canadian, thirty-six. Breast cancer.)

I wanted to be the kind of woman who could do without a prosthesis. Sometimes I am. Quite often I don't wear it. But I have to be selective. In the swimming pool I wear a special cossy. Whereas before I would take my costume off in the changing room, now I don't. I know that other people will be shocked. I intend to do it soon, but shall make sure I do it around my friends. When I was nursing, every time I saw a woman with a mastectomy, my feeling was compassion, not shock horror. I have to believe that other women's feelings will also be compassionate.

(Merle.)

Workplace ideology influences women's decisions.

I always wear it at work. I do so because I don't want my one breast to be the first thing people see. Even though a lot of my clients know, I don't want to be 'the mastectomy woman' first. Even though I will do political stuff around cancer, I don't want it to be my career. It mustn't be my whole person

(Merle.)

Ironically health professionals, more than most, feel clients should not be expected to worry about their health. 'I'm in a job where my role is to see how other people are. Clients can't take me on. I work almost entirely with women and breast cancer is what most women dread. It's our biggest killer so it's realistic to dread it!' (Merle.)

How do women deal with sensitivity over shape? Merle went on a Buddhist retreat.

A lot of Buddhist talk and thought is about death and impermanence so it was very useful. I did a huge angry drawing about my trauma about shape. My prosthesis is called 'True Life' (the name of the company). It was so utterly revolting, that falseness, I drew my True Life pinned by a dagger through the door of the surgical appliances office! Then I cried for three days and felt much better!

Friends' support. Partner's support. They can be critical in restoring women's self-esteem. 'My women friends were fantastic, cooking, giving me showers, washing my hair, just being there for me. They cared that I was suffering. I shall remember them almost like a prayer because I felt so held.' (Merle.)

Working in Italy, where for Italian women it would be madness not to wear a falsie, made me an outcast. Normality to them is looking well-groomed, well-dressed, and having two tits. I had my mastectomy four weeks ago and I'm still wearing a shirt with everything flat. I will get one so that my clothes hang correctly but it won't do anything for my femininity. I've always felt my femininity was precarious. I'm boyish, don't have a fully curvy body. But I have the support of a man who makes it clear every minute that he's not in love with me because I've got tits and a bum. I've just joined a group of Italian women who all have mastectomies, their support is great. Only our views on shape differ.

(Marie, thirty-six. Breast cancer. Rome.)

In Italy, the task of acquiring a prosthesis on health benefit is challenging. Listen to Marie, some weeks later.

The Italian bureaucracy for poor women is terrible. If you want the falsie and the bra that matches it on the National Health you go to your doctor, get a certificate which labels you as a certain kind of invalid. Then you get a second certificate from the surgeon who says it is true he operated. Then you go to a chemist, show them your papers and try the things on. Finally you get an estimate which you give to the health authorities who spend weeks, even months, deciding whether they are willing to pay for it. Why can't I just show them the scar and say: 'Come on! I'm not trying to rob you of this bloody falsie!'

If keeping up appearances is a hard issue, sexuality is harder.

It was six months after the operation. I met him at a dance. We dated for two months, I never took my clothes off. When I felt safe I told him. His face went blank but he said all the right things and held me tight. Our first night in bed, he tried but I knew it wouldn't work. He was obviously repelled. He kept touching my face and not looking at my body. God knows who he was fucking but it wasn't me!

(Melanie, American, thirty-four. Breast cancer.)

I had broken up with Julia my lover before the operation. I had those scars to heal as well as my breasts. Friends kept saying 'Try a club'. I loved dancing. I summoned up my courage. I took a book with me, not knowing how a one-breasted woman cruises. The lesbians in the club seemed incredibly young. None of them would have had mastectomies. They wouldn't understand. A really sexy woman came over and I flinched. She said she'd just read that book and wasn't it good? We talked all evening. She didn't pressure me to dance. I was scared rigid at her feeling my flatness. She called me a week later. We've taken it slowly, and last night we made love. She was amazingly gentle and asked if she could kiss both my breasts. 'I don't have any! Can't you see I don't have any?' I said angrily. 'You do to me. You feel fine to me,' she said.

(Sharon, British, thirty-eight. Breast cancer.)

We'd always had a good relationship and Dan was there when the bandages came off. Sexually he finds it much less difficult than me. I got terribly upset when I first saw him with an erection. I was distressed and thought this is freaky. That I felt the freak. He obviously didn't feel I was freaky. What was good was that he became quite assertive. My view of men in that situation is that they're usually very sensitive and try and take it at the woman's pace. He wasn't having any of that! I needed someone to show me I was still desirable. He was brilliant. Now I can sit and look at my top naked in front of a mirror with Dan watching me.

(Merle.)

When photographer Jo Spence was diagnosed with breast cancer, she courageously began to document through self-portraits, her illness and mortality, her internalised feelings about her body, the preciousness of her breasts, and her need for some kind of control even through surgery.

I looked at one of her photographs from her exhibition: 'From The Cancer Project' (taken in collaboration with Terry Dennett, 1982). It was a self-portrait in dark glasses, naked to the waist, with one breast marked in bold letters: 'Property of Jo Spence'. In a caption attached to the photograph called 'Framing my breast the night before going to Hospital', she explained: 'When I realised I was liable to lose a breast I decided I wanted a photograph of the spot that had been actually marked up for amputation. I wrote on the breast, 'Property of Jo Spence'. I took it into hospital like a magic fetish to protect me – to remind me that I had some right over my body.'

From the first diagnosis of cancer, when she refused a mastectomy in favour of lumpectomy supplemented by traditional Chinese medicine, for ten years she used photography to claim her right to define her body, producing a series of witty and disturbing pictures of scarring and debilitating disease.

Until her death in 1992, Jo Spence continued to combat cancer with courage and creativity. Always she shared with others her experience of woman-as-a-body and feminist-with-spirit, exploring hidden truths about illness and sexuality, embattled and engaged in the drive to lift the twin taboos around image and death.

How surgeons manage both the language of cancer and the handling of women's bodies makes a substantial difference to the response of patients.

'The doctor who diagnosed my cancer said to me, after unsuccessfully trying to jab a needle into the hard mass in my left breast, 'Well, it's certainly cancer. That one," pointing to my breast, "will have to come off." I completely fell apart and then looked for a second opinion.' (Judith Brady, American, forty-three.)[28]

> I took a friend with me for the first consultation but I was told firmly that the consultant only sees patients by themselves. I needed that friend as a witness for the doctor's safety as well as for my comfort. I was given no choices. The only choice was mastectomy. It felt brutal but I thought: 'Well, he's the expert.' It was a panic situation. No one ever said: 'Take a bit of time. Take more advice.' I received the impression if I didn't agree at once that would be it! Curtains for me! Within a week I was in hospital having the op. I wasn't offered therapy or breast counselling.
> (Doreen, Dentist. Breast cancer.)

After the first surgery Doreen was weepy, anxious, had panic attacks. Unaware of alternatives, she decided she could live with it. The cancer returned. Again she was given minimal communication, no choice, no control. After an incision made with a totally different technique so that her body is scarred in violently different ways (which she showed me on a series of painfully clear photographs), she has after great consideration entered into lengthy proceedings against the consultant, professing professional negligence.

> No attempt has been made even to line up the two incisions. Or to make them look similar. There are these wounds at totally different angles where my breasts were. I feel psychologically disturbed. Macabre thoughts went through my mind. Did he ritualise this? Is he a freemason? Did he get a kick out of doing this? In whose hands was I while under anaesthesia? The person who holds the scalpel always intimidates you, even if they're being nice. Which he wasn't. He intimidated me at every visit. He always insisted on seeing me on my own, always stripped to the waist. I

felt he constantly humiliated me. I was mute with fear. Never asked the questions I now know I should have asked. They were locked up in my voice box.

She did ask for a lumpectomy but the surgeon refused.

He said brusquely: 'I can't do a lumpectomy. It's too close to the nipple.' Then he got his hands and squeezed my breast roughly. I was afraid but thought he must be doing his job. Then he said: 'This is what your breast will look like if I just take the lump!' He squeezed until there was just a little blob left. He could have drawn it on a piece of paper, or shown me a photo. But he handled me. It was macabre and intimidating.

Doreen had been led to believe that there would be a mirror image of the surgical scar on her other breast.

But the scars are gross, not symmetrical. He kept saying: 'I could always slip in a couple of prostheses after two years.' You couldn't possibly do that. There is no way it could look acceptable. He took the incision down on to the sternum. There's no breast tissue. Even people with big boobs, which I did not have, don't have breasts on the sternum. Right up to the armpit is the scar. The longest line, the largest incision anyone could have made.

Doreen sat down and wrote the first of a sustained series of critical letters.

I said if he had gone to a mechanic for his fancy car, and needed a new wing, and the mechanic put a Beetle wing on a Mercedes car, and said 'Here's your car! A perfect job!' there's no way he would accept it. Well I am not going to accept this. I feel I've been brutalised. I've been totally wiped out. I've had to give up my job as a dentist. I feel like a woman who has been raped. I intend to try and get compensation at the rate of his gross annual income. If he treats women patients like I have been treated, he doesn't deserve to earn any money!

Doreen's account is not uncommon. It echoes the appalling experience suffered by writer Audre Lorde. Diagnosed as having liver cancer six years after her mastectomy, she wrote in her journal for 8 November 1986, New York City:

If I am to put all this down in a way that is useful, I should start
with the beginning of the story.

    Sizable tumour in the right lobe of the liver, the doctors
said. Lots of blood vessels in it means it's most likely malignant.
Let's cut you open right now and see what we can do about it.
Wait a minute I said. I need to feel this thing out and see what's
going on inside myself first, I said, needing some time to absorb
the shock, time to assay the situation and not act out of panic. Not
one of them said, I can respect that, but don't take too long about
it.

    Instead, that simple claim to my body's own processes elicited
such an attack response from a reputable Specialist in Liver
Tumours that my deepest – if not necessarily most useful – sus-
picions were totally aroused.

    What that doctor could have said to me that I would have
heard was, 'You have a serious condition going on in your body
and whatever you do about it you must not ignore it or delay
deciding how you are going to deal with it because it will not go
away no matter what you think it is.' Acknowledging my responsibility for my own body. Instead, what he said to me was, 'If you
do not do exactly what I tell you to do right now without questions you are going to die a horrible death.' In exactly those
words.

    I felt the battle lines being drawn up within my own body.[29]

On her visit to this specialist in liver tumours at a leading cancer
hospital in New York City, the first people in white coats who interviewed her from behind a computer were only interested in her
health-care benefits and proposed method of payment. Those crucial
facts determined what status plastic ID card she would be given.
Without a plastic ID no one at all, no matter how seriously ill, was
allowed upstairs to see the doctor.

From the moment I was ushered into the doctor's office and he
saw my X-rays, he proceeded to infantalize me with an obviously
well-practiced technique. When I told him I was having second
thoughts about a liver biopsy, he glanced at my chart. Racism
and Sexism joined hands across his table as he saw that I taught
at a university. 'Well, you look like an *intelligent girl*,' he said, staring at my one breast all the time he was speaking. 'Not to have
this biopsy immediately is like sticking your head in the sand.'
Then he went on to say that he would not be responsible when I

wound up one day screaming in agony in the corner of his office![30]

Audre Lorde tried to believe this doctor was sincerely motivated by a desire for her to seek what he saw as the only remedy for her diseased body. However her faith in that scenario was considerably diminished by his $250 consultation fee and his subsequent medical report to her own doctor which contained several supposedly clinical observations of her 'obese abdomen' and 'remaining pendulous breast'.[31]

I can think of no greater clash between the sickeningly sexist and disgracefully demeaning medical language and the language of a woman's body raped of response by such insensitive utterances.

How different the experience of a cancer diagnosis and treatment plan can be, if supportive (preferably knowledgeable) friends are allowed in to the consultation, if choices are offered and the patient invited to reflect upon them, if the surgeon behaves to the patient as if he understands her feelings.

> Italian doctors are not used to women wanting all the information. But I am an informed person. I am into having my rights. I didn't care if I gave the doctors a hard time by asking questions. I kept politely repeating in Italian: 'It is my right as a patient.' I'm not uppity. I try to be extremely polite but I intend to get what I want. I got all the information. The doctors found that they could be candid with me. I was given straightforward options. Decided I didn't want partial surgery. I'd seen my Dad die of cancer. I'd just seen my Mum die of cancer. They could cut it off. I wanted to minimise the risks. I wanted to be sure I could go at least another six years without worrying about getting another cancer. I was pernickety and persistent and they told me the truth.
>
> (Marie, Rome, 1994.)

Although many women initially fear losing a breast, most, like Marie, become remarkably realistic about recognising losing the cancer as their overriding concern.

Being an informed member of the health profession can be significant in assessing the options dealt out by the medical profession.

> I'm always amazed at the ignorance of ordinary people around medical matters. It's no wonder you get better treatment if you know what's going on. I was a teacher, then a nurse, now

involved in medicine for many years. You learn you can't pretend or faff around about death. You don't just say 'Oh that's a
small lump', you immediately ask 'Is it a tumour? Is it malignant? What grade is it?' I knew I was in a high-risk category that
fits the Western medical model. High-dose pill, no kids, middle-
class, ex-smoker. Smoked for fifteen years. So when I found the
lump I was prepared. I put all the medical things into gear
straightaway. Told lots of people because I wanted to talk
through all the options.

(Merle, Health visitor.)

Merle's two close friends were breast cancer counsellors. Sensibly she
insisted that one of them went with her to every appointment with
the consultant. 'She was a cancer nurse as well as a breast counsellor. The surgeon might have been intimidated but he took it pretty
well. It's different anyway talking to someone who isn't scared of the
language, who wants realistic options and the time to consider
them.'
Self-assertive and as calm as was possible, Merle was given maximum information and possible choices.

> I could have had a lumpectomy and radiation. But it was in an
> awkward place nearer the cleavage than under the arm. So you
> would be left with a strange shape. Also radiation tends to make
> the rest of the breast lumpier, more fibrous. I didn't want to end
> up with a strange hard fibrous shape. Because I wouldn't have
> been able to feel again if there was another lump inside it. I didn't
> want radiation burns. I didn't feel I would have been convinced
> about the remaining cells.

Merle's two advisers both suggested that though mastectomy would
be harder to deal with initially, in her case, it might prevent later
complications. She chose mastectomy.
A significant feature from Merle's account is the usefulness of
breast counselling, which Doreen was not offered until very late on
in the process. Because breast cancer is a disease with obvious implications for women, a start has been made on allotting it public
consideration as a women's issue, *though nowhere near enough is
being done*. In the UK breast cancer nurse counsellors are now
attached to some major hospitals, or are offered by some health
authorities. Their role can be seen as humanising the National
Health Service.

One liaison nurse with a breast unit told researchers at the Trans-Pennine Breast Cancer Group that her job is to help women by clarifying the meaning of the experience of breast cancer. Nurse counsellors also cope with such questions as 'Am I going to die?'; not necessarily by using their access to clinical records but by letting women talk about the possibility of dying.[32]

In the UK several national groups provide practical information. The Mastectomy and Breast Care Association of Great Britain, the British Association of Cancer United Patients, and Cancer Link all offer advice. A number of self-help groups for women with breast cancer in the UK can be located through health centres, doctors' surgeries or the local Community Health Councils.

It is crucial for women with cancer to find others with whom to talk through the issues, in language that is comprehensible and not scaremongering. It is not possible to know everything there is to know in order to make informed decisions. But the more information women receive, the more control over their cancer they will have.

'But attending my own health, gaining enough information to help me understand and participate in the decisions made about my body by people who know more medicine than I do, are all crucial strategies in my battle for living. They also provide me with important prototypes for doing battle in all other arenas of my life.' (Audre Lorde, 1986.)[33]

Audre Lorde, one-breasted proud black activist, has since died from cancer. She has however provided a model we can all learn from.

Women with cancer must live their lives not fear their deaths. When cancer writes itself upon the body, it is the body that speaks. The language of the medical profession must take account of that. There *is* cancer. So no more euphemisms. No more lies.

─────────── *Chapter Nine* ───────────

SONS?
DO I HAVE SONS?

I glanced at an excellent Open University text on death and dying. I noticed that it carefully calls sufferers of Alzheimer's disease 'she'.[1]

This is a substantial linguistic improvement on most medical texts where anti-sexist innovations in the language are rarely seen. Standard medical books consistently label victims of modern diseases 'he' irrespective of whether women and men suffer in different ways or have different physical, psychological or emotional responses to their condition.

However, the reason for the change in the pronoun in this case highlights an important fact but one that is seldom mentioned.

In several significant ways Alzheimer's is a women's disease.

The bulk of this chapter examines reasons for this little known fact, reviews the disease, delineates its meanings and documents the issues it raises for women.

But first, to understand how it affects women both as patients and carers, I looked for women to talk to.

'Talk to Janet Gibbons,' my medical friends said. 'She has a special interest in Alzheimer's.'

They did not tell me what her special interest in this disease was.

Janet was a consultant. She had emigrated many years ago from England to Canada. She had found a home, partnership, had retrained and extended her medical specialities, developed an interest in neurology. Ambitious and popular, her research had been well received. At nearly fifty she might have been expected to make some interesting career moves; but recently there had been some strange speculation that Janet might take early retirement. One rumour suggested she might be forced into it.

I was curious to meet her.

She had a strong-boned face, tough dark hair coiled efficiently into a single plait, and an attentive manner. I felt as if she was constantly on the alert for signs. But signs of what?

We sat in her flower-filled office and I said: 'I've been told you have a special interest in Alzheimer's.'

She barked a laugh. 'I do. Although I need to be precise and point out that it is not my specific field of research.'

She used the firm careful tone of a doctor familiar with the distinction between accurate prediction and idle conjecture. 'The greatest problem with Alzheimer's is that we have not found the cause. Doctors are like detectives. They despair when they cannot track down first causes. Without the cause we cannot yet find the cure.'

I know that scientists have so far looked in vain for both cause and cure because in allopathic Western medicine virtually every disease can be described in terms of cause and effect, and Janet's 'detectives', known as pathophysiologists, attempt to track down first causes. But what lies behind Alzheimer's and what Western medicine can do about it is still in frighteningly early stages. Like Janet, other doctors register despair:

> Among the greatest scourges of our time [is] the malady . . . called 'senile dementia of the Alzheimer type' [which] carries the additional vexation that its primary cause has continued to elude scientists since the problem was first brought to medical attention in 1907 . . . We know not a whit more about what might cure it than we do about what might cause it.[2]
>
> (Dr Sherwin B. Nuland, 1994.)

'Research may provide drug treatments which will slow down the progress of Alzheimer's disease or reduce the symptoms. A "cure" is however not a foreseeable prospect.' (Dr Nori Graham. Chairperson of the British Alzheimer's Disease Society.)[3]

At present there are no drug treatments that effectively prevent the disease from developing. Alzheimer's usually takes five to seven years to kill the sufferer; occasionally it slows up to continue for ten to fifteen years, but more often it will progress considerably more quickly taking only three to five years. And progress it will.

As if Janet had been following my thoughts she said: 'We know the disease is relentlessly progressive. There are no remissions. In every case the deterioration of the person's mind is irreversible. In every case it will lead to death. There is a heartbreaking descent from being a woman with contact with others and in control of oneself into losing all contact, all control. It is a descent into total cerebral atrophy. For those of us doctors and carers with a particular interest in the disease it is very hard.'

For a few seconds her steady authoritative voice was edged with sharp concern. Then flying a glance at her watch, gathering up her papers, she said briskly: 'My special interest in Alzheimer's is Ruth. I have to see her now. If you have time, if you want to know some of what I know, come with me.'

We drove ten miles through Ontario countryside to a leafy suburb. In the car she proffered further information. 'Ruth is fifty-two. For three years she has suffered from early onset Alzheimer's. It started before she was fifty. That's very young!'

Although this dementia is age related, Alzheimer's does affect a significant number of younger people, like Ruth, some as early as mid-forties. In the UK about one in a thousand people aged between forty and sixty-five get Alzheimer's. The British Alzheimer's Society estimate that there are currently about 17,000 younger people with dementia although they point out that this estimate is an underestimate of the real situation.[4]

In the USA Alzheimer's strikes more than 11 per cent of the US population over sixty-five but when you include younger people below sixty-five, the total is estimated at around 4 million.

Though the disease is rarer in younger women (one in a thousand people, two thirds of them women) the symptoms are the same but may produce even greater anxieties. If a woman has been holding down a job, taking an equal financial share in household management, leading a vigorous social life, consequences are lethal.

According to Dr Janet Gibbons that is what happened to Ruth.

Ruth had been a nurse at the hospital where Janet had formerly worked. When the disease started the signs were so tentative and so confusing that even the hospital staff appeared unaware of what was the matter.

'It was as if we all thought that nurses or doctors or health workers must be immune to the disease particularly if they were young. Did we believe that only non-medics could develop Alzheimer's? Today I cannot credit how stupid we all were. Ruth started losing her way in the hospital building where she had worked for years. She began to forget some of the names. She became irritable, seemed to lose her sunny nature and her gentleness. Once or twice she flared up. Got aggressive. Then she found she couldn't cope with the labels on the bottles, so she accidentally mixed up a few drugs. She put it down to failing eyesight or tension and we all went along. Initially the authorities interpreted her difficulties as absentmindedness, then stress, then they changed tack and decided she'd become slack. Finally there were threats of misconduct. It took a long time for doctors to realise what was happening. I blame myself for not spotting it sooner. I was too immersed in my work. I couldn't bear muddles at home. I couldn't see what was before my eyes. Maybe I didn't want to.'

Janet still spoke with detachment but there was a fierce undertone of regret. 'It is early in Ruth's disease but it is progressing rapidly. The worst is yet to come. I am experienced in dementia but in this case I doubt if it will help me sufficiently.'

Janet decided to tell me more about Ruth's condition so that I should not act surprised when I met her.

'Sometimes she still has residual memories of the recent past, even a vague hold on parts of the present. Sometimes she recalls she has been a nurse, sometimes she doesn't. I have of course told her that she has Alzheimer's disease. I did not find it easy, though as a doctor I have always been concerned to break down the taboos many doctors have about dying. So many of us see death as the enemy, we are taught to believe that with enough skills we can overcome. Well we can't yet overcome Alzheimer's so maybe it's a good thing I don't see death as an enemy, but as part of a process beginning with birth.'

At the start of her illness Ruth knew she would gradually lose all her functions until she died. She and her doctors talked about what that would mean to her home life now she had given up work. 'She was brave while she understood. Now her understanding is failing so the rest of us have to be brave.'

The car stopped. We had arrived at Redlands, a large house made in the characteristic Canadian clapboard style not much seen in Ontario.

'Ruth is from the east,' Janet explained. 'It was built specially.'

We walked through the garden gate into a mass of coloured blooms. A tall woman with gold brown hair flecked with grey was picking and sorting flowers into piles. At her feet were two huge vases and a small chalk board. On the board in bold black letters was a list:

GET DRESSED
BREAKFAST
MRS LLOYD COMING
COFFEE
SHOPPING WITH MRS LLOYD
PICK FLOWERS
JANET HOME
LUNCH WITH JANET

We walked over to Ruth and Janet, with that closely attentive air I had already noticed, checked the board. The first two items were scrawled through in a shaky hand. Janet confirmed that Mrs Lloyd, a part-time health worker, had taken Ruth shopping. 'This is Sally. She is writing a book on death and dying and how women go about it!' Her voice was ironic. 'She is talking to lots of women Ruth, women like us.'

I was more surprised at this earthy introduction than was Ruth. She half smiled at me then said: 'I was a nurse, wasn't I? I saw a lot of death . . . I think . . . didn't I?'

She turned for confirmation to the doctor. Janet said warmly: 'You were a very good nurse.'

The house was light, airy, filled with redwood and bamboo, the honey and rust shades giving it a warm rustic feel.

'I'll get lunch ready. Ruth, please will you lay the table.' Janet's voice was brisk, firm and kind. A woman given to instructing others.

Obediently Ruth moved into the living room, hesitated by the table, looked concerned, then with relief noticed some big red floor cushions and lay down on them a few feet from the dining table.

Janet walked in, saw her and laughed. But her eyes had misted over. 'I did not say "lie down" or even "lay down", I said "lay the table". Oh my poor Ruth, this is hard for you.'

She briefly stroked Ruth's hair then motioned me into the kitchen. 'You see how it is?'

'I think so. Ruth is not your patient?'

'No, not formally my patient. We have a doctor and a consultant. She is my partner so in another way of course she is my patient. We have known each other thirty years. Ruth was twenty-three, divorced, with three-year-old twin boys when we first met on my first visit to Canada. Later when I returned to become a resident, we decided to live together. So you could say that now she will always be my patient because she is my partner. What I shall choose to do about that I don't know.'

She tossed lettuce, whisked salad dressing, poked her head round the living room door to check on Ruth, then repeated: 'I don't know. Some days I feel I don't know anything. At present I am holding down my job, keeping my head together – just – and making a life for us by employing Mrs Lloyd in the mornings. I come back when I can at lunchtime and if possible teatime then return to work, then come back late and bring more work. These are early days, Ruth is still intermittently aware of her condition, but she can still help me help her. Soon it will not be like this.'

'And then?' I asked.

'Ah! And then? Then . . . I don't know . . .'

I recalled the rumours of her possible retirement. I asked about her career plans. Janet gave me a hard cynical look.

'Career or carer? Perennial women's problem that one! I owe a great deal to her, to our partnership, but I owe a lot to myself. To my work that can benefit hundreds of people. I love my work. There is also the frightening problem of finance. If I gave up work how would we live? For sure we couldn't live like this. But there is no way I would put her in a home. So I don't know – Let's go and join her and eat.'

Conversation over lunch was light and easy. Ruth relaxed now that Janet at home had taken charge. Janet talked in short simple sentences implying that I should follow suit.

Janet and I were still crunching through crisp salad and I was enjoying Canadian bagels with sprouts and cream cheese, when suddenly Ruth became restless. She began to shuffle plates and forks around, taking them off the table and stacking them up on the carpet. Janet kept an alert eye on her.

'There is no need to clear away yet love. We have not finished eating. Sit down until we have finished.'

Ruth's fingers fretted the tablecloth. Her eyes looked anxiously towards the door, taking in Janet's brief case.

'Will you be home late tonight, Janet?'

'No. I shall be home early tonight. Tom is coming to supper.'

'Tom? Who is Tom?' Ruth's anxiety was evident.

'Tom is your son, Ruth. One of your twin sons.'

There was a pause. Both women were silent as Ruth traced a pattern on the cloth.

'Sons? Do I have sons?'

The distress in her eyes was now reflected openly in her speech.

'Yes,' Janet said firmly. 'You have two sons. Twins. Tom and Andrew.'

'Do they come here often?'

'No they don't. They hardly come at all. That is why I shall be home early tonight.'

'Sons? Do I have sons? Twins. Goodness. Will you be late home tonight Janet?'

Janet encouraged Ruth to help her slowly clear the table and carry crockery into the kitchen. She erased the morning's list from the chalk board replacing it with the words:

REST AFTER LUNCH
PLANT BULBS
PUT ON MUSIC
JANET HOME EARLY
SUPPER WITH JANET AND TOM
TOM IS YOUR SON
TOM IS A TWIN

Janet persuaded Ruth to relax on the sofa whilst we washed up. 'Tonight will be a big occasion. Neither of her sons have visited for two years. Tom cannot bear to watch his mother deteriorating. He will find her changed tonight. Anything complex or convoluted is beyond her. She can't follow plays or films or make sense of television, or of fast conversation. Her reading has become slow and poor. I write in capitals on her slate. She is still fond of photographs but she doesn't always recognise the people. We used to go out for whole days with the cameras – it seems like a century ago.'

She sighed then angrily she talked about Ruth's other son. 'Andrew stopped visiting earlier. He is frightened stiff the disease can be inherited. It is true that with early onset Alzheimer's there are some genetic patterns. Both twins are worried but they seem to care more about their own skins than about their mother.'

Because Ruth's powers of recognition are fading this aspect distresses her less than it does Janet. Dr Jonathan Miller, President of the British Alzheimer's Disease Society, points out that the cruellest aspect of the disease is that the partner, friend or child of the sufferer who provides unremitting care and support will no longer be recognised. He adds: 'The fact that we are unable, as yet, to identify a cause or a cure merely compounds the tragedy.'[5]

Meanwhile, Ruth's failing recognition means the couple are becoming increasingly isolated.

'Friends who used to come over regularly can't cope with the fact she may not always know who they are. They get sad or angry or come less often. I have to face the fact that there will come a time when she will no longer recognise me. As a doctor I know this scientifically but emotionally I can't acknowledge it.'

How does a woman caring for a parent, partner, husband, sister, or friend anticipate the length of time before the patient is not merely unable to do up buttons or zips but actually forgets what buttons and zips are for? How long will it be before she forgets the names of her children, her parents, or her own name? What will occur when she forgets her own forgetfulness?

Janet is daily dealing with these unanswered questions as well with myriad practical problems in what has (as consultant Sherwin Nuland points out) been aptly called the Disease of the Thirty-six Hour Day. 'Soon she won't be able to be left alone even for short periods. Then I shall have to make major decisions. In the last three months I've watched her sense of time deteriorate. She is already having short phases of distorting night into day, though that isn't consistent. She has to have stable surroundings, she needs order. She becomes distressed in new environments.'

'Does that mean you don't go out much?'

Janet nodded. 'Hardly ever. Caring for someone with Alzheimer's even in the early stages is time consuming. And I have help that many women don't. But I know as she worsens the help will fall off. People don't want to be around Alzheimer's. Because it's both mental and physical, everyone sees them as loonies, or finally as vegetables. Many nursing homes or residencies won't take them.'

It seems that not only is Ruth losing some communication skills, but she has also started wandering, a persistent symptom of Alzheimer's.

'Early evenings are worst, she gets very restless. If she's not locked in then she may go out without proper clothes. I've seen her lose her way, just sit on the ground and cry. Sometimes she wakes at nights and tries to dress herself but she can't cope unaided so I'm getting very short of sleep. When I have to see patients early in the morning it's terrible. Occasionally she'll wet the bed. This will increase. Another year or two she'll be doubly incontinent. I know what to expect but I don't know how I am going to react.'

Other people's hostile reactions are beginning to shadow their lives. Ruth's lapses upset people so they have stopped inviting them out together.

'They still invite me,' Janet said. 'They feel I need rescuing from what they call "the situation". But I won't go without her. I'm happier at home trying to fit in some research when she is looking at gardening catalogues or when she finally falls asleep.'

For Janet there is irony in the situation that ten years ago she and her partner joked about how useful it was that Ruth the nurse had chosen a professional caring role.

'I used to say: "All the better to look after me!" What a bad joke. Now we rarely share a joke. Maybe for a few minutes there's a glimpse of the old funny Ruth, but no – mainly I've lost my companion.'

She sighed and stopped talking to me. Then as if commenting on something utterly impersonal she said coldly: 'It can only get worse. We must go now. I can't afford to be late.'

We put on jackets and headed for the door. Ruth was on her knees puzzling over the chalk board. Janet went across and hugged her. Ruth hugged her back. During my time at Redlands, not once had there been any evidence that Ruth's mind or body had forgotten who Janet was. I reminded myself of the doctor's words: 'This is early onset Alzheimer's. It is early in the disease but it is progressing rapidly. The worst is yet to come.'

Would the worst be when Ruth did forget who Janet was? Would the worst come if Janet made the decision to give up her flourishing career to care full-time for Ruth then later resented that decision? Or would it be worse if she decided not to give up work but to pay for full-time care or transfer Ruth to a home and face the distress it might cause Ruth and her own attendant guilt?

None of the choices were easy. None of the outcomes certain. Uncertainty is the keynote of this terminal illness. The only certainty was that Ruth would become daily more diseased until unable to think, learn, reason, remember, or control any of her mental or bodily functions she finally died. But when that would be was also uncertain. There is no way to estimate at what point death will occur.

As if she had read my mind, Janet appeared from behind me with my bag. 'So many uncertainties,' she said. 'No way of getting it right. Meanwhile we lurch from one crisis to the next, whilst I see to my other patients.'

She called across to Ruth: 'Try not to worry about anything. I shall soon be home.'

As if she had not heard, Ruth said: 'Will you be home late tonight, Janet?'

'No I shall be home early tonight. Tom is coming for supper.'

'Tom? Who is Tom?'

'Tom is your son, Ruth. You have two sons. Twins. Tom and Andrew. I have written it on your slate.'

'Slate? Yes. Son?'

As we opened the front door I heard Ruth whispering tearfully: 'Sons? Do I have sons? Twins? Goodness. Will you be home late tonight, Janet?'

Janet had an appointment in the city so agreed to drop me in the centre. She stopped outside a mainstream bookstore.

'Buy a lighthearted book. Take your mind off death!' she said humorously, waving me goodbye.

I drifted inside, willing my mind to be taken off. The books of Jane Rule, a fine Canadian novelist were prominent on the shelves. I selected a novel at random. Or perhaps it was not at random. Is there something else at work? The book was called *Memory Board*. Let me briefly tell you the start of the story and you may judge.[6]

David and Diana Crown are twins, now in their sixties, once close but estranged for forty years by conflicting loyalties and divergent lifestyles.

David has suffered an embittered wife and the demands of a large family. Diana has been a successful doctor who has spent half a lifetime living with Constance, once a vigorous independent gardener who, when the story opens, has grown frail, is losing her memory and appears to be in the first stages of what appears to be Alzheimer's although the disease is not given a clinical name.

Diana has given up her medical career to care for Constance. By strange coincidence, the first scene, where we meet the two women, almost exactly mirrors my first encounter with Janet and Ruth.

In Jane Rule's novel, the two women are in the bedroom. Constance stands irresolutely beside clothes put out by Diana the previous night.

'Have I had my shower?'

'No,' Diana said, smiling.

While Constance showered, Diana took up a small slate, . . . and began to write the list for today . . .

PUT ON YOUR CLOTHES
BREAKFAST
THE MORNING SHOW
LIFT BULBS IN THE BED BY THE GARAGE
LUNCH
REST

ERRANDS ON THE AVENUE
WALK ON THE BEACH
DINNER WITH DAVID[7]

Diana the doctor props the slate against Constance's gardening clothes and goes downstairs to prepare breakfast. Constance arrives at the table, dressed, slate in hand, with the first item crossed off.

"'David who?'" she asked.

"'My brother.'"

'Constance stared away from Diana at the blank slate of her memory.

"'My twin brother.'"[8]

In *Memory Board* Diana's twin brother, David, has decided, after a gap of four decades, to invite himself for dinner that evening. Although Diana tells Constance several times that her twin will be arriving she remains unsure that Constance will know who he is. Her fears prove to be correct. At dinner Constance politely asks David:

"'Do you know us?'" . . .

"'Not as I wish I did,' David replied . . .

"'Do you miss your work?' David asked, but he addressed his question to Constance rather than to Diana.

"'Did I ever work?' Constance asked.'[9]

During the meal with David, Constance's confusion deepens. She turns to David: "'I don't know who you are,' Constance said.

"'He's my brother, my twin brother, David.'"[10]

That evening after the meal and David's departure, Constance sleeps peacefully, every aspect of the evening erased from her mind. In the morning she will have no awareness that they had entertained a visitor. Nor will she ever be able to remember that Diana, her doctor/partner has a twin.

Twin? Have you a twin?

Jane Rule's novel uncannily and accurately mirrors the case study of Janet and Ruth. In these two stories there are remarkable similarities of symptoms and issues. We see the characteristic patterns that attach to the disease and to the dis-eased life of the caregiver in *any* situation where Alzheimer's is present.

The patterns, as we saw, include:

Difficulties of early diagnosis
Decisions of discretion versus disclosure
Employment problems for younger women with Alzheimer's

Early retirement of carers
Financial hardship
Lists and labelling as initial coping mechanisms
Behavioural patterns of sufferers:
    Mood swings
    Aggression
    Personality change
    Wandering
    Lack of recognition
Issue of home care versus institution
Sufferer's losses:
    Loss of memory, judgement, reasoning
    Loss of bodily functions
    Loss of control
    Loss of identity, selfhood
Carer's losses:
    Loss of companionship
    Loss of sexual partner
    Loss of parent, or relative
    Loss of confidante, speech partner
    Loss of energy; physical exhaustion; mental stress
    Emotional loss
Withdrawal by children
Social Isolation, social death
    Loss of outside interests, connections, friends
Anticipatory grief
Post-disease grief and guilt
Fear of genetic inheritance

The key theme however which underlies all the other patterns is that of *uncertainty*.

I shall look at each of the major issues, then look at uncertainty as the prism through which we may view women's total relationship to death and dying. But first, as the disease also attacks a great many men, it is important to establish in which ways Alzheimer's has implications for women, and which themes drawn from a study of Alzheimer's disease match themes threaded throughout this study.

What is known of Alzheimer's, a disease of excessive brain loss, is that relentlessly and progressively it attacks the nerve cells in the brain's cortex that is associated with our so-called higher functions of memory, learning and judgement.

What is overlooked is that it has three particular implications for women.

Firstly, substantially more women than men, roughly two women to every man, develop Alzheimer's, one of society's major killers. It is estimated that these numbers and this proportion will increase.

Although the disease can strike those in mid-life (forty to sixty-five), it is largely a severe condition attached to older age, and currently women live longer than men and are expected to continue to do so. Today more than half a million people in the UK alone (mostly over sixty-five) suffer from it.

In the UK, women are its major victims.

In 1991 Alzheimer's sufferers aged over forty numbered 500,000 of which about 334,000 cases were women. Over the next thirty years approximately 154,000 more cases will develop. We are talking about forty-two new cases of dementia every day for the next ten years in the same ratio of two women to one man with the strong probability that the proportion of women will keep increasing. By the end of this century it is foreseen that a total of at least 667,000 women – maybe up to 1,000,000 – will suffer from Alzheimer's.[11]

In the USA, as we saw, Alzheimer's strikes more than 11 per cent of the population over sixty-five. The total number of Americans affected by the disease (including those below sixty-five) is around 4 million. There is the same gender pattern.

In the USA women are its major victims.

Internationally, senile dementia, of which Alzheimer's is the predominant form, ranks as a great scourge of contemporary society. Worldwide, an estimated 50 million people over sixty-five are suffering.

Globally, women are its major victims.

The gender characteristics of the disease are consistent internationally. In less developed countries the difference in longevity between women and men is more pronounced. The World Health Organisation expects the number of older women with Alzheimer's to increase disproportionately.[12]

In the West, while improvements in our physical health mean that heart disease, strokes and cancer are decreasing or are becoming treatable, the irony is that consequently people live longer but are more likely to show failing mental powers, confusion and dementia.

Thus it is mainly women who are in receipt of medical technology's latest irony.

In an ageing society, an increasing majority are women, many of whom will unfortunately soon come to realise that there is a feminisation of ageing.

Until the age of forty-five, numbers of men and women are about equal, then the gap starts to widen. Today in this society the average woman may live up to ten years longer than the men she knows intimately. Feminisation of ageing means she will almost certainly outlive her husband and may outlive her eldest sons.

Between 1901 and 1970 the number of women over sixty-five increased twice as fast as the number of men. Today in the mid-nineties women over sixty-five are the fastest growing segment of the UK population. By the end of this century most of the one million people over eighty-five living in Britain will be women. It is all too likely that one in five of them will suffer from dementia and most probably it will be Alzheimer's.

The losses are incalculable. Women with Alzheimer's will lose their way, lose their faculties, finally lose their minds.

Looking after them will be ageing, often very frail carers of which two thirds to three quarters are likely to be women. This follows the pattern shown throughout this study of present day women doing the bulk of caring work attached to every terminal disease. Their losses too are a seldom-told story. Many women have lost their jobs and their finances to care for those with Alzheimer's who are daily losing their identity. No wonder that the women who care, often at best lose their patience, and at worst feel that they too are losing their wits.

The grave figures and grim facts of Alzheimer's present the *first* problem of significance to women.

Second is the linked issue of ageing and ageism.

In our ageist society with ageism particularly directed against women, ageing itself and the illnesses of ageing have very different connotations for the two sexes.

In Western culture ageism on its own (where separable from sexism) means that we all devalue older people who are no longer economically productive. We isolate old men and women. We dismiss their skills, discount their wisdom, deny them status, withold respect.

Ageism becomes a lethal tool when it is combined with our cultural death taboo because it means we deny the reality of the passing years, we deny our growing infirmity, we deny the approach of the dying time.

Signs of age herald signs of death so we disguise and ignore them.

In our masculist world, taboos around death and old age, when linked to our prevalent sexism, mean that while there is no official retirement age for women as carers, their work, while being taken for granted, is consistently devalued.

Think for a moment about the double standard for ageing. It leads us to define older men as 'craggy', older women as 'wrinkled'. We say a man's white hair is 'distinguished', but we believe a woman's grey head shows she is 'over the hill'.

How many of us start dyeing our salt-streaked hair a brilliant red, or a bold blue black from our early forties? I know from personal experience that once into the henna years it is hard to turn back. One's famous feminist politics have nothing to do with it! Take me: I'm a dyed-in-the-wool radical feminist, who stoutly asserts that the politics of appearance keep women oppressed. But once a month I can be spotted indulging in the regular fix of the dyed-in-the-bath black henna addict!

When women's bodies change and fail we are made to feel that a vital asset has been lost. Myths around maturity tend to make men feel sexually attractive, but make women feel grandmotherly or matronly. Even these terms only apply while women have their faculties. When a woman develops Alzheimer's, when that woman loses her faculties, she may be seen as even more useless, grotesque and threatening than a man with that disease.

Both men and women are subject to chronic illness, but some of the problematic issues of later years – poverty, continuous caregiving, surviving all relatives and friends – are predominantly women's problems. Yet because research and policy makers have mainly been men, women's special concerns have been overlooked. Because women are statistically and politically invisible *as women*, their needs have not been adequately addressed.

The *third* feature of Alzheimer's which has special significance to women is that more women than men act as carers for people with the disease.

This fact follows the gender-based pattern for the caring of all diseases in our society, shown in Chapter Four. In the UK of the 6 million carers of Alzheimer's sufferers, more than 60 per cent are women; of these women 2.1 million are the sole carers, twice as many as men.[13]

In a survey organised by the British Alzheimer's Disease Society it was discovered that more than half, 52 per cent of the female carers are under sixty-five years, three quarters of them care for a relative at home, and half of them spend more than eighty hours a week at it, more than double the average working week. The survey also showed that women carers were three times as likely to care for parents as were male carers. 33 per cent of the people they surveyed with this dementia were wives, and 24 per cent were mothers. It was predominantly female carers who looked after other women as well as spouses, male partners, brothers and friends.

These figures of course reflect only the position of carers who are members of the British Alzheimer's Disease Society.[14]

A more representative study would be likely to show thousands more women, impoverished and deprived, caring for those with progressive degeneration of the brain cells, knowing that as they themselves age, they too may become victims but with few remaining relatives or friends left alive to look after them.[15]

In non-western countries the situation is worse. In Africa, for instance, AIDS is decimating the middle-aged group who, under other circumstances, would be expected to care for older people, including those who are terminally sick. In countries with a new high death rate as well as a poor economic base, an increasing number of elderly female Alzheimer's sufferers may have to manage without much help.

When women do the caring for terminal illness, their caring goes largely unrecognised. Organisations that deal with the disease acknowledge this.

'It is now known . . . but not always remembered . . . that the majority of carers are women: wives, sisters, or daughters.'[16]

When men do the caring, an appreciative spotlight is focused upon them. In Alzheimer's, unlike some other diseases, some men do the caring, and it is on this minority that much of the media attention has been focused. It is after all what women are expected to do in the matter of Alzheimer's as in the matter of most other diseases.

What are the major issues that women carers have to deal with?

Misdiagnosis is a frequent problem. Ruth's case shows us how employers often misinterpret early Alzheimer signs in younger women as anything from stress to gross misconduct. Results may be dismissal or redundancy with attendant loss of pension and long-term service rights. Subsequent diagnosis of dementia rarely results in a reinstatement of those rights.

Doctors get it wrong too. In one recent survey, 92 per cent of carers said GPs desperately need more training to be better informed about how to identify the disease. A third of carers reported that doctors took over a year to correctly diagnose Alzheimer's.[17]

Alzheimer's Disease Society's Training Officer, and Assistant Director of the British Alzheimer's Association, Clive Evers, admitted that many GPs still respond to anxious family enquiries with: 'Well, what do you expect at her age?'

Patty, a British therapist at the Bristol Cancer Care Centre, who spent ten years caring for her mother, had this experience: 'The first signs were when she worked as a clerk in Bristol in a shipping office and she'd forget where the office was. She had to phone my father for directions. Our doctor told her it was the menopause and forgetfulness went with her brittle bones!'

Many women's uncertainties increase if subject to a difficult menopause, and are not helped by the arrant incompetence of a doctor like Patty's.

For women involved with someone who appears to have symptoms such as confusion, memory loss or personality change *in excess* it is critical to remember that they are not witnessing the ravages of ordinary senility. Alzheimer's is *not* the natural result of ageing. It is a disease. The distinction between ordinary forgetfulness and early onset Alzheimer's lies in the loss of the short-term memory that is part of dementia. A forgetful person can be reminded of the event she has forgotten. For the Alzheimer's sufferer it is as if the event of five minutes ago had never occurred.

Many of us start to lose things as we age. I sometimes forget my keys. But this is *not* a sign of Alzheimer's. It is when you forget what the keys are for that something is seriously wrong. Anyone can forget to stub out a cigarette but someone with Alzheimer's forgets why they need to. Similarly they may forget why it is essential to turn off the gas, pay bills, wash themselves, put their clothes on, clean the house. They forget the names of the tools they eat with, or how to eat. Some women unable to masticate may choke because they have forgotten how to chew.

In the early stages, using slates boards and lists, as did Constance and Ruth, can be useful aids.

Eva, a seventy-year-old American widow, said: 'I'm glad they told me I'd got Alzheimer's. Now I know what I have, I write down everything I need to do, then I cross it off my list as I do it.'

Anything a woman can do to keep her memory alert is worth trying. Clive Evers, Assistant Director of the British Alzheimer's Association, said that Reality Orientation Techniques, often used in day centres and hospital wards can be usefully transferred to the home. They include labelling each object, naming its place, labelling body parts, clothes, emphasising names of each person met, making constant reference to time, place, and reasons for being there, focusing on where things can be found, other people are, what relationship they have to the patient. Anything that helps preserve a woman's sense of identity may stave off the worst part of this disease a short while longer.

The problem for doctors is the blurred lines between the norma-tive features of ageing and early onset Alzheimer signs. It has been a problem for eighty-eight years.

Although it was 1907 when German neurologist Alois Alzheimer first observed the nerve cells in the brain becoming diseased in a fifty-one-year-old woman patient, and recorded the symptoms that led four and a half years later to her death, public concern and pro-fessional interest was very slow to develop. This was largely because of these blurred edges.

As we saw in Ruth's case, other medical conditions can mimic Alzheimer's. Women taking various medications may exhibit mem-ory loss, confusion, depression. Excessive use of alcohol may produce similar symptoms, as can anaemia or nutritional defi-ciency.[18]

Thyroid conditions, diabetes, kidney or liver problems, lung dis-ease, gall-stones and syphilis can also cause temporary mental confusion which may not be Alzheimer's. Brain and nervous condi-tions such as Parkinson's Disease or multi infarct-dementia (a series of small strokes) may also give rise to deteriorating memory.

Diagnoses are not easy.

The New York widow Eva's belief in the importance of knowing her diagnosis highlights another issue faced by doctors in the USA, Canada and the UK. Janet Gibbons (like many women doctors) stood firm that she should break through 'the taboo most doctors have about dying'. Aware that 'too many of us see death as the enemy' she determined to speak openly to Ruth about her death.

Decisions about discretion or disclosure are hard. A truthful diag-nosis implies a relentless progression towards death. It may help both patient and carer. This however depends on their characters. One woman patient, still lucid, who had been given an accurate diagnosis, told me she had far too much time to reflect on her terri-ble condition. Eva, the American listmaker, however felt relief.

Combating fear is part of that fight. Apprehensions range from terror at being alone to fear of being persecuted. Dread about being unable to 'name' objects correctly arises quickly. Remember Ruth who muddled 'lay the table' with lie down. Other women report husbands who rename 'city' as 'sea' and mothers who believe 'sea' is a bookshelf. There comes a frightening incongruity between the thought in one's head and the words needed to express that thought. One woman with Alzheimer's whom I saw in hospital wanted me to help her on with her nightdress, but she asked me to switch on the radio.

The exact nature of each sufferer's dementia, the severity of her case at any given time is proportional to the number and location of brain cells that have been affected. The fact that there is a decrease in nerve cell population is actually sufficient to explain disturbing memory loss and other drastic cognitive disabilities. However there is in addition a marked decrease in acetylcholine, the chemical used by the cells to transmit messages.

These are the basic elements of what is known about Alzheimer's at this time. It is not much. Indeed these elements are too few to provide a direct link between structural and chemical findings on the one hand and patients' specific manifestations on the other.

Although the cause is still unknown, some behavioural patterns can now be predicted. Strange thought sequences are matched by curious behaviour patterns. Abrupt mood swings are prevalent. Ruth's reported change from kindness to irritation is typical.

Angela, a British wife who cared for her husband for seven years, emphasised the distress that comes when a kind man becomes aggressive. 'He had never even shouted at our dog, suddenly he took the stick to me. He'd been a dignified kind Dad. Suddenly there he was wandering the streets with his vest but no pants on. In front of our sons he'd take down his pants and expose himself and shout at them with foul words.' (Angela.)

In the later stages the sufferer may have no idea what came before, no inkling of what might follow. One woman I saw in hospital used the word 'love' to a man she did not know and swung out at him violently. Another woman, once almost prudish in matters of hygiene, sat soaking in her own urine and, before the nurses could stop her, smeared herself with her faeces quite unaware of what she was doing.

Towards the end, lack of recognition (which together with difficulties in early diagnosis and financial hardship, are the three main problems which the British Alzheimer's Society deals with consistently) is the issue which confronts many women carers in the West. 'It wasn't too bad whilst he still knew I was his wife. But after four years he hadn't a clue. Looking after a man you've known all those years who stares at you with that dead stare is horrible. "Who are you? I don't know you. Get out!"' (Angela.)

'Mother would just look at me and say: "You're a nice girl. I used to have a daughter like you." She was like a blank television screen. Occasionally you could press a button and she'd come on.' (Patty.)

Constant restlessness is another feature, so frequently occurring at supper time that doctors have termed it the Sundowning Syndrome.

Some suggest that the body clocks have gone out of control so that restlessness occurs from wildly mistaken views such as the sufferer's belief that they are waiting for now grown-up children to come off a long-ago school bus, or the notion that they are waiting for a train to take them home from work.

In the case of Patty's Mum, wandering finally led to her death.

> She wandered frequently, totally naked out in the street. That whole year of wandering she was incontinent and sometimes knew it and it destroyed her. In her lucid moments she asked us to put a pillow over her head and kill her. In one of her wanderings in the dead of night she missed her footing, fell down the stairs, broke both her hips and subsequently died. My main emotion was huge relief that at last it had ended.
>
> (Patty.)

Patty's relief was turned to a new grief within hours after the funeral.

> I'd just got home from the funeral and gone to bed when in the early hours of the morning the police banged at my door to say my brother had crashed his car which had overturned and caught fire. I behaved like a gibbering idiot. 'This can't be!' I said. 'I've just been to my mother's funeral. You've got the wrong man.' But it was true. He was dying of burns in hospital. He survived as a burnt wreck, 65 per cent burns to his face and body, until in deep depression he killed himself leaving me to tell his two small children. The months of uncertainty around whether or not he would kill himself brought back all the uncertainty of my mother's years of Alzheimer's.
>
> (Patty.)

Patty, who had cared for her brother as well as her mother, was now left to support his two children and look after her very sick father who died with her beside him a year later. Patty's story of how she acted like an oak tree perpetually ready to collapse is told throughout the pages of this book. As a survivor of a series of family deaths all within two years she said it felt like a 'family holocaust'.

However what she learnt initially from being an Alzheimer's carer was the strength and singlemindedness ('like an oak tree' she repeated constantly) needed to combat Alzheimer's uncertainties and the growth she could gain as a constant carer. 'I think death is feared because it isn't talked about. But even though I saw my whole family wiped out within months of each other, I still kept on talking to them about death. I don't fear death. I have grown from it.' (Patty.)

In thinking about her mother's disease she focused on two aspects:

1. The fact that she felt she had no choice but to act as a carer.
2. The issues of uncertainty that mark out that dementia.

These indeed are the twin features of women's relationship to Alzheimer's, so it is with an analysis of each that I conclude my exploration of this disease.

This study has already shown that in this society women become primary carers of the terminally ill less often from personal choice than from the internalisation of society's expectations.

Daughters, sisters, wives, girlfriends who feel obligated to care for others, rarely spend less than twenty hours a week caring. Sometimes this rises to eighty hours.

Most of these women are over fifty-five, half of them look after someone over seventy-five. 80 per cent of them care for a relation. Half of them care for parents or parents-in-law. 20 per cent of them have been doing this unpaid exhausting task for more than five years.

In most cases there are men around – husbands, sons, brothers – who could share or take over that responsibility. In most cases the men don't.

These are facts. These facts are built on the unfair expectations about caring in our society.

The fact that women bear the brunt of caring has an impact on their employment prospects. A recent Alzheimer's Survey indicated that 60 per cent of carers of working age had been forced to give up jobs or take early retirement to provide full-time care. The survey discovered considerably more women than men gave up jobs to do this. Of those who became carers under sixty-five 41 per cent lost their full pension rights by doing so.

Janet, when considering whether or not to give up medicine to care full-time for Ruth, recognised it would bring sure financial hardship. The difference between Janet and many other women carers is that as a doctor she had some resources and some choice. Most women have neither.

Despite the optimistically named Equal Pay Act and Sex Discrimination Act we do not yet have anything like equal pay or non-discrimination. Dementia in a household means untold extra expense for women whose incomes are invariably lower than men's. The poverty rate for women over sixty-five is more than double that for men over sixty-five. 42 per cent of those on low incomes at or below the 'poverty level' are people over sixty-five, which because of our life expectancy means most of these are women.

The causes of women's poverty, critically increased through caring for Alzheimer's, are political. If the hidden expectation that women do the caring forces their withdrawal from the workforce, if and when they attempt to return (after the death of an Alzheimer's patient), they are pressured into jobs with low wages or find themselves 'unemployable' for lack of recent experience. Low wages, low rates of benefits, non-availability of sufficient social care, are the result of political decisions that shape society and not simply accidental events in individual women's lives.

Many benefits for which women carers or patients apply are still assessed on the basis of marital status and assume women's financial needs are met through a heterosexual relationship with the person they live with. The stories of Ruth, Janet, Diana, Constance, Patty, Eve, Angela and the others show the insidiousness of such policies. Sex discrimination, heterosexism, racism, and low valuation of women's unpaid care tinge many Alzheimer's situations.

The new government policy in the UK to transfer an increased proportion of care costs to community carers, will scandalously affect women. In Britain, carers over eighty who are most likely to be caring for a partner with dementia are paying the most for being a caregiver. 20 per cent of over-eighties surveyed in 1992 spent more than £300 a month of their income on caring. This, at £66 a week, is greater than the current basic state pension for a single person (£54.15) and five times the carer premium (£11.55) The majority of the over-eighties penalised are women.

Recent research showed that what we call 'community care' is in reality 'women's unpaid care'. This saves the state between £15 billion and £24 billion per year.[19]

In the Alzheimer's Report 1992 it says: 'The most widely available treatment (for Alzheimer victims) is the love and support that a carer can give.'

Undeniable.

But this 'widely available love and support' is largely given by women for whom the costs are financial hardship, physical illness, social deprivation, stress, loneliness, exhaustion and total lack of societal recognition.

An illustration of exactly how taken-for-granted women's caring role often is in Alzheimer's can be seen clearly in a major case study by an eminent American consultant on death and dying. Dr Sherwin B. Nuland describes the case of one Mrs Whiting who cared devotedly for her Alzheimer's-stricken husband first at home then day-and-nightly with nurses' help in a nursing home. Her three children neither helped her nor visited their father, formerly a strong man, now a urine-soaked vegetable.

> The three children found it impossible to be witness to the destruction of their adored father, and it was a good thing that this was so. They succored the soul of their mother, seeing to it that she was fed the emotional sustenance to carry out the tasks they knew she must undertake.[20]

Dr Nuland's evident acceptance that it was solely Mrs Whiting's duty to care for her husband and that the grown-up children had a perfect right to absent themselves is outrageous.

Dr Nuland believes not only that Mrs Whiting did what 'no nurse, no doctor, no social worker . . . could do', but that Mrs Whiting *should* do it because she is a woman, a mother and that man's wife.[21] Dr Nuland tells us:

> The nobility and loyalty of a Janet Whiting are not unique, may even be, to a greater or lesser extent, the norm. By so much is Janet's behavior not exceptional in fact, that those who provide the professional help come almost to expect that FAMILIES (my caps) will rarely question their own roles in the caretaking process.[22]

Dr Nuland states that 'Janet did what almost everyone in her anguished situation does. She determined to take care of Phil herself for as long as she could.'[23]

Dr Nuland, I must administer a severe correction. Not *everyone* in that anguished situation does do that. Or believes that they should do it. The Whitings' own grown-up children did *not* do that. Ruth's own twin sons did *not* do that. But almost every *woman* in that anguished situation does do it or feels they should do it. It is not *families* who rarely question their roles as caretakers, it is the *women* within those families.

In 1990 the House of Commons Social Services Committee stated that: 'For too long carers have been the unrecognised partners in our welfare system. Their services have been taken for granted. They have been regarded as a resource but not as people with their own needs.'

In the USA and Canada, as in Great Britain, the bulk of the carers of dying people are women. It is women as carers who have long been the unacknowledged partners. It is women who are not seen as people with their own needs. When it comes to an analysis of the carers of dying men and women there is absolute gender blindness.

This study and this writer refuses to partake in that.

The debilitating, but hidden, cost of caring is one of the few certainties attached to Alzheimer's. All else is uncertain as Patty, Janet, Eva and the other women bore witness. Perhaps the most worrying uncertainty felt by carers is the fear that they too might develop the disease.

I cared for Mum for three years. At first she lashed out then in the last year she sat curled up on the floor making mewing sounds. She examined her toes as if they didn't belong to her. I couldn't cope and started shaking and forgetting things. Soon she couldn't feed herself so the doctor said to take out her dentures, so she wouldn't choke. She knew her face wasn't right and she kept mewing and spitting at me. After another year looking after her alone I became very confused and panicked that I was getting it.

(Jean.)

Jean's panic is characteristic of many carers. Research shows stress can produce certain kinds of confusion particularly in the aftermath of caring when someone has died. In one British study over 50 per cent of carers were troubled by anxiety, memory loss, insomnia and high blood pressure.[24]

Alzheimer's disease however is not contagious. You cannot 'catch' it.

Whether or not there is a genetic tendency, as Ruth's twin sons Andrew and Tom feared, is less certain. Research suggests there may be a basis for a genetic inheritance but the evidence is restricted to early onset (forty–sixty-five) Alzheimer's.

Research indicates there is an abnormality on chromosome twenty-one causing the production of too much amyloid, a protein which has been found in the brain of Alzheimer's sufferers. However the case for genetic predisposition has not yet been satisfactorily proven. Certain physical and biochemical changes have been found to accompany the disease process but their role is not clear. One example is that a biopsy of a patient's cerebral cortex shows a 60 to 70 per cent decrease in levels of acetylcholine, a major factor in chemical transmission of nerve impulses. Some scientists believe that acetylcholine may play a strong role in regulating the body's production of amyloid. It seems that when acetylcholine levels are low, then amyloid increases.

Scientific controversy rages. Some neurobiologists believe amyloid causes the degeneration of nerve cells. Others believe it is merely the result of the breakdown of those cells. While scientists score points and debate the issue, women with Alzheimer's and women related to them go on worrying. And men too. Like Ruth's twin sons. Like Jean's two brothers and two sons, who all spoke to me of their fears. All that we can say accurately at this time is that relatives of patients who developed Alzheimer's between forty and sixty-five may be at some genetic risk, though it does not affect all that person's descendants. It may miss a generation.

Fortunately the under sixty-five group is relatively small. Families of the over sixty-fives can feel much less anxious about genetic disposition as it has not been convincingly proven.[25]

Genetic uncertainty ties into the range of uncertainties that are the hallmark of Alzheimer's. It is because of this feature, and because it is a disease that profoundly and particularly affects women, that it can be used as a metaphor for the many uncertainties women confront when they face dying and death. Many women in the early stages of Alzheimer's or caring for someone with the disease, used talk and tears as their way of dealing with the uncertain certainty of death.

Though uncertainty is a condition of life itself, it is now partly a function of improvements in modern medicine. Now that skilful scientific interventions delay death, uncertainty in relation to dying and death is on the increase.

The uncertain, lengthy, chronic illness has come to predominate over possibly more certain black and white cases of terminal illness leading to speedy death. Advances in medical technology have created new stresses for dying women and their carers.

Technological innovations mean life is often prolonged at all costs regardless of the quality of that life. This has led to increased concern among women patients and carers. In the case of Alzheimer's, too often there is hardly a 'real life' to be prolonged at all. But movements towards recognising grounds for limiting treatment have of course created new uncertainties about the relationship between professionals in the health-care industry and those who are dying.

'The widening range of therapeutic and technological options in the management of advanced illness may aggravate the medical uncertainties about how far to pursue a policy for living rather than a policy for dying.'[26]

In most illnesses there is a measure of uncertainty. In Alzheimer's disease the policies for the dying, and the policies for the living, who in an emotional sense are dying with them, are riddled with uncertainties.

In facing death from this dementia, women confront not merely practical uncertainties but they also face existential uncertainties. Those about the very meaning of existence. As identity slips away, as selfhood blurs, women must ask themselves and each other: what does it mean to be a person? What does it mean to be a woman? What does it mean to be a mother?

As a mother myself I wonder what it must be like not to recall the first time your daughter swam to the end of the pool? The first time she stayed out so late you could have throttled her? The irritating times your son ran up your telephone bill? Or the amazing times your children brought you flowers and hugs?

What must it be like not to know whose children they are? Or finally not to understand what the concepts mother and daughter, or mother and son, mean? What if you still knew your children but they did not want to visit you?

A recent report on Alzheimer's Disease states baldly: 'Sons and daughters are often unable to come to terms with the fact that a parent is suffering from dementia.'[27]

What does it mean to be a mother when you no longer know you have sons?

Sons? Do I have sons?

Chapter Ten

SUICIDE: SHOCK AND STIGMA

Many mothers are held back from suicide even when in deepest depression by the thought of the effects on their children. There are however a few for whom their children's welfare ceases to be a sufficient deterrent.

I had just written the lines above when I received a note from a woman friend which tragically underlines that statement.

'Sorry to break this to you in a note, but Pearl's body has been washed up in the river near Oxford.'

Pearl, a forty-eight-year-old mother of two young children, Gilly and Sam, had been my neighbour for a decade in a Northern city. We had worked at the Women's Centre together, had been involved in the Peace Movement, had shared the experience of Greenham Common.

Pearl wore outrageous coloured clothes and tied her hair with scarlet ribbons. I think she was a deeply angry woman and a very funny one. I suddenly recall her on a women's march, in floral dungarees, waving her fluorescent striped woolly hat in one hand and a banner in the other. Funny what you remember when someone has taken their own life.

Pearl had been savagely depressed, in and out of hospital, had already made one suicide attempt. I thought that 'because of the children' she would refrain from a second serious attempt. That may be a stereotyped notion, but one borne out by research. I was wrong. Pearl went missing last week. Nobody knew where she had gone. She had last been seen on a bridge over the river by Gilly, now fifteen, who, discovering her mother would not come home, ran to get help from some adults. That was the last time the teenager saw her mother alive. When she arrived back at the river her mother had disappeared. Twenty-four hours later the police found Pearl's body, face down, in the river.

How will Gilly and Sam cope with Pearl's death? What questions will they ask themselves?

It seems savagely ironic that Pearl, a woman committed to non-violence, peace, and community action, should finally have died in early middle years, in violence and alone. She must have asked herself: how did I miss the path? Where did I go wrong? I ask myself: where did we, her community, her women friends and acquaintances go wrong?

Rationally I know both her questions and mine are irrelevant. They are the wrong questions. But they happen to be the ones asked both by those about to commit suicide and those left behind. I asked them of myself when I attempted suicide. I asked them when my mother attempted suicide and then died. I ask them now that Pearl has killed herself.

Although suicide appears to be the ultimate individual act it has far-reaching social consequences.

The repercussions which affect *any* survivor irrespective of his or her gender or race have been boldly documented by researchers such as Wertheimer and Staudacher.

Evidence shows that *all* survivors are in crisis situations which pose problems rooted in the shock, stigma, violence, guilt, sense of blame and inability to fathom the reason why, which surround suicide.[1]

What has been given less attention is that suicide is an act largely carried out by men and boys which has profound, often catastrophic, effects on women and girls.

How many survivors are there?

Bernhardt and Praeger (1983) estimate each suicide will involve a minimum of five family members or 'significant others'. Lukas and Seiden (1987) suggest that between seven and ten people will be 'intimately affected'.[2]

The grief chain is long.

There are likely to be between 40,000 and 80,000 new survivors each year in Britain, for deaths *recorded* as suicide. Great numbers of deaths misnamed as 'accidents' or given open verdicts will have grieving survivors that stretch into dozens.

It is useful to consider first statistics which illustrate the predominance of male self-destruction, the reasons for gender disparity, and consequences for women.

However, the significance of women's relationship to suicide is not merely part of a numbers game. Thus secondly I consider specific issues for female suicide survivors shaped by the sexual politics attached to women's identity as primary parents, sisters, or partners. Differential gender socialisation results in differently-perceived effects on women of problems that affect all survivors. Cultural conditioning which focuses women on the meaning to be found in relationships heightens differences in how women deal with guilt, feelings of powerlessness (which arise from their structural situation but are compounded by surviving a suicide), chronic grief intensified by rejection, and anger which many women find difficult to express.

The stigma and silence which intensifies the death taboo is hard on women who wish to talk about suicide to an extent that men do not.

Thirdly I consider the legacy of the characteristic *modes* of male suicides (usually violent) on female survivors.

The first three considerations relate to women's position as suicide survivors. A fourth consideration is an analysis of the factors which predispose women to inhibit them from committing suicide themselves.

Statistics: Gender Disparity in Suicide and Consequences for Women Survivors

An analysis of the suicide rates shows that two thirds of adult suicides are males who leave women grieving, guilt-ridden or occasionally relieved.

This century, the ratio of male to female suicides has fluctuated considerably. Although more women kill themselves today than in the early 1900s, men still account for approximately 67 per cent. This gender disproportion is increasing.

In the UK currently 4,667 male deaths have been recorded of an official total of 8,000 people per year: a huge underestimate of actual figures. The major reason for this tip-of-the-iceberg syndrome is the stigma associated with suicide.

According to the Samaritans, male suicides increased by 38 per cent between 1975 and 1987. Numbers grow daily. Female suicides however increased by only 20 per cent over the same period. In the USA a similar pattern shows men are three times more likely than women to kill themselves.[3]

Who are these men?

Evidence from the USA provides insights. A substantial group is elderly. In America, white men over fifty form approximately 10 per cent of the total population but constitute 28 per cent of suicides.[4]

Doctors suggest that men give in to the stress of physical illness, loneliness and depression. Sociologists suggest that male deaths which occur after retirement may be precipitated either by a reduction in a man's capacity to work or by a lessening of his capacity to function independently, or by a diminution of his means of exercising control. *These three precipitating factors are seen to be more essential to the way men run their lives than to the way women organise theirs.*[5]

Do these male deaths relate to or affect any particular group of women? Are we for instance to make something of the fact that many of these men are single, without women in attendance as caregivers, comforters, and cooks?

Apparently we are.

Male suicides, particularly in middle age, are often unmarried, frequently have suffered the recent death of their mother. Several studies indicate adult single men who live with their mother are greatly at risk of suicide if she dies. As early as 1971 Bunch showed that 60 per cent of single men who committed suicide had lost their mother in the preceding three years, compared with only 6 per cent of single men who did not commit suicide. Loss of parents among married male suicides and among female suicides is by contrast relatively uncommon. Today's surveys confirm these mother and son patterns.[6]

The other important category is adolescent boys, who form two thirds of a new teens-to-twenties high risk group. (Possible reasons for suicides of teenage girls are discussed later.) Both sexes will usually have living mothers as the primary parent.[7]

Today in the USA suicide is the third leading cause of death for young males. A 1991 survey conducted by the USA Government Centers for Disease Control found that 27 per cent of 11,631 high school students had 'thought seriously' about killing themselves in the previous year. One in twelve had actually attempted it.[8]

In Britain sixteen to twenty-four-year-old boys and girls are the most vulnerable group, but for the boys, suicide is the second most common cause of death, second only to road accidents.[9]

Following the pattern in our culture of perceiving the activities of males (even when dead) as more valuable than those of females, research work continues to explore the question of why men kill

themselves. Less research has been done on what effects such suicides have on women survivors.

Colin Murray Parkes points out that family structure and functioning are always changed by bereavements, but bereavement by
suicide is often seen as a rejection of the central supportive function
of a family.[10]

It is crucial to emphasise firstly that it is the *mother* who is most
often the supportive person at the centre, and secondly to re-emphasise
the particular significance of *rejection*, for women..

Counsellor Dorothy Jones suggests:

> Many women find divorce, separation and relationship break-ups
> worse than death because most cases of death are not chosen, so
> they don't feel that terrible rejection. The one death which mirrors
> and exceeds that is suicide because that too is chosen. Grief then
> is often unresolvable.

If that grief is a mother's, the task of dealing with that repudiation
seems Herculean. Mothers of children who have killed themselves
described their emotions:

'Feeling blotted out'

'Excommunicated'

'Feeling exiled as a parent'

'Discarded as a mother'

'Thrown aside'

'Feeling emotionally denied'

'Wasted'.

I shall not draw up a scale of loss, as every death of a loved person is devastating for the survivor. However sociological research
and women's experiential reports suggest firstly that *any* death by
suicide, because self-chosen, self-inflicted, may be harder to cope
with; secondly that a *child's* death by suicide will be harder for both
parents than other parental bereavements. Where mothers are the
primary child carers, a child's suicidal death ties in with notions of
maternal bonding as well as with anxieties about rejection.

Mothers have been forced to take on a new role. They have
become unwilling maternal suicide survivors. Mothers of the Dead.

That maternal survivors, as a special group with needs of their
own, have so far been insufficiently investigated, results partly from
the fact that all survivors' needs have been overlooked; partly from
a lack of acknowledgement that women's responses to suicide differ
from men's.

Until the 1970s, survivors' needs were sublimated to the socio-logical attention paid to victims. Eventually researchers Barraclough and Shepherd (1976, '77, '78) Carol Staudacher (1988), and Alison Wertheimer (1991) investigated experiences of those left behind but even they did not pay sufficient attention to needs specific to women.[11]

Conflicts Faced by Mothers

What special issues are faced by maternal survivors?

They will have key characteristics in common with women left to survive any sudden death, including shock, lack of preparation, no farewells. There will have been no opportunity to talk about crucial issues with the dead person. Questions raised by the relationship can never be answered. Conflicting emotions cannot now be voiced. They will share with other bereaved mothers that feeling of ampu-tation, which Shirley Cooklin called the 'Mark of Cain'. But Mothers of the Dead, deprived through suicide, will have additional burdens to bear.

Annie's story may offer insights. Common threads in Annie's story might diminish the isolation of other women suicide survivors.

I talked to Annie, in the old farmhouse in a quiet country village, where she, her husband Rick, and her remaining children moved after her twenty-two-year-old son, Greg, killed himself in their London house four years ago.

The first thing I noticed was how her four children and two stepchildren seem to be strewn across her life and her body.

As we talked she clutched on to Maisie, a squirming ginger-haired four-year-old, before she kicked her way through a spiral of toys to monitor eight-year-old Eddy's progress on the computer, picking up a photo album as she passed.

There's Eddy, a bit wild as usual. Maisie's another redhead like Greg. The only one in the family. There's only this one photo of them together. I'd just had Maisie. I'd just given birth while I suppose Greg was preparing to die. Weird, isn't it? Maisie was premature, in an incubator, I was in intensive care so I couldn't see her. Rick shot a load of film, got it developed in an hour so I could see my new baby. Look, there's Maisie! There's Greg behind her grinning. At the time I thought 'Bloody hell typical Greg! I just want photos of my baby. I don't want your great mush in it!'

That's the only photo I've got of them together. Two weeks later Maisie was out of the incubator, I was out of intensive care, and Greg was dead.

The phone in the farmhouse rang. Annie excitedly took an international phone call from her daughter Poll (the eldest, since Greg's death) who is teaching in Spain. 'Poll is about to go and work in the Far East. I'm anxious already. Ever since Greg died I worry unceasingly about the kids who are left.'

Annie had been a 'reasonably calm' mother before Greg's death. Now she is fearful. That fear, which arises during pregnancy, when bitterly validated by a child's death, is a uniquely female experience.

Taking the album from Maisie she turned to a photograph of her son Jack, now working at the BBC. In the photo Jack is leaning shoulder to shoulder with Greg, grinning at a joke. The sun, inevitably, is shining. It was the summer before Greg's death.

They were very close as brothers. All my children belonged to The Woodcraft Folk, so they did a lot together, had friends in common. Rick's children, Dolphus and Jemma, are the same age as my big ones, they lived with us too some of the time. We had fun as a family . . .

Her voice trails of. Annie is aware of her new preoccupation with her young. As a medical sociologist, formerly very career-oriented, she hasn't always been like that.

Greg's death has focused me on the kids. As a feminist . . . before he died . . . I think I spent a lot of time sort of rather resenting the demands of the kids, and his death has actually softened my feelings. I chose to have them, they have certain needs, the situation where both partners are working and kids are in day-care – this may well be sacrilege – but I don't think it is very satisfactory. There have to be other solutions.

Ironically, in view of Annie's changed ideas, at the funeral she was verbally attacked by one of her family.

My eldest sister, an absolute cow, put it about that she wasn't surprised Greg had committed suicide because I'd always been such a terrible mother and put my career first. Before he died I could have laughed off a line like that. But now I can't. You don't just feel guilty when your child dies, you have no confidence. You have to completely re-evaluate your parenting skills.

Annie's feeling that her mothering role has been called into question is a characteristic reaction. For some mothers suicide means the loss of an only child and with it a sudden cessation of their parental identity.

Someone said to me that I was 'covered' by having other children. That it would be worse to lose your only child. I can't say that. *There is no scale*. I've still lost Greg. It is losing that person that is unbearable. The unbearable sadness of not seeing their dreams materialise won't be different whether you have other children or not.

Annie reiterates the theme of inconsolable loss and relational response to death repeated by women. There is no scale. Although we cannot assume that the death of a child by suicide is necessarily worse than the loss of a parent or sibling, there is no doubt that mothers of suicide victims felt it to be the most grievous loss they could ever face.

Dealing with chronic grief that follows suicide is made harder by society's attitude. People are uneasy with the thought that someone chooses death. The topic arouses powerful emotions. Keir suggests: 'We do not in truth really want to know . . . Contemplation of the deed itself, the manner of its execution – the overdose, the drowning, the hanging – fills us with horror.'[12]

Being unable to find people with whom to talk is a consistent issue for women survivors, and appears more important to them than it does to men. In Alison Wertheimer's study her fifty interviewees comprised thirty-six women and fourteen men because 'fewer men than women were apparently willing to talk about their bereavement'.[13]

Wertheimer s experience matches those of Lukas and Seiden (1987) who discovered that in the USA male suicide survivors were consistently less willing to talk. They suggested that this was because men thought they had less need to talk to other people about grief.[14]

I found that women's desire for intimate discussion (of anger, guilt, or difficult family dynamics) was exacerbated not merely by public silence but by private resistance from male partners, brothers or sons. In several cases where couples were involved in a family suicide, having initially approached the woman, when I later approached the man, most declined to talk. During the research period spent with Annie, I asked Rick, her husband, whether he would find it useful to talk to me about Greg's death. In a friendly, pleasant way he said: 'You're better off talking to Annie. You wouldn't get much out of me.'

It was a response characteristic of many males in couples who confront suicide.

Several years after a child's suicide mothers still wish to relive details: 'Four years after Greg's death it is more taboo. People want you to shut up. What you are craving is for someone to say, like you did: "What was he like?" You were the first person for years to say that. Nobody ever asks.' (Annie.)

What was he like? Shy, quiet, with 'a sort of presence, safe and nice to have around'. He never sought attention, was unusually calm as a teenager, did not have a troubled adolescence. 'I used to tell people: "I never had any trouble with Greg. Greg was always amazing."'

Interestingly, this view of Greg as a 'model child' was echoed in descriptions of suicide victims by other parents. Mothers frequently said the dead child was 'special', 'amazing' or most often 'no trouble'. *This did not seem to be paralleled in the reports of children who had died by other means.* Remember how Juno described her daughter as 'an extremely fiery, independent pest'.

Part of Greg's apparent 'untroubled adolescence' lay in shyness rooted in acute dyslexia, which I suspect troubled him more than his family suggest. He did not match up well intellectually in his household. His stepbrother Dolphus, the same age, was academically and socially highly skilled. His sister Poll, only nine months younger, was in his class, caught him up, and surpassed him in a term.

'His spelling was appalling, his writing illegible, we all teased him. Because he took it in good part maybe we didn't know how painful it was.' (Annie.)

Inevitably Greg found difficulty with application forms. At home Annie helped him. At University, when his friends filled in job applications, Greg, without his Mother's support, 'gave it a miss'.

He got a Third at college, became stressed. Never came up. Felt he could have done better. He'd cut off some of his choices. He was in terrible debt, no job to go to. In past summers he'd come home, got temporary jobs. But this summer he wouldn't come home. He said: 'No I can't. No! I've got to be independent.' He had a strong sense his childhood was over. He'd got to be grown up. But he felt he hadn't done well enough . . .

Obviously Greg did not commit suicide for a single reason such as feeling a failure scholastically. He had a mother and stepfather who loved and helped him. But it may have been a significant element. As Elisabeth Kubler-Ross points out, our children, in a competitive, career-based, goal-oriented society, are made to feel they have to prosper on its terms. Kubler-Ross tells the story (as it was recounted to her by the anguished mother) of an eleven-year-old boy who killed himself.

> He came home from school with a long face. Nobody paid much attention, except for my husband, who confronted him shortly before dinner. He cannot stand long faces at the dinner table. To his father's inquiry, 'What's the matter with you?' our son confessed that he had brought home two bad grades from school. My husband was angry and said, 'So you don't care. If you don't care, we don't care.' He ordered the rest of the family not to look at my son during the meal . . .

Early the next morning they heard a shot and found him dead. Dead, because he brought two bad grades home from school! As Kubler-Ross comments:

> I think this is the tragedy of our achievement oriented society, that we tell our children a thousand times, 'I love you if you bring good grades home. I love you if you make it through high school. God, would I love you if I could say one day 'My son, the doctor'. And so our children prostitute themselves to please us, to buy our love – which can never be bought.[15]

If this is another example of our cultural norm adopting the male achievement-oriented attitude towards life, and achievement-oriented response to death, patently it would be more productive to adopt instead the largely female relational response to both. Children, as Kubler-Ross emphasises, are lovable whether they achieve or not.

Annie sees the conflict for non-competitive youngsters as an 'eighties dilemma'. 'Greg wanted a soft job, he was a caring sort of person, but in 1989 everyone was competitive, thrusting, into making lots of money. He did want to be solvent. He was in that sort of tension.'

This conflict is one shared by many adolescents. Take the case of Amy, a young American college student. Shocked and grief struck for three years after her nineteen-year-old brother Tim hung himself from a hook in their den, she reached nineteen herself, to witness her twenty-four-year-old boyfriend Toby (her dead brother's best friend) gas himself to death in his father's car.

> I'm frightened all the time about who will be the next guy in our group to top himself. I came back from college and found him in the car. It was only three years after Mom came home from the supermarket to find Tim like that, hanging from the hook, in the den. I'm never going to forget the way Mom screamed. I can't tell you how horrible he looked, hanging like meat, bleeding. They said he'd used a razor first. Why did they do it? Tim was just about to start training as an occupational therapist. Some people said it was a sissy job for a guy, but he was keen. How could he do it to all of us, we were so close as a family? Toby and I were going to live together. I was training as a lawyer so we programmed him for a house-husband for our first kid, till I got established. Some people thought us weird, but we were cool. Now everything is upside down in my mind. Maybe he wasn't that happy. Obviously I didn't know enough about him, or I wouldn't be screaming, 'Why did he do it?

Greg's desire for a 'soft job', his personality as a 'caring person', like Tim's plan to be an occupational therapist which some saw as 'sissy', and Toby's decision to become a house-husband, may all have stronger gender implications than are acknowledged in Annie's version of an 'eighties dilemma'.

Gender Implications

Reasons behind young men's self-inflicted deaths are not easy to decipher. One researcher suggested that adolescent suicides occur in 'a family background high in ambivalence, with open hostility and unresolved dependence'.[16]

Other researchers disagree. In some cases this may be accurate, but it cannot account for the huge – and rising – number of young male deaths. In households where I talked at length to mothers, sisters, girlfriends, I found some male-female conflict, I found some unresolved dependence, often (as in Greg and Annie's case) an unwilling push-and-pull dependence upon mothers, sometimes on older sisters. One case in point was Janine, a psychiatric social worker, whose younger brother, a high-pressured BBC executive, threw himself off Centrepoint, one of London's highest buildings.

> From childhood I played the older sister role. But in our family we
> didn't talk about the messiness of feelings. So when he became
> bizarre, depressed, we did not explore it. He became completely
> withdrawn. Did not talk to me or his wife. I identified with her
> anger about how little he did in the home and I stopped having an
> interactive relationship with him.

Janine, who even throughout his marriage had mothered him
through crises, 'sort of gave up on him'.

> When he no longer talked, and there was no closeness, I got fed
> up playing that role. I became impatient that he couldn't get in
> touch with his feelings. I don't think men are good at it. They
> compartmentalise their lives. So when he was in real emotional
> danger, he didn't talk. He planned to die, then he jumped. I felt
> overwhelming guilt. I know it wasn't my responsibility. There
> was nothing I could have done because he didn't make himself
> available. But there I was, a trained psychiatric social worker, a
> sister, all those caring things, and I hadn't seen the pattern.

Several case studies confirm Janine's view that men do not feel they
have permission to talk about emotions. Many do not wish to. Some
women survivors said they had not tried hard enough to talk
through the issues.

> I never understood how low Toby felt after Tim died. Maybe guys
> don't talk about what they feel for each other. I didn't ask. He kept
> saying he was a 'bit depressed'. I kinda didn't take it in. Like
> because he loved me, I thought we'd work it all out. I guess I
> never talked things through enough with him. It makes me won-
> der what I've done. I feel I'm kinda to blame, I know I'm not but
> that's what I feel. (Amy.)

Like Janine, Amy knows rationally the suicide was not her responsibility, yet feels guilt and self-blame. Annie too feels regret over
insufficient communication. 'I was pregnant with Maisie, the pregnancy was going very badly, I had to care for three-year-old Eddy
who was disturbed because they kept rushing me into hospital. I
went up to see Greg one evening, found myself thinking "It's really
hard to talk to Greg."'

Greg had a breakdown while taking what Annie saw as 'ridiculous jobs for a reticent boy' as a double-glazing salesman and a cleaner, which didn't cover his rent, but kept him from returning home.

He got deeper and deeper into trouble. I was bound up with the pregnancy. Finally he visited on his birthday in October to talk about taking a job as a Care Assistant in a home for mentally handicapped children. He was interested in nursing, he was a socialist, he wanted to care. He decided to take the job but he felt low. His version was he was '*a bit depressed*'. How I interpreted that was that he was in debt. I arranged to drive him there and settle him in. Then I went into the first of my big bleeds, so Rick had to take him. That was another big regret.

Greg's words 'a bit depressed' exactly mirror Toby's words. Neither cue was overt enough for the women to pick them up. Annie's situation as the mother of a large demanding family is familiar to many women. Giving equal time to everyone is impossible. Greg visited, told her he was dealing badly with a challenging handicapped child. She, meanwhile, handicapped by a challenging pregnancy, was rushed to hospital ten days before Greg's suicide.

My pregnancy kept going wrong. Bleeding, bleeding. Greg said he felt a bit of a misfit, felt alienated, said he was a failure, not a good person. I just kept bleeding, eventually they took me into hospital where I haemorrhaged so badly that Maisie was delivered early by emergency caesarean. They thought I might die. So all the kids rushed home including Greg. But I couldn't see them. You're not allowed visitors in intensive care.

Many young men like Greg, like Tim, like Toby, felt in some sense 'a failure'. Several of my case studies indicate that there is as much pressure on boys to take up competitive roles as there still is to force girls into more caring occupations. Boys who wish to act in gentler ways, or embark on less pushy professions, are still urged into the 'tougher' jobs. Several young men who took up work in the caring professions, or indeed preferred to stay at home and mind the children, found it hard to do so whilst simultaneously feeling appropriately masculine.

Some of those boys are now dead.

I am not suggesting that this was either a primary cause in their suicide, or even that it accounts for a vast number of deaths, but it was a frequent element I noticed in descriptions of young dead males. Many had had ambivalent attitudes towards their homes and their mothers, ambivalent in the sense that they were intensely attached to them but felt they should strike out on their own, often to pursue occupations they did not feel suited to.

The causes of suicide cannot be studied from a single perspective. The act of suicide is not a single act that can be isolated and analysed without examining the total life and background in which it took place. *Suicide is part of a process.* It is rooted in conditions of long standing, effected by psychological motives, social, cultural, ethnic and religious factors.

Gender (like class and ethnicity) is one significant strand. *But it is a strand that has been neglected.* To explore it may help to make sense of some deaths that appear to the survivors to be senseless.

This study shows repeatedly that differences exist in the ways men and women view death. Many men expressed the view that life is about 'doing' or 'activity'. When activity appears over, for some it is like death itself. When we examine a suicide victim's emotional history, we have to look at the social pressures and cultural expectations. In our society these are gendered. Research shows that many suicide victims had high expectations, a desire for perfectionism, made unrealistic demands upon themselves. Gender is an important element that fits into the coalition of these external and internal forces which results in suicide.

Are there ways in which women rely on 'experts' or are treated by doctors, police, coroners, that have gender implications or intensify traumatic responses?

Annie's description of her son's death shows several key factors.

> Still bleeding from the after-effects of the hysterectomy, trying to breast feed baby Maisie, I went home. The next time I saw Greg was the day he came home to die. He arrived at five a.m., cold, wet and dirty. Quite dishevelled and distraught. He told Rick he'd suddenly upped and just left the job. He seemed peculiar and strange, but I was very bound up in myself.

An hour later Greg came down from the top floor where the older children slept and had their own bathroom, to set up camp in Annie's bathroom, which was in a rather public place. Leaving the door open he took from the cupboard aspirin, paracetemol, diarrhoea tablets, rehydration pills, put them in a circle around him, then ritualistically started to take them. His stepfather spotted him, moved quickly, cuddled up his crying stepson, told him to come home so that they could look after him. Then believing the episode was over, went to tell Annie.

> He came in and said: 'I don't want to worry you but Greg has tried to take an overdose, but I'm sure it's just a cry for help. He hasn't taken anything.' I accepted Rick's words at face value. When I talked to Greg, he said he had swallowed pills. So I made him drink salt water. He was sick . . . wouldn't say where he had been all night. But suddenly he produced this carrier bag with a bottle of wine and a box of chocolates that he'd bought for us. He had obviously come home with some sense of hope but couldn't hack it. He got more strange. Made strange sounds – noises – not talking, just 'heurgh . . . huh . . . heurgh'. He was just clearly mad. Incredibly difficult to deal with. Not aggressive. Just withdrawn. You asked a question but he simply grunted. Like a mad person.

Annie's immediate decision to involve experts like her GP and a psychiatrist received a poor response. When she asked her doctor to come out and see Greg, he asked her to bring him to the surgery. 'I said I'm not supposed to drive. I've had a hysterectomy. I've got a premature baby not yet at term. It's pissing with rain. My son is trying to die. Please will you come?'

Reluctantly the GP called, agreed that Greg was suicidal, suggested he contact a psychiatrist, attempted to do so, failed, then forgot to phone a second time. Meanwhile Greg's 'madness' came and went.

> Some minutes from being mad, he'd have these windows when he was sort of normal. He wandered down at one stage and got himself a cheese sandwich and a great big pint glass of milk just like the old Greg. Although I was panic struck, because I thought I'd set in motion professional help, because I believed a pyschiatrist would come, I was reassured.

Women, even mature intelligent women, are socialised into accepting the views of male experts. In this case reassurance did not last long. No psychiatrist called. The rain poured. Greg in Doc Martins, no socks, wearing his boxer shorts, looking wild and acting strange, pushed open the front door and rushed out. Annie attempted to stop him.

That was the moment when I thought something terrible is going to happen. Is he going to jump under a train? We lived near a railway bridge. I rushed out saying 'Greg, please don't go.' He looked me in the eye and pushed me back. It was: don't interfere. That was not how Greg would ever behave.

Several hours passed. Still it rained. Annie, in desperation, called her friends to start a search. Then she rang the GP, finally the police. 'When the police arrived I thought he might already be dead. The police were so laborious. They kept saying "Have you got a photograph? We can't search without a photograph!" At that moment Greg fell in dripping wet through the front door. "Heurgh heurgh, grunt grunt".'

This time the GP recognised the urgency, sent for a psychiatrist. When her children and husband arrived, momentarily Annie recovered.

Although I'd accepted in my head that he was broken down *I felt soon there would be expert help*. I begged him not to go out again. He sort of smiled and said, 'Oh, I won't Mum'. Did he know then what he would do or was it another window through which the real Greg looked? I sat with him a long time. I had a strong sense he shouldn't be on his own. But what we all have to live with is that he was actually impossible to be with. Too painful. I went downstairs to feed the baby, begged Poll and Jack not to leave him alone.

The youngsters, too upset to stay long, instead returned to make him soup and tea. 'We all found him impossible just to be with. You want to do something so you make a cup of tea. We all wanted to do something but we didn't want to be with him.'

Ten minutes later Greg was alone again lying on the landing. Wet coat. Bare feet. Suddenly a terrible crash. Greg had shot through the door onto the roof terrace, then dived off head first.

We had bought the house because of its incredibly high roof terrace. Panoramic views of London. It's bloody ironic. Earlier, I'd hidden all the pills and razor blades but I hadn't thought of this bloody roof terrace. I was feeding the baby when Jack came down and said: 'He's lying in the garden next door.' I went into adrenaline. 'Poll, quick, go go.' But she said 'I'm not. I'm not going.' Then I said 'Jack go. Please go'. He said: 'Mum: I can't.' So I stopped feeding Maisie and thought, well I'll have to go. He was lying beatifically in the pouring rain. No blood. I tried to push him so that he didn't vomit or choke. Then he made this awful noise in his throat, *kkkrch*. So I ran in, phoned for an ambulance. When the police and doctor arrived, I still hoped because the professionals took him over.

Annie's presence of mind was extraordinary. She gathered up nappies and baby wipes, bundled up Maisie, put on her coat, tried to step inside the police van where they had put Greg.

The policeman said: 'There's no room in here! *Who are you any-way?*' I said: 'I'm his mother.' The policeman said, '*Well, no, you can't come in, you'll have to travel behind.*' I now know he had cracked the back of his head like an eggshell. They knew there was no hope. But I didn't know. The experts' manner was so dismissive and horrible.

By the time they arrived at the hospital, Annie, following behind the police, everyone but Greg's mother knew he didn't stand a chance. She was put in the relatives' room to wait for news. Despite her distress, Annie's reliance on authority continued. At intervals a nurse reported that Greg was having X-rays, a scan, was on a ventilator, could not breathe.

Because they put it in medical language it seemed something manageable. Suddenly I felt euphoria. I was suffused with well-being. I felt wonderful, hopeful, optimistic. Everything was going to be all right. It was such a powerful feeling that I glanced at my watch. It was 7.30. I thought this is the moment when they'll say he started breathing again. A few minutes later I heard someone say: 'Have you sent for the Chaplain?' Then I knew. They told me he died at 7.30.

For Annie as for many survivors, the next trauma came with the breaking of bad news.

I was pacing around the room. Nothing happened. Then a nurse came in. 'Sit down.' Why do you have to sit down? Will you keel over? Then the doctor came. He didn't just say: 'Your son has died.' He gave a great rigmarole of every medical intervention, all the clever things they had done. Then the great big climax: 'Sorry, we couldn't save him!'

A maternal suicide survivor, like murder survivors, needs the strength to wear her personal sorrow in a public place. For characteristic of death by suicide is the involvement of the police, the media, and stressful publicity hounds who turn a private grief into public news. When those experts are unhelpful or dismissive the strain is unbearable.

The dramatic death of a young person is always a tragedy and therefore news. For the press, bad news becomes good news. For the survivor, bad grief becomes worse.

> The night of Greg's death I heard a nightingale sing. You don't have nightingales in Greenwich in December. The next day the police came. Would Maisie die too? She constantly shivered. Should I put her in bed with me? No, she'd suffocate. Should I lay her down? No, she'd die of cold. The police made sure it wasn't a suspicious death. Bureaucracy took us over. Maisie was jaundiced, couldn't breathe. I'm a passionate breastfeeder, but my milk dried up before they opened the inquest. I howled like an animal the day after the funeral. I couldn't pay enough attention to Maisie. She'd die of malnutrition. I dealt with the post-mortem. Then a wonderful woman came from the Special Baby Care Unit, who gave me permission to give a supplementary feed, give my body a rest. She looked at Maisie: 'Is she smiling yet?' Smiling! Come on, don't be ridiculous! All I can do is look at her and howl. Everyone looked at her and cried. Nobody smiled at her. I panicked that she'd grow up with all her emotional wiring wrong. So I had to decide. Well either you die, in which case get on with it. Or you live, you've a new baby, a three-year-old, other lovely children, in which case do it reasonably properly. That meant dealing with all those officials. It meant forcing smiles. So I smiled at her, smiled at the officials, and have been left for four years engorged with unshed tears. To this day I grit my teeth, don't express my grief because I have so many people to think of.

Just as Amy's case shows us ways in which men are not given cultural permission to express their feelings or talk through issues, so Annie's case illustrates women's socialisation to nurture others at the expense of themselves. **In crisis situations, both women and men are culturally constricted, often cannot help each other.**

As in many suicide cases, significant facts at the inquest were mismanaged.

At the inquest they actually got it all wrong! I'd reached a version of what had happened that I would have to live with. Greg had chosen to die. I would have to bear that. *Then the Coroner erased my version.* He said that what I knew to be true wasn't true. He wouldn't give a verdict of suicide. I knew from my reading of Durkheim and Douglas that this was supposed to protect me. But it didn't. Coroners will do anything to give an open verdict, because of the stigma, unless there's an actual note saying 'I've killed myself because nobody loves me!' The suicide statistics are just a laugh! I didn't want an open verdict. I didn't care about any stigma. I cared that Greg was dead. The Coroner said: 'We don't know it wasn't just a bit of attention seeking that went wrong.' Now this kid had suffered all day waiting for a moment to be alone to do it. Yet they were raising this horrible possibility.

In Greg's case the pathologist and other officials were even less accurate.

They got every fact wrong! The pathologist said: 'This was a young man of five foot six.' Greg was over five foot ten! Who are they talking about? Can't the law give him the dignity of measuring him right? These small facts matter. They mismanaged measurements of the height of the roof terrace and the distance from the house. People like that are supposed to be able to measure! They can't even do that properly.

Coroners' Verdicts

Greg's case shows the kind of traumatic effects a misdiagnosis can have on women survivors. Sociologists (Durkheim, Douglas, Atkinson) have suggested that suicide stigma is a prevalent reason for coroners' frequent mislabelling of deaths.[17]

The bias of coroners' verdicts makes accurate estimates of the extent of suicide difficult. In Britain, the *official* figure is 4,361 suicides a year (1989 figs. England and Wales). Translated to a global scale, an estimated one thousand people a day take their lives: nearly one suicide a minute. But those are only *recorded* suicides.[18]

These notoriously unreliable figures grossly underestimate the extent of the problem worldwide.

Alvarez (1974) suggested an accurate estimate might be between a quarter and a half as many again. Chambers and Harvey (1989) suggested the actual rate is more than double published figures.[19] This huge statistical disparity results from the conscious rela- belling of suicides as domestic accidents, shooting accidents, heart attacks, or accidental overdoses. In Britain inquests must be held, victims' intentions must be strictly proven. Coroners who choose not to bring in a verdict of suicide use the hidden agenda that suicide will harm a family's reputation. But women on the receiving end of this well-meant action may find it utterly unac- ceptable.

Other causes for the disparity of figures are:

The family's desire to avoid guilt, blame and disgrace. Some sur- vivors even appeal to sympathetic physicians to write something else on the death certificate.

Survivors' subconscious desire to see suicide as an accident.

A well-meaning and silent conspiracy of investigators, family, friends, who call suicide an 'accident' in order to assure the sur- vivors of insurance benefits.

Sometimes the suicide victim has disguised the suicide to look like accidental death to save the family further hurt.

Research shows that cover-ups produce denials, evasions, fan- tasies and extra guilt. Denial makes it harder to get to grips with grief. Falsely naming a suicide means survivors do not have to believe that person chose to die. In order to support that false claim the survivor may deny negative feelings either that had been felt by the victim or that the survivor is left with as a consequence of being abandoned.

As Adrienne Rich says in *Women and Honor: Notes on Lying*: 'In lying to others we end up lying to ourselves. We deny the impor- tance of an event, or a person, and thus deprive ourselves of a part of our lives. Or we use one piece of the past or present to screen out another. Thus we lose faith even with our own lives. The uncon- scious wants truth, as the body does.'[20]

An honourable relationship between a woman and her intimate who has taken his or her life has to be a process of truth telling, *and those truths must continue even though one of the two is dead*. Because women as a powerless group function in a society constructed on the lies of the powerful, women have a profound stake in cleaving to the truth of their own experience even when it brings acute pain.

Stigma and Sexual Politics

Stigma makes suicide a death others fear to mention. Social unacceptability subjects survivors to a conspiracy of silence. It encircles their loss with shame.

As Barraclough says: 'Self-blame for failing to prevent the death and a sense of stigma may be longer lasting.'

As Raphael emphasises: 'The death itself brings shame, stigma and guilt. Complicated maybe pathological bereavements seem a likely outcome for the survivors.'[21]

Colin M. Parkes points out that one of the saddest features of suicide is the fact that it may become the only thing that is remembered about the *victim*, and remembered with fear.[22]

But women who *survive* a suicide face the same problem. 'I've become the woman with that defining characteristic: I'm the woman whose son committed suicide. That one shocking fact. That's how people talk about you, but not to you. It raises difficult social interactional things like when and how to tell people.' (Annie.)

Stigma must also be faced by sisters, daughters, girlfriends. Patty, the therapist, whose brother killed himself after being burnt in a car crash, the day after their mother died of Alzheimer's, was left not only with her twin bereavements (and an elderly dying father), but also with the distressing knowledge that no one cared about his suicide.

> His friends who rallied round him after the car crash and the terrible burns now gave up. They sort of felt the death was shameful. People had been very kind to us after my mother's death, and during my brother's accident and illness, but with suicide you don't get the same reaction. People would cross the road. I felt I should go down the road with a bell and say: 'Unclean!' I felt I should put a placard round my neck saying: 'Keep away! Keep away!' Believe me people did keep away. It is suicide we are talking about here!

Deena, whose father gassed himself, is unusual in acknowledging stigma, without feeling she should lie.

> My brothers think there's shame attached to Dad's death. If anyone asks them what happened, they normally say he died of a heart attack. I don't feel that shame. And I won't lie. In fact I'm quite proud of it. It sets me apart. Everyone looks so shocked. Everyone knows that people do it but no one ever knows anyone who has a relative who's done it. I won't keep quiet about Dad's death.

What are the roots of this shame?

The context is both religious and scientific. Those who are religious view suicide as a sin, a moral crime and an unnatural act. From a religious perspective suicide will be taboo. Those who are scientific view suicide as a topic for clinical research, reducing human agony to cold statistics. Both groups, in particular the medical profession, see suicide as essentially shocking because it runs counter to our venerated idea of human life as sacred.

Consultant neurosurgeon Carys Bannister was especially concerned over young people's suicides. 'One can feel angry with them because they seem to be valuing their lives very poorly. I sympathise with them but I still feel it is a wasted life.'

US consultant Sherwin Nuland, who believes 'taking one's own life is almost always the wrong thing to do', speaks for many doctors who see only two exceptions to this viewpoint. One is 'unendurable infirmities of a crippling old age', the other is the 'final devastations of terminal disease'.[23]

Health professionals are firmly behind the suicide-as-stigma syndrome. Evidence from studies as early as Sudnow (1967) and as recent as Littlewood (1992), suggest that even at the point of death, in hospitals and amongst doctors, considerations of social worth and status are paramount. *Attempted suicides have the lowest social worth of all dying people.*[24]

Different amounts of effort are made to revive people suspected of being 'dead on arrival'. This depends on their respectability. If the person is rich, renowned or respectable, attempts at revival may be made. If this proves impossible their attempted suicide will be relabelled an 'accident' as this is seen as having higher worth.

'This incredibly respectable Cornish doctor was found by a colleague with his throat half cut, his razor by his side, and later his suicide attempt was called an "unfortunate accident". They don't take that much trouble with your ordinary man!' (Jessie, former hospital nurse.)

What happens with suicides within the hospital structure is a process of depersonalisation. Premature death by disease or unprovoked violence can be viewed dispassionately by only very few in the legions of those who care. But premature death through self-destruction evokes a very different mood.

That mood is not dispassion . . . The very word suicide appears as a discomfiting tangent. We seem to separate ourselves from the subject of self-murder in the same way that the suicide feels himself separated from the rest of us when he contemplates the fate he is about to choose. For those left out and left behind it is impossible to make sense of the thing.[25]

As women identify corpses, they are not 'making sense of the thing' but at that point they are less likely to be making the cold judgements of the medical staff. Of more relevance is the fact that *their* responses and their lives will be affected by such judgements. Surgeons have assured me that though medical staff feel suicide is inexplicable they do not generally feel compassion. **It is significant that even women survivors, if they are also health professionals, are likely to share this tough attitude.** 'People who attempt suicide and land up in hospital are a total waste of time. They take up precious beds and precious energy of those of us trying to care for sick people who matter.' (Jessie, ex-hospital nurse. Suicide survivor.)

'Failed suicides are treated differently. Taking overdoses, wanting attention! You're taking a bed from someone genuinely sick. You could say they're sick mentally to have tried but it isn't always that. It's the little girls who say "Well, I'll make you love me. I'll pop a few pills."' (Deena, hospital nurse whose father gassed himself.)

Nearly half the women who overdose (women's preferred method) will die. The remainder who land up in hospital will be dismissed not only by male medical staff, but also by other *women* in the hospital service. Do 'successful' suicides that arrive at the hospital as corpses receive better treatment? 'They go straight to the mortuary. We don't get them on the ward. They won't get a lot of respect there either!' (Hannah, hospital nurse. Suicide survivor.)

Research studies show that Hannah is right. *Less respect is shown to a suicide corpse than to a corpse from any other cause of death.* The theory is that if people did not value their own lives then the social constraints which prevent others from desecrating their corpses need not apply.

Families frequently feel themselves to be stigmatised by association. Circles of silence enfold a grieving household. Anxiety about which member of the household will be the next to die is an unspoken fear. Children may verbalise it as a threat.

'How long have I got till Mum dies?' (eight-year-old Eddy to Rick, his father, four years after Greg's death.) Later, angry, when Annie had chastised him for naughtiness, Eddy said: 'You obviously don't love me. I'm going to go home and jump off the roof like Greggie did.'

Kids can be cruel. They may want to hit out. Pay someone back. Maybe their mother. After all, in their eyes their mother did not prevent the suicide. She failed to prevent a loss children do not understand. Not a loss like a lost marble or ball. Chances are the ball will be found. Must have rolled somewhere. Even a shiny glass marble won't have smashed. Won't have broken in pieces. Not like a head. The head of a brother that smashed on the ground hundreds of feet below the roof that he jumped from. When something happens like that, it is no wonder that some children grow wild. Or angry. Maybe introverted or silent. Suicide is a savage situation within a family.

'I kept a diary during the last four years of the way Eddy grieved, because children don't grieve in the way you expect. He says things like, "I just feel terror in my tummy like I'm haunted. Even trying to talk about it to you makes me feel I'm haunted."' (Annie.)

Insanity?

Stigma around suicide is rooted in the myth of insanity. Social constructions of mental illness mean that in different cultures or at different times suicide victims may be deemed 'sane' or 'insane', *but there is no evidence to suggest that suicide is a necessary product of mental illness*. Killing oneself is not by definition an indication of a form of insanity. What the research tells us is that suicide acts have in most cases been committed by those who were desperately unhappy but not necessarily mentally ill.[26]

Some women choose to believe that the dead person was 'temporarily insane'. 'My brother had been suffering an illness where he seemed quite psychotically depressed, so, though I think people have the right to commit suicide, he was not in his right mind to have that right. He'd managed to mask it brilliantly but he was deluded, he was mad.' (Janine, about her brother.)

Her view partly came out of her psychiatric training, but later her work as a feminist led her to reflect on her initial diagnosis. 'That could be my own rationalisation because I don't want to confront the fact that he chose to die.'

Sometimes the problematic label 'mental illness' may be used by a survivor about the victim as a defence against her own feelings of powerlessness.

Annie, as a medical sociologist, was highly familiar with the dubious concept of 'madness' but found it hard to throw off in the case of her son's death. Although she stood firm in her belief that the court should have labelled Greg's death 'suicide', because he had made a 'rational' choice; nevertheless later she re-evaluated his rationality. At the time when Greg said he was 'a bit depressed', she did not query his sanity, any more than Amy did when Toby used the same phrase. When Greg felt 'a bit of a misfit', Annie's interpretation was that he was having job difficulties. Today Annie's re-evaluation is that in those last days Greg vacillated between 'being mad' and 'having windows' of normality.

Female survivors may take refuge in the idea of mental instability as a defence against feeling rejected. Tragically they will never know if theirs is an accurate assessment. But in the long run emotional dishonesty distorts the woman survivor's grief. The fact is that many women and men who are in the accepted sense of the word 'sane' do choose to take their lives.

Because suicide is often linked to mental illness it means that survivors may also speculate about whether the 'disease' is 'hereditary'. In the clinical sense of the word suicide is not a disease and cannot be inherited. There remains however the problem that mortality risks for those who survive a suicide are greater than for other comparable groups through depression rather than through heredity.

Many survivors, particularly children of parents who have killed themselves, attempt suicide, and some succeed. The evidence is conflicting. Although Lukas and Seiden's study showed that of seventeen children of parents who had committed suicide, five made suicide attempts and two killed themselves; by contrast Alison Wertheimer's study showed that though death no longer seemed alien to suicide survivors, they did not actively contemplate it.[27]

My own study has borne out Wertheimer's positive findings. Though many suicide survivors longed for death at some point, and several contemplated it briefly, not one suicide survivor took her own life.

Violence

When a death is violent, many women feel more strongly that mental disturbance was a factor. Several women whose husbands or fathers had hanged themselves felt the men 'had to be mad' to do something 'so dreadful'. 'When I thought about my husband hanging himself from that spike in the shed, I felt the way he did it to himself is as disturbing as him doing it at all.' (Susan.)

Suicide is an act of aggression, but the methods used can be more or less violent. **In our society, men generally use violent methods to kill themselves. Women do not.**

Men most often kill themselves with firearms, by hanging, stabbing, or leaping from tall buildings. Women most often overdose.

Evidence suggests that this is related to the fact that male violence is the most disturbing feature of our routine life. Men frequently commit violent acts against women, often those with whom they are in intimate relationships. As women are expected to deal with sexual abuse, battering, sexual harassment and rape in their everyday lives, it makes it less surprising, even predictable, that women are left to deal with the effects of male violence in death.

In the USA increased death by violence is now the province of *young* males. It is the third leading cause of death amongst the young. The number of deaths due to firearms is per capita seven times the figures for the UK. The frequency of suicide has doubled among children and adolescents in the last thirty years, an increase significantly due to firearms. Guns are used in 55 per cent of suicides in the USA.

According to Dr Sherwin B. Nuland, when American men do not choose firearms they choose what he temperately calls 'old fashioned' methods such as hanging and stabbing.[28]

In Britain there is a similar picture. The most common male choice of method (three out of ten) is hanging. Sometimes hanging is combined with other methods. By contrast less than one fifth of female suicides die by hanging.

If stabbing, firearms or hanging do not work first time, a man may add pills and gas. Sometimes a poorly planned suicide is botched. In desperation the man will keep trying until he succeeds. I discovered that men who wished to die were highly goal oriented. 'First Dad took paracetemol and whisky. When that didn't work he attached the vacuum hose to the car and gassed himself. He had to get it right.' Deena, Nurse.)

'My boyfriend leapt under a train in Germany, our home. He had to choose a method where he could not be saved. He wrote in his note that he asked himself which method he should use and that for him the worst would be if he were still alive when he tries to kill himself.' (Clara, German survivor.)

Persistent violent methods can result in the discovery – usually by a woman – of a body that has been lacerated, shot, poisoned and finally hanged.

'One doctor cut his throat totally round, then to make sure, he cut the arteries in both wrists, then bleeding three ways he went and sat in this boiling hot bath. His wife, of course, she was the one to find him.' (Jessie, former hospital nurse.)

Jessie's father-in-law used a variety of violent methods, before his wife found him.

> Will's father had been renting all his life. When his Dad got the money he bought a bungalow, couldn't bear the responsibility, got depressed. One day he three quarters cut his throat then lay till Will's Mum stumbled over him, bleeding all over their new carpet. Because he was respectable the doctor hushed it up. If they hadn't he might have got sectioned, saved us all from something worse. The second time he swallowed every tablet in the house then he finished himself off with a bottle of paraquat. You die in total screaming agony with convulsions. Poor Will's Mum found him writhing behind the sofa in his death throes.

The case of an American couple, Tom and Madeleine, a retired doctor and schoolteacher, is similarly characteristic of many male suicides. The couple who had planned for years to make agreeable use of retirement suddenly discovered Tom had no taste for a life without professional care for others. He sank into despair. One afternoon after they had been pruning their fruit trees, Madeleine drove off to see her mother. 'On my way, I suddenly realised I'd left behind Mom's birthday gift. So I headed back into the drive. I could see the garden. Tom was swinging from one of the trees. Thank God I got there in time to cut him down. But I shall never get over that image.'

Tom's suicidal motivation fits the male pattern that often occurs after retirement. There is also Tom's individual psychology to add to the equation, and the feeling of total dislocation all would-be suicides experience. But his choice of violent method, like Jessie's father-in-law's, takes no account of a wife's reactions.

Violence intensifies disbelief and the sense of unreality. Barbaric methods produce complex grief responses. 67 per cent of such suicides are committed by men. Women, primary caregivers and caretakers, pick up the tab. And the pieces.[29]

There is one suspected reason for death by hanging (particularly in young males): the contemporary cult of 'auto-eroticism'. This involves hanging whilst masturbating or indulging in sado-masochistic rituals, where the projected end result is not death but a spectacular orgasm. In many cases this event goes wrong and the young men die.

Simpson and Knight have this to say:

Exceptions to suicidal hanging occur in young men as mishaps during experimental tying-up or suspension for the masochistic enjoyment of simple restraint or pain or in sex perversions. Such subjects are often found naked, or may be clothed in women's attire, chained, padlocked, bound with strips of adhesive plaster and found with pin-up types of alluring female nudes set out within view. *Girls do not indulge in this dangerous perversion . . .* These cases must not be mistaken for suicides; they are misadventure – the verdict used by the coroner.[30] (My emphasis.)

Despite Simpson and Knight's warning, these cases are often mistaken for suicides because of another curious coroner's quirk. Instead of the verdict 'accidental death' or 'death by misadventure', the coroner may bring in a verdict of suicide because he believes this will offer greater protection to a mourning family. Again, as in the reverse procedure, it drastically alters the suicide statistics, and makes adequate grieving based on an honest verdict difficult for those left behind.

Several homeopaths have posited an interesting reason for gender differences in suicide methods. They see hanging symbolically as a severe separation of the head from the body. 'When men think the head no longer works, that things aren't getting achieved, then that head is literally cut off from the rest of the body. The intellectual process is severed.'[31]

Some sociologists see the violent male method of leaping from tall buildings as illustrating the 'moral career' of a man from a feeling of success down (a long way down) to absolute failure. Confirmation of this view is the number of male suicides that occurred during the period of the Wall Street crash when businessmen leapt to their death from skyscrapers.

These perspectives, which confirm men's reliance on achievement, typically omit the consequences of violence on women and children. 'My daughter Biddy refused to divorce her husband. So Kevin swallowed an overdose, then rushed round their house with an axe chopping down all the furniture and terrifying Biddy and six-year-old Bunny. The child still talks about her Dad and the chopper.' (Jessie.)

American researcher, E.S. Shneidman (1982), reports that survivors of violent suicides who discovered the body, or were witnesses to violent suicide attempts, may take years to come to terms with that shattering experience. Images may never disappear entirely.[32]

Where methods are violent, women survivors are often advised by medical personnel or police not to view the body. Some women may appreciate this but it does deny them the reality of that death, it gives them no chance for leave-taking, and may give them wilder fantasies about the horrors of the body.

Factors That Predispose Women towards or Inhibit them from Committing Suicide

My findings in this area are interesting but tentative and confirmatory research would be useful. Two exploratory patterns however have so far emerged.

1. Women who have been *sexually abused* or subject to severe forms of male sexual violence appear to be more predisposed towards suicide than women who have not been.

2. Women who have *dependent children* often feel inhibited from committing suicide, as long as they do not fall into the category of incest survivors.

1. Incest Survivors/Survivors of Sexual Abuse

I looked at two groups of women. The first group were the young adolescent girls who make up the remaining one third of adolescent suicides.

Research shows that many adolescent girls who have been sexually abused consistently contemplate suicide, frequently attempt it; some succeed.

Elisabeth Kubler-Ross, writing in 1983 when suicide in the USA among children aged six to sixteen was the third most common cause of death, and when in many communities where she worked up to 30 per cent of teenagers had attempted or committed suicide, pointed out that 'many little girls have lived through years of incest and physical abuse, unable to confide in a grown-up because of threats to her life if she did so.'

From Kubler-Ross's first hundred incest cases involving little children, more than half the children were threatened with death if they were to as much as insinuate that 'something happened to them'.

'Needless to say, they were petrified when left in the care of an abusing father, grandfather or uncle, and several of them preferred to die of their own choice rather than endure the tortures any longer.'[33]

The second group of women were adults who were incest survivors prior to becoming suicide victims. According to bereavement counsellors, many were mothers, but motherhood held no positive meaning for them in terms of suicide deterrent.

'Several women I see regularly have experienced acute violence either as children or in their young adult years. This leads them to make several attempts before finally they succeed in killing themselves.' (Donna, Bereavement counsellor.)

> This woman, abused as a child, took her low image of herself around the world, picked up men who treated her like dirt. This confirmed her view of herself. When she finally managed a relationship with a nice guy who treated her well, she said to me: 'It's no good. I don't deserve to live and look after my kids.' She tried to kill herself.
>
> (Dorothy. Bereavement counsellor.)

Dorothy counselled suicidal women who had been routinely sexually abused. She felt they may eventually kill themselves from despair rooted in past family abuse which resulted in continuous self-blame.

> One woman lived in emotional grot. All her relationships were dirt. Her Mum used to tell her as a kid never to come out of their bathroom without being fully dressed or one of the men in the family would have her. One day when she was eight she rushed out in just a towel and her brother and her brother's friend raped her repeatedly. They continued this for years. She blames herself for coming out in a towel. She still can't see it wasn't her fault.
>
> (Dorothy.)

The woman married, had three children, wishes to kill herself. Her marriage repeats the themes of her childhood.

> He made her have sex with their dog. Then he killed himself. Now she feels she can't go much lower and can't go on living. She has nightly dreams in which she hears her dead husband's voice saying 'Go on! Go on! Kill yourself!' She has always obeyed him so she feels she should. I am hoping that my work with her may help.

Fortunately my exploration also came up with more positive findings. The majority of women I spoke to are *not* predisposed towards suicide.

Group 1: Women Bereaved by Non-Suicidal Deaths
Would they contemplate suicide? If so under what circumstances? A few women said they would contemplate it for one or more of these reasons:

1. If old, incontinent, or left alone without family or friends.
2. If they had become a 'terrible burden' on others, or believed they would be 'better out of the way'.
3. If they had a 'free autonomous choice' and circumstances warranted it. Some women qualified this statement by saying they did not feel they had a free choice because their lives were bound up with other lives.

Several women said they would contemplate suicide if:

1. They had motor neurone disease, or were terminally ill with no hope of recovery. Several women suggested suicide would be more likely if they were not connected to family or friends.

The majority of women said irrespective of grief/illness they would not commit suicide for one or more reasons:

1. Strong religious beliefs.
2. A strong spiritual feeling (not aligned to any specific religion) that we are all connected to a life process and that it would be wrong to kill oneself.
3. They felt 'life affirming'. Despite pain or ill health they wanted to get the best they could from this life.
4. It was their job to see others through.
5. They had a responsibility for their children.
6 They could not bear to leave behind those they loved.
7. They had hopes for their future when their dependants grew up. No matter what their difficulties they wished to see those hopes through.
8 Suicide was selfish.
9. They rejected violence, and saw suicide as violent.

Conclusions: Women bereaved by non-suicide deaths felt a sense of spirituality, connection with family and friends, or desire for peace and hope for the future would inhibit them from suicide.

Group 2: Suicide Survivors: some statements:
'I'll never understand why. I'll never cope. I'll just look like I am coping. I'm so angry. How dare she leave me like this. If I could punish everyone by dying I would – but then I probably wouldn't.' (Gay. Daughter overdosed.)

'The guilt doesn't go away. I still think it was my fault. But I can't put that on them, they rely on me.' (Sarah. Son jumped off bridge.)

'I feel bereft and very scared. I want to take care of everyone I have left. I don't want to leave them like I've been left.' (Kathleen. Husband shot himself.)

'My brother's leap to death has not made me contemplate suicide, because I see suicide as a negation of life. It has made me think more about life. I feel connected to the life process.' (Janine. Brother leapt from building.)

'I think about her all the time. For years she wanted to give up on pain and I tried to stop her. I feel as desperate now as maybe she felt but I'm not ill, just desperate. I am quite a spiritual person so I won't kill myself.' (Susie. Woman partner overdosed.)

'I can't imagine taking my life. I've been haunted by Dad's death. But I'm not brave enough or loopy. I've got two kids who were his grandchildren. He didn't think of that. It's an extremely selfish act.' (Deena. Father gassed himself in car.)

'What you want to do if your child has died is die too. I lay in bed with pneumonia working out how to take the kids with me. When I recovered I felt I had to carry on because of the two little ones, Maisie in particular. Somebody said: "She'll be your ray of sunshine."' (Annie. Son leapt to death.)

'I feel betrayed so I'm angry and relieved after all those years of tension. You're never supposed to feel relieved. Sometimes I think it would be better to get out, then on another day I think I'm too much in my life to do that.' (Shirley. Brother leapt under train.)

Conclusions: Suicide survivors: **Evidence which suggested they might be more likely to contemplate suicide proved wrong.** Life affirmation, passivity, responsibility for children, dislike of selfishness, spirituality, and awareness of effects of suicide acted as deterrents.

Reviewing comments from both groups, several patterns emerge that might begin to explain why women find it harder to commit suicide than men do.

1. They had lived through the effects of a suicide
2. Greater sense of connectedness
3. Significance of spiritual feelings
4. Socialisation to nurture others
5. Less awareness of own needs
6. Recognition of emerging needs/hopes for their future
7. Anti-violence feeling
8. Suicide seen as negative or selfish
9. Sense of responsibility for offspring

10. Fear of leaving loved ones (in a table of fears people of both sexes have about death, women's biggest fear was the fear of leaving intimates behind. 54 per cent of women offered a choice of fears chose that).[34]

Within these ten patterns (many of which are linked to one another), the most consistent amongst women who were bereaved mothers was their ongoing sense of responsibility for their children. In terms of women's relation to suicide this gives ground for optimism.

Chapter Eleven

AIDS: THE SOCIAL DEATH KEPT UNDER WRAPS

AIDS can affect anyone. Women. Men. Children. Heterosexual. Homosexual. Black or white.

AIDS is not a gay disease. AIDS is not a male disease. AIDS affects women.

Why am I saying this? Do we not know this already? Is the truth not something we hear on the news? See on television? Read in the magazines?

Well, maybe.

In the small print. As a footnote to the still prevalent media mythology that implies AIDS happens to others. To the gay who are now not-so-gay (and quite right too!) I have heard that a great deal. Witnessed stories to that effect. Seen reports that imply AIDS is not a women's disease. Well, not a straight women's disease. Encroaching homophobia even imperceptibly blemishes lesbians who are actually the group of people *least* at risk physically. Media mythology persuades us that AIDS does not much concern other women. Other women's families. Other women's children. Initial hysteria in 1981 (when the first cases reported concerned gay men) promoted a fallacious view of a 'gay male plague' and invisibilised the risks for all women. I repeat AIDS is not a gay male disease. The virus does not discriminate. People do.

It is time for figures. Time for facts.

AIDS can affect anyone.

Today (which happens as I write to be World AIDS Day, 1 December 1994) the latest figures show $19\frac{1}{2}$ million people worldwide are HIV positive. In the UK alone at least 21,718 people have contracted HIV; of these 9,025 have developed AIDS and over 6,000 have died (figs. to March 1994). Many more people are infected than we know about, who may not know themselves, who may be frightened to find out, because of the prejudice and discrimination they will be forced to combat.

AIDS can affect women.

Although the exact level of HIV infection among women worldwide is not known, evidence shows that millions are already HIV positive and millions more likely to become infected before the turn of the century. The World Health Organisation reports that HIV infection in women is set to become 'one of the major challenges to public health, health care and social support systems worldwide'.[1]

The global picture in 1990 according to WHO showed that of the more than ten million people – by 1993 this was 13 million men, women and children – infected with HIV, the virus which leads to Acquired Immune Deficiency Syndrome (AIDS), about one third were women, most of whom contracted the virus through heterosexual intercourse. **Globally in 1993 three out of four HIV infections were through heterosexual sex transmissions.**

Despite the fact that in industrialised countries including the UK and USA the WHO emphasises that globally the major route for HIV transmission is heterosexual intercourse (which by 1993 accounted for well over 60 per cent of all infections), there is *still* the impression that HIV and AIDS only affects certain minority groups such as homosexual men, injecting drug users, recipients of blood transfusions or blood products.[2]

In Africa, where HIV infection among women is believed to be the most widespread, the disease has affected several thousand women. The WHO 1992 estimates for sub-Saharan Africa projected for the start of 1993 a total of 600,000 cases of AIDS in women and a similar number in children. In Central Eastern and Southern Africa, and some parts of the Caribbean women and men have been infected with HIV *in equal numbers. Primarily through heterosexual sex.* Though the first appearance of AIDS in Latin America and the Caribbean was in men who had unprotected homosexual sex, because a significant number of men in those regions have intercourse with both sexes, infection has spread increasingly to women.[3]

In Europe and the USA although the majority affected at present are gay or bisexual men, a significant number of women have contracted the disease. Many women are partners of bisexual men, drug users, or haemophiliacs; many women have contracted the infection through injecting drugs, some are recipients of infected blood transfusions. In the UK by December 1992 the Department of Health had recorded 19,000 cases of HIV and almost 7,000 of AIDS in Britain.[4] Though three out of four of these 7,000 cases were in homosexual or bisexual men, because AIDS can take at least ten years to become symptomatic, today's pattern of AIDS cases reflects the pattern of HIV transmission of a decade ago. *By 1993 the pattern had changed so that one in three HIV infections were in heterosexuals.*

By June 1994, in the UK alone, of the 22,101 people with HIV, there were 2,995 women. In the UK in 1988 there were 61 cases of AIDS in women. By September 1994 figures show that of the 9,865 reports of AIDS cases since reporting began in 1982, 837 were female. 68 per cent of the total are known to have died. In the UK for one year to September 1994 while the number of AIDS cases in men rose by 12 per cent the number of AIDS cases in women rose almost as much, by 11 per cent from 196 to 218. Statistics put out for World AIDS Day on 1 December 1994 show that the 37 per cent increase in AIDS among women in Great Britain was particularly high for the previous year as was the rise in those infected through heterosexual sex, a rise of 42 per cent.

The British projection through till 1997 is that AIDS incidence may peak but not get any higher amongst homosexual men *whilst incidence in those exposed heterosexually is expected to increase steadily throughout the forthcoming period from 1994 for the next three years.* This will have severe effects on women and children.[5]

Where else in the Western world are women affected?

The USA reports the greatest number of HIV affected women in the industrialised world. By the end of 1990 over 13,000 women and over 2,500 children had been affected by AIDS, the largest number of AIDS cases affecting women and children in the industrial world. These cases only represent the tip of the iceberg and have continued to increase. In the USA women account for over 10 per cent of AIDS cases. Estimates from twenty-four states suggest three out of every 2,000 childbearing women nationwide are HIV positive and levels of infection are five to fifteen times higher for black women, an indication of the underlying factor that helps the virus spread in many parts of the world: disadvantage and poverty. New York is the worst affected state, accounting for about a quarter of all AIDS cases in the country, of which more than 17 per cent are women.

The major cause of death for women between the ages of twenty-five and thirty-four in New York City is AIDS. In the USA, though drug injecting accounts for the majority of female cases, over one-third results from heterosexual sex.[6]

Figures. Figures. Figures.

A roller-coaster ride of frightening and sensational statistics.

Yes. But . . .

What these figures and facts show is that AIDS can affect anyone. Women are not immune. Women are at risk.

As a society which still brushes away AIDS as a gay male disease, we have not acknowledged these facts. This means that the impact of HIV and AIDS on women is still little recognised and insufficiently documented. Partly this problem has come about because when AIDS was first reported in the USA, it appeared primarily to affect men, gay men, who had the power and the money to make the disease and research around it a prime political and social concern, something that for instance has not been achieved by women workers in the field of breast cancer.

Today, however, women can no longer afford to ignore AIDS any more than they can afford to ignore breast cancer. Women need financial support and political power to fight invisibility as well as the disease itself. AIDS-related problems concern women. Some AIDS issues are specific only to women. Where women are at risk, so too are any future children they may have. Infection can be passed between sexual partners and from mother to new-born infant. Estimates for the year 2000 are that the mothers of 10 to 15 million children globally will have died of AIDS.[7] The specific problem AIDS creates for women, and only for women, is the possible transmission of infection at birth to the foetus. In addition to risks to themselves and their children, the task of caring for those with AIDS, as with any disease, falls on women. Though AIDS is not a gay disease, its early description as that, and the immediate response by the gay male world, also involved and still involves lesbians as health-care workers and political workers within AIDS projects. Like gay men they have been smeared, sullied and silenced not merely by the general taboo around any death, but by the extra discreditation of death by a disreputable disease. The two issues most relevant to this study are: where women fit into the AIDS debate and how AIDS slots into the silencing around death.

Women's Place in the AIDS Debate

Current information at the time of writing shows that worldwide women account for 40 per cent of AIDS cases and that worldwide 10 per cent of people with AIDS are children born to mothers who are

HIV positive.[8] Insufficient research has been done on patterns of
infection in women, though an interesting on-going study in San
Francisco called AWARE (Association for Women's AIDS Research
and Education Project) studied 550 women to analyse their risk for
HIV infection as a result of heterosexual contact. The women either
had a heterosexual relationship with a man at risk for AIDS in the
previous three years or had had multiple sexual relationships with
men (defined as five or more sexual partners) during the previous
three years. Preliminary reports show over 5 per cent to be antibody
positive. This is too small a number to report anything significant,
but what it does reveal is that compared to women who had a negative test result, the 'positive' group were more likely to have had
bisexual or injecting drug use partners, or partners with AIDS.[9]

Women are at risk of acquiring the HIV virus if they:

Inject drugs and share needles, syringes, other equipment.

Have unprotected sexual intercourse with an HIV infected man.
(This may be voluntary or may be rape. Women may be in personal sexual relationships or they may be prostitutes. They may
be sexual partners of intravenous drug users or haemophiliacs.)

Are artificially inseminated by an HIV infected man. (Today this is
very unlikely if official channels are used because sperm samples
and donors are tested and re-tested at intervals.)

Receive a blood transfusion with HIV infected blood. (In the USA
and UK this risk is largely eliminated.)

One female funeral director talked about blood transfusions: 'If
someone has died of AIDS it's all hush-hush. People walk up to you
and whisper: "You won't spread this about will you?" Why should
they be ashamed? The last person I dealt with got AIDS through
blood transfusion. Why be ashamed about that?' (Mandy Walker,
Funeral Director.)

Why indeed?

In the USA figures for women with AIDS are believed to be an
underestimate because doctors still do not expect women to get
AIDS. There is another problem attached to discovering AIDS in
women. Because the disease was initially defined in terms of symptoms first seen in gay men, the opportunistic infections which may
be part of AIDS-related diseases *in women* still go undetected.
Another reason for invisibility is that women may be ashamed to
admit they are at risk through injecting drugs or through having
bisexual partners.

I knew Sam had been gay but when he asked me to live with him, he and I both believed those days were over. They weren't, but I didn't know that until after our marriage when he became sick. When I told my parents, my father said 'How could you have married someone like that?' Sam died last year, I am HIV positive, and holding out very little hope. But despite my family's reactions I don't regret my relationship with Sam in any way..

(Alice, New York woman, thirty-three.)

In the USA the largest group of women with AIDS, about half, is those who inject drugs. In England recent figures suggest between 10 and 20 per cent of women who inject drugs are already HIV infected. In Edinburgh it is higher, nearly half. This reflects the difficulties of obtaining sterile needles at least in the past – an outcome of police attempts to regulate drug use by restricting hypodermic needles.

Giving up drugs doesn't always save a woman.

She had all sorts of problems . . . skin rashes, dizziness, sensitivity to sunlight, stomach pains and terrible fatigue . . . Joan thought she might have AIDS, but since she hadn't used needles since 1980 or '81 I figured it was just panic . . . Of course she should have gone to a doctor, but Joan didn't have health insurance, and we didn't have much money . . . she ended up applying for welfare in order to receive Medicaid. She could barely get out of the house . . .

Joan was diagnosed with AIDS in February 1987 in New York City. Her lover Jennifer Brown recalls the mistakes made during her hospitalisation.

'One day when I came to visit, Joan's left arm and wrist were both rigid, her neck was contorted, and her mouth dropped at the corner. I thought she'd had a stroke.'

The doctors took no notice until she lay almost immobile. Joan, convinced she had an adverse drug reaction, proved to be correct. Her paralysis was a side effect of the drug Compazine, taken to combat nausea. For a time she improved, left hospital and was in her partner's care. But she suffered from the shame and silence around both AIDS and drugs.

'She shied away from seeing most of our friends. She didn't want them to know she had AIDS because of the drug history behind it.'

By late June, due to an undiagnosed AIDS-related infection she began to lose her vision. She decided to kill herself.

Joan's death was horrible and unexpected, even though we'd often discussed her desire to die. I found this message in our home . . . 'Time to end inhumanity. We need to lobby for merciful deaths for terminally ill people on this earth. An overdose of opium, morphine, or heroin would have made mine a painless, less ugly and less violent type of death.

Jennifer Brown, still in grief for her partner, now committed to AIDS work, believes: 'This is a very threatening subject to most people. Even though death is as great a taboo as sex once was, we must start talking about our schizophrenic attitudes towards it. It shouldn't be hidden away.'[10]

Many women who inject drugs are doubly at risk of developing AIDS: both directly at risk from infection, and also as sexual partners of men who inject drugs.

In the USA where 73 per cent of women with AIDS are black or Hispanic, health officials suggest it reflects a more widespread use of injectable drugs among black and Hispanic women. But social conditions for black women's lives, including poor access to health education and great poverty, as well as racism and sexism, put them at greater risk. This must also be taken into account by health officials.

Some female drug users who are antibody positive have been denied dental treatment, surgical operations, even medical care for their drug problems. This partly stems from health workers' unfounded fears that they may contract HIV (they at least should know better!); partly it is related to the punishing ideology that drug users (like gay men) get what they deserve.

Women in some countries are particularly vulnerable to HIV infection from heterosexual contact as they may be severely financially dependent on men, may rely on husbands or male partners for even the roof over their head, or may have been sold by their families into prostitution. These women will have little power to insist men wear condoms during intercourse.

A recent survey in Rwanda in Central Africa found more than one third of women aged nineteen to twenty-one who claimed to have slept only with their husbands were HIV infected. Organisations like the Society for Women and AIDS in Africa currently campaign to protect women's health by improving their social status. Education may be one way to promote opportunities to earn money without resorting to prostitution.[11]

Researchers believe it is easier for men to transmit the virus to women during heterosexual intercourse than it is for a woman to pass it on to a man. This again places women in a highly vulnerable position. The substantially higher figures for women developing AIDS through heterosexual contact with men, than the reverse, indicates a highly significant finding: while heterosexual contact to date has been less important than homosexual contact in the spread of AIDS among men, *in women heterosexual sex is a very significant risk factor.* Even five years ago, in the USA, of the total reported cases of people with AIDS where the only risk factor was heterosexual contact, over 75 per cent were women. Five years on, this percentage has increased.[12]

Bereavement Problems for Women in Partnership With Men With AIDS
The fact that AIDS is contagious means that a partner or wife of someone dying of AIDS has to confront the question of whether she will also develop the disease. Facing the possibility of her own death at often a tragically young age complicates her bereavement in a way that does not happen to women bereaved by other illnesses. It can drastically affect her attitude towards the dead partner. I met women whose love for their men was now confused and ambivalent.

'I feel angry and betrayed not merely abandoned', was one woman's phrase subsequently repeated – over and over – by other women.

These emotions compounded by the stigma around the disease meant some female survivors were rejected by other people in their grief.

Are Lesbians at Risk from AIDS?
It is lesbian sexual partnerships which have generally been regarded as those involving least risk from HIV and AIDS. Certainly there have been very few reported cases of woman-to-woman transmission. However, risks belong not to identifiable social groups but to patterns of activity, and lesbian sexual orientation or lesbian political identity are not in themselves a protection. Injecting drugs or *possibly* unprotected oral sex is as risky for lesbians as for anyone else.

Some lesbians may occasionally have sex with men who may be at risk.

Some lesbians who now only have sex with women used to have sex with men.

Some lesbians are prostitutes who, under pressure from pimps or for financial reasons, may be forced to agree to intercourse with male clients without using condoms.

Some lesbians inject drugs or share equipment.

Some lesbians may have received blood transfusions before screening from 1985 onwards largely eliminated the element of risk.[13]

Many lesbians, alone or in female partnerships, wish to have children and plan this through artificial insemination which can put them at risk.

With AIDS the risk is not how you label yourself but what you do. It is essential in talking about how AIDS affects women to discuss behaviour not how women identify themselves.

Though in practice lesbians appear to be the least-at-risk group, their social and political lives have been affected adversely by the strengthening of homophobia and anti-lesbianism which the mass media portrayal of AIDS has led to. The link between fear of AIDS and gay phobia may affect the rights of lesbians (as well as gay men) in such areas as housing, insurance, employment etc. Lesbians have reported greater violence towards them because of AIDS. As health-care workers and as workers in AIDS projects (for which they volunteer in substantial numbers) they are daily involved in the care of women and men with AIDS. For many lesbians considering artificial insemination, the desire to have a child is quite a separate issue from wanting to have sex with someone. Another reason for lesbians' preference for babies by artificial insemination is to attempt to ensure sole guardianship and custody of their child. The current reluctance of British and American courts to grant custody and often access to lesbian mothers is already well documented and is based on the nonsensical assumption that lesbians do not make 'good mothers'. Increased anti-gay hostility during the AIDS crisis has given courts a new objection to lesbian motherhood. In the USA a lesbian mother was denied visitation rights because the judge feared that she might give her children AIDS.

If leaders in the legal profession can show such ignorance and homophobia it is hardly surprising that lesbians meet it everywhere else.

Recently both artificial insemination (the use of a syringe rather than a penis to introduce sperm into the vagina) and self-insemination (where women do it themselves without the help of doctors or official donor organisations) have become areas of concern. Initially this was due to four Australian cases of women artificially inseminated with infected semen, and subsequently to some clinics discarding samples of donated sperm; other clinics are closing their doors. Most clinics now screen would-be donors for HIV infection, and some British lesbians have been successful in obtaining artificial insemination through the National Health Service, but in general the British medical profession regards artificial insemination as a way of helping heterosexual couples to conceive a child. Costs of using a sperm bank are prohibitive for women on low incomes. Women who then decide to self-inseminate could be at risk if they use semen without first screening their donor.

Women as Carers of People with AIDS

Though women do contract AIDS themselves, it is their role as carers which has allowed AIDS to have the greatest impact on their lives.

Society expects women, as wives, partners and mothers, to care for their sick children, spouses, male partners, and parents. As we have seen in earlier chapters, the financial and social burdens this places on women are debilitating. Caring for people with AIDS, however, is considerably more complex. Several mothers of homosexual sons talked about the dual shock they received when they discovered both the disease and their sons' orientations, which made caring an ambivalent process.

> I had always suspected Richard was gay but his father and I never mentioned it. It felt too terrible. He lived away and only occasionally brought his 'friend' home. Of course we gave them separate bedrooms. When Richard became iller and iller after his 'friend' died, I feared the worst but my husband never suspected a thing. I decided to bring Richard home, look after him until he died, but I asked him never to spell out his disease to the family. It has taken eighteen months of horrors, he passed away last year, and soon, for my own peace of mind, I am going to tackle what really happened with his Dad and younger brother.
>
> (Mary, British mother, fifty-eight.)

Seventy-year-old poet, April Ryedale, was another mother who talked openly about the feelings she encountered during the time she spent caring for Christopher, her son who died of AIDS.

> Before he got it I knew little about the disease, only that it had become the plague. My husband died eight years before Christopher. Thank God he died. I don't know how he would have coped. He'd have found it harder to accept than I did. In the

process of being counselled I found only my top liberal self was accepting, my emotional half was very angry with Christopher.

Christopher himself was highly aware of how the stigma affects families.

He didn't want it known it was AIDS. He said my grandchildren who lived near us might be in trouble at school if people knew their uncle had AIDS. Sexually he was gay and straight, and he had been on drugs. He was thirty-six, he always said he belonged to all the risk groups. There wasn't anything he hadn't done that couldn't have been the cause! So, yes, I was angry, but I felt my task was to be at his side. When he told the family I wrote warmly and said feel free to come when you are ill. I was able to feel protective towards him if I thought of him as a woman, not as a dull man who had done a stupid thing. The whole time I was carrying him I thought of him as a girl. I called him Mary Judith then out popped another little boy. So in the end it was easier to care for him as if he was a girl. I never realised what nursing that illness meant. I felt as a carer who was his mother my standards would be expected to be higher. He stayed with me, sick, so sick, until near the end. I felt when Christopher wants to die, I will help him die. I was absolutely clear as his mother that was what I was here for, and would do.

However Christopher told his counsellor he wished to die alone.
'It was a terrible mishearing between us. I thought he wanted me to help him shorten his life when the end got terrible. But Christopher couldn't die as long as he knew I wanted him to.'
April recalls the tensions in the mother-son relationship.

Coping with Christopher in the house at all after a few weeks is hell, even though we were close. He needed a mother like me to rebel against, even at the end. He needed to get his teeth into my arm. But mothers aren't ever supposed to want their sons to die. It was a terrible decision to let him go. To stop my caring. But he was doubly incontinent. The opportunistic infections were crowding in. He had herpes, thrush, everything. He had warts on his prick. But finally I knew I couldn't and shouldn't keep him with me any longer. Whatever it was I was supposed to be doing for him something in him fouled it up.

Christopher was transferred to a Sue Ryder home for his last weeks.

> I saw him several times. He was on a morphine drip but he would whimper when he was fully under. This is the only dying person I've ever attended. This is my son. When I visited him when he was in a coma, I tried to keep out of sight of his slightly half-opened eyes. I held his hand so as not to bring him back. It was very hard that I had to be *not* his mother. Very hard. Sons either reject their mothers or they cannot separate. We had not resolved our relationship. I did my grieving as he lay dying. When he was dead I summoned up my sister and my daughter to come and look at him. He was in a foetal position on the pillow. Little head bowed sideways. Six feet long. I kissed him and went. They have to burn them. They don't want AIDS bodies lying around. I was writing poems about Christopher. That morning at 8.30 I just howled at the cosmos. I said 'You cannot burn the body of my son'. When we got the ashes a month later I put together four poems and called them 'My Son, My Son'. We scattered the ashes in my daughter Laura's garden under an ash tree. Today there are snowdrops and daffodils growing there.

April Ryedale like other mothers in this study believes she will never get over her grief, but her poetry is the positive outcome of her son's death.

'Becoming a poet so late in life comes absolutely directly from the pain that needs some form of expression. I'd always wanted certainty, now I accept there is no certainty. But however painful this separation may be I never see it as final.'

Where AIDS Fits Into the Censure and Silence Around Death

We might suppose that funeral firms who deal daily with death would merely regard AIDS as a disease. This is not so. Listen to the voices of the female funeral directors:

> Some funeral firms refuse to have anything to do with AIDS cases. I was approached by the local AIDS helpline because several firms had turned them down. The helpline lady said: 'You know he'll come out of the hospital in a special sealed bag. There will be a zip! Are you prepared to do it?' When I reassured her, she was

quite overcome. Thought us dealing with AIDS was the best thing
since sliced bread.

(Sally Smith, Funeral Director.)

Whenever we collect an AIDS or HIV body from hospital there is
a great plastic tag on the toe to signify this body has died of something nasty. We don't embalm because you can catch it from body
fluids. We always wear surgeons' gloves anyway, but with AIDS we
put on a mask. Some of the men in our firm say: 'Oh the dirty
gits!' or 'He's a queer old boy!' Men in the funeral trade look on
AIDS more grossly than women do.

(Sally Smith.)

Female funeral directors discover friends of those who died of AIDS
are reticent about obituaries. 'People are afraid to put an advert in the
paper saying what the body died of. Or they say give money to cancer research instead of to AIDS. They want to say something in the
newspaper but they don't dare. I help them place a loving message
that is discreet.' (Mandy Walker, Funeral Director.)

Obituaries are instructive. They tell us about attitudes to death.
They tell us about attitudes to AIDS. They reveal homophobia.
Revelations of stigma and silence. An effective shroud. Obituaries do
not mention that AIDS can affect anyone. Men. Women. Children.
Heterosexual. Homosexual. Black or white. They are selective in
their discretion. Conservative of nuclear family values, prejudicial in
their presentation of any alternatives. Although intimately concerned with mortality, they support the silencing of certain deaths.

Tania, sister and friend to Toby, who died of AIDS when only
thirty-two, showed me her brother's obituary advertised by the
American funeral home. Toby's obituary and Tania's story illustrate
how AIDS has become one side of a three-sided polygon, that trian-
gle of compulsory quietude, whose remaining and connected two
sides are homosexuality and death.

The obituary did not of course mention the nature of his disease.
It merely confirmed his 'brave fight against a long illness', eulogised
him as a 'beloved son' of his caring parents, 'dear brother' of his
three older siblings and 'affectionate uncle' towards his sister Tania's
three children and his 'dear brother' Bob's three children.

What I noticed was the last line of the obituary. Tucked away dis-
creetly at the bottom, before the date of the memorial service and the
suggested donations not of course to AIDS charities but to Amnesty
International, an excellent and significantly respectable cause, was

the phrase: 'He is also survived by his close companion Robin Godstone.' 'Close companion' was the nearest a traditional obituary came to commemorate the grief of a same-sex lover, his partner for fifteen years, who was with him when he died.

Note the word 'also'.

Tobias Gee, Toby to his extended family and wide circle of friends, was born in London, educated at Oxford and Yale, Assistant Professor of Political Science at an American University since 1988, specialist with an international reputation in Latin American politics, groundbreaking writer on the experience of Uruguay's torture victims, composer, tenor, jazz pianist with a taste for Jerome Kern and Cole Porter. His sisters, both writers, Ellie, forty-five, and Tania, forty-three, recall his large fluent hands moving over the piano keys as he played and sang: 'Every Time We Say Goodbye' and 'The Way You Look Tonight'.

Toby Gee, the golden boy. Golden with promise. Much of it fulfilled. Youngest by several years in an emotionally knit family of four. AIDS the adversary of that promise. Tarnishing him for five years unsuspected by – or at least not revealed to – the family who treasured him. Within that household at least three members, his father, his mother and his sister Tania, consistently denied the reality of exactly who he was, what dangers he was subject to (not because he was gay – AIDS I repeat is not a 'gay disease' – but because his unsafe *behaviour* put him at risk of infection), and what illness ultimately he contracted.

Every time he visited England during his last five years, the way he looked tonight worsened. Every time they said goodbye, thoughts of a stigmatised disease lurked below the conscious surface of Tania's mind. The stigma prevented her from acknowledging it to herself, and certainly from talking about it to him. Or from discussing it with her parents.

It was an odd relationship because I was a sort of second mother to him. I was eight years old when he was born. My feelings were maternal as well as sisterly. I worried about him terribly. He came out as gay when he was twenty-one, at Oxford. I remember my father saying: 'But I don't want a queer for a son!' My mother said: 'We should never have sent him to Oxford.' To be absolutely honest my reaction was: 'Oh God, how awful! How dreadful!' *I felt bereaved when he told me.* To be perfectly honest, and that means not being at all politically correct, I have to say I thought it was a sort of pathology. I thought there was something wrong with him.

I loved him very much and couldn't bear the idea of him being an outcast from society, a 'different' person. I wanted him to have marriage. I wanted him to have children. I've changed my attitude a lot, but I still have a basic feeling that homosexuality is a kind of problem, a wrongness, but I keep very quiet about it because I know this isn't an acceptable thing to say.

Toby's parents, like his sister, had a discrepant personal and public attitude.

My mother said it was the most awful thing that had ever happened to her. She said it was the biggest tragedy of her life. She didn't think she'd ever get over it. That was what she said privately but her public act was completely broad-minded. They welcomed his boyfriends to the house. One Christmas his lover, a French guy, came and my parents gave him a bottle of Chanel No.5 as a Christmas present! It was publicly okay but there was chortling, giggling and laughing behind Toby's back.

After Toby's death in 1991, his elder sister Ellie, a British journalist, wrote an open and moving tribute to her brother. Ellie recalls how at Tania's wedding, Toby set Ogden Nash to music, pivoting his composition around the verse: 'Well I'd be in less danger, from the wiles of a stranger, If my own kin and kith, were more fun to be with.'

Ellie's wry comment was that it was 'an accurate statement, I'm afraid'.[14]

Tania believes he contracted the illness from bath houses in New York in his early twenties.

Toby said later he got AIDS through having affairs outside his relationship with Robin. He felt guilty about being unfaithful. His partner Robin was not promiscuous at all. I felt Toby's promiscuity was unnatural. I don't like to admit it but I felt then that this unnatural promiscuity brought this upon him.

Intellectually Tania knew that sexuality is socially constructed, that anyone can choose a homosexual lifestyle. Intellectually she knew that heterosexuality is constructed as normative which makes it seem 'the right and normal thing to do' rather than merely one of a possible series of sexual choices. Emotionally however she felt her thinking had been heavily conditioned.

'I was locked into an equation that said a bad sex life could equal disease, could end in death.'

Tania's remarks about promiscuity highlight a major piece of misinformation about AIDS. As well as being viewed initially as a gay disease, AIDS has always been associated with promiscuity. In their book *AIDS: The Deadly Epidemic* Graham Hancock and Enver Carim tell us that HIV is definitely transmitted through 'the shared use of needles by drug abusers and promiscuous sex of any kind', obviously with an infected person.[15]

There are several problems with this statement. Firstly the authors fail to specify exactly what is meant by 'promiscuous sex'. Their words suggests that it is less the *way* you have sex that matters than the *number* of different people with whom you have sex. They imply that if you restrict your sexual activity to one person you will probably not get AIDS. However being monogomous is no protection against AIDS if your partner is already infected with HIV. Nor does monogamy assist you if you engage in sexual acts that allow transmission of the virus.

The second problem with the idea that 'promiscuous sex' transmits AIDS is that people may believe that everyone infected with HIV or who has AIDS must have been 'promiscuous'. *This is not the case.* As Diane Richardson points out there is substantial evidence to show that people who have had only one sexual encounter have later developed AIDS. Although your chance of becoming infected with HIV increases with repeated exposure, as with pregnancy, you only need to have intercourse once to contract the virus.[16]

A third issue to arise from Tania's statement is that not only does 'promiscuous' mean different things to different people, but (though Tania used it derogatorily about her brother) it generally has different implications depending on whether it is used about a woman or a man. The fact that in our society we have a sexual double standard means it is more acceptable for men to have more sexual partners than it is for women. If women indulge in what is termed 'casual sex' this is seen as more blameworthy than it is for men. A case in point is the way that prostitutes and not their male clients are singled out for blame in spreading AIDS through heterosexual transmission.[17]

Although the number of partners may affect our chances of becoming infected with the virus, 'promiscuity' does not cause AIDS. It is vital to recognise that cutting down on the number of sexual partners will not significantly reduce infection risks if safer sex is not also practised. Tania thought that 'promiscuous people' (in relation to her brother this meant gay men) were a high risk category.

It is not certain groups of people who are high risk but certain kinds of behaviour.

The concept of risk groups may lead people who do not identify with those groups but whose behaviour puts them at risk, to feel AIDS will not affect them. Many married or partnered men, for instance, do not identify as gay or even bisexual, but may have high-risk sexual activity with another man which has serious implications for their wives or partners whom most often they do not tell.

At one level Tania understood this because later she pointed to differences in types of sexual behaviour, safer versus unsafe (as well as differences in numbers of partners) evidenced by Toby with his partner Robin and Toby with other men. But at another level she had bought into the notion that gayness itself, irrespective of safer or riskier behaviour, was a pathway to a disease that invariably results in death.

Toby did not take an HIV test until 1985 when, living with Robin in the USA, he visited his father, who had a by-pass operation at St Mary's Hospital, England.

> Later he told me he received the news in an outrageous way at that same hospital. He'd been an outpatient at the VD clinic. He was walking down the corridor having just seen my Dad, when a doctor stopped him and said: 'Oh by the way your test was positive!' Dad was just the other side of a glass partition.

The importance of the way in which bad news is broken has been a constant theme in this study. The way in which Toby learnt the news of his possibly fatal illness is evidence of appalling – indeed unforgivable – bad practice in the medical field.

At the time and throughout Toby's long illness, Tania denied any evidence of the truth. When AIDS-related symptoms began to appear she refused to recognise them. When Toby visited depressed or distressed, she refused to ask relevant questions.

> Later I realised that for years he had been asking me to say the word to him. But I hadn't picked up any of the signals. He kept sending photographs of himself. I thought: why more photographs? I knew in my heart he sent them because he was going to die. Looking back at the photos, he looked terribly thin and strained. He and his partner visited at Christmas. He was terribly thin, terribly anxious. All the vibes were telling me they were both worried about AIDS. I deliberately didn't ask him. On one

visit he wouldn't kiss my children. He kissed the air. That was before we knew how it got transmitted. The ignorance was appalling. Another time, he was licking an icecream. I grabbed it from him and said: 'Let's have a lick!' He sprang back as if I'd stabbed him. He grabbed it back and said 'No! No!' I should have known then. Well I must have known, but I just wasn't accepting.

Tania was not, and is not, alone in her ignorance. Even today many people believe it is possible to get AIDS through normal everyday contact with an infected person. *This is not the case.* No one can contract HIV simply by being near, eating with or touching a person who is infected. No one can become infected by touching objects used by someone who has the virus. No one has become infected by drinking out of the same cup, swimming in the same pool, sharing clothes or towels. HIV is fragile. It is easily killed outside the body. There is no evidence that it can be spread through the air or by casual social contact.

However, when Toby contracted AIDS his family, like many families today, saw the disease as a monster. Surrounded the subject with a silence through which really useful knowledge could not penetrate.

Of course underneath I worried about AIDS. But death wasn't ever spoken about. There certainly wasn't much grieving or mourning done openly about any death. We only knew horror stories. My aunt had a lodger who died of AIDS. I remember my mother saying she just couldn't let the flat after he died because nobody would rent it. They thought it had to be fumigated.

At one of Toby's visits, I made a joke at the dinner table about how lucky I was that I'd started puberty when the pill first came on the market, that I'd managed to get married just before AIDS. I joked and he looked tense. I thought: 'Oh is that tactless of me?' Then I pushed away the thought. He nearly died of hepatitis B some time before he really got AIDS. Nobody picked up on that. Nobody asked, 'Why has Toby got this dreadful illness?' He'd just come back from South America so the family thought he'd picked it up drinking the water. Nobody wanted to know . . .

As AIDS became a public and controversial issue, Tania and Ellie suspected their brother might be in danger. After Toby already had his positive test results, Ellie, who also lived in the States, phoned him to ask if he'd taken the test as a precaution.

'I didn't dare ask him. But he told Ellie he wouldn't take the test because he'd rather not know. To think when we were just starting to edge towards thinking about it he had already tested positive.'

In another newspaper article which Ellie wrote after Toby's death, she suggested that his decision to hide his illness from his family until an unbearably late stage was typical of his urge to outstrip threatened negativity and pessimism, whilst protecting those dear to him. She saw it as a personal decision on his part, but of course society's taboo and callous attitude – internalised by Toby's family – constructed that decision. Ellie suggests that it was Toby's fear of the depressing and disfiguring symptoms of dementia, lesions, dysentery, blindness, TB and folliculitis, the typical 'Hard Death' (as it is known in medical circles) made harder when shame and guilt are added, which made it terribly difficult for him to admit to the illness. Today Tania believes he needed to talk, and she for one did not allow him to break through the taboo.

> I feel bad I didn't help him unburden himself. Now I know he had been asking me to do that for years. He even got AZT posted to him by a British doctor friend via my mother. My mother needed to be obtuse. Finally when she rang the doctor and said: 'Why am I sending this stuff to Toby? Is he HIV positive?' this guy just said 'It's as well to take this stuff whether you're positive or not!'

In order to multiply HIV needs an enzyme called 'reverse transcriptase'. A drug that stops this enzyme from working should stop the virus reproducing itself. AZT (azidothymadine), an antiviral drug, is thought to work in this way. AZT, made by Burroughs Wellcome, which despite its toxic side effects, which can produce severe anaemia, has been known to prolong the life of some AIDS patients. It is not a cure for AIDS because although it stops the virus from multiplying it does not destroy it. It is not yet clear what the long term effects of taking AZT will be but it has had a certain degree of success. This is one reason why Toby had it sent from England. The other reason was his vain attempts to send across the sea a message in a bottle.

In the summer of 1989 he came for his bi-annual family visit. At this point, recalls Tania, he had nightsweats, cancer on the roof of his mouth, and had been stricken by the form of skin cancer, Kaposi's sarcoma, known as KS. This is one of the two most common illnesses found in people with AIDS which can cause death.

I picked him up at the railway station. Suddenly I could see that he had AIDS. I just saw it. It was absolutely awful. I said: 'Toby, your hair's falling out. What's the matter with you?' He said: 'No, it's not, it's not! I'm perfectly all right. What are you talking about?' He deposited the suitcases. I went for a walk in the rain, tears pouring down my cheeks, thinking if he'd said: 'Oh God is my hair falling out, really?' that would have been the Toby I knew because he was very vain. But the fact that he said 'No it's not!' made me finally realise. He has been trying to tell me this for years and I just haven't allowed him.

It took seven more days before, washing up the supper dishes with his sister, Toby broke through the silence and forced Tania to be open about AIDS.

Suddenly he said in a terribly formal voice: 'My counsellor tells me I have to tell you some very bad news.' He slipped in the word 'counsellor' because he knew I'd have to pick that up. I said: 'Counsellor? Why are you seeing a counsellor?' He said: 'I've got this awful news to tell you.' Basically he didn't want to have to say the word. He wanted me to say it for him. I said: 'I know what you're going to tell me.' He said: 'What am I going to tell you?' I still couldn't get there. I said: 'You're going to tell me you're HIV positive.' He said: 'I'm afraid it's worse than that.' I burst into tears, cried on his shoulder. He said: 'I haven't got any tears left. I've cried all my tears. I've known about this for five years . . . I've accepted it now.' Suddenly Dad walked into the kitchen and said 'What's going on?' We made some flimsy excuse. I said: 'Nothing! Nothing!' Dad walked out of the kitchen and Toby said: 'I've got absolutely no regrets. I've had a wonderful life. I'm not ashamed of anything I've done. I've done everything I wanted to do. When they said I was HIV positive I could either have given up or carried on, achieved everything I wanted to achieve, that's what I've done.

Initially Toby's lack of shame, and self-regard was not echoed by his sister or family.

'It was absolutely awful. I felt this is the worst thing I can imagine. It is my worst fears confirmed . . . But in a way that was the worst moment. Subsequently nothing was quite as awful as that awful blow.'

Toby told his parents who refused to believe it. Tania recalls:

My father said: 'Come on Toby, come on Toby, it's just your high anxiety state. You're just being silly. You're just worrying about nothing.' My mother reads fiction avidly if she's upset. Immediately she buried herself in a book. She had this book at all meal times. She wouldn't talk, she couldn't stop reading. I was chosen to tell my sister. Someone told my brother.

But outside the immediate family a new silence fell.

'Immediately Toby told us, it was like a family instruction: "Don't tell *anybody*. Keep this very secret, we don't want anyone to know." My father and mother were absolutely determined. I've always been very submissive to my parents.'

That year Toby, desperately ill, organised their mother's seventy-fifth birthday party. Dozens of relatives came and went, bringing presents and champagne, ringing up later to ask why Toby looked so terrible.

'Those who knew he was gay asked me 'Has he got AIDS?' I found I said: 'No, no! Of course not. What makes you say that? He's just been overworking.' I told my best friend, I had to tell someone, but mainly I told lies.'

While Tania suffered and prevaricated, Toby became iller. He was again hospitalised in England in a new wing opened by the Princess of Wales.

'That was very important to my mother. She thought this is an unspeakable social disease but if the Princess of Wales says it's okay then maybe it's okay.'

Tania visited him constantly, offering him support whilst trying to sort out her own feelings.

He was a walking skeleton covered in sarcomas. Very disfigured. He'd lost all his hair and had this ridiculous wig. There was so much putting on a brave front. Trying to keep your face from looking shocked. We are rather an emotionally repressed family. To say 'I love you' is impossible . . . So I brought him presents, tapes, tried to distract him. One time he said: 'Tania, I enjoy your visits more than anybody else's.' That was his way of saying 'I love you'. I tried to make sense of his illness. I suppose I knew you could be heterosexual and get AIDS, but I thought more about drug use, or haemophilia, I thought it wasn't so much from sex . . . but I still thought – oh how awful it sounds – that AIDS was a punishment for sin. I can't deny there was an element of that in all our thinking, though of course we all said: 'Of course you haven't sinned or done anything awful. Oh anybody could get it!' Or we said 'What's wrong with being gay? Nothing is.' But in our heart of hearts I don't know if we were believing it. For me there was ambiguousness. Trying to come to terms with my own homophobia . . . it could be that I was, or perhaps still am, ambiguous about myself, my sexuality.

While Tania wrestled with her sexual feelings, Tania's mother, who also visited daily, struggled with her own problems.

My mother kept saying: 'Where did Toby get this from? Who gave it to Toby?' When I said that he'd told me he probably got it from many different sources, may have been infected many times over, she couldn't hear that. She wouldn't listen. It was her son. She couldn't think of him being promiscuous. At the time she didn't really understand what being gay was. She thought it meant having a romantic love for another man. Not any more.

Toby's mother is not the only one I met who found it difficult to face the issue of a sexual experience between their son and another man. However, by the time Toby was sufficiently well to leave hospital and return to America, his mother had decided that if his illness worsened she would fly over to care for him. Within weeks of his return to the States Toby contracted another blood disease. His parents flew out so that his mother could share the care with Robin of Toby's last months. Now denial of death, rather than of AIDS, was the controlling attitude.

'I felt I should talk about death to him. But my mother constantly said: "We mustn't ever depress him. That's what we are here for. We must never give in, never give up."'

Tania, under her mother's instruction, told people Toby had lung cancer. 'At the time I kept smiling. Didn't tell my three children. Of course they know everything now, they came to his funeral, but at the time I handled it very badly.'

Toby deteriorated. Their mother made a transatlantic call to Tania. As a sister-mother Tania now faced her final conflict:

It was the day war was declared in Iraq. They said people shouldn't fly. My mother rang and said: 'He may have less than a week left. You'd better come right now.' What was I to do with the kids If I fly to America without them I might get stuck. I felt I should drop everything! But I didn't drop everything. My husband

and I had planned to go there the following week, taking the children, because my parents believed seeing the children might give Toby a new burst of energy. So I waited. We got there after he had died. For a long time I felt terribly guilty that I hadn't dropped everything. I was faced with that choice: my kids or my brother. But also I was afraid of going, afraid of what I was going to see.

It was a conflict many sisters who are mothers, many women shaken by the way in which AIDS can lay waste and devastate the human frame, will empathise with.

Tania arrived in time for the cremation.

The funeral parlour seemed surprised the family wanted to see him cremated. We drove to a huge warehouse, like an aircraft hangar. In it was a great big incinerator. Because this state was very ecological they told us recycling was important so they wouldn't waste resources on a beautiful wooden coffin. He was in a body bag inside a massive cardboard box, ecologically friendly! It was wheeled in on an old rusty trolley. My father, my sister, my brother and myself stood there. My mother didn't come. Stood in a row just like in a factory. These big burly men heaved the cardboard box off the trolley then they dropped it! It crashed down. We thought it would burst open. My father said: 'Yes, he always was a big boy!' My sister and I burst into tears. Howling and sobbing. I hadn't cried like that. I'd been smiling for so long. Just before they pressed the button which makes the flames burst out my father said: 'Excuse me, can I do that?' He'd always got on badly with Toby. Now tears were rolling down his cheeks. Then he pressed it.

There was a small hurried funeral arranged by his mother. Tania said: 'Strangely there were no gay men there. My mother was a committed Christian, though Toby wasn't, so it was more of a Mum-thing than a Toby-thing. Much later there was a memorial for him which was more relevant.'

Four years later Tania is still grieving. Still trying to work through her feelings about homophobia, death and AIDS.

His death has made me more hypochondriac, worry more about the children. I am still ambivalent about gayness but struggling with it. I miss Toby terribly, not like a brother, more like losing a sister I suppose because he was gay. Ellie has become very involved in AIDS political work in San Francisco. I am supporting the Terence Higgins Trust. When I have come to terms with my feelings I should like to become a 'buddy'. I wrote an open letter to the *Guardian* following an article on homophobia saying that we must all look into our hearts and see the homophobia that lies there. His death, and the letters we received, have taught me how to act towards somebody who has just lost a loved one. Some people were hopeless at it. I was outraged by people who said nothing, who wouldn't acknowledge his death. But those who did write honestly were very consoling.

There have however been several positive outcomes:

The best thing is that my mother and I talk about the experience. We are actually talking about death. Slowly we are all changing. If Toby hadn't died, my parents would still be mourning the fact that he was gay; because he is dead they are mourning his death. My father is much less homophobic. The positive outcome for me is I have learnt to love people for who they are while they are here. Not to hold back your feelings. To tell people you love them when you love them.

Tania's painful experience forcefully brought home to her the truth of Susan Sontag's critical point in her book *AIDS and Its Metaphors* that the savage reputation of the illness adds to the suffering of those who have it, forcing them to endure the extra secrecy of shame.[18]

Tania's relentlessly honest appraisal of her attitude to AIDS has allowed her to grow through the suffering of her brother's death to a point where today she recognises that, despite the stigma and social death of the disease, it is ultimately only a disease. A disease that can happen to anyone of any sexuality. Men. Women. Children. Homosexual. Heterosexual.

As powerful evidence of this, Clare Williams, twenty-three years old, heterosexual, a young woman who routinely practised safe sex and was not a drug user, wrote to the *Guardian*, eleven months after being diagnosed as HIV positive, to say: 'The ignorance and complacency of people terrifies me. When will people realise that we are all at risk? If I can get HIV, then everyone can.'

Clare was raped.

The fear of being raped is a form of male oppression which is shared by all women of any colour, age or sexual orientation. It shapes women's daily lives, restricts women from going out alone at night, ironically increases their dependence on male protection. Recent statistics on sexual violence confirm this fear is well-founded. Since 1980 rapes in the UK have increased by 100 per cent. AIDS adds a new dimension to this fear. The rapist may be infected with HIV which can be transmitted during forced intercourse with a woman. If the woman suffers lacerations, bleeding or internal bruising, it becomes easier for the virus to enter the bloodstream. Some women under attack have said they were HIV positive as a means to prevent rape. Occasionally this has worked. Sometimes this has provoked extra violence. Public acknowledgement of the possibility of either party contracting AIDS through rape has not so far led to a decrease in rape. Some researchers suggest rapists may now use condoms or may attempt other forms of sexual violence as well as or instead of intercourse.

Clare Williams was unable to prevent her attacker.

'I'm a child of the AIDS age, you see. I know the dangers. I had unprotected sex once . . . I was raped and I didn't really get the chance to ask my attacker if he'd be so kind as to wear a condom. So henceforth my blood will test sero-positive.'

Following the trauma, she was tested in a clinic and found in her own words to be 'one of them'.

'The sort of people who, if they admit to their condition, may lose their job, their partner, may watch friends disinfecting the cups they have drunk from and find their best friend suddenly won't let them into the same room as her newborn baby . . . "I feel awful but you know how it is".'

Today Clare knows – what eleven months previously she could not have dreamt of – exactly how it is. Suddenly her life has become filled with catch phrases like 'T helper cells'. Suddenly she has become a threat to her oldest friends. At first she did not even tell her partner. Her family still have no idea. Later she decided it was important to her to lift the taboo.

'I want my friends to know, even though actually telling them is so difficult. I find myself sounding out their views, how much they know about AIDS, whether they would realise I am no threat to them, how discreet they will be.'

A few minutes before she discovered her test result, she had her photo taken outside the clinic. She was dressed in jeans and a scarlet tee-shirt, with her hair falling over her face.

I haven't changed. I still have that shirt, those jeans. My hair still falls over my face . . . I look the same as I did eleven months ago,

I still fall in love, I still enjoy long suppers with friends over a bottle or three of wine. I'm still the same person. It is your society, my society, that sees me as different, as a threat to your cosy way of life. I'm a twenty-three-year-old, heterosexual, non-drug using, safe sex practitioner.

In one way – miraculously – Clare has become a different person.

It isn't all bad news. My life is fuller now . . . I daren't waste a second. That sort of thing sounds like a cliché until it applies to you. Losing my job was a blessing; I decided to go to college. My relationships are far more intense now. I go to the theatre, the cinema, the ballet as often as I can . . . I've a lifetime of happiness to fit into maybe ten years. I surround myself with the people I love and feel a new freedom to ignore those I don't. I now make the most of everything.

You don't appreciate life until you think it's going to be taken away. I feel that I've been given a second chance to live as wonderful a life as I can. In so many ways, I'm very lucky.[19]

Clare is self-aware. Conscious of what might be termed a cliché-ridden stance. Alert to the dangers of sentimentality. Sentiment, the dark side to a disease clouded by stigma. She genuinely feels her uncertain future has strengthened her ability to live fully. AIDS can affect anyone. Any woman. We are all children of the AIDS age. It is our society which sees those who are HIV positive as different. As a threat to a cosy way of life. Strength not sentimentality can be women's tools to see the disease differently. To grow up.

Chapter Twelve

UNACKNOWLEDGED
LOSSES

Irish poet Mary Dorcey describes the emotional landscape of a
woman dying in a Dublin nursing home. At her bedside is another
woman.

Our hands clasped together on the white sheet
seemed to tick soft and loud as a time bomb
in the sterilized cosiness of that place.
'No sickness or grief here please' where
wounds are freshly dressed each day and
nights are tucked in with 'little sleepers', . . .

. . . Husbands come and go, devotion comfortably
contained within the appropriate visiting hours, . . .

. . . As evening comes the television
chatter shrouds our fitful conversation,
but our hands embracing on the white sheet
vibrate with a violence that we know must pierce
each tactful barricade of earphone and raised
newspaper. And when at last i leave, i am stalked by
every eye, until Mrs Kavanagh the chosen mediator,

Exorcizing any shadow of disquiet
in a voice made suave with homeliness

declares 'You have a lovely sister!'
But that last night,
strained beyond embarrassment or caution
when i took your face between my hands
and kissed your mouth a slow goodbye,
it seemed the bomb would explode
in a shower of brilliant sparks that

Might have set the ward alight were
it not for the immediate action of fire-
fighting nurses, who with the ice composure
of a lifetime's training in temperature control
drew screens, plumped pillows, inserted
thermometers, and asked me to wait outside
while they changed your dressings.[1]

You have a lovely sister.

Yes, but she is not my sister. How sad to lose your lovely sister. Yes, but she was not my sister. How you must miss her, how you will grieve, such a lovely sister. Yes, but it is not my sister I am missing. I know it would be more comfortable, a sister's devotion, contained like a husband's within the appropriate visiting hours. Within the appropriate scale of sorrow. Within an acknowledged framework of grief.

But it is not like that.

There are griefs that rage outside the castle walls. Safe inside, other women and men do not recognise those griefs. Would not want to if they could. Safer (they think) to stay inside.

There is however no underlying or long term safety in refusing to understand the risks some women take with their lives. In refusing to recognise the impact that certain deaths shrouded in silence may have on any of us. Deaths of women who loved other women. Whose love could set the ward alight. If the ward would let it. Wait outside the ward, the woman in the Dublin nursing home was told. Wait outside the castle walls.

Why do we do exclude some women's suffering?

Are we afraid that grief for a loss we cannot share will defile our own? Denial of same-sex pain is denial of difference. It is a denial that has been reported to me by lesbian women of every age, class and colour. More women than one can imagine have used the pretence of sisterhood, the fraudulence of family, to protect themselves, to gather information.

When my partner of many years standing, with whom I no longer lived, went into hospital with cancer, I became frightened. I wasn't even her 'pretend family' any more. They would never understand. I knew the hospital rules. 'I'll say I'm your sister,' I said to her before she went in. 'That way they'll keep me informed. They'll let me visit constantly.'

(Anna, lesbian bereaved woman.)

Anna visited daily. The doctor amiably gave her the medical reports on her 'sister's' progress. They give reports to family. Anna knew she could offer her former partner only sisterly hugs. Remember in the introductory chapter the woman whose lover came daily. 'She knows how much I am longing for her to touch my body. But because she is a woman the staff don't take her presence in my life seriously.' In that hospital nurses drew back the curtains, did not allow same-sex lovers' privacy. In the eyes of the staff she was not a relative. Would that she had been. Family grief has a validated place in our simulated scheme of loss.

Dudley Cave, founder of the Lesbian and Gay Bereavement Project in the UK, stresses how often similar situations occur: 'Sometimes the admitting nurse won't put the partner's name in the "next of kin" slot. At other times nurses appear not to realise that the friend who comes in to visit the patient is clearly a "special" friend. So they are not taken into consideration if the patient becomes sicker or dies.'[2]

Anna was determined this would not happen to her. So she compromised. She lied. Thus she was not able to express her emotions openly. The showers of brilliant sparks of an illicit love remained a memory. Bombs did not explode in the ward. Fire-fighting nurses did not see (or did not choose to see) a fire that needed extinguishing. The staff were solicitous, concerned, friendly.

Anna's former partner died of cancer. The hospital sympathised with her distress. They felt they knew what losing a sister was like.

She was not Anna's sister.

Another woman dying of breast cancer in a hospital told me: 'When we'd summoned the ambulance, I told Janey she must say she was my sister. My real sister was in Australia. I knew they'd let Janey come with me. No questions would be asked. My daughter was my next of kin so both of them could be there.' (Aileen, dying lesbian woman.)

No questions were asked. Later, after Aileen's death, Janey told me how much she had hated that subterfuge. 'I felt the reality of her death had been wrested from me.'

Countless other women feel compelled to connive in a system

that constantly excludes them. This system will continue to oppress some women who are dying or grieving unless we put a stop to it. In the early years of this second stage of the Women's Movement, the slogan 'Sisterhood is Powerful' stood for a united feminist front. It stood for freedom from discrimination for *all* women, not for a select number. How ironic that a spurious sisterhood should be used today in the service of bereavement censorship.

Death revives passion. How often we have noted this in the preceding pages. But some passions, even in death, are disallowed. We saw in Chapter Nine the plight of Dr Janet Gibbons passionately caring for her partner Ruth, dying of Alzheimer's. If Ruth dies before Janet – a strong possibility – Janet may find she will be treated more as a carer than a partner. Many people will find it easier to sympathise with her loss in that way.

Society's socialisation system which restricts women to nurturing roles and needing approval from men, means that lesbian women may find it harder than gay men to act openly against the grain, even though legal punishments historically were not inflicted on them for their sexual or political choice. What lesbians faced was invisibility in life, which they may also face around death. The consequences of this socialisation system may also mean that lesbian women's care for their lovers may be more easily seen as 'sisterly' or as 'nurturing'. The kind of thing women are supposed to do. The kind of thing Janet Gibbons is still doing. Lesbian partners who have also been carers may have additional bereavement burdens, which in bereavement research is scarcely addressed.[3]

The majority of bereavement literature currently addresses the loss of a relative: a spouse, a child, a sibling, a close family member. Clinicians and bereavement counsellors are well provided with guidelines to help clients through the grieving process when the deceased and the survivor are heterosexual.

But others, who see themselves as intimate family members, but who do not live in traditional nuclear families, may not feel able to talk about their grief to neighbours, colleagues or family. The Lesbian and Gay Bereavement Project points out that 'those who love in secret will have to mourn alone'.[4] Same-sex griefs are forbidden. Losses are unacknowledged. Neighbours are often unaware that two women (or men) sharing a house may be lovers. One woman who was referred to the Project had no contact at all from her neighbours after her lover died until one neighbour suddenly knocked on her door to inquire if she had a spare room to rent now that her flatmate had died.[5]

Researchers Siegal and Hoefer point out that 'there is a paucity of literature dealing with the grieving process of gay persons who encounter the cruelty of society's antihomosexual stigma while simultaneously mourning the loss of a lover or "spouse." . . . Because society conditions its members to feel apprehensive towards those who lead alternative lifestyles, it is more difficult for gay men and women to receive support while they mourn their loss.'[6]

Society does not sanction intimate same-sex relationships, and it is this lack of sanction that prolongs, that complicates, the grieving process. Bereaved lesbian women experience a double stigma. Their grief, like their life, may go underground. They may need help from bereavement counsellors as well as from friends. They may not know where to find it.

Lesbian mothers may be particularly affected, for there is an additional stigma, almost a feeling of incomprehension, attached to the two concepts: lesbian and mother. In our society there is still a simple equation: mother equals good, lesbian equals bad. The way the law courts seldom award custody of children to lesbian mothers bears this out.

Some excellent organisations for bereaved mothers and fathers, such as the Alder Centre and the Compassionate Friends are still largely white and heterosexual. They do not actively reach out to lesbians who may be co-parenting either a child born to one of them before their partnership, or a child born to them as a lesbian couple through artificial insemination. A Compassionate Friends worker said about same-sex parents: 'I'm not aware we have any couples of that kind involved in Compassionate Friends.' But children's deaths affect couples 'of that kind' just as they affect heterosexual couples. Both female partners, not merely the biological mother, may need counselling. Both certainly need those deaths to be validated.

Sonia was the boys' biological mother. She had them when she was married before we lived together. I helped bring up Tom and Kevin for fifteen years. When Tom was killed in that car crash everyone sympathised with Sonia's terrible grief. I couldn't believe that they didn't see what I was going through. Tom was my child just as if I'd borne him. Even people who knew us well suddenly saw me as the 'helping friend'. They thought I should support Sonia. Of course I did. But there was desperately little room or support for me.

(Rory, bereaved lesbian co-parent.)

In an attempt to deal with some of these issues in the UK, Bernard Williams and Dudley Cave, a lay assistant minister, set up the Lesbian and Gay Bereavement Project which works to help any bereaved lesbian or gay person. Twelve years ago Cave established a support group for widows in his congregation, then he realised how few of the ordinary lines of support were available to bereaved lesbians and gay men. Initially he envisaged a similar self-help group where lesbians and gay men could come together for support in their bereavement. But as word spread he recognised that what people needed was a telephone support and counselling service. A heterosexual minister was involved in the initial counselling until Cave realised: 'We were certainly not offering what was needed.' Today everyone providing counselling has to be lesbian or gay and comfortable with their own homosexual identity.

Teams of volunteers take calls every night from 7 p.m. from both the recently bereaved, and those bereaved perhaps years ago, who may have had no chance to express their emotions. Bernard Williams, the co-founder, reports that most callers are overwhelmingly glad they no longer have to pretend. Expressions of anger about the death and about society's attitude towards same-sex bereavement together with grief predominate. Some callers can be referred for psychotherapy if they wish it.

On offer from the project is a range of practical advice such as suggestions of sympathetic doctors and solicitors, information about sympathetic clergy who are willing to conduct memorial services for same-sex couples; and information and positive encouragement to lesbian and gay couples about making wills. The Project prints its own will form, and emphasises that without a valid will, a same-sex partner cannot inherit, and the estate will go to relatives of the deceased, or if there are none, to the state.

I met several bereaved partnered lesbian women whose deceased partners had failed to make a will. In almost every case enormous financial hardship (even to losing the roof over their heads) ensued. When this was added to the emotional stress of battles with the deceased woman's family, the situation of these women was described by them as 'unspeakable' or 'feeling under attack constantly' or 'feeling like a leper in a hostile world'.

It is attitudes within this 'hostile world' which the Project workers try to alter. Dudley Cave gives talks to interested groups and to nurses at various hospitals. Other organisations like the Terence Higgins Trust, a support and counselling organisation for AIDS sufferers and their families, have also campaigned for several years to bring the needs of bereaved same-sex partners to public attention. The Lesbian and Gay Bereavement Project has a team of committed lesbian counsellors. But it cannot do everything. It cannot reach every woman.[7]

The existing bereavement counselling and befriending organisations, which mainly serve white heterosexual bereaved people, must find space for black and lesbian bereaved women, for lesbian mothers and co-mothers, for those who are social parents as well as those who are biological parents.

When the deceased is lesbian, problems about bereavement may start with or be complicated by the issue of funerals. We saw earlier (Chapter Five) that if a funeral is to be the starting point for the slow healing process of letting go, of adjusting to life without that particular person, it should be right for those intimately concerned. The most effective funerals are those that are an expression of solidarity amongst the affected as well as being relevant to the deceased. Where a funeral has no relevance to the person's life or where, worse, it contravenes something essential to their identity, it may actually harm the remaining group.

When lesbians die, funerals cannot always work meaningfully for all participants. When a lesbian woman dies, if she and her partner had been highly closeted, the bereaved woman may be entirely excluded from the funeral.

Writer Alison Wertheimer tells the story of Mary and Betty who had lived together for more than twenty years and who were running a nursing home for elderly people in a small village when Betty died. No one in the community knew they were lesbian lovers. It was generally assumed that Mary had merely lost her business partner. Faced with the loss of her lover, the subsequent loss of her home and her livelihood, Mary had no one to turn to. Even worse, on the day of the funeral, she had to go on caring for the elderly residents, unable publicly to acknowledge the nature and magnitude of her loss. As Wertheimer emphasised, if Mary had been situated within a heterosexual marriage somebody in the village would have made sure that at least on the day of the funeral Mary did not have to think about her elderly charges.[8]

The stigma that forces some lesbian couples (today more perhaps who are elderly) to live their lives in isolation, reinforces that isolation when the issue of funerals and final leave-takings is paramount.

If a deceased lesbian woman is partially 'out', perhaps out to her partner, her children and her friends but not out to her parents, there may be conflict over funeral arrangements. Her intimates, particularly her partner, may want an appropriate lesbian funeral, whilst her parents may be determined, unthinkingly or otherwise, to have a traditional 'straight' Christian service.

Remember Tania's story of how brother Toby's funeral was a 'Mum-thing' not a 'Toby-thing': a Christian funeral with no gay men present. Yet Toby, gay and non-Christian, had been out to his family! Many bereaved lesbians suffer similarly. Sometimes blood relatives make arrangements, take over the funeral organisation, minimise the bereaved partner's or intimate women friends' participation or exclude them from the service altogether. If the partner attends she may be left to sit at the back away from the formal expressions of sympathy directed to the acknowledged 'chief mourners' at the front.

Allie and Nichole had lived together as a sexual couple for eleven years. They were 'out' to their friends and to Nichole's mother, but not to Allie's family.

> Last summer Allie went rock climbing with her brother. The plan was for her to stay a week with the family then come home. She never phoned and never returned. She had been killed climbing. The parents didn't think about letting me know though they knew we lived together. Obviously at some level they 'knew' our relationship was sexual. When I told them I would do everything necessary for the funeral they were icy. 'There's nothing for you to do. Her family are doing everything to try and make up for our poor girl's life. If she hadn't moved away to that peculiar life with you and your lot she would be alive today! There will be no need for you to attend the funeral.'
>
> (Nichole, bereaved lesbian partner.)

Even if all participants are united in wanting a memorial that honours the lesbian identity or politics of the deceased woman, it is not always easy to find clergy or lay leaders to conduct the service in an appropriate spirit of acceptance. One priest at a gay funeral prayed for God's forgiveness of the deviant lifestyle of the deceased![9] The Lesbian and Gay Bereavement Project is building up a list of 'sympathetic' priests, ministers and rabbis who are prepared to conduct a funeral in accordance with the wishes of the bereaved person, and who can offer continuing support. In the UK the Project is currently being aided in its attempts to find appropriate people to lead lesbian funerals by the Lesbian and Gay Christian Movement, Quest, the Gay and Lesbian Humanist Association, the Unitarian Church and the London and various regional Lesbian Switchboards.

Another choice women may make before a cremation is to organise a simple but relevant ceremony themselves at which the dead woman's favourite music might be played and her life as a lesbian, a family member, a friend, a mother if she was one, can be celebrated through readings and tributes read by her friends and family. This is only possible if friends and family are in agreement and if there is total disclosure.

Sometimes compromises are attempted. To see how this works I shall look at the case of the friction over the family funeral followed by the lesbian memorial for Phyllida, the thirty-three-year-old lesbian mountain climber (out to her friends, closeted to her family) who was one of the women killed in the Kathmandu air disaster in 1992.

Phyllida, a women's health worker, intent on improving health services for women, involved in setting up a well-women's service, spent her leisure time climbing. Many of her women friends were climbers and canoers. I spoke to three: Lana, a college lecturer, Kirsten, a community worker, and Marny, ex-nurse and health worker, whose views of Phyllida were remarkably consistent. She came across as idealistic, principled, very single-minded, therefore an achiever, yet often hard on other people less politically strong-minded than herself. She had no partner, lived alone, her ongoing intensely affectionate support came from her women friends. She was part of a close lesbian feminist network in her city. By all three accounts she was a young woman who drove herself furiously to her limits. Her climbing before her death had been moderate. She had not climbed any big mountains. Then at the time of her death, she decided to fly with a group of virtual strangers in order to trek and climb more challenging ranges on her own.

Her 'holiday climbing' friend Lana said goodbye to her on Friday. Kirsten, who had been her close friend for eight years, saw her for Saturday breakfast.

She was anxious she would be too slow. Perhaps nobody would like her. She had all sorts of anxieties. She even got in a tizz about not being able to fit everything in her rucksack, so I packed it for her. She left me a letter in case she didn't come back. It was in the form of a will but it wasn't a legal will. Then she went off down to her parents who were to take her to the airport on Sunday.

The plane crashed Monday lunchtime. Lana received a message on her ansaphone. 'It said ring a friend. I rang and she said "Have you

heard the news about the plane crash?" I said: "Oh no! It can't be
them!" Then I listened to the 6 o'clock news on the radio. It was!'

Marny, who describes Phyllida as 'the closest person to me since
I have been an adult', also heard the news of her friend's death on the
radio.

> I couldn't believe it. Not her death on the radio. I went through
> this process of thinking it couldn't be them, they couldn't be on
> that plane, then I thought oh yes, they could, they were. Then it
> was confirmed. What I found hardest about Phyllida's death was
> because it came as a shock, I couldn't understand the process of it.
> If you die in an aircraft there's no process, there's no understand-
> ing. I couldn't sort that out. One minute she was alive, the next
> absolutely nothing. People said she wouldn't have felt anything.
> That's not the point! What happened to her mind and her feelings
> in that instant? I am haunted by that question and about what has
> happened to her extraordinary energy. Also about what happened
> over the funeral.

Kirsten listened to the same news broadcast.

> I was driving home from work. I had to pull in to the side of the
> road. I tried to talk myself out of it. Maybe she wouldn't be
> among the forty or more dead. By the 7 p.m. news I knew there
> wouldn't be any survivors. So I opened the letter she left, then
> rang her parents. Her Mum had seen it on teletext. The terrible
> preparations had to begin. Ringing around. Getting identification
> details out to Pakistan. Her life with us and her life down south
> with her parents were very separate. They may have known she
> was a lesbian but she hadn't told them and it wasn't talked about.
> They did realise they didn't know who their daughter was or
> who those close to her were. So at first they were grateful to me
> for ringing.

It was a hard time for both groups, for Phyllida's parents not least
because they knew so few of the intimate details of her life. Phyllida's
friend Lana flew to Kathmandu with identification details

> All the parents knew was what she was wearing when she got on
> the plane. We knew Phyllida's dentist so Lana could take the den-
> tal records. I'd packed her rucksack and I'd packed a little parcel
> for her to take. She must have told her Mum because her Mum

rang and asked me what I'd put in the parcel. I felt for them at the time that it must all be quite difficult.

(Kirsten.)

The friends' emotions worked in various ways. Lana on her return from Kathmandu felt relief.

Going to the crash site was very painful but it helped me enormously. You still saw the tail of the plane coming out of the hillside. For ages afterwards every time I saw a plane it was like seeing that one. It was: why them? Why her Why that plane? But I was comforted by the feeling they probably died incredibly quickly.

Marny derived no comfort and felt great anger.

I didn't so much feel angry that she was dead but that, bloody hell, she'd made me feel this about her or that about her, she was my closest person, and now she is dead. So I was angry with her! I've worked with bereaved people so I know it's all right to feel that anger. There had been times when I'd wanted to keep Phyllida more at a distance, when she'd died I felt the guilt of: 'Oh, I pushed you away! Why did you make me push you away?' Now you are dead.

Personal anger was soon transferred into a group anger about how the friends were treated by the family. When the family announced they would organise the funeral, despite the efforts at understanding by Phyllida's friends, there was increasing strain. A coachload of fifty women decided they wanted to attend the funeral. 'We wanted to go but it was not in any way what we would have planned. We had no idea of what to expect.' (Kirsten.)

Subsequently the friends decided to organise a lesbian feminist memorial service, which Phyllida's doubtless apprehensive parents said they would attend.

At the time I felt it was important to her family for them to organise the funeral. Phyllida had left this letter saying what she wanted doing with her house and money but not what to do with her body. I felt we could go to their family service and they could come to ours. I had no idea they would ignore us and our needs.

(Marny.)

Dealing with her father, a most controlling man, was difficult. But we accepted the family had the right to sort out the funeral. We did not know what Phyllida would have wanted. We did know she preferred cremation so I told her parents. Apart from that there was no other way they involved us. They did not ask us to speak. They did not ask us what we wanted. They told us not to take flowers. Then one friend got angry and said: 'Look we understand you don't want millions of flowers from everybody. But there is a coachload plus several cars going from her city. Surely we can bring one tribute from all of us!' There was no way they took us into account. They didn't even wait for us to arrive before they started the service.

(Kirsten.)

The women's coach and cars got held up. When they arrived at the funeral, no places had been saved for them, the friends were split up, most of them had to stand right at the back. The family remained immobile at the front as the women piled in.

Arriving a little late we had to squeeze past the coffin. I didn't like her funeral at all. It was a pretty awful event. A very straight funeral. No connection with her life in any way. I felt very tearful . . . I was glad I had said my goodbyes to her at the crash site.

(Lana.)

One woman was left standing in the aisle with her kid in a buggy because the coffin was brought in. The funeral had nothing to do with the Phyllida we knew. A lay preacher uncle of hers talked. What he said made us very angry. It had been Remembrance Sunday the day before so he talked about war and violent death. Phyllida was an out-and-out feminist and pacifist, utterly opposed to war and violence, and quite anti-men in those ways. This man talked about how Phyllida had been a bossy sister who had gone to university after which her family had spared her to go and do good works among the poor and needy in a northern city! No reference in his talk to her life, her network, her friends.

(Kirsten.)

When the coffin was taken out this produced further severe reactions from the group of friends.

For a lot of us who hadn't been to straight funerals, it was a shock seeing these men pick up Phyllida's coffin. It should have been us! I had these strong inhibitions that I couldn't rush forward and say: 'What the hell do you think you're doing? I'm going to carry her out! She is my friend!' That's what I wanted to do.

(Kirsten.)

The funeral was bizarre. Here was this lesbian feminist being buried by her traditional straight family. She was carried in a coffin by God knows how many men. It felt totally inappropriate. This was just not right. I had to keep remembering that this wasn't being done for Phyllida but primarily for her family.

(Marny.)

The women told me that they felt not merely were their needs overlooked by the family, but in the pressure to organise car and coachloads of women to attend the funeral, they too had failed to discuss in advance what their needs might be, and how to deal with being excluded. As it was, most of the large gathering of women came away feeling excluded and disturbed.

Most of us came away from that funeral feeling angry. I think her family's grief and pain was very real but they did not consider our pain. It never occurred to them to ask Marny or I to speak. We were completely alienated. Whoever it was they felt they knew and whoever it was we felt we knew were probably two different people.

(Kirsten.)

'What came out of that funeral was that we have no rights. Even though without a doubt Kirsten and myself were far more important to Phyllida than her family, it was clear we had no rights. *Friends have no rights, only family have rights*.' (Marny.)

If the funeral had raised the issue of a hierarchy of grief and unacknowledged losses, organising the memorial which was to validate the loss of Phyllida as a lesbian, a feminist and a friend, raised new issues. The first was the differing ways we all view a dead person and how easily we can fall into the trap of claiming the deceased as a certain person. They can become who we say they were.

Because Phyllida did not have a partner her friends sorted it out. Although we didn't all know each other, we felt bonded together. It was easy to talk, easy to cry. It was useful arranging it with other

women because we were forced to learn certain things. We started
with: 'No, that was Phyllida!' or 'No, Phyllida wasn't like that!'
Finally we came to terms with the fact that though Phyllida had
been one woman to us and a different woman to her parents, she
had also been a very different person to each of her friends. But
hearing all those things about her life made me feel terribly lonely.
Why wasn't she here? Someone said 'This is an enriching experience!' I wish my life hadn't become a richer thing through this!

(Lana.)

A second issue was related to the strong community support
Phyllida's death evoked. For some women this was comforting. For
others it felt almost threatening.

Phyllida had had an impact on even people in the community she
hadn't known well. There was community sorrow. I got cards
from women I hardly knew, but who knew how important she
had been to me. Whereas at work all my colleagues said was:
'Had she married? Did she have children?' As if only family could
miss her.

(Kirsten.)

Phyllida was part of the feminist lesbian community. You can be
lesbian or feminist but not be part of that network. I am not. I find
it too incestuous. She was my separate private climbing friend.
Other women felt because they were close friends of Phyllida that
friendship would be transferable to me. I was expected to do my
grieving inside this close network.

(Marny.)

The third issue was how much concealment or revelation of
Phyllida's lesbianism there should be at the memorial.

We spent days thrashing out whether we could out Phyllida to her
parents. If we were to have the memorial we needed, she would
have to be outed. Her parents were quite clear they intended to
come. At first we thought we would write to them, tell them who
Phyllida was, and say if you still want to come you are welcome.
Then we decided as Phyllida had chosen not to be out to her parents we would have a memorial that was suitable for a woman and
a feminist at which nobody stood up and said Phyllida was a lesbian. But if you wanted to hear it, it was there in everything that

was said. A Judy Grahn lesbian poem was read. There was a chant which ten of us spoke with bits like: 'I could touch any woman's lips to remember you.' A lot of strong material about close female friendships.

(Kirsten.)

Whether the memorial succeeded better for Phyllida's parents than their funeral did for Phyllida's friends is not clear because I do not have the parents' version. I suspect her mother and father may have felt a similar degree of exclusion no matter how generous-spirited the friends had attempted to be. What it is important to stress however is that the loss of a daughter to heterosexual parents is one that is validated beyond any shadow of doubt. The loss of a lesbian woman from the life of her community and from the lives of her female friends is a loss that is seldom given its due in our society.

What Phyllida's story throws up is not merely the issue of lesbian bereavement but also that of the place of *friendship* in our system of recognised or approved losses.

Just as certain deaths such as miscarriages, still births, neonatal and perinatal deaths are frozen out, just as the griefs of those whose relationship has no legal status or social approval such as common-law wives, unmarried partners, lesbian lovers, are forbidden, so too is friendship ranked low in terms of bereavement.

Researchers Holmes and Rahe drew up a scale of stressful life events. They claimed that a score of over 150 indicated a stress level that could give rise to health problems. At the top of their scale was the death of a husband or wife. This merited 100 stress points. Fifth on the list came the death of a close member of a family with a stress score of 63. Way down on the list at number fifteen was death of a close friend which in their view was worth 37 stress points.[10]

In this book I have consistently claimed that there can be no scale of loss. Stress from a particular bereavement affects different women in different ways according to their strengths and spirit, and precisely what had been their relationship with the dead person. Scales of loss do not take account either of the cognitive perspective of the woman experiencing that loss or of the social context of the death. As long as society attempts to quantify suffering we shall be separated from one another and we shall remain powerless.

In history and literature women's friendships have always been of great significance. They often last when heterosexual love affairs fall apart. In Chapter Six (Widows and Other Leftover Lives) I referred to the longstanding friendship between Charlotte and

Claudia in Joan Barfoot's novel. Claudia recalls their friendship starting age six: she was more blissfully thrilled to be Charlotte's partner at school than she ever was when she fell in love. It is Claudia's husband Bradley who has died and Charlotte as her best friend is there to comfort and sustain her, to lead her towards a new life. How will one friend cope when the other, who has seen her through her life's vicissitudes, dies? More significantly how will the world outside their relationship react? When my friend Carol died, I was fortunate in that my close friends and family comprehended my grief. Another friend of Carol's was less lucky. When she went to work, a colleague seeing her distress, said, 'Well, it was after all just your friend, it's not quite like family.'

I recall Marny's words after Phyllida's funeral: 'Friends have no rights. Only family have rights.'

Grief for a friend, like grief for a same-sex lover, is not pathological. It is simply a different form of grief. Women grieve for husbands, for male or female lovers in varying ways. They grieve for friends in other ways. I miss my friend Carol because she was integral to the life of my spirit. The life of the senses. We shared a life of politics, passion, extravagant treats and silly jokes. The loss of my friend Carol is not number fifteen on a scale of stressful life events. It cannot be equated with the allotted 37 stress points for the death of a close friend. I cannot equate it with anything I know about. The loss of my particular woman friend from my daily life is incalculable.

As I am sure is the loss of your friend from your life.

We must work towards acknowledging such losses.

If a book about the sexual politics of death and dying is to be accurate it must record the dying situation and the griefs of female friends who, like lesbian lovers, contravene the patriarchal process but who may have brought joy into some women's lives.

Chapter Thirteen

POSITIVE GAINS

Although the problem of unacknowledged losses remains to be dealt with, there have however been some positive gains made by women in other directions related to the denial of death. I devote this chapter to three strong, spiritual women whose imaginative philosophies and radical work challenge the notion of denial and discrimination. They accept and are inspired by death. They have made creative innovations in dealing with death.

First: *Helen Passant*. Today a complementary healer, who as a former hospital ward sister saw that elderly dying patients were not living life to the full and decided on a revolutionary new approach to nursing the dying. Against predictable opposition she successfully implemented aromatherapy, massage and visualisation techniques into hospital and clinical practice.

Second: *Josefine Speyer*. Buddist psychotherapist, co-founder of the Natural Death Centre which spearheads the natural death movement. She runs regular workshops on organising funerals, DIY coffin-making, the best way to die at home, near-death discussions, and gives information on all aspects of death and dying. The centre even holds Death Dinners at which between fifty and a hundred people eat a gourmet meal and discuss mortality. Last year the Centre put on the first British Day of the Dead modelled on the lively and irreverent Mexican Festival.

The third woman is *Dame Cicely Saunders*, a former nurse and social worker, later a doctor, who is the founder of the global Hospice Movement. Founded on her principles of compassion, care, communication and solid scientific research it has built into its fabric both openness about death and enrichment of the life of the dying. Through her trail-blazing work in pain relief she pioneered the principle that pain relief should be given in steady doses, which has done much to alleviate a major fear around dying.

All three women have made profoundly creative and highly successful attempts to lift the taboo around death. Not only do they encourage people to talk, but they have altered the discourse so that it allows dying people and their friends and family to see death as positive, exciting and even comic, as well as ensuring that conversation takes place in a comfortable space where people can make their last spiritual search.

In their daily work with the terminally ill, these are three of the many women currently transforming our standard approach to dying by making it a life-enhancing experience until the very last day of each person's life. In their contact with the bereaved, through their efforts to change the normative, generally negative viewpoint on death, these three women are substantially altering other women's experience of bereavement, and men's also.

Helen Passant

Helen Passant, now sixty with two children and two grandchildren, had wild hair, a peaceful manner and a strong presence. Touch is important to her. After many years in orthodox nursing, where patients were angry, shattered, often demented, with physical problems so complex that neither surgery nor drugs could finally help them, her despair and dissatisfaction with traditional methods led her to seek another way. Ten years ago at her first conference workshop on touch and massage she suddenly decided that touch is the gateway to thought and vision in the care of patients.

Daily she massages elderly and dying people, touching limbs that are gnarled, twisted and torn, touching old scars and wounds, emotional breakages that have been hidden for years. She holds elderly men and women in a way they say they have not been held since childhood. One woman whom she had massaged told her: 'I have waited ninety-three years for that!' The woman was ninety-six.

As we talked, she used her hands all the time, touching my hand to make a point, touching my hair or her own as we laughed at some of her more comic stories. As I listened I had the curious feeling that I was being protected. Indeed it is protection which Helen

Passant sees as necessary for her work with the dying. The idea
came to her early as a child of thirteen.

> I was a nosy little girl. Always snooping around. I listened to a
> conversation between my mother and her friends. They men-
> tioned a woman dying of cancer. They whispered the word.
> Someone said: 'Shocking . . . cruel' then they revealed this woman
> was dying in a shed. Her husband couldn't bear the smell, so he'd
> put her down the garden in a bed in the shed! I knew where they
> lived so I crept down the road and in through their gate. It was a
> hot summer holiday, the shed was made of wood, and the smell
> was awful. But oh that poor woman. She was on a bed with cov-
> ers, that's how she was, dying in the garden. We can't bear death
> so we put people away and her husband had put her as far away
> as possible. All the neighbours knew but not one of them went
> and got her out of the shed. As I stood by her bed and took hold
> of her hands, I decided I had to protect people like her. I had to
> become a nurse.

Two years later, the minister in Helen's church asked if anyone would
visit the sick at home. Helen's first visit was to a woman dying of
tuberculosis. 'It was a terrible experience because it really did smell.
She died later in hospital, and once she was dead her family refused
to see me or talk to me. They thought I was religious, coming from
the church. Nowadays I'm not religious, well I don't go to church.'
 Helen Passant however is deeply spiritual. She sees spirituality as
the core of her caring.

> Professionally it is crucial in my work. When I talk to patients, I
> talk to their spirits. They can't answer me, sometimes they can't
> speak at all. I just talk to that part of them; I believe they speak to
> my spirit even when they can't answer. Patients are brought in
> who are said to be 'at the end of the line'. I think they are at the
> beginning. They may die on a ward, when I worked on wards, or
> now they may die in my care, but I hope they will die whole
> because we try by bringing mind and body together to allow the
> spirit to shine through.

If spiritual care is not about religious beliefs, what is it about? For
women like Helen, spirituality is a search for meaning, and religion
is one particular expression of that.
 Helen Passant, at the time Ward Sister on a long-term elderly

ward at the Churchill Hospital, Oxford, found that spiritual attention as well as good nursing care was not often possible within the conventional medical model. She knew she had to make changes. She also knew they might not be popular.

I was driven to it because I felt I wasn't communicating with my patients. They had Parkinson's Disease, or dementia or strokes. I was *doing* things to them, but I wasn't getting through. Once I'd experienced my first massage which made me want to sing and dance and laugh, I thought maybe this could help. At first the staff were incredulous about my ideas on massaging patients with herbal oils mixed with essential oils from flowers, leaves, roots, berries. They've been used through the centuries as remedies and relaxants but never in the health service! Some nurses thought I was potty! At first the doctors were delighted, so as the nurses couldn't beat me they joined me.

They saw how patients improved immediately. Massage helped them talk about their dreams, get in touch with their fears about death. One widow called Violet, almost silent with fear, started telling her dreams. At Christmas she said she was fed up with the hospital. I said: 'Do you want to join your husband?' She said, 'Oh no! Not yet.' A few months later I was massaging her when she said: 'I dreamt I was sitting on my husband's grave and he said "What kept you then dear?" I knew she was ready to die. The massage and the oils helped her get in touch with her fears.

Helen Passant and her staff played music and healing sounds of earth, water, fire and air on the ward. Sometimes staff and patients held hands and used visualisation techniques, taking imaginary walks through bluebell woods. They found that touching in an asexual way brought many benefits. Patients discovered, some for the first time, an expression of unconditional love.

It was surprising how much the men loved it. By the feel of their muscles, even if they couldn't speak, I could feel their enjoyment. Those poor men with strokes, faces all crooked, sometimes dribbling, eyes half closed, people didn't automatically want to come and hug them. Men didn't often mention their death. They rarely asked: 'Am I going to die?' Women frequently said: 'Will you be with me when I die?' Yet of course the women generally lived longer.'

When she worked with patients with multiple sclerosis, there were two separate wards for men and women. Working upstairs on the men's ward, she said to one doctor: 'It is physically darker here and the men are miserable.' He said: 'Well, that's a fact. You'll find that men can't cope with strokes and MS the way women can.' Helen Passant told me: 'It really was physically and emotionally lighter on the women's ward because women spoke and sang and did things. When men had strokes or MS they just sat. But women live longer with their disability, so they learn to be creative.'

On both wards, and many others in the hospital, Passant brought light. But despite her extraordinary success amongst the dying – or perhaps because of it – she began to encounter hostility amongst the senior staff.

> It grew because people talked about the work, people visited the ward, I was asked to give talks everywhere, I taught massage in other wards, then things got difficult. The hospital became a Trust. The Director of Nursing Services wanted to change my role to Clinical Nurse Specialist which sounds grand but it meant I taught nurses in a clinical setting so I wasn't allowed to teach massage. At first I still practised massage and aromatherapy but we took on a new Ward Sister who didn't approve of such techniques. I felt if I couldn't encourage nurses to work in this way, I didn't want to stay.

After ten invigorating years Helen Passant took early retirement. 'You've got to be on the top before you can change anything. I had to be a Ward Sister before I could try things my way. But if you want to change anything you have to be brave! Sometimes bravery means letting go.'

Today her bravery has led to her running a small clinic in Oxford where part of the time she massages patients with tumours, multiple sclerosis, cancers, Parkinson's and other diseases. The rest of the time she teaches at hospices, private hospitals, self-care units and clinics. She also teaches patients how to massage their carers and teaches home carers how to massage patients.

Many of her patients today have cancer.

> One of the ways we help them face the world is through both having massage and learning to massage others. Many of the cancer patients are women and the carers men, and the dynamic works

wonderfully. Something taken away from patients is their ability to give because everything is done for them. If you can't give, something dies within you.

The way Helen Passant has restored a feeling of use to her patients is remarkable. One woman with cancer who had no fingers and only one leg was propped up on a chair while a nurse lay on the floor with her foot on the patient's lap, and with one of her crippled knuckles the patient massaged the nurse's leg. A few minutes later they swapped around. The woman with cancer and no fingers smiled quietly to herself. 'It's like playing an instrument. I feel I'm playing a harp,' she said.

For those who are sceptical about the importance of touch, there have been several medical studies which endorse its productiveness. In an analysis of the significance of touch within palliative care, S. Sims reported: 'Touch is not experienced solely as a physical sensation, but is also experienced as an emotion. Comfort measures involving touch may therefore not only provide a pleasant sensation, but also comfort the psyche.'[1]

Sims suggests that massage brings about physical, psychological and combined body-mind effects which include:
1. Stimulation or sedation of the central nervous system
2. Muscular relaxation
3. Increased flexibility, stretching of adhesions between muscle fibres
4. Alleviation of pain
5. Dilation of blood vessels, increased circulation and drainage of lymphatics
6. Loosening of bronchial secretions
7. Alleviation of anxiety, soothing the mind
8. Facilitation of a close relationship and the disclosure of problems and concerns.[2]

Dying people often suffer from water retention or oedema, usually in their limbs. The skin swells.[3] Massage is frequently medically prescribed to treat lymphoedema (swellings) as well as for patient comfort. 80 per cent of dying people find they suffer from weakness with accompanying despondency.[4] This despair through their progressive loss of power or mobility can be improved through discussion. A very significant contribution massage makes to dying patients is the way it enhances communication. Dying people want to talk and Passant's treatments help them do just that.

I train my nurses in the power of silent as well as spoken communication. If nurses pay enough attention, their unspoken words can vibrate and help heal. I ask them to keep their minds on their patient, use a mantra or a word like love or peace or joy, concentrate on that silently in their heads as they attend to dying people. Instead of thinking: 'I'm feeling hungry', or 'How much longer till my break?', when they attend to patients, I ask them to centre themselves. Once they realise that patients who are dying can pick up the slightest nuance, they become much more concentrated.

Helen Passant believes sickness is an uncovering. That for patients who are dying, layers peel off so that they hear more, smell more, feel more. 'When they recover, they no longer hear your silent sounds, because they've covered themselves up again. We all do it.'

Like many nurses and some women doctors, Helen Passant is not into curing but healing. 'Healing means getting rid of the rubbish so that underneath will be something pure. Healing is acceptance and love, the ability to give it as well as receive it. I believe that is what the dying need.'

While Helen Passant continues to teach and practise not only in England but now also in the USA where she has just become a consultant nurse, the complementary therapies she has used so successfully are being increasingly introduced into conventional medicine.

Alternative health-care now provides emotional relief as well as pain control for the sick and dying in many institutions. As the end nears, many practitioners and patients are convinced that complementary therapies such as Passant's massage, visualisation and aromatherapy, or homeopathy, osteopathy, acupuncture, reflexology, herbalism and spiritual healing can alleviate physical and emotional distress in dying people. Medical visualisation can be used in treatment of AIDS, acupuncture is frequently successful in pain relief, spiritual healing can be productively directed at the dying person's psyche, massage and aromatherapy which give dying people a sense of well-being can be taught to informal carers and hence can be provided at home. Homeopathy, of which I have considerable highly successful personal experience, is a holistic healing process which may prevent sickness, can maintain good health, and can aid terminal illness.

Another successful illustration of alternative philosophies is exemplified by the Bristol Cancer Centre which uses dietary and behavioural methods to treat those with cancer. The availability of alternative therapists obviously varies from area to area. Sometimes services are provided free in some hospices and hospitals. In other places they are only available privately, which limits their use for those financially pressed, though often there are concessionary rates. It is, however, always worth asking if such treatment is available.

Josefine Speyer

Back in 1975 Josefine Speyer was pregnant. During pregnancy she held on to a dream of travelling through the countryside by horse and cart. Her husband, social inventor and psychotherapist Nicholas Albery, took a long spell off work to help her fulfil her fantasy. For £3 a week, they rented Patience, from the Heavy Horse Preservation Society, found a converted manure tip car, turned it into a reasonably comfortable caravan and set off through the wilder parts of Wales looking for a cottage for the winter and the birth.

Josefine recalls: 'I was determined to have the baby at home. I wasn't ill so why should I go into hospital?'

They found a place by the river Teifi and a willing doctor. 'I don't mind if you give birth on a haystack,' he told Josefine. 'I'll come wherever you want.'

Raspberry leaf tea, natural breathing exercises, and visualisations had prepared Josefine for a quick, pain-free natural labour and birth. Natural birth 'at home' had been so 'ecstatic' she began to think about natural death. Surely most people would like to die in the comfort of their home with loved ones around? Why was home no longer the natural place for people to die?

The spark of her idea for the Natural Death Centre was ignited.

A few years later when her father-in-law died peacefully at their home, the couple felt even more strongly that there was a need for a natural death movement to parallel the natural childbirth movement. 'We wanted to spread the tenets of good hospice care to home care for those dying of all causes not just cancer. It might not suit everybody but why shouldn't those families who wanted it be fully supported by the NHS in caring for dying people at home? Why shouldn't there be financial and practical aid for carers?'

In 1991 Josefine Speyer, together with her husband, started to implement their dream. They set up the Natural Death Centre in their London house, to try and combat people's ignorance and prejudice around death. They established a charity to campaign to make it easier for people to leave hospital and return home to die.

'The Centre acts as a society for home death. We use the power of the media and every other means to promote the idea that people should be able to die at home, which is what the majority want.'

Speyer's speculation is correct. Most people do prefer to die at home. But preferences do not prevail. Every year in the UK 650,000 people die; 15,000 of those deaths occur to the under twenties. 180,000 children under sixteen grow up in families where one parent has died. Death, however, is no longer in the midst of life, for the majority of those deaths occur away from home. In 1984 three out of every four deaths occurred elsewhere. In the mid-nineties more than 60 per cent of deaths occur in hospitals. In urban areas the proportion is as high as 70 per cent.[5] In Scandinavia institutional settings prevail to an even greater extent. In 1991 90 per cent of all deaths occurred in hospital.[6]

Despite the away-deaths statistics, the fact is that home-deaths remain an ideal for many. In a 1990 study of terminally ill cancer patients, well over half indicated they wished their final care to be at home.[7] A study by Wilkes discovered only 31 per cent of the relatives of people who had died at home subsequently stated the deceased would have preferred a hospital death.[8] Josefine Speyer's work, which suggests that a humane and friendly response to death is harder when it occurs in impersonal institutions, strongly confirms this research.

The Natural Death Centre is environmentally conscious. It offers advice and information about cheap 'green' burials, and leads courses in coffin-making from recycled paper or wood. Josefine and her team have run into opposition from professional undertakers and funeral parlours.

> Most cemeteries will not accept home-made coffins or home-done funerals. If all you want is a coffin, which we can get made for about £45, almost no funeral service will supply that. They will charge anything upwards of £400. Many people want personal involvement in death but they don't want to dress it up in a glossy way so that it becomes removed, impersonal. Spending money you haven't got doesn't necessarily help your grieving.

Her belief that lifting the death taboo warrants discussions and good food has resulted in both serious workshops and lighthearted dinners where death is the topic of the night. She invited therapist

Christianne Heal who runs death workshops to join as a co-director of the Centre.

In her workshops Heal asks participants to talk about what has influenced their ideas on dying: parents, TV, books. Then people pair off for role-playing exercises. At one workshop which I attended she asked each of us to speak about dying while the partner remained absolutely silent. She did not however tell us how long we were to talk before she stopped us. I felt quite disturbed, out of control, at not having a time limit, never knowing when the hammer would fall. When I talked to her later about my discomfort she laughed. 'But that's just what death is about. Uncertainty and how to cope with it.'

Certainly at the workshops I attended people discovered how talking about death led directly back into thinking about life. In my group we all decided we would go away and ruminate on what we wished to change about our lives. Suddenly I became aware that there *is* only today. I made three resolutions. The first was to clear the loft and throw away the years of accumulated junk. The second was to make less lists for the future but to actually achieve everything I decided upon for a given day. The third was to try in my current partnership not to follow my old unsuccessful pattern of avoiding tense emotional issues, but to confront them as openly as possible, as soon after they had raised their beastly heads!

I have to report none of this has been easy! Working on death, as Speyer acknowledges, is a lifetime's occupation.

Speyer's Death Dinners, with their excellent vegetarian food and wine at a candlelit table, offer an elegant, witty ambience in which guests discuss the socially invisible subject of mortality. There are guest speakers who have talked about near-death experiences, spiritual phenomena, surviving suicide, and how to care for the dying.

The Centre's first vivid and irreverent English Day of the Dead included a hand-painted coffin display, debates on euthanasia, death-related poetry and music, exhibitions of paintings, photographs and glass engravings on death themes, a will-writing service, and exquisite memory boxes and memorial tablets with fossil, flower and trowel engravings to commemorate the lives of friends and relatives. There was a New Orleans jazz band which played thumping good funeral music; harps and flutes accompanied songs and dances of death; there was an improvised play on gravestone epitaphs with lively audience participation, and finally a death-inspired Anglican Evensong in the church next door to the festival hall.

Josefine and her husband Nicholas also launched the publication of their *Natural Death Handbook*. This offers a good funeral guide, advice on how to draft a Living Will (which limits the amount of high-tec intervention to which one can be subjected in hospitals), training for practitioners in the areas of sickness and dying, a description of a legal alternative to active euthanasia for the terminally ill, and several deeply moving personal accounts of brave and 'conscious' deaths. There is information on hospices, hospitals, support structures for home care, and sturdy practical advice about washing, hygiene, bedsores, even bowel management for those involved in looking after dying relatives and friends. The handbook focuses on some extraordinary near-death encounters as well as surveying death rituals in other cultures. Its aim is to prepare people for death. Their own and other people's.

'We want to help people take back control of their lives,' said Josefine Speyer. It is significant that the book's range – from spiritual and mystical to practical and administrative – comes out of her own quirky mixture of those four key elements.

Her notion of spiritual need as both a search for meaning and the ability to enter into the individual experience of each dying person is at the core of the Centre's philosophy. 'We try to help people find good relationships with others at the end of their lives because that is what they seem to want.'

Predictably, initial reactions to Josefine's idea for setting up a death centre were hostile.

'Unless somebody is terminally ill, or has just been bereaved, they don't chat about death. People thought we were mad! But we would not give up.'

Who are the clients at the Centre?

We don't get many young people, except for young mothers in great distress because their children have died. We counsel many of them over the phone or in person. Generally we meet older people. Often they are terrified of death. They worry about what will happen to their children, their family; they worry about pain. We discover that for some of them the real problem is they are afraid of living. Through the talks and work here they become more confident about their lives and through that about death.

Whatever the reasons for people attending the centre, one problem is central. 'Many are so tied up in life that they don't want to die. They haven't yet done what they wanted to do. So they find it hard to accept that death is inevitable.'

Josefine Speyer sees the Centre as a useful resource for doctors and nurses.

Some doctors were resistant.

> They feel it is madness. I believe the medical profession should go to death workshops. I've been reading about the doctor-nurse-patient triangle. The doctor is God/father, the nurse is the maid/mother, the patient is the little prince/princess, an absolute useless lump with nothing to say at all. So the drama for doctors is they become isolated because they are supposed to make life and death decisions but they are not in touch with dying patients the way nurses are. So there is this power struggle where doctors who see themselves as saviours make decisions which sometimes nurses feel are violating the patients. But nurses must carry them out. Meanwhile patients co-operate because they believe doctors have the knowledge to save them. But as long as doctors see death as failure that drama will continue and patients can't face death realistically.

In Speyer's view, saving people from death has taken precedence over facing death in what she calls a proper manner. She believes that in order to die 'properly' or to support a dying person 'properly' you need to live 'consciously'.

> 'To die well, you have to respect others, without abusing anybody or any relationship. That whatever happens between them and you there is trust. It's hard to do this if you feel angry and want to lash out. I've had to learn to develop compassion for my own frailties and weaknesses too.'

Like many women practitioners in this study Josefine Speyer sees one major difference between male and female attitudes.

> I see men as Martians and women as Venusians. The Venusians let it all out while the Martians take it all in then cook up something inside. Marriages where children have died are often broken up because of this. Suddenly the two people can't understand each other or can't cope with two different ways of grieving. When we see men they have become rational because that's where they feel secure, while the women want to talk, to talk a lot. But often there isn't a place for them to talk.

In terms of how the sexes deal with death itself Speyer has found women to be more emotionally open.

Those who have given birth always feel that death is a part of them. Even women who aren't mothers feel death is something inside like the possibility of birth. Those women who have had a natural birth are more likely to feel death is part of a way of life. Everything that applies to childbirth applies to dying. That's why I think women have an easier attitude towards death.

Using the natural childbirth notion, Josefine Speyer is trying to pioneer the idea of having midwives for those who are dying. 'When you go into hospital terminally ill, you should have this woman who is like a spiritual counsellor, psychotherapist, nurse, guide all rolled into one person to sustain them, to help bring about the death, like a midwife brings about the birth.'

What has running the Natural Death Centre done for Josefine Speyer herself? Has it better prepared her for losses of her own? Has it taken away any of her anxieties around death?

I used to fear loss of control, being lost, having no ground; today less so. This morning I felt strong. I felt it would be blissful to die. It was like letting go of attachment. I stopped holding myself together so that even on a physical level the atoms I'm made of dispersed. I felt I had become loose droplets of light, that I was no longer strung up with all those thoughts, feelings and desires. It's a Buddhist idea.

The first time I met her, Josefine Speyer was dealing with a personal bereavement. Graham, her close friend and colleague, had just died.

Those kind of meditations as well as my work at the Centre have made the reason for my specific pain today, that of losing someone I cared deeply about, much easier. I worked with Graham in psychotherapy, he was an analyst. Because death is in my consciousness every day now, when it happened it wasn't an alien feeling. Strangely, every time someone dies I feel more alive, depending on how close they are to me. Through Graham's death I felt intensely alive. I felt that what he had been giving me . . . what I thought *he* had . . . I suddenly found in myself.

She believes relevant funerals can aid grief.

He was lying there in his clothes in a very plain simple coffin. You could look at his body for three days. It had a Quaker feel. You could stand up, say what you wanted, even sing. Two tables, loads of flowers. Photographs of him with his daughter. A little Buddha head. His daughter, his girlfriend, his ex-wife, they arranged it. Women arrange very relevant funerals.

In her personal life Speyer tries consciously to hold on to the idea of death every day. 'I am aware each day that I could see my son or my husband for the last time. We all die. We have no idea when. I think of dying as a long goodbye. Because I expect death all the time, I'm a bit less hooked into painful states like hating people or being sorry for myself.'

If she was faced with an imminent death, as the writer Jill Tweedie was when she discovered she had motor neurone disease with but a few months to live, would she rage publicly against the dying light as Jill did, or is raging not a part of proper dying?

'I'm sure I would rage. But when that anger died down I'd have an enormous goodbye party, a funeral-party-in-life with everyone there. I'd have it before I felt very ill. I would talk about the kind of funeral I wanted and help plan it. Taking control of your death, being thoroughly in charge of it, is a big help.'

Although sudden death is the hardest for mourners to come to grips with, it is often the death that people say they would prefer. But not Josefine Speyer.

'I wouldn't like to die of a heart attack. I would hate a sudden death. It's a lovely thing to have cancer because you have time to think about it. I want to be "there", within my dying, when it happens. I want to feel involved in the process of my death.'

For Speyer (as for Helen Passant), brave and conscious deaths, taking responsibility for your dying, and communicating gently but honestly with others, is the model she promotes at the Natural Death Centre.

Dame Cicely Saunders

Three Polish men, two now dead, one dying, influenced one British woman's work. That one woman's work influenced the Western world's approach to death and dying.

This is no small matter.

The woman is Dame Cicely Saunders. The work: the founding of the inspirational Hospice Movement. More than most, this woman has striven to ensure that death, especially by cancer, is neither a taboo word nor a stigmatised experience. As an internationally renowned doctor she is fierce about the importance of hard scientific research. As a former nurse and social worker she crusades for care, compassion and communication with dying patients.

The men? Two were Poles dying on her hospital wards at different times, with whom she formed intense emotional attachments, for whom she cared until they died. The third Pole is her husband, now ninety-three, whom she did not marry until she was in her sixties and he eighteen years older. Today he is frail and ill and in her daily care at St Christopher's Hospice.

Her story is romantic. It captures the imagination. Her vision, however, is rooted realistically in bricks, mortar and the under-standing of people's inner needs. It has enhanced the lives and changed the deaths of thousands of people.

Where did it begin?

David Tasma was a Polish waiter dying of cancer in St Thomas's Hospital, London, where young Cicely, twenty-eight, was a social worker, shortly after the war. They fell deeply in love. Tasma felt that he had not achieved anything in his life, that he would not have left a ripple on the pool when he died. He and young Cicely talked of somewhere that might have been more helpful to him than the busy surgical ward in which he lay dying. In their imaginative search for a place both healing and heartening, the seed of the modern Hospice Movement was sown.

One day he asked her to say something to comfort him. Immediately she recited the 23rd Psalm. He told her to carry on. But when she suggested reading to him, he said: 'No, I only want what's in your mind and in your heart.' It was those words which formed one of the founding principles of Dame Cicely's hospice philosophy: 'Everything of the mind, everything we could bring of research and understanding, but with the friendship of the heart.'[9]

When Tasma died at forty, he left young Cicely £500 with the words: 'I will be a window in your home.' A home he hoped she would open to help the dying. For twenty years she held on to their dream and the money. For three years previously Cicely Saunders had been searching for meaning in her life. Waiting to discover what was the right thing for her to do. She saw Tasma's words and his bequest almost as a sign from God. It took until 1967 for her to use that bequest as the starting point for a money-raising campaign which successfully launched a new kind of hospice, St Christopher's in London.

She had read politics, philosophy and economics at Oxford, had moved from social work to nursing, against parental pressure, trained at St Thomas's Hospital and one day when a qualified nurse she had suddenly decided she would attempt to become a doctor.

> I was thirty-three. I had no scientific education. But I had always believed people matter. Recently I had become aware that they mattered most at the end of their lives. But that was when no one cared about them. I read medicine entirely to get that message across. I had to do something about those who were dying. It was the neglected area of medicine. A doctor I knew told me I wouldn't be able to achieve my aim as a nurse. He said: 'Go and read medicine. It's the doctors who desert the dying. There's so much more to be learned about pain. You'll only be frustrated if you don't do it properly. They won't listen to you.

Like Helen Passant, who knew she could only achieve her radical goals from a position of authority, Cicely Saunders recognised that her medical colleague was correct. Power was imperative. 'He was absolutely right. The fact that a considerable number of people have listened is due to what Mr Barrett said to me back in 1951.'

She decided that symptom control and communication would be the cornerstones of her medical approach. 'The moment you want to properly address and analyse pain, you have to communicate. Quickly I recognised there was a total pain picture, not just physical, but social and spiritual. Pain is about the whole person. That is what I set myself to address.'

After she qualified at thirty-eight her decision to study pain control at St Joseph's Hospice led her to encounter the second Pole to have a profound influence on her life. He was Anthony Michniewicz, another dying patient, this time under her medical care as a doctor. She has described their relationship as the most intense, liberating and peaceful experience of her life, though it lasted but a few months. One day he asked her if he was going to die. Without any prevarication she said 'yes'. He asked her how long and she told him 'not long'.

'He said "Thank you, it's hard to be told, but it's hard to tell too . . ." After that encounter we had a month in which we were never alone, we were always in the ward, yet we somehow managed to communicate at a very deep level.'[10]

They held hands, he kissed her hand several times, they kissed once. 'But once was enough . . . What was important was that at the end of that month there was nothing we'd said that we regretted, and there was nothing we might have said that we hadn't. It was very happy but it was absolutely devastating when he had gone.'[11]

The reason for her devastation was that she and Anthony had no memories. No past. She felt she was forced to grow up in that bereavement. To make something creative out of it. She wanted to express her appreciation for the love she had found and she wanted that love of a dying man to carry on in her work for other dying people. She sees her bereavement as the power behind all her work that went into finding funds and building St Christopher's which became the home around David Tasma's window. Seven years after Anthony's death she opened her hospice.

The word 'hospice' was first used from the fourth century onwards when Christian orders welcomed travellers, the sick and those in need. It was first applied to the care of dying patients by Mme Jeanne Garnier who founded the Dames de Calvaire in Lyon, France, in 1842. The name was next introduced in Dublin by the Irish Sisters of Charity when they opened Our Lady's Hospice in 1879. In 1905 these Irish Sisters of Charity (the same order) ran St Joseph's Hospice in Hackney where Cicely Saunders started her initial pain relief research. St Joseph's together with St Luke's Hospital (Home for the Dying Poor 1893) were the major inspirations for the modern hospice she founded which had a twin focus on medical and psychosocial enquiry. Twenty-seven years later in the UK alone there are now nearly 200 hospices providing in-patient care, all of which adhere to Dame Cicely's philosophy. Today it has become a worldwide philosophy breaking both political and religious boundaries. The ideals of hospice care have spread to five continents, adapting to the needs of different cultures and settings. Sixty countries now have established or planned hospice services.

While she was grieving for Anthony and raising funds for St Christopher's she met her third Pole: Marian Bohusz-Szyszko, a prominent Polish artist.

She came across his work before she came across him. In 1963 she suddenly saw one of his pictures through a gallery window. It was the last half-hour of his one-man show. She discovered the painter was the same age as Anthony had been and came from the same city in Poland. She had never bought a painting in her life. But she purchased a small picture and took it home excitedly. Then she wrote to the unknown painter, thanking him for painting something so beautiful, assuring him when they finally opened the hospice she would see that they purchased a larger painting for the chapel. He wrote

back and said her letter was the most important thing to have
occurred so far in his life. They met and began a lifelong attachment.
Marian was married at the time to a woman who was still in Poland.
He and Cicely Saunders have now known each other for thirty years
but they did not marry until she was sixty-one and he seventy-nine.
Today, in his nineties, after many happy years of companionship he
lies upstairs ill and weaker day by day, in the hospice where Cicely
hung his first painting, where today many more of his paintings
crowd the walls, bringing pleasure to the other patients cared for, as
he is cared for, by his wife Dr Saunders.

As a doctor and a woman, Cicely Saunders is highly critical of the
medical profession's behaviour, and interested in the extent to which
the traditional masculine medical ethic is altering within the hospital structure.

I hope it is changing. But I was very depressed by a recent newspaper headline that said: 'Doctors can let terminally ill patients
die. Doctors can stand back.' I have dictated a letter saying that is
the last thing we as doctors can do. There is a great deal doctors
can do. We can give appropriate treatment, give family support. I
think it is indicative of the fact that doctors have not fully
accepted how much challenge there is in helping people to live
until they die as fully as they can with their own potential.
Doctors can not only help people die peacefully but they should
help them come up to death having fruitfully filled in as much
time as possible.

In hospice and palliative medicine there is still a higher proportion
of women than men. But Dame Cicely feels optimistic about the
male doctors she works with. 'There are now a lot of men about, at
least in this area, who do not see death as a failure, but see death as
the patient's possible last achievement.'

This is a sacred tenet of hospice practice.

What exactly is hospice and palliative care?

Palliative care, as recognised by the World Health Organisation, is
the active, total care of patients whose disease no longer responds to
curative treatment, for whom the goal must be the best quality of life
for them and their families. In the UK it is now a distinct medical
speciality. Offering a unique combination of care both in hospices
and at home, it focuses on controlling pain and other symptoms,
easing suffering and enhancing the life that remains. It integrates the
psychological and spiritual aspects of care, to enable patients to live

out their lives with dignity, as well as offering support to families both during the patient's illness and their bereavement.[12]

At St Christopher's there are no rigid hospital rules. Nurses in bright blue have time to laugh and chat and cry with the patients whom they know well, treat like friends. Compassion is the quality Dame Cicely insists on in her staff. 'We are pretty selective. Usually nurses come because they are already interested in our ideas. The Chief Nurse who employs more than anybody else will look for a warm, compassionate, resilient person who has a degree of security within themselves, and a degree of enquiry and aim to learn more and to give more. Their basic commitment must be to the care of patients.'

To Dame Cicely the word hospice 'is about living until you die, and it may be much longer and hopefully very much better than you ever expected. Hospice doesn't only mean bricks and mortar. It means attitudes and skills. It means principles.' Her own attitude towards dying embodies several vital principles, every one of which comes out strongly against a denial of death:

1. That people matter because they are themselves and they matter until the last moment of their lives.

> If we can do anything for people in a hospice it is to help them lay down their lives with a sense of 'I'm me and somehow it's all right.' I look after my own ninety-three-year-old husband here in the hospice from 3.30 in the afternoon until 9 a.m. the next day which means I am often on duty all night. He is very frail and is always saying 'It's time I died.' Because he is a proud Pole it is hard for him to be dependent, but often he will sit back and say: 'I am completely happy.' Why is he so happy when he is sure he is dying? It is because he is satisfied with what he has done with his life and because he knows he is cared for as a person. That is what I want for all our patients because I see death as a summing up of life, and I want them to be able to sum it up well.

2. That a hospice (for those with advanced cancer, motor neurone disease, or HIV related illnesses) should offer sufficient specialised pain relief so that there is freedom from fear and a comfortable space for dying people in which they can explore individual feelings and needs.

Dame Cicely learnt very early when she was working together with the Sisters at St Joseph's that pain is not only physical.

It is psychological, it's family pain, it's spiritual pain. We have to deal with the pain of the whole person. We try and meet everyone's needs. Some patients have the wrong idea about what St Christopher's can do. They are not aware that each person is looked on as an individual case and will be treated in the most appropriate way. The other day our Medical Director went to see a patient in his own home with the suggestion that he come into the hospice. It was obvious the man didn't like the idea at all. He thought we would just fold our hands and let him die, or that we would perhaps hasten his death even. So what the Medical Director said to him was: 'We will help you fight, because we do. If people want to fight, we will help them.' And that made all the difference

Does Dame Cicely see women as a group with particular wishes? 'Women have special needs. They have a very strong feeling of unfulfilled commitments. That is the hardest thing for them to leave.'

One need frequently voiced by patients is to die at home. This too is a need met by Cicely Saunders's team. One in four people return home from St Christopher's once their symptoms have been controlled. The home care team, started in 1969, helps people to stay in their own homes living comfortably until their death. 'Only about half of our home care patients need to go into the hospice. Our policy is to have people at home if they possibly can be. With the back up of the hospice and its skills.'

Originally the home care policy was planned as a consultant service to family doctors and primary health teams, with advice on symptom control, counselling and a twenty-four-hour on-call service, always with the promise of a bed. 'Today we have upwards of two hundred patients at home and only sixty-two beds. So we can't always keep that promise. So we are starting more respite care nurses to go out to people at home. This works well.'

When carers desperately need time to recharge their batteries, home patients are welcomed at the day centre where they can learn to paint, write, take up pottery, indoor gardening, have a massage or simply chat to others in similar situations.

'We try to banish depression and isolation because that in itself is disabling. We take a great deal of care to make people look nice, have pretty bedclothes, things like that are even more important to women than men. I think women are very concerned with body image so we have a hairdressing salon which has proved very therapeutic.'

3. That a hospice is a place where people can regain some control over their lives. They can *talk* about dying . . . or about anything else . . . easily. With family. With intimates. With the hospice staff. Without holding back.

> I know what it means not to be able to talk about death! Death was taboo in my family. When my grandmother was dying, I was about eight. My two brothers and I were sent away to the country and not allowed back until after she'd died. We were never told anything. People find it very difficult to know what to say to somebody who is mortally ill, or to their family. They're just as bad when someone is bereaved. They think they have to say something so they stay away. I think the old Irish tradition is much better. People come along, they don't stop to talk long, they just say 'We'll remember you at Mass', or something similar, but they *do* actually come. I find because people want desperately to talk about death, they do it easily in a hospice. I hope the hospice movement has given us a new language for dying. Because it started with my being able to listen to patients and express some of their needs and announce their achievements, we have been able to get over the message that people matter and they matter at this part of their lives, when they are dying.

4. That a hospice is an extension of life not a place to wait for death. It is life-enhancing. It allows people creative opportunities they may never have had before.
At St Christopher's men and women take up painting, become involved in creative writing, some explore philosophy, others begin to birdwatch. Family life carries on at St Christopher's. Elderly patients help grandchildren with puzzles and colouring. Relatives bring in pet dogs or cats to visit. Birthdays and anniversaries are celebrated.
5. A hospice should be a spiritual place though non-denominational. You can be Jewish or Muslim or a card carrying atheist and feel comfortable within its walls.
Dame Cicely is Christian but points out that though St Christopher's is Christian in its commitment to care, and though it holds Chapel services every morning, it has never proselytised. Its cornerstone is spirituality rather than religion. 'Death is about searching for deeper values, and we are creating a climate for the dying to make that last search. We try and provide a spiritual home for patients to ask their last questions and to find their own answers. We don't ever give answers, we just listen.'

Part of the ease she feels as a constant carer for her elderly husband comes from their shared spiritual values. 'He is a very believing Catholic and he says God will know what to do with me after he dies!'

What is the response of patients to this environment? I hope Dame Cicely is delighted at the affirmation she receives. Many patients report that their pain has been spectacularly improved. Others enthuse at the ways in which their emotional and creative lives have been empowered. Within the walls and the gardens of the hospice people feel able to be themselves. They openly express what they feel about dying and death. They talk about what their lives have meant to them. Dame Cicely and her team encourage dying patients to expand these lives. They help them create new opportunities, new ways of looking at the world, even within their last months or even weeks.

Not only is it a place for patients to view dying in a new and positive way, it is also a place where relatives, parents, children, partners, close friends, are offered emotional support, spiritual involvement and any kind of back up they need, both before and after someone close to them dies. Many families return to the hospice after a death, and through specialist bereavement counselling they are helped with the process of coming to terms with their grief.

In the study centre social workers and teachers share the experience of how adults and children come to terms with bereavement. Medical staff learn about controlling the symptoms of terminal illness. Police officers learn how to break bad news. They are taught to understand processes of grieving.

When Cicely Saunders talks about grief she does not talk about 'resolution' but about growth. 'I think when you lose someone dear to you, that gap is always there. Although things come round it. But I think every time, every loss has a potential for growth in it. Certainly the bereavements that I have been through have very much led to my growth. Life is a discovery along the way, all the time until we die and afterwards.'

Other women in this study who are in mourning echoed her words. They taught me that if you have to live with grief, it is possible to live and grieve creatively. Patty, who works at the Bristol Cancer Centre, spoke for many women when she said that grief was a process, that it will always be there in some form.

It is not like a tunnel in which you go in one end and come out the other. You never come out the other end. There are twists and turnings. Something will suddenly trigger it off. There is the will to happen, the anger, the disbelief. There is no set route. You can't conform to a grief manual. But there are wonderful things along the way. There is the communication between other women who have suffered loss, who speak the same language, who can help each other through talking. You can grow from it.

Within a hospice grief and growth, death and hope are threads in a patterned rug. People pull at the threads. Sew fabric into new shapes. Learn from each other. Cicely Saunders too has learnt from her work in the hospice.

I have learnt a lot about God and a lot about mankind and a certain amount about myself. My greatest challenge has been learning to let go. Having started the hospice myself, gathered together a small group, raised the money, got it opened, and been Medical Director for years, handing on to my successor has not been easy. But the next successor who is already on board is no threat to me and no problem. I like what he is doing very much. I am much more the elder statesman now. So I hope I have learnt a certain amount along the way to meet that challenge.

On a personal level her learning has been to confront two issues. 'I have had to learn to keep my priorities right. At present it is keeping the balance between how much I do for my husband and how much I do here in the hospice, and what talks I agree to give and which ones I feel I can't.'

The second issue relates directly to her husband's probable death.

When he says 'It is time for me to die' I have to ask myself am I ready to let him go? I think: yes, I'm sorry that you are occasionally incontinent, that you are very dependent, that you cannot walk without someone to help you. It's hard for a proud independent person to be so dependent. That tears at my heart. Just like it tears at my heart to walk around the hospice and see two people part, one of them a dying patient. Sometimes I see the deep weakness of the one, and the relationship between them both, that is still there after all those years. So, yes, it is hard to let someone go.

But with my husband, unlike that other one, we have memories. With Anthony there were no common memories because he was ill when I met him. So I had nothing to go back on, to think that we had a good time. That is not true now. I've had more time to become maturer in a relationship. I have memories. This will

make it a good death in one way but it will make it an even bigger gap in my life.

What kind of death does Cicely Saunders wish for herself? Like
Josefine Speyer and Helen Passant she eschews the short, sudden,
unknowing finale and wishes to be involved in the process. 'I want
to have a death in which I have time to say "I am sorry" and "thank
you" and tidy things up a bit.'
  She believes that a 'good death' is one that is right for that particular person.

  It's important we don't have a preconceived idea of what should be
  a good death for somebody else. There are some people who feel
  it is right that they go out raging because that is them. But that is
  not a high number. I feel more satisfied if somebody appears to
  have been reconciled with themselves, with their families, and
  with what is happening.

Cicely Saunders and almost every woman in this study saw death,
like grief, as a process. They saw death not as failure but as part of a
cycle. Patty, the Bristol Cancer Centre therapist, said:

  The feeling I have that everything is connected gives me the
  strength to carry on despite seeing my whole family wiped out by
  death within a few months. In a workshop on death we made
  sacred shields like the native American Indians do. We decorated
  huge pieces of cardboard with symbols and words. We recognised that life is but the flash of the firefly in the night, the breath
  of a buffalo in the winter time, it is the little shadow that runs
  across the grass and loses itself in the sunset. The shield was not
  against death but to give us the courage to face it.

Another kind of shield is the act of writing. Many women put pen
to paper in order to deal imaginatively (or therapeutically) with
grief. When you have suffered a loss, writing about it is a way of
recovering. Writing down your story helps to keep the memory
alive.
  In this book I have written down the stories of women who are
grieving, women near to dying, women who are care-giving. I have
written their stories and I have written my own. Many of us have
changed through the process. Come to terms with uncertainty.
  The ultimate uncertainty is what – if anything – happens to us

after we die. We cannot choose *not* to die. But we can and do choose
what to fear or what to revere about death and dying.

Do men and women have different or opposing fears and rever-
ences about death? Are they presented as equal and equally
admirable options? Can we face death and its uncertainties in ways
appropriate to us as individuals and as women, or are some kinds of
dying, some ways of dealing with doubts about death, more validated in this society?

Let us listen to the words of two people who when terminally ill,
faced their fears of death publicly. Both writers, both white, both
male.

Harold Brodkey, sixty-three, American, was recently told he had
AIDS. Brodkey is a talented mythmaker. His major myth has been
that after one well reviewed book of short stories published in 1958,
he would someday get his act together and write The Great
American Novel. It took him nearly thirty years to write it and it has
been considered to be not that great after all. But by this time his literary reputation has been firmly established.

Then he fell desperately ill. When his doctor told him his AIDS
diagnosis, he informed readers of several British newspapers that his
writer wife, Ellen Schwamm (not a mythmaker, but a productive talented writer), said that he was 'heroic'.

'Ellen says I was heroic,' he repeats.

Being heroic is crucial in the face of death.

Seated in the small hospital room with Ellen and his doctor, he
said that he felt 'too conceited to have this death'.

At that moment he felt that 'death . . . and AIDS . . . are a com-
monplace'.

Commonplaces should not happen to brave men, to major myth-
makers, to heroes. Ellen and his doctor, being more ordinary people,
are caring and concerned for him. He has had a shock. He has been
told he is about to die. Brodkey reassures them:

'"I'm OK" I said and went on grandly, "Look it's only death. It's not
like losing your hair or all your money. I don't have to live with this."
I wanted them to laugh. I wanted them to admire me.'[12]

When Brodkey finally left hospital, he decided to write an article
to show: 'How my life ended and my dying began'. He emphasised
throughout the article that 'something one must bear beyond the
claims of religion [is] not the idea of one's dying but the reality of
one's death.' He says: 'one schools oneself in all acceptance of the terror.'[13]

The schooling is done with style. With wit. With irony.

Brodkey wishes to illustrate Hemingway's grace under pressure. The macho badge of courage. No tears. Make 'em laugh. Exit on the upbeat. Face dying as a hero. *Ellen says I was heroic.*

What does Ellen think? Is Ellen emulating the laugh lines?

Our second hero is Dennis Potter. White, British, male, a playwright.

On 5 April 1994, Potter gave a moving, brave and enthralling television interview. Potter, who had just learnt he had inoperable cancer of the pancreas and had been given three months to live (though sadly he lived only two months until 7 June 1994), said that all his life he had lived with the fear that he might be a coward. Now he tells viewers proudly, he has found 'at the last I am not a coward'. He said he felt able to respect himself because since he heard the news of his terminal illness, an illness with no hope of a cure, he 'had not shed a tear'.

In the interview he laughed at himself, he made the interviewer laugh, and I am sure also many viewers, who must simultaneously have been moved to tears.

Like Brodkey, he was facing death with wit but also with hard work on two new plays. I suspect that when he revealed his particular fear of cowardice and his particular reverence for no tears in the face of death, he spoke for a great many men.

He also spoke for and to me. As a former Fleet Street journalist reared in the Hemingway stoical school of prose and life, I find this masculist way of facing death and its attendant uncertainties particularly attractive. I used to think tossing away fears or doubts about death with a witty line, denying their reality, was not merely the best way, but the only way.

But now I know it is *not* the only way.

It is merely one way to face death. There are others. Facing death with tears, with unashamed emotion, with talk, with long emotional discourses on the reality and pain of dying or the frightening uncertainty of death and what may lie beyond. These are other ways.

They too should be seen as acceptable.

Throughout this study we have seen many women patients and carers, many women doctors and consultants who are not ashamed to shed tears, who believe talk and tears are part of the process of dying, and who wish to become involved in that process. They have talked emotionally about the issues of death and dying with those at death's doorway or with those whose family and friends have passed through it. They have been keener on compassion than cure. They have opted for discussion rather than denial.

For these women tears and emotions are not cowardice. As Juno, the mother whose child could not be saved by the doctor who broke down in tears as she told her, said: 'When the doctor cried I knew how much she cared . . .'

Ellen said Brodkey was heroic. Can Ellen act in a different way about death and also be called heroic?

Silent stoicism is not necessarily bravery. Tears and talk are not necessarily cowardice. Conversation, openness and willingness to discuss death are not necessarily unheroic. They might be part of a new courage. The courage of talk and tears. It is through this that women strive to lift the taboo.

The death that women in the forefront of lifting the taboo wished for themselves, and wished for me, is one I wish for anyone who has read this far.

It is a gentle death. It is a strong death. At peace with yourself. Still in possession of your senses. Near to those you love and who care for you. Knowing you have achieved some of your possible goals. Knowing you have lived creatively. Knowing you have tried to change things for the better.

And I have lived to read this to the end
~ and changed by the reading.
shared with Tej at the dining table.
Wednesday 20/8/97.
• Where 'k' is 'talk of' this book is 'talking about'. (Tej)

NOTES

Background to the Book

1. *Memories, Dreams and Reflections*, C.G. Jung, quoted in *A Special Scar*, Alison Wertheimer, Routledge, London, 1991, p. vi.
2. Although the word 'survivor' is sometimes used to describe people who have survived a suicide attempt, my decision to use the word 'survivor' for those bereaved by someone's suicide follows the example of American suicidologist Albert Cain and British writer Alison Wertheimer. Like them I believe the word has positive connotations, for example a survivor can continue to live, even live well, in spite of difficult experiences or situations.
3. 'Help for those Bereaved by Suicide', D.M. Shepherd and B.M. Barraclough, *British Journal of Social Work*, 9, 1979, pp. 67–74; 'Bereavement from Suicide', M.I. Solomon, *Psychiatric Nursing*, July–Sept, 1981, pp. 18–19, *op. cit.*, Alison Wertheimer, 1991.
4. *Survivors of Suicide*, Albert Cain (ed.), Charles C. Thomas, Springfield, Illinois, 1972, p. 24.
5. *Women Celibacy and Passion*, Sally Cline, André Deutsch, 1993; Optima, 1994, p. 246.
6. 'Resume' in *Enough Rope*, *The Penguin Dorothy Parker*, Dorothy Parker, Penguin, Harmondsworth, 1966, p. 99.
7. *The Female Experience. An American Documentary*, Gerda Lerner, Bobbs-Merrill Educational . Publishing, Indianapolis, Indiana, 1977.
8. *Dorothy Parker: What Fresh Hell Is This?: A Biography*, Marion Meade, Minerva, London, 1991, p. 393.

Chapter One: Breaking the Silence

1. Malcolm Muggeridge, *The Observer*, 20 February 1970.
2. *Radio Times*, 24 February 1990.
3. Sally Smith, Cambridge, 1994.
4. *The Facts of Death*, M.A. Simpson, Prentice-Hall, Englewood Cliffs, N.J., 1979.
5. Open University Course: 'Death and Dying, Workbook 1 *Life and Death*, prepared by Alyson Peberdy, Open University Department of Health and Social Welfare, 1992, p. 28.
6. *Women Celibacy and Passion*, Sally Cline, André Deutsch, 1993, Optima 1994.
7. *The Change: Women, Ageing and the Menopause*, Germaine Greer, Hamish Hamilton, London, 1991, p. 134.

8. *Ibid.*, p. 314.

9. Anna Haycraft (writer Alice Thomas Ellis) in *Perspectives for Living*, Bel Mooney, John Murray, 1992, p. 90.

10. 'Grief: Its Nature and Significance', J.R. Averill, in *Psychological Bulletin*, 70, 1968; *On Death and Dying*, E. Kubler-Ross, Macmillan, New York, 1969: *Bereavement*, C.M. Parkes, International Universities Press, New York, 1972.

11. *Aspects of Grief*, Jane Littlewood, Tavistock Routledge, London, 1992, p. 54.

12. *Perspectives for Living: Conversations on Bereavement and Love*, Bel Mooney, John Murray, 1992, p. 212.

13. Germaine Greer, *op. cit.*, p. 318.

14. *The Meanings of Death*, John Bowker, Cambridge University Press, p. 211. Bowker discusses the idea that ultimately there are no other acceptable terms for living fully than those of death.

15. *A Protestant Legacy: Attitudes to Death and Illness Among Older Aberdonians*, R. Williams, Clarendon Press, Oxford, 1990, in Nicky James *op. cit.*, p. 77.

16. *The Female Experience: An American Documentary*, Gerda Lerner, Bobbs-Merrill Educational Publishing, 1977, pp. 147–9.

17. *Ibid.*, p. 147–9.

18. Mortality Statistics 1989.

19. Nicky James in Alyson Peberdy, *op. cit.*, p. 77.

20. 'Childhood Gender Roles: Structure and Development', J. Archer, in *The Psychologist*, September 1989, 9, pp. 367–70, in Nicky James, *op. cit.*, p. 77.

21. *Ibid.*, James, p. 77.

22. Birth Statistics and Abortion Statistics 1989.

23. *Husbands at Home*, J. Wheelock, Routledge, London, 1990.

24. Nicky James, *op. cit.*, p. 77.

25. *Women and Death*, Beth Ann Bassein, Greenwood Press, Connecticut, 1984, p. 194.

26. *Femicide: The Politics of Woman Killing*, Jill Radford and Diana E.H. Russell, Open University Press, 1992, p. xi.

27. Bassein, *op. cit.*, p. 194.

28. *The Sexual Division of Labour*, S. Dex, Wheatsheaf, Brighton, 1985, in *op. cit.*, Nicky James, p. 77.

29. *Women Celibacy and Passion*, Sally Cline, André Deutsch, 1993; *Reflecting Men at Twice Their Natural Size*, Sally Cline and Dale Spender, André Deutsch, 1987; *Man Made Language*, Dale Spender, Routledge and Kegan Paul, 1980; *In a Different Voice*, Carol Gilligan, Harvard University Press, Cambridge, Mass, 1982, 1993; *Mapping the Moral Domain*, Carol Gilligan, Jane Victoria Ward, Jill McClean (eds), Harvard University Graduate School, 1988.

30. *You Just Don't Understand: Men and Women in Conversation*, Deborah Tannen, Virago, 1991.

31. Nicky James, *op. cit.*, p. 77.

32. *Dealing With Death*, Jennifer Green and Michael Green, Chapman and Hall, London, 1992, p. xi.

33. *Western Attitudes Towards Death*, Johns Hopkins University Press, Baltimore, USA, 1974; *The Hour of Our Death*, Philippe Aries, Peregrine Books, Aylesbury, 1983.

34. 'Modern Death: Taboo or not Taboo?', Tony Walter, p. 36 in *Death, Dying and Bereavement*, Donna Dickenson and Malcolm Johnson, Open University and Sage Pub., London, 1993.

35. CSO 1989, Table 7.2.

36. Nicky James, *op. cit.*, p. 48.

37. CSO Table 2.20, Deaths analysed by cause 1989; *How We Die*, Sherwin B. Nuland, Chatto and Windus, London, 1994, p. 64.

38. *Ibid.*, p. 78.

39. *Ageing: the Facts*, Nicholas Coni, William Davison, Stephen Webster, OUP, England, 1992, p. 177.

40. 'Death and Development Through the Lifespan', R. Kastenbaum, 1977, in *New Meanings of Death*, H. Feifel (ed.), McGraw Hill, New York, 1977, p. 42.

41. *Death and the Family*, Lily Pincus, 1976, in *op. cit.*, Bel Mooney, p. 6.
42. 'Terminal Care: Home, Hospital or Hospice?', C.M. Parkes, *The Lancet*, 1985.
43. 'Dying Now', E. Wilkes, *The Lancet*, 28 April 1984, pp. 950–52.
44. *Life Before Death*, A. Cartwright, L. Hockey, J. Anderson, Routledge and Kegan Paul, 1973; *Domiciliary Terminal Care*, D. Doyle, Churchill Livingstone, Edinburgh, 1987; *Dying With Dignity*, J. Griffin, Office of Health Economics, London, 1991.
45. 'The Household Structure of the Elderly Population in Britain', A. Dale, M. Evandrou and S. Arber, in *Ageing and Society*, vol. 7, 1987, pp. 37–56.
46. Wilkes, *op. cit.*, 1984.
47. Nicky James, *op. cit.*, p. 29.
48. 'Not Going Gently', David Widgery, extract from *Some Lives*, Sinclair-Stevenson, London, pp. 124–38, in Donna Dickenson and Malcolm Johnson, *op. cit.*, p. 17.
49. *Funerals and How to Improve Them*, Tony Walter, Hodder and Stoughton, London, 1990, p. 33.
50. 'Nursing the Dying', D. Simpson (1975) in *Nursing the Dying*, D. Field, Routledge, London, 1985.
51. *Death, Grief and Mourning in Contemporary Britain*, Geoffrey Gorer, Cresset Press, London, 1965.
52. *AIDS and its Metaphors*, Susan Sontag, Penguin Press, 1988, p. 11.
53. *Ibid*, p. 44.
54. Peter Tatchell, 1986, in *Aspects of Grief*, Jane Littlewood, Tavistock Routledge, 1992, p. 4.
55. 'Cremation Research Project', D. Davies, *Pharos*, Vol. 57, No. 1, 1991, pp. 22–9.
56. Geoffrey Gorer, *op. cit.*, 1965.
57. Philippe Aries, *op. cit.*, *Western Attitudes Towards Death*; Philippe Aries, *op. cit.*, *The Hour of Our Death*.
58. 'Silence and truth in death and dying', David Armstrong, in *Social Science Medical*, Vol. 24, No. 8, 1987; Philippe Aries, *op. cit.*, *The Hour of Our Death*, p. 592.
59. *The Denial of Death*, Ernest Becker, The Free Press, New York, 1973, pp. 292–4; 'Thoughts for the Times on War and Death' and 'Totem and Taboo' in John Bowker, *op. cit.*, p. 12.
60. *Maxims*, La Rochefoucauld (1613–80), in *The Oxford Book of Death*, (ed.) D.J. Enright, OUP, Oxford, 1983, p. 39; Ernest Becker, *op. cit.*, 1973.

Chapter Two: Earlier Times, Other Cultures and Religions

1. Registrar General's Report 1839, in *Dealing with Death*, Jennifer Green and Michael Green, Chapman and Hall, London, 1992, p. 6.
2. *Between Pulpit and Pew*, David Clark, CUP, Cambridge, 1982, pp. 128–38, abridged in *Death, Dying and Bereavement*, Donna Dickenson and Malcolm Johnson (eds), Open University and Sage, London, 1993, pp. 4–10.
3. *Ibid.*, p. 9.
4. *Ibid.*, pp. 4, 5.
5. *Ibid.*, pp. 5–7.
6. Many British health authorities, now aware of staff insensitivity to religious and cultural issues, are currently writing policy documents to ensure that all patients have the right to have their way of dying respected.
7. Jennifer Green and Michael Green, *op. cit.*, pp. 150, 151, 155; 1987 figs.
8. 'The adult patient: Cultural considerations in palliative care', I. Ajemian and B. Mount, in *Hospice: The Living Idea*, C. Saunders et al (eds), Edward Arnold, London, 1981, pp. 25, 26.
9. *The Meanings of Death*, John Bowker, CUP, Cambridge, 1991, p. 75
10. Bel Mooney, *op. cit.*, p. 91.
11. *Ibid.*, p. 91.
12. John Bowker, *op. cit.*, p. 75.
13. *Ibid.*, p. 81. This idea of God's comfort being available to all people on the basis of faith and trust was an enormous step away from the Jews who believed that those possibilities were only

allowable through the Torah and confined to the people of Israel. For other Jews of Jesus's time, the consequence of God was mediated by the Torah and interpreted by the rabbis. The followers of Jesus began to see Him as the 'intermediary' between individuals and God, and to believe that through Him people may live eternally. This means that death is not the last word.
14. From the Jewish point of view, Jesus's perspective was aberrant in that he tied all his teaching and his action to God as the immediate source and direction of his life, and suggested the only necessary mediation was faith. If Jesus had stayed in Galilee he could have avoided the issue of his own authority. Other rebel teachers of his time were repudiated but not crucified, because they stayed away from Jerusalem, the centre of Jewish authority. By insisting on going to Jerusalem, where he was seen as a threat to the Temple, Jesus made his most critical challenge. In that context it is not surprising that the Last Supper and the time later in Gethsemane became the setting for his voluntary, inevitable, and unevaded death. (Ibid., p. 84.)
15. Statements like this from women in grief and loss make it clearer why the Christian understanding of death does not begin with the Crucifixion but with the eucharist. The historical reconstruction of exactly what happened at the Last Supper is uncertain, but what is indisputable is the way in which the eucharist has been seen through the history of the Church as the epitome of human salvation achieved through Jesus's death and more significantly involving and incorporating other Christians in that death through baptism.
'For each individual the incorporation into Christ's death is by baptism. The effect of this incorporation is renewed and made continually manifest by the eucharist: the eucharist links the passion and resurrection with what happens to us.' Response by the Church of England to the Agreed Statements by ARCIC, in Ibid., p. 86.)
16. Barrett, 1990, in J. Green and M. Green, op. cit., 1992, and Whitaker's Almanac, 1989.
17. The Jewish Book of Why and What, Lucien Gubbay and Abraham Levy, Shapolsky Publishers Inc., New York, 1989, p. 77.
18. The Jewish Way in Death and Mourning, Jonathan David, New York, 1988, quoting 'Ethics of the Fathers', chapter 4, p. 215.
19. Ibid., pp. 216, 217.
20. J. Green and M. Green, op. cit., p. 205.
21. North West Surrey Health Authority Training Video. Dr Abduljilil Sajid.
22. Ibid.
23. John Bowker, op. cit., p. 105.
24. 'Approaches to death in Hindu and Sikh Communities in Britain', Shirley Firth, p. 27, in Donna Dickenson and Malcolm Johnson (eds.), op. cit, 1993.
25. Ibid., p. 29.
26. Ibid.
27. J. Green and M. Green, op. cit., p. 188.
28. John Bowker, op. cit., pp. 168–70.
29. Ibid., p. 169; Majjhima Nikaya 1.77–9.
30. Buddhist teaching suggests that by destroying greed, hatred and delusion, which are the causes of all suffering, people can attain perfect enlightenment. The truth which the Buddha recognised, upon which Buddhist understanding of death is based, is the fourfold nature of 'dukkha', the subjection of everything to change and impermanence, and the suffering that inexorably accompanies it. The epitome of 'dukkha' is death.
If one thinks there is an 'I' which continues, one is deluding oneself. Buddhists work to achieve the realisation that there is no 'self' which can continue from life to life, that every aspect of the appearance which we regard as 'ourselves' is ultimately subject to change and death. What we have is only the process of change which produces apparent forms, some, like the forms of gods, enduring longer than others. Another possible comfort is removed, when you accept that you cannot hide from impermanence in sexual activity for neither does that last.
31. Ibid., p. 174.
32. Ibid., p. 188.
33. Ethnic Variations in Dying, Death and Grief: Diversity in Universality, Donald P. Irish,

Kathleen F. Lundquist, Vivian Jenkins Nelsen (eds), Taylor and Francis, Washington DC, USA.

34. *Ibid.*, pp. 13, 14, 15. Irish used work by V. Wikan (1988), 'Bereavement and Loss in 2 Muslim Communities: Egypt and Bali Compared', *Social Science and Medicine*, 27, pp. 451–60.
35. 'The Myths of Coping with Loss', C.B Wortman and R.C. Silver, *Journal of Consulting and Clinical Psychology*, 57, 3, pp. 349–57, 1989.
36. Lillian Burke MD in Irish, Lundquist, Nelsen, *op. cit.*, p. 170.
37. *The Death Rituals of Rural Greece*, Loring M. Danforth, Princeton University Press, New Jersey, 1982.
38. *Ibid.*, p. 55.
39. *Ibid.*, p. 14.
40. *Ibid.*, p. 19.
41. *Ibid.*, p. 19.
42. *Ibid.*, p. 20.
43. *Ibid.*, p. 23.
44. Thomas Chan, North West Surrey Health Authority Training Video: Death and Care of the Dying.
45. *The Labyrinth of Solitude: Life and Thought in Mexico*, Octavio Paz, Greve Press, New York, 1961.
46. Maria Antonieta Sanchez de Escamilla in *The Skeleton at the Feast: The Day of the Dead in Mexico*, Elizabeth Carmichael and Chloe Sayer, British Museum Press, London, 1991, p. 119.

Chapter Three: Mortal Messages

1. *The Denial of Death*, Ernest Becker, The Free Press, New York, 1973, p. ix.
2. *To Have or to Be*, Erich Fromm, Sphere Books, London, 1979, p. 127.
3. *The Inward Road and the Way Back*, Dorothee Soelle, Darton, Longman and Todd, 1978, p. 13.
4. *Living With Dying*, David Carroll, Paragon House, New York, 1991, p. 89; Vernon, 1970, p. 204, in Carroll, p. 89.
5. 'Death and Dying: Perspectives and Attitudes in Italy', F. Toscani, L. Cantoni, G. Di Milo, M. Mori, A. Santosuosso, M. Tamburini, in *Palliative Medicine*, 1991, 5, pp. 334–43.
6. *Attachment and Loss*, John Bowlby, 1969, Vol 1: *Attachment* (1972) Vol 2: *Separation, Anxiety and Anger* (1980) Vol 3: *Loss, Sadness and Depression* (1982), Hogarth, London.
7. *Loss and Change*, Peter Marris, Routledge, London, 1974.
8. *Bereavement Studies of Grief in Adult Life*, Colin Murray Parkes, Pelican Books, London, 1975.
9. *On Death and Dying*, Elisabeth Kubler-Ross, Tavistock, London, 1970; *Death: The Final Stage of Growth*, Prentice-Hall, London, 1975: *Death, Grief and Caring Relationships*, R.A. Kalish, Brooks Cole (2nd Ed.), California, 1985.
10. *Aspects of Grief*, Jane Littlewood, Tavistock Routledge, London, 1992, p. 17.
11. *Ibid.*, p. 53.
12. *Social Work with the Dying and the Bereaved*, C.R. Smith, Macmillan, London, 1982; *The First Year of Bereavement*, I.O. Glick, R.S. Weiss and C.M. Parkes, Wiley, New York, 1974.
13. Jane Littlewood, *op. cit.*, p. 54.
14. Anna Haycraft (novelist Alice Thomas Ellis) in Bel Mooney, *op. cit.*, p. 89.
15. *Ibid.*, p. 88
16. *What is found there. Notebooks on poetry and politics*, Adrienne Rich, Norton, New York, 1993, p. 16.
17. *Western Attitudes Towards Death*, P. Aries, Marion Boyars, London, 1976; *The Hour of our Death*, P. Aries, Penguin, Harmondsworth, 1981.
18. Gary L. Grammens in *Ethnic Variations in Dying, Death and Grief. Diversity in Universality*, Donald P. Irish, Kathleen F. Lindquist, and Vivian Jenkins Nelsen (eds), Taylor and Francis, Washington DC, p. 166.

19. Jane Martin, *Guardian* 'First Person', 5 April 1989, quoted in Donna Dickenson and Malcolm Johnson, *op. cit.*, pp. 83–4.

Chapter Four: Dutiful Daughters: Private Caring

1. *Of Woman Born*, Adrienne Rich, Virago, London, 1979, p. 37.
2. Adrienne Rich, *op. cit.*, p. 219.
3. Phyllis Chesler in *Our Mothers' Daughters* (Introduction), Judith Arcana, The Women's Press, London, 1981, p. xv.
4. *Memoirs of a Dutiful Daughter*, Simone de Beauvoir, André Deutsch and Weidenfeld and Nicholson, London, 1959.
5. Adrienne Rich, *op. cit.*, p. 46.
6. *Little Women*, Louisa May Alcott, The Studley Press, Ewell and London, 1946.
7. Judith Arcana, *op. cit.*, p. 15.
8. *Have the Men Had Enough?*, Margaret Forster, Penguin, London, 1989, pp. 34, 175–6.
9. 'General Household Survey: Carers in 1990' (emphasis mine).
10. *Ibid.*
11. *Ibid.*
12. *The Forgotten People*, J.A. McCalman, Kings Fund Centre, London, 1990; *Carers Perceived: Policy and Practice in Informal Care*, J. Twigg and K. Atkin, OUP, Buckingham, 1993.
13. 'Asian elders' knowledge and future use of community social and health services', K. Atkin, E. Cameron, F. Badger, H. Evers, *New Community*, 15, 2, pp. 439–46; 'Black Old women, disability and health carers', E. Cameron, F. Badger, H. Evers, K. Atkin, in *Growing Old in the Twentieth Century*, M. Jeffreys (ed.), Routledge, London, 1989a; 'Cancer support and ethnic minority and migrant work communities', C. Baxter, CancerLink London 1989; 'Ageing minorities: black people as they grow old in Britain', S. Fenton, Commission for Racial Equality, London, 1987.
14. 'How a survey led to providing more responsive help for Asian families', C. Walker, *Social Work Today*, 19, 7, 1987, pp. 12–13; Cameron, *op cit.*, 1989a; 'Helping Asian families in Smethwick', Janjit Uppal, Carelink, 4, 3, 1988; 'Working for black carers', M. Bould, *Mutual Aid and Self Help*, 15, 1–3, 1990b; 'A special case for treatment', I. Cocking and S. Athwal, *Social Work Today*, 21, 22, pp. 12–13, 1990; McCalman, *op. cit.*, 1990; 'The Needs of Women Carers whose first language is not English', Report of the Director of Law and Administration (Women's Unit), London Borough of Camden, 1990.
15. Cameron, *op. cit.*, 1989a.
16. Walker, *op. cit.*, 1987; 'Asian families with a pre-school handicapped child: a study', M. Powell and E. Perkins, *Mental Handicap*, 12, pp. 50–52, 1984; 'Health of infants and use of health services by mothers of different ethnic groups in East London', E. Watson, *Community Medicine*, 6, 1984, 127–35; Janjit Uppal, *op. cit.*, 1988; McCalman, *op. cit.*, 1990; *Elderly of the Minority Ethnic Groups*, Anwaal Bhalla and K. Blakemore, All Faiths Once Race, Birmingham, 1981; *We don't buy sickness, it just comes*, J. Donovan, Gower Press, Aldershot, 1986; Cameron, *op. cit.*, 1989a.
17. Celia Haddon, *The Times*, 30 August 1994.
18. *Terminal Health*, Sally Cline, (unpublished novel).
19. *Nothing to Forgive: A Daughter's Life of Antonia White*, Lyndall Hopkinson, Chatto and Windus, London, 1988, p. 14.
20. Celia Haddon, *The Times*, 30 August 1994.
21. Celia Haddon, *The Times*, 30 August 1994.
22. Lyndall P. Hopkinson, *op. cit.*, pp. 13, 14–15.
23. *Aspects of Grief: Bereavement in Adult Life*, Jane Littlewood, Routledge, London, 1992, p. 162.
24. Mavis Nicholson in conversation with Maya Angelou, 'Moments of Crisis', Channel 4, 8 July 1993.
25. *Ibid.*

Chapter Five: Female Funeral Directors

1. Shirley Firth, in Donna Dickenson and Malcolm Johnson, *op. cit.*, p. 27.
2. *The Sense of God*, Bowker, Clarendon Press, Oxford, 1973.
3. *The Rites of Passage*, Arnold Van Gennep, Routledge and Kegan Paul, London, 1960.
4. 'The Original Vision', Edward Robinson, The Religious Experience Research Unit, Oxford, 1977.
5. Francis Chappell and Sons, Funeral Directors, London.
6. In the UK those already on certain social security benefits are entitled to a basic funeral including a car. The catch is that for entitlement from the Social Fund it must be the bereaved person who is already claiming benefit not the deceased who might have been. Any Social Fund payment must be repaid later from the estate of the person who died. If no one is willing or able to arrange and pay for the funeral the local council or in some cases the health authority may do so. Financial aid from the Social Fund, at the time of writing, covers:
   Collecting the body
   Transporting the body home or to chapel of rest or undertakers
   One return journey to the funeral
   Death Certificate
   An ordinary coffin
   A car for coffin and bearers
   One following car
   Flowers from the person arranging the funeral
   Fees for undertaker, chaplain and organist at a basic funeral
   Cemetery or crematorium fees
   Up to £75 extra costs because of the religion of the dead person.
   In the UK the local council has a duty to bury or cremate a deceased if no other arrangements have been made. If they have reason to believe the deceased did not wish to be cremated they will not do so. They make a claim on the deceased's estate to pay for the funeral. The health authority may arrange the funeral of someone who dies in hospital if the deceased's relatives cannot be traced or cannot afford to pay for it. They too may make a claim on the deceased's estate.
7. Melanie Hunnaball, quoted by Sarah Boseley, *Guardian*, 19 November 1994.
8. *Ibid.*

Chapter Six: Widows and other Leftover Lives

1. Sally Cline, *op. cit.*, 1993.
2. *Ibid.*
3. *The Treasure Upstairs*, Margaret Powell, Pan, London, 1972.
4. *When the crying's done. A journey through widowhood*, Jeanette Kupfermann, Robson Books, London, 1992, pp. 88, 89.
5. *Dictionary of Word Origins*, Joseph T. Shipley, Philosophical Library New York, 1945; *Womanwords*, Jane Mills, Virago, London, p. 259; *The Flowering*, Agnes Sligh Turnbull, 1972, in Jane Mills, *op. cit.*, p. 259.
6. *The Widow. A Women's Ministry in the Early Church*, Bonnie Bowman Thurston, Fortress Press, Minneapolis, 1989.
7. *Ibid*, pp. 9, 11, 13, 14, 15.
8. *Women in Mediaeval Life*, Margaret Wade Labarge, Hamish Hamilton, London, 1986.
9. *The Weaker Vessel. Woman's Lot in 17th Century England*, Antonia Fraser, Methuen, London, 1985.
10. *Widow*, Lynne Caine, William Morrow and Co., and Macdonald and Co., 1974, p. 166.
11. *Women as Widows*, H.Z. Lopata, Holland: Elsevier, New York, 1979.
12. *Recovery from Bereavement*, C.M. Parkes and R.S. Weiss, Basic Books, New York, 1983; 'Effects of bereavement on physical and mental health – a study of the medical records of

widows', C.M. Parkes, in the *British Medical Journal* 2, pp. 274–9; 'Risk factors in bereavement outcome', C.M. Sanders, *Journal of Social Issues*, 44, 3, 1988, pp. 97–111.

13. Figures taken from Widow's Advisory Trust: Widows Benefit Information, 1994.

14. *After Marriage Ends. Economic Consequences for Midlife Women*, Leslie A. Morgan, Saga Publications Inc., Newbury Park, California, 1991, pp. 82, 154. Initial sample of 5083 women aged thirty to forty-four in 1967. Women surveyed between 1967 and 1982.

15. 'Foreigners in our own Land', Ngahuia Te Awekotuku and Marilyn J. Waring, in *Sisterhood is Global*, Robin Morgan (ed.), Penguin, London, 1985, pp. 483, 484.

16. 'Pakistan: Women – A Fractured profile', Miriam Habib, in *ibid.*, p. 536.

17. 'Sudan: Women's Studies and a New Village Stove', Amna Elsadik Badri, in *ibid.*, pp. 654, 655.

18. 'Marriage and the Family in Iran', J. Rudolph-Touba, in *The Family in Asia*, M.S. Das and P.D. Bardis (eds.), Vikas, New Delhi, 1978, pp. 233–4, cited in *The Change: Women, Ageing and the Menopause*, Germaine Greer, Hamish Hamilton, 1991, p. 71.

19. Jeanette Kupfermann, *op. cit.*, p. 109.

20. 'Japan: The Sun and the Shadow', Keiko Higuchi, in Robin Morgan, *op. cit.*, pp. 388, 389, 390.

21. 'A Little Widow is a Dangerous Thing', A.L. Cochrane, *International Journal of Psycho-Analysis*, 17, 494, 1936.

22. *Ibid.*

23. *Death and the Right Hand*, R. Hertz, trans. R. and C. Needham, Free Press, New York; *Celebrations of Death. The Anthropology of Mortuary Ritual*, Richard Huntington and Peter Metcalf, Cambridge University Press, 1979.

24. 'Ghana: To Be A Woman', Ama Ata Aidoo, in Robin Morgan, *op. cit.*, p. 261.

25. The Koran, N.239 Sura 11 Al-Baqara: This states: 'If any of you die and leave widows behind, they shall wait concerning themselves four months and ten days.'

26. *Burying SM. The Politics of Knowledge and the Sociology of Power in Africa*, David William Cohen and E.S. Atieno Odhiambo, Heinemann, Portsmouth, NH; James Currey, London, 1992, pp. 31, 32, 33, 71, 115, 116.

27. 'Nandi Widows', Regina Smith Oboler, in *Widows in African Societies*, Betty Potash (ed.), 1986, Stanford University Press, California, 1986.

28. Christine Obo in *ibid.*, p. 85.

29. *Ibid.* Note: Matrilineal is descent or kinship through the female line. Matrilocal is the marriage pattern where the couple live with the wife's family.

30. 'Greece: A Village Sisterhood', Margaret Papandreou, in Robin Morgan, *op. cit.*, pp. 276, 277; *The Death Rituals of Rural Greece*, Loring M. Danforth, Princeton University Press, 1982.

31. 'Israel: Up the Down Escalator', Shulamit Aloni, in Robin Morgan, *op. cit.* (The Knesset, to which Aloni has several times been elected, is the Israeli Parliament.)

32. *Mother India*, Katherine Mayo, cited in *Gyn/Ecology: The Metaethics of Radical Feminism*, Mary Daly, The Women's Press, London, 1979, p. 119.

33. *Ibid.*, p. 117.

34. *Bereavement: Studies of Grief in Adult Life*, Colin Murray Parkes, Penguin, London, 1972, p. 29; *Violence Against Women: New Movements and New Theories in India*, Gail Omvedt, Kali for Women, New Delhi, 1990.

35. *Women in India and Nepal*, Michael Allen and S.N. Mukherjee (eds.), ANU Printing, Canberra, 1982, pp. 27, 43, 62.

36. *Status and Role Perceptions of Middle Class Women*, Shashi Jaln, Puja Publishers (Rega), New Delhi, 1988.

37. Germaine Greer, *op. cit.*, p. 72.

38. Jeanette Kupfermann, *op. cit.*, pp. 70, 71.

39. *Charlotte and Claudia Keeping in Touch*, Joan Barfoot, The Women's Press, London, 1994, pp. 14, 17.

NB: *Note on the treatment of widows cross culturally:*
Nepalese writer Manjula Giri suggests that 'The Hindu sacred laws are categorical in their demands for female submission.' She further indicates that the Hindu 'Sati system', Chinese

footbinding, and the Muslim veil are all customs which fit like tiles into a mosaic. The Asian woman, in particular the Asian widow, endures as a living example of the abyss into which the human self may be forced to descend. ('Nepal: Women as a caste', Manjula Giri, in *Sisterhood is Global*, Robin Morgan (ed.), Penguin, 1985, p. 28, 464.)

Just as the custom of female genital excision, for instance, predates Islam and is nowhere recommended in the Koran, yet is fanatically defended by some as a holy Islamic practice, so comparably is the practice of Sati, also omitted from sacred texts, defended as a holy act for a Hindu woman. Giri's article offers the idea that the way Hindu tradition has relegated women to second place makes the husband the *raison d'être* of an ideal woman, so for the widow, the practice of widow-burning becomes their logical end.

Mary Daly cites the case of the wretched existence of 7,000 widows of Brindaban, living spectres whose life has been eroded by another's death. Poverty-stricken, with shaved heads, wearing only a white cloth over their bare bodies, they chant praise every morning for four hours in order to get a small bowl of rice. A typical case was that of a sixty-nine-year-old widow, who had been married at the age of nine, widowed at eleven, who has been waiting ever since for her 'day of deliverance'. Her view is that what happens to widows in countries where widow-burning has been revived is less the savage consequence of a cultural death taboo than explicit violence committed in cultures worldwide out of direct and horrifying misogyny. Atrocities which happen to widows in other cultures heighten and reinforce violence (such as battering, rape and sexual abuse) which happens to women in cultures such as our own no matter what their marital status, no matter what their relationship is to death. (Mary Daly, *Gyn/Ecology*, The Women's Press, London, 1978, p. 114, 127.)

Chapter Seven: Deaths That Haunt: Mothers Lose Children

1. *Aspects of Grief: Bereavement in Adult Life*, Jane Littlewood, Tavistock-Routledge, London, New York, 1992, p. 122.
2. Compassionate Friends. Leaflet, 1994. 53 North St, Bristol, England.
3. 'A Comparison of Adult Bereavement in the Death of a Spouse, Child and Parent', C.M. Sanders, *Omega*, 10, (4), 1979–80, p. 303–23.
4. Anne Chisholm in Bel Mooney, *op. cit.*, p. 38.
5. *Parental Loss of a Child*, A.T. Rando (ed.), Research Press Co., Illinois, 1986, p. 30.
6. 'The Loss of a Baby: Parents' Needs and Professional Practice after Early Loss', Nancy Kohner, in Dickenson and Johnson, *op. cit.*, p. 286.
7. Jane Littlewood, *op. cit.*, p. 123.
8. Jenni Thomas talking to Marina Cantacuzino, *Guardian*, 1 November 1994.
9. Jane Littlewood, *op. cit.*, p. 131; *Recovering from the loss of a child*, K. Donnelly, Macmillan, New York, 1982; *The Anatomy of Bereavement: A Handbook for the Caring Professions*, B. Raphael, Hutchinson, London, 1984.
10. B. Raphael, *op. cit.*, p. 270.
11. Jane Littlewood, *op. cit.*, p. 132.
12. 'Psychosocial Intervention with the child cancer patient and family', C.M. Binger, *Psychosomatics*, 25, 1984, pp. 889–902; 'Death of a child at home or in the hospital: Subsequent psychological adjustment of the family', R.K. Mulhern, M.E. Lauer, R.G. Hoffman, *Paediatrics*, 71, 1983, pp. 743–7; 'Psychosocial aspects of Leukemia and other Cancers during childhood', J.R. Mann, in N.K. Aaronson and J. Beckman (eds.), *The Quality of Life of Cancer Patients*, Raven Press, New York, 1987.
13. 'Effective Parental Coping Following the Death of a child from Cancer', J.J. Spinetta, J.A. Swarner, J.P. Sheposh, *Journal of Paediatric Psychology*, 6(3), 1981, pp. 251–62.
14. *Brigie: A Life: 1965–1981*, Janet Taylor, Hodder and Stoughton, London, pp. 11, 161.
15. 'Parents' coping and communication following their infants' death', N. Feeley and L.N. Gottlieb, Omega, Vol. 19 (1), 1988, p. 53.
16. 'The myths of coping with loss', C.B. Wortman and R.C. Silver, *Journal of Consulting and Clinical Psychology*, 57, 3, 1989, p. 351.

17. 'Long term effects of losing a spouse or child in a motor vehicle crash', D.R. Lichman, C.B. Wortman and A.F. Williams, *Journal of Personality and Social Psychology*, 52, 1987, pp. 218–31.

Chapter Eight: Image, Sex and the Language of Cancer

1. Woman with breast cancer talking to Sandra Steingraber, a woman with bladder cancer, Judith Brady, in 'We all live downwind', Sandra Steingraber, in *One in Three: Women with Cancer Confront an Epidemic*, Cleis Press, San Francisco, 1991, p. 40.
2. *A Burst of Light*, Audre Lorde, Sheba Feminist Publishers, London, 1988, p. 55.
3. Judith Brady, *op. cit.*, pp. 9, 13.
4. *Always a Woman: A Practical Guide to Living With Breast Surgery*, Carolyn Faulder, Thorsens, 1992, p. 15.
5. Age standardised mortality rates for Canadian women, reported in Canadian Cancer Statistics 1989, p. 27, show breast cancer as the highest with a rate per 100,000 population fluctuating between 23 and 25 throughout the period of 1970 to 1987.
6. Canadian Cancer Statistics 1989, National Cancer Institute of Canada, Toronto, 1989, p. 26. Incidence of breast cancer, women only, was at 62 per 100,000 in 1970 and 71 per 100,000 in 1984. These figures available 1991.
7. *Alternatives*, Kushner, Rose, Warner Books, New York, 1984, p. 66, cited in Judith Brady, *op. cit.*, p. 62.
8. UK Statistics; *Always a Woman: A Practical Guide to living with Breast Surgery*, Carolyn Faulder, Thorsons, London, 1992, pp. 9, 27–8. Canadian Cancer Statistics 1989. Survival rates for breast cancer in Canada are 74 per cent, colon cancer 51 per cent, lung cancer 15 per cent.
9. *How We Die*, Sherwin B. Nuland, Chatto and Windus, London, 1994, p. 215.
10. *Ibid.*, p. 215.
11. *Ibid.*, p. 215.
12. *Ibid.*, p. 215.
13. *Ibid.*, p. 215.
14. *Ibid.*, p. 213.
15. 'The Goose and the Golden Egg', Judith Brady, in Judith Brady, *op. cit.*, p. 13, 14.
16. Sherwin B. Nuland, *op. cit.*, p. 207.
17. *Ibid.*, p. 210.
18. *Ibid.*, pp. 207, 211.
19. *Ibid.*, pp. 206, 207.
20. *Aids and its Metaphors*, Susan Sontag, Allen Lane The Penguin Press, London, 1989, p. 9.
21. *Ibid.*, pp. 9, 10, 11, 12; *Illness as Metaphor*, Susan Sontag, Penguin, London, 1979.
22. *Ibid.*, 1989, p. 14.
23. *Stigma: Notes on the Management of Spoiled Identity*, Erving Goffman, Penguin, Harmondsworth, 1963.
24. *The Vital Balance*, Karl Menninger, in Susan Sontag, *op. cit.*, 1979, p. 6.
25. Audre Lorde, *op. cit.*, p. 127.
26. *Ibid.*, pp. 127, 128.
27. 'On Cancer and Conjuring', Janice Coombe Epps, in Judith Brady, *op. cit.*, p. 227.
28. *Ibid.*, p. 21.
29. Audre Lorde, *op. cit.*, p. 112 (emphasis is mine).
30. *Ibid.*, p. 113.
31. *Ibid.*, p. 113.
32. 'Choice and Control in Breast Disease', Judith Emmanuel, Laura Potts, Lesley Thompson, Mary Twomey, in *The New Our Bodies Ourselves*, Angela Phillips and Jill Rakusen (eds.), Penguin, England, 1973, pp. 535–56.
33. Audre Lorde, *op. cit.*, p. 116.

Chapter Nine: Sons? Do I Have Sons?

Note on Alzheimer's Disease
Originally the term 'Alzheimer's Disease' referred only to the under sixty-fives like Ruth. The medical profession still tends to use the laborious phrase 'Senile Dementia of the Alzheimer's type' for patients over sixty-five. However evidence has accumulated which shows that both forms are characterised by the same microscopic pathology, which means there is no validity differentiating between them except for their social or psychological effects. For this reason I am following the British Alzheimer's Society's use of the simple term Alzheimer's for both groups.

Statistics on Alzheimer's Disease

INTERNATIONALLY: Worldwide by the year 2025 there could be a population of 1 billion who live beyond sixty-five years. 50 per cent of those will suffer from severe dementia. Half of all dementia victims will have Alzheimer's. The majority of Alzheimer's worldwide will be women. (World Health Organisation.)

USA: By the year 2030 projections indicate that there will be over 60 million Americans who live beyond sixty-five. Currently Alzheimer's attacks more than 11 per cent of the USA population over sixty-five. This number is expected to increase. Alzheimer's accounts for 50–60 per cent of all dementias. The majority of the over-sixty-five sufferers of Alzheimer's will be women. (*How We Die*, Sherwin B. Nuland, Chatto and Windus, London, 1994, pp. 103, 107.)

UK: Alzheimer's represents half to two thirds of all demential illnesses. It will rise steadily over the next thirty years. By the year 2021 an estimated three quarters of a million people will have dementia. By the end of this century, an estimated 8,324,000 people over sixty-five will live in the UK. This is 15 per cent of the total UK population. As a result of developments in medicine and healthcare the UK population stands greater chances of living beyond eighty. Women are living longest. As women age, so their chances of getting Alzheimer's increase.

How Alzheimer's Affects Us As We Age

(UK Figures)

Age Group	Prevalence of Alzheimer's Disease
40–65 years	0.1% (1 in 1000)
65–70 years	2.0% (1 in 50)
70–80 years	5.0% (1 in 20)
Over 80 years	20% (1 in 5)

NB: Women comprise the majority of the over-80 group.
(Alzheimer's Disease Society Figures)

1. Open University Course: *Death and Dying*, Donna Dickensen and Margaret Allott (eds.), Open University, 1992.
2. *How We Die*, Sherwin B. Nuland, Chatto and Windus, London, 1994, pp. 90–91.
3. Dr Nori Graham, Chairperson of the British Alzheimer's Disease Society, 1993.
4. British Alzheimer's Disease Society Report, 1993.
5. Jonathan Miller, British Alzheimer's Disease Society Report, 1993.
6. *Memory Board*, Jane Rule, Macmillan of Canada, Toronto, 1987, (caps mine).
7. *Ibid.*, p. 2.
8. *Ibid.*, p. 25
9. *Ibid.*, pp. 29, 31.
10. *Ibid.*, p. 32.
11. Dr Nori Graham, 1991.

12. World Health Statistics, and Sherwin B. Nuland, *op. cit.*, pp. 89–117.
13. General Household Survey, 1988.
14. British Alzheimer's Disease Society Report, 1993.
15. British Alzheimer's Disease Society Report, 1993.
16. British Alzheimer's Disease Society Report, 1993, p. 10.
17. British Alzheimer's Disease Society Carers' Survey, 1993. NB: The British Alzheimer's Disease Society, 1993, point out that carers who are members of the society who took part in the survey are likely to be in a better position both financially and socially than other women, with better access to information and services. This picture of women carers of people with dementia cannot be taken as entirely typical of carers throughout even Great Britain.
18. *Just Desserts: Women and Food*, Sally Cline, André Deutsch, London, 1990.

NB: Nutritional deficiency especially the lack of Vitamin B12/folic acid can sometimes contribute to confused states. Women as they age are prone to nutritional problems. In a previous study, *Just Desserts: Women and Food* (André Deutsch, 1990) I researched on food I discovered many women living on their own frequently stopped cooking for themselves and might survive on a diet of tea and biscuits.
19. National Carers Association, 1992.
20. Sherwin B. Nuland, *op. cit.*, pp. 98–9.
21. *Ibid.*, p. 99.
22. *Ibid.*, p. 105.
23. *Ibid.*, p. 96.
24. Alyson Peberdy, Open University, *op. cit.*, 1993, p. 14.
25. Sherwin B. Nuland, *op. cit.*, pp. 115, 116.
26. *Guardian*, 19 March 1994.
27. Deprivation and Dementia Report, British Alzheimer's Disease Society.

Chapter Ten: Suicide: Shock and Stigma

Note: In discussing suicide I am following the lead of Albert Cain and Alison Wertheimer in using the term 'survivor' to mean the person bereaved by suicide rather than a person who has attempted suicide and survived that attempt. I use it in this sense for positive reasons as many of the bereaved women I interviewed used it optimistically to mean they were continuing to live and grow in spite of their experience.

1. *Survivors of Suicide*, A.C. Cain (ed.), Charles C. Thomas, Springfield, Illinois, 1972; *A Special Scar: The Experiences of People Bereaved by Suicide*, Alison Wertheimer, Routledge, London, 1991.
2. 'After Suicide: Meeting the Needs of Survivors', G.R. Bernhardt and S.G. Praeger, Paper: Annual Convention of American Personnel and Guidance Association, Washington DC, March 1983; *Silent Grief. Living in the Wake of Suicide*, C. Lukas and H. Seiden, Charles Scribner's, New York, 1987.
3. *Beyond Grief. A Guide for Recovery from the Death of a Loved One*, C. Staudacher, Souvenir Press, London, 1988.
4. *How We Die*, Sherwin B. Nuland, Chatto and Windus, London, 1994, p. 152.
5. *Ibid.*, p. 158.
6. 'Suicide Following the Death of Parents', J. Bunch, B. Barraclough, B. Nelson, P. Sainsbury, in *Social Psychiatry*, 6, pp. 193–9, 1971; *Bereavement: Studies of Grief in Adult Life*, C.M. Parkes, Penguin, Harmondsworth, 1986, p. 142.
7. *The Anatomy of Bereavement*, B. Raphael, Hutchinson, London, 1985; *Suicide: Clinical and Epidemiological Studies*, Brian Barraclough and Jennifer Hughes, Croom Helm, London, 1987.
8. Sherwin B. Nuland, *op. cit.*, p. 156–8.
9. Alison Wetheimer, *op. cit.*, p. 4. NOTE: Though it is the case that suicide is no particular respector of age, for instance in 1986 there were 303 recorded suicides of people in Britain aged sixty-five to sixty-nine and 331 recorded suicides aged twenty to twenty-four, these

figures mask critical differences. In the older age group the suicides accounted for only 0.5 per cent of all deaths, while in the younger age group, suicides accounted for nearly 14 per cent (Wertheimer, p. 4).

10. *Ibid.*, p. xiii.

11. 'Public Interest: Private Grief', B.M. Barraclough and D.M. Shepherd, in *British Journal of Psychiatry*, 129, 109–13; *British Journal of Psychiatry*, 131, 1977, 400–4; letter in *The Lancet*, 1978, ii, 795; Carol Staudacher, *op. cit.*, 1988, Alison Wertheimer, *op. cit.*, 1991.

12. *I Can't Face Tomorrow. Help for those troubled by thoughts of Suicide*, N. Keir, Thorsens, Northants, 1986, p. 13.

13. Alison Wertheimer, *op. cit.*, p. 32.

14. C. Lukas and H. Seiden, *op. cit.*, 1987.

15. *On Children and Death*, Elisabeth Kubler-Ross, Collier Books, New York, 1983, p. 110.

16. B. Raphael, *op. cit.*, 1985.

17. *The Social Meanings of Suicide*, J. Douglas, Princeton University Press, USA, 1967; *Suicide: A Study in Sociology*, Emile Durkheim, Routledge and Kegan Paul, London, 1970; *Discovering Suicide. Studies in the Social Organisation of Sudden Death*, J.M. Atkinson, Macmillan, London, 1978.

18. C. Staudacher, *op. cit.*, 1988; Sherwin B. Nuland, *op. cit.*, p. 158.

19. *Suicide and Attempted Suicide*, E. Stengel, Penguin, Harmondsworth, 1973; *The Savage God: A Study of Suicide*, A. Alvarez, Penguin, Harmondsworth, 1974; 'Inner Urban and National Suicide Rates: A Simple Comparative Study', D.R. Chambers and J.G. Harvey, *Medicine, Science and the Law*, 29, 3, pp. 182–5.

20. Adrienne Rich, pamphlet by Onlywomen Press, 1979, p. 2 reprinted from *On Lies Secrets and Silence*, W.W. Norton and Co., New York, 1979.

21. B. Barraclough, *op. cit.*, 1987, p. 134; B. Raphael, *op. cit.*, 1985, p. 280.

22. C. Parkes in Alison Wertheimer, *op. cit.*, p. xi.

23. Sherwin B. Nuland, *op. cit.*, p. 140–62.

24. *Passing On: the Social Organisation of Dying*, D. Sudnow, Prentice-Hall, Englewood Cliffs, New Jersey, 1967; *Aspects of Grief: Bereavement in Adult Life*, Jane Littlewood, Tavistock-Routledge, London, 1992.

25. Sherwin B. Nuland, *op. cit.*, p. 150.

26. C. Staudacher, *op. cit.*, 1988.

27. C. Lukas and H. Seiden, *op. cit.*, 1987; Alison Wertheimer, *op. cit.*, 1991.

28. Sherwin B. Nuland, *op. cit.*, p. 144.

29. *Ibid.* Note: Nuland gives evidence of a curious feature about hanging, the preferred choice of men. The same effect could be accomplished by less violent means which most men would have access to and knowledge of. A would-be suicide could hook up one end of a hose to an automobile exhaust pipe and inhale at the other, thus taking advantage of the affinity that haemoglobin has for carbon monoxide, which it prefers by a factor of 200 to 300 over its life-giving competitor oxygen. The victim dies because his brain and heart are deprived of an adequate oxygen supply. Hanging accomplishes much the same thing but by a mechanism significantly less gentle. The weight of the victim's body provides enough force to tighten the noose and bring about mechanical obstruction of the upper airway. According to Nuland, because the constricting noose cuts off drainage through the jugular and other veins, deoxygenated blood is damned back up through the tissues of the face and head. The discovery usually by a wife, mother or partner, of a grotesquely hanging corpse whose swollen sometimes bitten tongue protrudes from a bloated blue grey face with hideously bulging eyes is, Nuland assures us, a nightmarish sight which only the most hardened cases can gaze on without revulsion.

30. *Forensic Medicine*, K. Simpson and B. Knight., Edward Arnold, London, 1985, pp. 104–5.

31. Joel Jaffey, 1994, private discussion.

32. *Voices of Death: Personal Documents from People Facing Death*, E.S. Shneidman, Bantam Books, New York, 1982.

33. Elisabeth Kubler-Ross, *op. cit.*, 1983, p. 110.

34. Alyson Peberdy, *op. cit.*

Chapter Eleven: AIDS: The Social Death Kept Under Wraps

1. World AIDS Day statistics 1 December 1994. National AIDS Trust, London; Chris Carne, Consultant, Addenbrookes Hospital, Cambridge. Director of Clinic 1A for East Anglian HIV and AIDS patients under the care of Addenbrookes Hospital. Committee of the Cambridge AIDS Helpline, March 1994, using 1992 figures; 'Epidemiology: current and future dimensions of the HIV/AIDS pandemic in women and children', J. Chin, in *The Lancet*, 28 July 1990, Vol. 336, No. 8709, pp. 221–224, and *Triple Jeopardy: Women and Aids*, Panos Dossier, The Panos Institute, Budapest, London, Paris, Washington, 1990, p. 11.
2. Panos Dossier, *op. cit.*, p. 1; AIDS dossier in *Focus: The World in Perspective*, (ed.) Mick Hurrell, June 1993.
3. Panos Dossier, *op. cit.*, pp. 5, 8.
4. Mick Hurrell, *op. cit.*, 1993.
5. Communicable Disease Report 21 October 1994, Vol. 4 No. 42; World AIDS Day Action Kit Fact File 2 Latest Statistics; National AIDS Trust, London SE1, 1 December 1994.
6. *Matters of Life and Death: Women Speak Out About AIDS*, Ines Rieder and Patricia Ruppelt (eds.), Virago, London, 1989, p. v; *Women and the AIDS Crisis*, Diane Richardson, Pandora, London, 1987, p. xiii; Panos Dossier, *op. cit.*, pp. 1–7.
7. Mick Hurrell, *op. cit.*, 1993.
8. Information from Chris Carne, Consultant at Addenbrookes Hospital, Cambridge, Director of Clinic 1A which deals with East Anglian AIDS and HIV patients; Cambridge AIDS Helpline Committee, March 1994.
9. Diane Richardson, *op. cit.*, p. 27.
10. Ines Rieder, and Patricia Ruppelt, *op. cit.*, pp. 42, 43.
11. Mick Hurrell, *op. cit.*, 1993.
12. Diane Richardson, *op. cit.*, p. 37.
13. Diane Richardson, *op. cit.*, p. 74.
14. In her articles written for British and Irish newspapers 'Ellie' uses her own name and her brother's real name. It is in keeping with the policy of this book which gives fictionalised names to the women interviewed, and at the suggestion of Toby's sister Tania, that all family names have been altered. All other facts are accurate and have been provided by Tania in a series of interviews or come from documented sources such as newspaper articles, faculty documents, private correspondence and published books.
15. *AIDS: The Daily Epidemic*, G. Hancock and E. Carim, Gollancz, London, 1986.
16. Diane Richardson, *op. cit.*
17. *Ibid.*, pp. 15, 16.
18. *AIDS and Its Metaphors*, Susan Sontag, Penguin, London, 1988, 1991.
19. Clare Williams, *Guardian*, 'First Person', 29 May 1991.

Chapter Twelve: Unacknowledged Losses

1. 'In a Dublin Nursing Home', in *Kindling*, Mary Dorcey, Onlywomen Press, London, 1982, p. 13.
2. Dudley Cave, co-founder of the Lesbian and Gay Bereavement Project. Report by Pamela Holmes in *The Nursing Times*, 13 January 1988, Vol. 84, No. 2, reprinted and distributed by the Lesbian and Gay Bereavement Project, Vaughan M. Williams Centre, Colindale Hospital, London NW9 5HG. Tel: 0181 200 0511; staffed weekdays 3.00–6.00 p.m.
3. *Ibid.*
4. *Ibid.*
5. *Ibid.*
6. 'Bereavement Counseling for Gay Individuals', Reva Lee Siegal and David D. Hoefer, in *American Journal of Psychotherapy*, Vol. XXXV, No. 4, October 1981, p. 518.
7. The Lesbian and Gay Bereavement Project, *op. cit.*
8. Alison Wertheimer, *New Society*, 17 April 1987.

9. The Lesbian and Gay Bereavement Project, *op. cit.*
10. 'The social readjustment scale', T.H. Holmes and R.H. Rahe, in *Journal of Psychosomatic Research*, 11, 1967, pp. 213–18.

Chapter Thirteen: Positive Gains

1. 'The significance of touch in palliative care', S. Sims, in *Palliative Medicine*, 2, 1988, pp. 58–61.
2. *Ibid.*, p. 60.
3. 'Oedema in advanced disease: a flow diagram', C. Badger and C. Regnard, in *Palliative Medicine*, 3, 1990, pp. 213–15.
4. 'Weakness in terminal illness', L. Lichter, in *Palliative Medicine*, 4, 1990, pp. 73–80.
5. *Domiciliary Terminal Care*, D. Doyle, Churchill Livingstone, Edinburgh, 1987.
6. 'Dying with dignity', J. Griffin, Office of Health Economics, London, 1991.
7. 'Terminal Cancer Care and Patients' Preference for Place of Death', P. Townsend, A. Frank, D. Fermont, S. Dyer, O. Karran, A. Walgrove, M. Piper, *British Medical Journal*, Vol. 301, 1990, pp. 415–17.
8. 'Dying now', E. Wilkes, *The Lancet*, 28 April 1984, pp. 950–52.
9. Cicely Saunders talking to Sue Lawley, 'Desert Island Discs', BBC Radio 4, 1994.
10. *Ibid.*
11. *Ibid.*
12. *Guardian*, 19 March 1994.
13. *Ibid.*

BIBLIOGRAPHY AND FURTHER READING

Act Up New York Women and AIDS Book Group, *Women, AIDS and Activism* (South End Press, Boston, MA, 1990).

Albery, Nicholas; Elliot, Gil and Elliot, Joseph (eds.), *The Natural Death Handbook* (Virgin, London, 1993).

Alvarez, Alfred, *The Savage God: A Study in Suicide* (Bantam, New York, 1972).

Aries, Philippe, *Western Attitudes Towards Death* (Marion Boyars, London, 1976).

―――― *The Hour of Our Death* (translated from the French by Helen Weaver) (Penguin, Harmondsworth, 1981).

Augenbraun, Bernice and Neuringer, Charles, 'Helping Survivors with the Impact of a Suicide' in Albert C. Cain (ed.), *Survivors of Suicide* (Charles C. Thomas, Springfield; Illinois, 1972).

Baro, F., 'International perspectives in Alzheimer's disease' in Desmond O'Neill (ed.), *Carers, Professionals and Alzheimer's Disease* (proceedings of the fifth Alzheimer's Disease International Conference, 1989) (John Libbey and Company, London, 1991).

Barraclough, Brian and Hughes, Jennifer, *Suicide: Clinical and Epidemiological Studies* (Croom Helm, London, 1987).

Bassein, Beth Ann, *Women and Death: Linkages in Western Thought and Literature* (Greenwood Press, Connecticut, 1984).

Bean, Constance, *Women Murdered by Men They Love* (Haworth Press, New York, Forthcoming).

Beauvoir, Simone de, *The Second Sex* (Bantam, New York, 1968).

Beck, Frances, *The Diary of a Widow: Rebuilding a Family after the Funeral* (Beacon Press, Boston, 1966).

Becker, Ernest, *The Denial of Death* (Free Press, New York, 1973).

Bell, Anne Oliver (ed.), *Diary of Virginia Woolf. Vol. l: 1915–1919* (Hogarth Press, London, 1977).

―――― *Diary of Virginia Woolf. Vol. 2: 1920–1924* (Hogarth Press, London, 1978).

―――― *Diary of Virginia Woolf. Vol. 3: 1925–1930* (Hogarth Press, London, 1980).

―――― *Diary of Virginia Woolf. Vol. 4: 1931–1935* (Hogarth Press, London, 1982).

―――― *Diary of Virginia Woolf. Vol. 5: 1936–1941* (Hogarth Press, London, 1984).

Benefits Agency, *What to Do After a Death* (Leaflet D49) (BA Publications, Lancashire, April 1993).

Benn, June (ed.), *Memorials: An Anthology of Poetry and Prose* (Ravette, London, 1986).

Bennett, Olivia (ed.), *Triple Jeopardy: Women & Aids* (Panos Publications Ltd, London, 1990).

Blum, Arlene, *Anna Purna: A Woman's Place* (Granada, London, 1980).

Boston, Sarah and Tresize, Rachel, *Merely Mortal: Coping with Dying, Death and Bereavement* (Methuen, London, 1987).

Bowker, John, *The Meanings of Death* (Cambridge University Press, Cambridge, 1991).

Bowlby, John, *Attachment and Loss* (Hogarth, London, 1969).

——— *Attachment and Loss. Vol. l: Attachment* (Hogarth, London, 1972).

——— *Attachment and Loss. Vol. 2: Separation: Anxiety and Anger* (Hogarth, London, 1980).

——— *Attachment and Loss. Vol. 3: Loss, Sadness and Depression* (Hogarth, London, 1982).

Brady, Judith (ed.), *I in 3: Women with Cancer Confront an Epidemic* (Cleis Press, Pittsburgh and San Francisco, 1991).

Brownmiller, Susan, *Against Our Will: Men, Women and Rape* (Bantam, New York, 1975).

Broyard, Anatole (ed.), *Intoxicated by My Illness and Other Writings on Life and Death* (Fawcett Columbine, New York, 1993).

Buford, Bill (ed.), *Death* (Granta 27, Penguin, Harmondsworth, 1989).

Burns, Edward (ed.), *Staying on Alone: Letters of Alice B. Toklas* (Vintage, London, 1975).

Butler, R.N., 'Alzheimer's Disease into the 1990s' in Desmond O'Neill (ed.), *Carers, Professionals and Alzheimer's Disease* (proceedings of the fifth Alzheimer's Disease International Conference, 1989) (John Libbey and Company, London, 1991).

Cahill, S. and Roseman, L., 'Care-giver Considerations in Institutionalizing Dementia Patients' in Desmond O'Neill (ed.), *Carers, Professionals and Alzheimer's Disease* (proceedings of the fifth Alzheimer's Disease International Conference, 1989) (John Libbey and Company, London, 1991).

Cain, Albert C. (ed.), *Survivors of Suicide* (Charles C. Thomas, Springfield, Illinois, 1972).

Cameron, Deborah and Frazer, Elizabeth, *The Lust to Kill: A Feminist Investigation of Sexual Murder* (New York University Press, New York, 1987).

Campbell, Alistair Vincent and Higgs, Roger, *In That Case: Medical Ethics in Everyday Practice* (Darton, Longman and Todd in association with the *Journal of Medical Ethics*, London, 1982).

Cantacuzino, Marina, *Till Break of Day: Meeting the Challenge of HIV and AIDS at London Lighthouse* (Heinemann, London, 1993).

Caputi, Jane, *The Age of Sex Crime* (Bowling Green State University Popular Press, Bowling Green, Ohio, 1987).

Carmichael, Elisabeth and Sayer, Chloë, *The Skeleton at the Feast: The Day of the Dead in Mexico* (British Museum Press, London, 1991).

Carroll, David, *Living with Dying: A Loving Guide for Family and Close Friends* (revised edition) (Paragon House, New York, 1991).

Chesler, Phyllis, *About Men* (Simon and Schuster, New York, 1978).

Chitty, Susan (ed.), *Antonia White Diaries. Vol. l: 1926–1957* (Constable, London, 1991).

——— *Antonia White Diaries. Vol. 2: 1958–1979* (Constable, London, 1992).

Cline, Sally and Spender, Dale, *Reflecting Men at Twice their Natural Size* (André Deutsch, London, 1987).

Cline, Sally, *Just Desserts: Women and Food* (André Deutsch, London, 1990).

——— *Women Celibacy and Passion* (André Deutsch, London, 1993).

Coffey, Maria, *Fragile Edge* (Chatto & Windus, London, 1989).

Cooper, David, *The Death of the Family* (Penguin, Harmondsworth, 1972).

Daly, Mary, *Beyond God the Father* (Beacon Press, Boston, 1973).

——— *Gyn/Ecology: The Metaethics of Radical Feminism* (Beacon Press, Boston, 1978).

Davenport-Hines, Richard, *Sex, Death and Punishment* (Collins, London, 1990).

Dickenson, Donna and Johnson, Malcolm (eds.), *Death, Dying and Bereavement* (Sage Publications in association with The Open University, 1993).

Dinnage, Rosemary (ed.), *The Ruffian on the Stair: Reflections on Death* (Viking Penguin, London, 1990).

Dufour, G., 'The Family and Dementia' in Desmond O'Neill (ed.) *Carers, Professionals and Alzheimer's Disease* (proceedings of the fifth Alzheimer's Disease International Conference, 1989) (John Libbey and Company, London, 1991).

Durkheim, Emile, *Suicide: A Study in Sociology* (translated by John A. Spaulding and George Simpson) (Routledge and Kegan Paul, London, 1970).

Dworkin, Andrea, *Woman Hating* (E.P. Dutton, New York, 1974).

Ehrenreich, Barbara and English, Deirdre, *Witches, Midwives and Nurses* (Writers and Readers, London, 1976).

Elias, Norbert, *The Loneliness of the Dying* (translation by Edmund Jephcott) (Basil Blackwell, Oxford, 1985).

Elliott, Janice, *Necessary Rites* (Hodder and Stoughton, Kent, 1990).

Ellis, Alice Thomas, *The Birds of the Air* (Penguin Group, London, 1983).

Emanuel, Judith; Thomson, Lesley and Twomey, Mary, *Thinking About Breast Cancer: A Guide for Women who may be Well, Worried or Facing Treatment* (National Extension College, Cambridge, 1988).

Enright, Dennis Joseph (ed.), *The Oxford Book of Death* (Oxford University Press, Oxford, 1987).

Fanthorpe, Ursula A., *Standing To* (Peterloo Poets, Calstock, Cornwall, 1982).

—— *Selected Poems* (Peterloo Poets and King Penguin, Harmondsworth, 1986).

Faulder, Carolyn, *Always a Woman: A Practical Guide to Living with Breast Surgery* (Thorsons, London, 1992).

Feifel, Herman (ed.), *The Meaning of Death* (McGraw Hill, New York, 1965).

—— *New Meanings of Death* (McGraw Hill, New York, 1977).

Fiedler, Leslie, *Love and Death in the American Novel* (Criterion, New York, 1960).

Field, David, *Nursing the Dying* (Routledge, London, 1989).

Fitzgerald, Penelope, *Charlotte Mew & her Friends* (Collins, London, 1984).

Forster, Margaret, *Have the Men Had Enough?* (Penguin Books, London, 1990).

Freud, Sigmund, *Mourning and Melancholia: Collected Papers. Vol. 4* (Basic Books, New York, 1917).

Garnett, David (ed.), *Carrington: Letters and Extracts from her Diaries* (Oxford University Press, Oxford, 1979).

Gerzina, Gretchen, *Carrington: A Life of Dora Carrington 1893–1932* (John Murray Publishers Ltd, London, 1989).

Gittings, Clare, *Death, Burial and the Individual in Early Modern England* (Routledge, London, 1984).

Glaser, Barney G. and Strauss, Anselm Leonard, *Awareness of Dying* (Aldine Publishing Company, Chicago, 1965).

—— *Time for Dying* (Aldine Publishing Company, Chicago, 1968).

Goate, A. M., 'Molecular genetics of Alzheimer's Disease' in Desmond O'Neill (ed.), *Carers, Professionals and Alzheimer's Disease* (proceedings of the fifth Alzheimer's Disease International Conference, 1989) (John Libbey and Company, London, 1991).

Gorer, Geoffrey, *Death, Grief and Mourning in Contemporary Britain* (Cresset, London, 1965).

Graham, N., 'The Silent Epidemic: Who Cares?' in Desmond O'Neill (ed.) *Carers, Professionals and Alzheimer's Disease* (proceedings of the fifth Alzheimer's Disease International Conference, 1989) (John Libbey and Company, London, 1991).

Green, Jennifer and Green, Michael, *Dealing with Death: Practices and Procedures* (Chapman & Hall, London, 1992).

Grigson, Geoffrey (ed. & Intro.), *The Faber Book of Epigrams and Epitaphs* (Faber & Faber, London, 1977).

Hanmer, Jalna and Saunders, Sheila, *Well-founded Fear: A Community Study of Violence against Women* (Hutchinson, London, 1984).

Hartman, Mary S., *Victorian Murderesses* (Schocken, New York, 1977).

Hemer, June and Stanyer, Ann, *Handbook for Widows* (Virago, London, 1978).

Hill, Susan, *In the Springtime of the Year* (Penguin, Harmondsworth, 1977).

—— *Family* (Michael Joseph Ltd, Penguin Group, London, 1989).

Houlbrooke, Ralph Anthony (ed.), *Death, Ritual and Bereavement* (Routledge, London, 1989).

Humphreys, Sally C., *The Family, Women and Death: Comparative Studies* (2nd edition) (Ann Arbor, University of Michigan Press, 1993).

Ignatieff, Michael, *Scar Tissue* (Chatto & Windus, London, 1993).

Ivan, Leslie P. and Melrose, Maureen E., *The Way We Die* (Angel Press, Chichester, 1986).

Jantzen, Grace M., *Julian of Norwich: Mystic and Theologian* (SPCK, London, 1987).

Jarman, Derek, *At Your Own Risk: A Saint's Testament* (Hutchinson, London, 1992).

Jones, Mary, *Secret Flowers. Mourning and the Adaptation to Loss* (The Women's Press, London, 1988).

Jung, Carl Gustav, *Modern Man in Search of a Soul* (1933) (reprinted) (Routledge and Kegan Paul, London, 1973).

Keir, Norman, *I Can't Face Tomorrow: Help for Those Troubled by Thoughts of Suicide* (Thorsons, Wellingborough, Northants, 1986).

Kelly, Liz, *Surviving Sexual Violence* (Polity Press, Cambridge, 1988).

Killeen, J., 'Dementia: Priorities for Care, Strategies for Change' in Desmond O'Neill (ed.), *Carers, Professionals and Alzheimer's Disease* (proceedings of the fifth Alzheimer's Disease International Conference, 1989) (John Libbey and Company, London, 1991).

Kingston, Maxine Hong, *The Woman Warrior: Memoirs of a Girlhood Amongst Ghosts* (Pan, London, 1981).

Krementz, Jill, *How It Feels When a Parent Dies* (Victor Gollancz Ltd, London, 1983).

Krishnamurti, *On Living and Dying* (Victor Gollancz Ltd, London, 1992).

Kubler-Ross, Elisabeth, *Death: The Final Stage of Growth* (Prentice-Hall, Englewood Cliffs, New Jersey, 1975).

——— *Living with Death and Dying* (Souvenir Press, London, 1982).

——— *On Children and Death* (Macmillan, New York, 1985).

——— and Warshaw, Mal, *AIDS: The Ultimate Challenge* (Macmillan, New York, 1987).

——— *On Death and Dying* (Tavistock/Routledge, London, 1989).

Lamm, Maurice, *The Jewish Way in Death and Mourning* (Jonathan David Publishers, New York, 1973).

Lerner, Gerda, (ed.) *Black Woman in White America* (Vintage, New York, 1973).

Lester, David and Lester, Gene, *Crime of Passion: Murder and the Murderer* (Nelson Hall, Chicago, 1975).

Levine, Stephen, *Who Dies?* (Anchor Books, New York, 1982).

Levitt, Paul M. and Guralnick, Elissa S. with Dr A. Robert Kagan and Dr Harvey Gilbert, *The Cancer Reference Book* (Harper & Row Ltd, London, 1984).

Lewis, Clive Staples, *A Grief Observed* (Faber & Faber, London, 1966).

Lindemann, Erich and Greer, Ina May, *A Study of Grief: Emotional Responses to Suicide* in Albert C. Cain (ed.), *Survivors of Suicide* (Charles C. Thomas, Springfield, Illinois, 1972).

Liss, L., 'Environmental Factors in the Pathogenesis of Alzheimer's Disease' in Desmond O'Neill (ed.), *Carers, Professionals and Alzheimer's Disease* (proceedings of the fifth Alzheimer's Disease International Conference, 1989) (John Libbey and Company, London, 1991).

Littlewood, Jane, *Aspects of Grief: Bereavement in Adult Life* (Routledge, London, 1992).

Longford, Lord, *Suffering and Hope* (HarperCollins, London, 1990).

Lopata, Helena Znaniecki, *Women as Widows* (Holland Elsevier, New York, 1979).

Lorde, Audre, *A Burst of Light* (Sheba Feminist Publishers, London, 1988).

Lukas, Christopher and Seiden, Henry M., *Silent Grief: Living in the Wake of Suicide* (Papermac, London, 1987).

Mace, Nancy L. and Rabins, Peter V., *The 36-Hour Day: A Family Guide to Caring for Persons with Alzheimer's Disease, Related Dementing Illnesses, and Memory Loss in Later Life* (Johns Hopkins University Press, Baltimore, Maryland, 1981).

McIntosh, John, 'Suicide as a Mental Health Problem: Epidemiological Aspects' in Edward J. Dunne; John L. McIntosh and Karen Dunne-Maxim (eds.), *Suicide and its Aftermath: Understanding and Counselling the Survivors* (Norton, New York and London, 1987).

Magdalen CSMV, Margaret, *Transformed by Love: The Way of Mary Magdalen* (Darton, Longman and Todd Ltd, London, 1989).

Manning, Rosemary, *A Corridor of Mirrors* (The Women's Press, London, 1987).

Mars-Jones, Adam and White, Edmund, *The Darker Proof* (New edition) (Faber & Faber, London, 1988).

Meade, Marion, *Dorothy Parker: What Fresh Hell is This? A Biography* (Minerva, London, 1991).

Middlebrook, Diane Wood, *Anne Sexton: A Biography* (Virago Press Ltd, London, 1992).

Miller, Mary, *Suicide After Sixty* (Springer Publishing Company, New York, 1979).

Millett, Kate, *Sexual Politics* (Ballantine, New York, 1969).

Mok, Jacqueline, 'Children with Aids' in John David Baum et al. (eds.), *Listen, My Child Has a Lot of Living to Do* (Oxford University Press in association with the Institute of Child Health, Bristol, 1990).

Molloy, Dr William and Mepham, Virginia, *Let Me Decide* (Penguin, London, 1993).

Mooney, Bel, *Perspectives for Living: Conversations on Bereavement and Love* (John Murray, London, 1992).

Morgan, Robin (ed.), *Sisterhood is Powerful* (Random House, New York, 1970).

Neuberger, Julia, *Caring for Dying People of Different Faiths* (Austen Cornish Publishers in association with the Lisa Sainsbury Foundation, London, 1987).

—— and White, John Austin, *A Necessary End: Attitudes to Death* (Macmillan, London, 1991).

Nuland MD, Sherwin B., *How We Die* (Chatto & Windus, London, 1994).

Pagelow, Mildred Daley, *Family Violence* (Praeger Publishers, New York, 1984).

Palmer, Elsie and Watt, Jill, *Living and Working with Bereavement: Guide for Widowed Men and Women* (Detselig Enterprises Ltd, Calgary, Alberta, 1987).

Parkes, Colin Murray, *Bereavement* (Tavistock, London, 1972).

—— *Bereavement: Studies of Grief in Adult Life* (Revised edition) (Penguin, Harmondsworth, 1986).

Peabody, Barbara, *The Screaming Room: A Mother's Journal of her Son's Struggle with AIDS* (Avon, New York, 1987).

Pearson, Carol, *Good-Bye, I Love You* (Random House, New York, 1986).

Phillips, Angela and Rakusen, Jill (eds.), *The New Our Bodies Ourselves* (Penguin, London, 1989).

Pincus, Lily, *Death and the Family: The Importance of Mourning* (Vintage Books, New York; Faber & Faber, London, 1976).

—— and Dare, Christopher, *Secrets in the Family* (Faber & Faber, London, 1978).

Pitt-Rivers, Julian, *The Fate of Shechem or the Politics of Sex* (Cambridge University Press, Cambridge, 1977).

Radford, Jill and Russel, Diana E.H. (eds.), *Femicide: The Politics of Woman Killing* (The Open University Press, Buckingham, 1992).

Raphael, Beverley, *The Anatomy of Bereavement: A Handbook for the Caring Professions* (Hutchinson, London, 1985).

Rhodes, Dusty and McNeill, Sandra (eds.), *Women Against Violence Against Women* (Onlywomen Press, London, 1985).

Rich, Adrienne, *Of Woman Born: Motherhood as Experience and Institution* (Virago, London, 1977).

—— *Women and Honor: Some Notes on Lying* (Onlywomen Press, London, 1979).

Richardson, Diane, *Women and the AIDS Crisis* (Pandora, London, 1989).

—— *Safer Sex: The Guide for Women Today* (Pandora, London, 1990).

Rieder, Ines and Ruppelt, Patricia (eds.), *Matters of Life and Death: Women Speak about AIDS* (Virago, London, 1989).

Rosenblatt, Paul C; Walsh, R. Patricia and Jackson, Douglas A., *Grief and Mourning in Cross-Cultural Perspective* (HRAF Press, New York, 1976).

Rule, Jane, *Memory Board* (Pandora, London, 1987).

Ryedale, April, *My Enemy My Friend: Poems* (Janus Publishing Company, London, 1993).

Salvo, Louise de, *Virginia Woolf: The Impact of Childhood Sexual Abuse on her Life & Work* (The Women's Press, London, 1989).

Sarton, May, *As We Are Now* (The Women's Press, London, 1983).

—— *After the Stroke: A Journal* (The Women's Press, London, 1988).

—— Endgame: *Journal of the Seventy-Ninth Year* (The Women's Press, London, 1993).

—— Encore: *Journal of the Eightieth Year* (The Women's Press, London, 1993).

Saunders, Cicely (ed.), *The Management of Terminal Malignant Disease* (2nd edition) (Edward Arnold, London, 1984).

——— 'The Evolution of the Hospices' in R.D. Mann (ed.), *The History of the Management of Pain: Early Principles to Present Practice* (Parthenon Publishing, 1988.).

——— and Baines, Mary, *Living with Dying: The Management of Terminal Disease* (2nd edition) (Oxford University Press, Oxford, 1989).

——— (ed.), *Hospice and Palliative Care: An Interdisciplinary Approach* (Edward Arnold, London, 1990).

Schneidman, Edwin S: Foreword in Albert C. Cain (ed.), *Survivors of Suicide* (Charles C. Thomas, Springfield, Illinois, 1972)

——— *Voices of Death: Personal Documents from People Facing Death* (Bantam Books, New York, 1982).

Shapiro, Jean (ed.), *Ourselves Growing Older: Women Ageing with Knowledge and Power* (British version of original text by P.B. Doress and D.L. Siegal, and the Midlife and Older Women Book Project in cooperation with the Boston Women's Health Book Collective) (Fontana/Collins, London, 1989)

Simpson, Joe, *This Game of Ghosts* (Jonathan Cape, London, 1993).

Sontag, Susan, *Illness as Metaphor* (Allen Lane, London, 1978).

——— *AIDS and its Metaphors* (Allen Lane, London, 1989).

——— and Hodgkin, Howard, *The Way We Live Now* (Jonathan Cape, London, 1991).

Spalding, Frances, *Stevie Smith: A Critical Biography* (Faber & Faber, London, 1988).

Stanley, Liz and Morgan, David (eds.), *Sociology* (The Journal of the British Sociological Association, Volume 27, Number 3, BPCC Wheatons Ltd, Exeter, 1933).

Staudacher, Carol, *Beyond Grief: A Guide for Recovering from the Death of a Loved One* (Souvenir Press, London, 1988).

Stengel, Erwin, *Suicide and Attempted Suicide* (revised edition) (Penguin, Harmondsworth, 1973).

Stocker, Midge (ed.), *Cancer as a Women's Issue: Scratching the Surface* (Third Side Press, Chicago, 1991).

Storr, Anthony, *Solitude* (Fontana, London, 1989).

Stott, Mary, *Forgetting's No Excuse: The Autobiography of Mary Stott Journalist, Campaigner and Feminist* (Virago, London, 1975).

——— (ed.), *Women Talking: An Anthology from the Guardian Women's Page, 1922–35 and 1957–71* (Pandora Press, London, 1987).

Sudnow, David, *Passing On: The Social Organisation of Death* (Prentice-Hall, Englewood Cliffs, New Jersey, 1969).

Tannen, Deborah, *You Just Don't Understand: Men and Women in Conversation* (Virago, London, 1991).

Tatelbaum, Judy, *The Courage to Grieve: Creative Living, Recovery and Growth through Grief* (Heinemann, London, 1981).

Tavanyar, Judy, *The Terrence Higgins Trust HIV/AIDS Book* (Thorsons, London, 1992).

Taylor, Janet, *Brigie: A Life, 1965–91* (Hodder & Stoughton, London, 1984).

Truman, Jill, *Letter to my Husband: Notes about Mourning & Recovery* (Hodder & Stoughton, London, 1988).

Vanessapress (eds.), *Bits of Ourselves: Women's Experiences with Cancer* (Vanessapress, Alaska, 1986).

Van Gennep, Arnold, *The Rites of Passage* (Routledge and Kegan Paul, London, 1960).

Wagner, Linda W. (ed.), *Sylvia Plath: The Critical Heritage* (Routledge, London and New York, 1988).

Walker, Susan, *Memorials to the Roman Dead* (British Museum Publications Ltd, London, 1985).

Walter, Tony, *Funerals and How to Improve Them* (Hodder & Stoughton, London, 1990).

Weisman, Avery D., *On Dying and Denying: A Psychiatric Study of Terminality* (Behavioural Publications, New York, 1972).

Wertheimer, Alison, *A Special Scar: The Experiences of People Bereaved by Suicide* (Routledge, London, 1991).

Williams, Rory, *A Protestant Legacy: Attitudes to Death and Illness Among Older Aberdonians* (Clarendon Press, Oxford, 1990).

Woolf, Leonard Sidney, *The Journey not the Arrival Matters: An Autobiography of the Years 1939 to 1969* (Hogarth Press, London, 1969).
Worden, William J., *Grief Counselling and Grief Therapy* (Tavistock, London, 1983).

Journals, Papers

Bankoff, E.A., 'Aged parents and their Widowed Daughters' (*Journal of Gerontology*, 38: 226–230, 1983).
Barraclough, B.M. and Shepherd, D.M., 'Public Interest: Private Grief' (*British Journal of Psychiatry*, 12: 109–13, 1976).
———— 'The Immediate and Enduring Effects of the Inquest on Relatives of Suicides' (*British Journal of Psychiatry*, 131: 400–4, 1977).
Barry, H. Jr.; Barry, H. III and Lindemann, E., 'Dependency in Adult Patients Following Early Maternal Bereavement' (*Journal of Nervous and Mental Disease*, 140, 3:196, 1965).
Barry, M.J. Jr., 'The Prolonged Grief Reaction' (*Mayo Clinic Proceedings*, 48: 329–35, 1973).
Bowlby, J., 'The Making and Breaking of Affectional Bonds, I and II' (*British Journal of Psychiatry*, 130: 201–10; 421–31, 1977).
Bowlby-West, L., 'The Impact of Death on the Family System' (*Journal of Family Therapy*, 5: 279–94, 1983).
British Medical Association, *The Euthanasia Report: Report of the Working Party to Review the British Medical Association's Guidance on Euthanasia* (London, 1988).
Buckman, R., 'Breaking Bad News: Why is it Still So Difficult?' (*British Medical Journal*, 288, 1: 1597–9, 1984).
Bunch, J,; Barraclough, B; Nelson, B. and Sainsbury, P, 'Suicide Following the Death of Parents' (*Social Psychiatry*, 6: 193–9, 1971).
Cain, A.C., 'The Legacy of Suicide: Observations on the Pathogenic Impact of Suicide upon Marital Partners' (*Psychiatry*, 29: 26–8, 1966).
Callahan, D., 'Can We Return Death to Disease?' in C.S. Campbell and B.J. Crigge (eds.), *Mercy, Murder and Morality: Perspectives on Euthanasia* (Hastings Center Report special supplement, January–February, 1989).
Cameron, J. and Parkes, C.M., 'Terminal Care: Evaluation of Effects on Surviving Family of Care Before and After Bereavement' (*Postgraduate Medical Journal*, 59: 73–78, 1983).
Clayton, P.J.; Halikas, J.A.; Maurice, W.L. and Robins, E., 'Anticipatory Grief and Widowhood' (*British Journal of Psychiatry*, 122: 47–51, 1973).
Cochrane, A.L., 'A Little Widow is a Dangerous Thing' (*International Journal of Psycho-Analysis*, 17: 494, 1936).
Coleman, S,; Hemphrey, A,; Scraton, P. and Skidmore, P., *Hillsborough and After: The Liverpool Experience* (Centre for Studies in Crime and Social Justice, Edge Hill College of Higher Education, Ormskirk, Lancs, 1990).
Earnshaw-Smith, E. and Yorkstone, P., *Setting Up and Running a Bereavement Service* (St Christopher's Hospice, 1986).
Gerber, I; Rusalem, R. and Hanon, N., 'Anticipatory Grief and Aged Widows and Widowers' (*Journal of Gerontology*, 30: 225–9, 1975).
Henley, S.H.A., 'Bereavement following Suicide: A Review of the Literature' (*Cruse Academic Paper No. 1*, CRUSE, Richmond, Surrey, 1984).
Hill, S., 'Personal Experiences of Bereavement' (*Bereavement Care*: 29–33, Winter 1988).
Johnson, I.S. *et al.*, 'What Do Hospices Do?: A Survey of Hospices in the United Kingdom & Republic of Ireland' (*British Medical Journal*, 300: 791–3, March 1990).
Kane, B., 'Children's Concepts of Death' (*Journal of Genetic Psychology*: 134–41, 1979).
Katz, J.T.S., *Context and Care: Nurses' Accounts of Stress and Support on a Cancer Ward* (unpublished Ph.D. thesis, University of Warwick, 1989).
Klein, M., 'Mourning and its Relationship to Manic Depressive States' (*International Journal of Psycho-Analysis*, 21: 125, 1940).
Lehman, D.R.; Wortman, C.B. and Williams, A.F., 'Long-term Effects of Losing a Spouse or

Child in a Motor Vehicle Crash' (*Journal of Personality and Social Psychology*, 52: 218–231, 1987).

Lewis, E. and Page, A., 'Failure to Mourn a Stillbirth: An Overlooked Catastrophe' (*British Journal of Medical Psychology*, Vol. 51, 1978).

Lindemann, E., 'The Symptomatology and Management of Acute Grief' (*American Journal of Psychiatry*, Vol. 101: 141–8, 1944).

Littlewood, J.L.; Cramer, D.; Hoeskstra-Weebers, J.E.W.M. and Humphrey, G.B., 'Gender Differences in Parental Coping Following their Child's Death' (*British Journal of Guidance and Counselling*, 19, 2: 139–48, 1991a).

McIntosh, J., 'Survivors of Suicide: A Comprehensive Bibliography' (*Omega*, 16, 4: 355–70, 1985–6).

Maddison, D.C. and Viola, A., 'The Health of Widows in the Year Following Bereavement' (*Journal of Psychosomatic Research*, Vol. 12, 1968).

The Open University Course Team, *Death & Dying* (Workbooks 1–4. Dickenson, Donna; Peberdy, Alison; Katz, Jeanne and Sidell, Moyra (eds.), (The Open University Department of Health and Social Welfare, Milton Keynes, 1992)

Parkes, C.M. and Brown, R., 'Health After Bereavement: A Controlled Study of Young Boston Widows and Widowers' (*Psychosomatic Medicine*, 34, 1972).

Parkes, C.M., 'Bereavement Counselling: Does it Work?' (*British Medical Journal*, 281: 3–6, 1980).

—————— 'The Risk of Suicide After Bereavement' (*Bereavement Care* 1(1): 4–5, Spring 1982).

—————— 'Depression: When is it an Illness?' (*Bereavement Care* 4(1): 5–6; 11, Spring 1985).

—————— 'Bereavement as a Psychosocial Transition: Processes of Adaption to Change' (*Journal of Social Issues*, 44 (3): 53–65, 1988).

Passant, H., 'A Holistic Approach in the Ward' (*Nursing Times*, Vol. 86, No. 4).

Range, L.M. and Calhon, L.G., 'Responses Following Suicide and Other Types of Death: The Perspectives of the Bereaved' (*Omega*, Vol. 21 (4): 311–20, 1990).

Raphael, B., 'Preventive Intervention with the Recently Bereaved' (*Archives of General Psychiatry*, 34: 1450–54, 1977).

Rees, W.D., 'The Hallucinations of Widowhood' (*British Medical Journal*, 4: 13, 2 October 1971).

Sanders, C.M., 'A Comparison of Adult Bereavement in the Death of a Spouse, Child and Parent' (*Omega*, 10: 303–22, 1979–80).

—————— 'Risk Factors in Bereavement Outcome' (*Journal of Social Issues*, 44, 3: 97–111, 1988).

—————— 'Caring to the End' (*Nursing Mirror*, 151 (12): 52–3, 4 September 1980).

—————— 'On Dying Well' (*The Cambridge Review*: 49–52, 27 February 1984).

Savishinsky, J.S., *Dementia Sufferers and their Carers: A Study of Family Experiences and Supportive Services in the London Borough of Islington* (Polytechnic of North London, 1990).

Sidell, M., *Gender Differences in the Health of Older Women* (Research Report, Department of Health and Social Welfare, The Open University, Milton Keynes, 1992).

Sklar, R. and Hartley, S.F., 'Close Friends as Survivors: Bereavement Patterns in a "Hidden" Population' (*Omega*, 21 (2): 103–12, 1990).

Tallon, J. and Hayworth, M. (eds.), *Helping Each Other Through the Seasons of Grief* (The Compassionate Friends' pamphlet, Bristol, 1991).

Taylor, H., *The Hospice Movement in Britain: Its Role and Future* (Centre for Policy on Ageing, London, 1983).

Wrobleski, A., 'The Suicide Survivors Grief Group' (*Omega*, 15, 2: 173–84, 1984–85).

—————— 'Guilt and Suicide' (*Afterwords*, October 1986).

INDEX

women, nationality – *contd*
  Egyptian 58
  European 5, 279
  Greek 59
  Indonesian 58
  Italian 210–11, 216
  Turkish 17
  West African 97
women's bodies 25, 27, 58, 67–8, 92, 96,
    154, 196–7, 204, 208–9, 211–13,
    215–16, 218, 233, 250, 262, 306, 339
Women's Liberation Movement 23, 29–30,
    93, 103, 158, 307
Working Party on 'Perspectives of Living
    and Dying' x, 6–7
World Health Organisation 31, 279, 337

Wortman, C. 58–9, 193, 195
writers 4–5, 9, 14, 17, 20, 35, 47, 66–7, 76,
    89–90, 106, 108, 110–11, 113–15,
    147–8, 151, 154, 157, 159–61, 175–6,
    183, 197, 202, 205, 214–16, 223,
    228–9, 242, 310, 344–5
  writing 14–15, 17, 69, 90, 115, 189, 196,
    343
  creative 4, 339–40

Young, Lady (Sasha, Lady Young of
    Dartington) 111
Young, Michael 111
young people 33, 36, 59, 62, 68, 83, 130,
    152, 165, 175, 221, 229, 234, 262–3,
    266, 280, 285, 301, 303, 312, 330